Gothic Mash-Ups

Lexington Books Horror Studies

Series Editors: Lorna Piatti-Farnell, Auckland University of Technology, and Carl Sederholm, Brigham Young University

Lexington Books Horror Studies is looking for original and interdisciplinary monographs or edited volumes that expand our understanding of horror as an important cultural phenomenon. We are particularly interested in critical approaches to horror that explore why horror is such a common part of culture, why it resonates with audiences so much, and what its popularity reveals about human cultures generally. To that end, the series will cover a wide range of periods, movements, and cultures that are pertinent to horror studies. We will gladly consider work on individual key figures (e.g. directors, authors, show runners, etc.), but the larger aim is to publish work that engages with the place of horror within cultures. Given this broad scope, we are interested in work that addresses a wide range of media, including film, literature, television, comics, pulp magazines, video games, or music. We are also interested in work that engages with the history of horror, including the history of horror-related scholarship.

Titles in the Series

Gothic Mash-Ups: Hybridity, Appropriation, and Intertextuality in Gothic Storytelling
  edited by Natalie Neill
Japanese Horror: New Critical Approaches to History, Narratives, and Aesthetics
  edited by Fernando Gabriel Pagnoni Berns, Subashish Bhattacharjee, and Ananya Saha
Violence in the Films of Stephen King
  edited by Michael J. Blouin and Tony Magistrale
Dark Forces at Work: Essays on Social Dynamics and Cinematic Horrors
  edited by Cynthia J. Miller and A. Bowdoin Van Riper

Gothic Mash-Ups

Hybridity, Appropriation, and Intertextuality in Gothic Storytelling

Edited by
Natalie Neill

LEXINGTON BOOKS
Lanham • Boulder • New York • London

Published by Lexington Books
An imprint of The Rowman & Littlefield Publishing Group, Inc.
4501 Forbes Boulevard, Suite 200, Lanham, Maryland 20706
www.rowman.com

86-90 Paul Street, London EC2A 4NE

Copyright © 2022 by The Rowman & Littlefield Publishing Group, Inc.

All rights reserved. No part of this book may be reproduced in any form or by any electronic or mechanical means, including information storage and retrieval systems, without written permission from the publisher, except by a reviewer who may quote passages in a review.

British Library Cataloguing in Publication Information Available

Library of Congress Cataloging-in-Publication Data

Name: Neill, Natalie, 1974- editor.
Title: Gothic mash-ups : hybridity, appropriation, and intertextuality in gothic storytelling / edited by Natalie Neill.
Description: Lanham : Lexington Books, [2022] | Series: Lexington Books horror studies | Includes bibliographical references and index.
Identifiers: LCCN 2021056384 (print) | LCCN 2021056385 (ebook) | ISBN 9781793636577 (cloth) | ISBN 9781793636591 (paperback) | ISBN 9781793636584 (ebook)
Subjects: LCSH: Gothic fiction (Literary genre)—History and criticism. | Horror films—History and criticism. | Horror in mass media. | Intertextuality. | Appropriation (Arts)
Classification: LCC PN3435 .G66656 2022 (print) | LCC PN3435 (ebook) | DDC 809.3/8729—dc23/eng/20211116
LC record available at https://lccn.loc.gov/2021056384
LC ebook record available at https://lccn.loc.gov/2021056385

I dedicate this odd and wonderful mash-up of a book, with great love, to my mother, Sharon Neill, and to the memory of my father, Robin Neill.

Contents

Acknowledgments ix

Introduction xi
Natalie Neill

PART I: FILM AND TELEVISION MASH-UPS — 1

1. Do the Monster Mash: Universal's "Classic Monsters" and the Industrialization of the Gothic Transmedia Franchise — 3
   Megen de Bruin-Molé

2. Adapting Monstrous Creation: *Lisztomania* and *Gothic* as Gothic Mash-Ups — 21
   Kevin M. Flanagan

3. Gothic Exploitation: Transnational Appropriation, Hybridity, and Originality in Continental Horror Cinema, 1957–1983 — 37
   Xavier Aldana Reyes

4. Queer(ly) Mash(ed) Up: Portraits of Neo-Victorian Others in *Penny Dreadful* — 55
   Sarah E. Maier and Rachel M. Friars

5. Horror, Humor, and Satire in *Get Out* — 73
   Chesya Burke

PART II: LITERARY MASH-UPS — 89

6. Anne Boleyn, Tudor Vampire — 91
   Stephanie Russo

7	The Holmes-Meets-Dracula Mash-Up *L. N. Rosales*	107
8	Orgiastic Authorship in *The Picture of Dorian Gray* and *Teleny* *Sandra M. Leonard*	123
9	Rewriting Indigeneity in the Canadian Gothic: Monsters, Mash-Up, and *Monkey Beach* *Kelly Baron*	139

PART III: MORE MASH-UPS: COMICS, PERFORMANCE, AND GAMES — 153

10	"The crawling thing within me": Marvel Comics and the Return of the Gothic Body *Matthew Costello and Mary Beth Tegan*	155
11	*Misty,* Mash-Ups, and the Marginalized in British Girls' Comics *Julia Round*	173
12	Mashing Up Magick: Bizarre Magick and the Fuzzy Gothic *Nik Taylor*	189
13	Gothic Gaming, Queer Mash-Ups, and *Gone Home* *Ewan Kirkland*	205
14	Hypertext of Horrors: A Post-Mortem of *Evermore: A Choose Your Own Edgar Allan Poe Adventure* *Adam Whybray*	225

Index — 241

About the Contributors — 259

Acknowledgments

I am grateful to Judith Lakamper, Lesley Higgins, and Jennifer Judge for their enthusiasm and good advice at various stages in the project. My deep appreciation goes to the contributors of the volume, who prevailed despite the extraordinary stresses of the pandemic. I would also like to acknowledge my "peeps" Elicia Clements, Cheryl Cowdy, and Alison Halsall, my students at York University, my family, and my sweet dog Watson. Thank you to Arc Indexing for preparing the index.

Above all, affectionate thanks to my husband, Paul Cnudde, for his love, encouragement, and sense of humor. There is no one with whom I would rather be in lockdown.

Introduction
Natalie Neill

GOTHIC MASH-UPS, NOW AND THEN

"Gothic is everywhere and nowhere," Fred Botting writes memorably of the genre's place in twentieth-century culture (1996, 155). His expression captures the ubiquity of the Gothic and the difficulty of containing it. Gothic turns up in unexpected places. It appears in new forms and combinations. "Like a malevolent virus," observes Catherine Spooner, "Gothic narratives have escaped the confines of literature and spread across disciplinary boundaries to infect all kinds of media" (2006, 8). The genre is subject to mutation (to continue a metaphor so fitting in our current COVID-19 world). Gothic is always being reinvented—undone, redone, repurposed, reconstituted, recycled—and yet, somehow, it is always still recognizable.

Adding to recent work on Gothic adaptation and intertextuality (e.g., Spooner 2017; Piatti-Farnell 2019; de Bruin-Molé 2020), the present collection explores the way that Gothic stories and elements lend themselves to appropriation and recombination. This characteristic of the genre is seen most clearly in the Gothic mash-up texts of the twentieth and twenty-first centuries, in which characters and storylines from two or more Gothic sources are combined or in which Gothic stories are crossed with stories of other kinds. Examples include filmic "monster mashes" such as *Frankenstein Meets the Wolf Man* (1943) and *Billy the Kid vs. Dracula* (1966); TV shows such as *The Munsters* (1964–1966), *Dark Shadows* (1966–1971), and the animated cartoon *Groovie Goolies* (1970–1971); neo-Victorian pastiches such as the graphic novel *The League of Extraordinary Gentlemen* (1999–) and Showtime's *Penny Dreadful* (2014–2016); dark spin-offs such as the video game *American McGee's Alice* (2000) and teen drama *Riverdale* (2017–); and mash-up novels such as Seth Grahame-Smith's *Pride and Prejudice and*

Zombies (2009) and *Abraham Lincoln, Vampire Hunter* (2010)—to name but a few. *Gothic Mash-Ups: Hybridity, Appropriation, and Intertextuality in Gothic Storytelling* starts from the assumption that mash-ups like these merely exaggerate a propensity on the part of all Gothic storytellers to borrow from earlier texts and make new stories out of older ones.

The recent flurry of self-consciously hybrid Gothic texts has attracted scholarly attention and prompted wider formulations of the genre. In *Post-Millennial Gothic* (2017), Spooner explores the diversification of the Gothic in the twenty-first century through a study of the "growing number of Gothic texts that [. . .] hybridize Gothic with comedy or romance" (2017, 3). *Gothic Afterlives* (2019), edited by Lorna Piatti-Farnell, focuses on contemporary remakes or "reincarnations" of iconic horror narratives. In her introduction, Piatti-Farnell notes the "rise not only in remakes and 're-imaginings,' but also [. . .] a broad scope of genre-bending remixes" (2019, 1). Most recently, Megen de Bruin-Molé (a contributor to the present volume), in *Gothic Remixed* (2020), coins the term "Frankenfiction" to describe her object of study: "commercial narratives, which insert zombies, vampires, werewolves, and multiple other [. . .] monsters into classic literature and popular historical contexts" (2020, 2). All three studies suggest the paradoxical way in which Gothic has adapted and remained up-to-date as a genre through the reanimation and remixing of earlier stories.

What accounts for the pervasiveness of mash-ups in the late twentieth and early twenty-first centuries? And what can Shelley Jackson's Frankensteinian hypertext mash-up *Patchwork Girl* (1995) or Sherri Browning Erwin's *Jane Slayre: The Literary Classic with a Blood-Sucking Twist* (2010) tell us about the Gothic as a whole? Such mash-ups reflect the postmodern penchant for retelling and remaking. In our age of "cultural recycling," argues Linda Hutcheon, we are surrounded by adaptations of every kind, across every medium (2006, 3). Mash-up novels like *Pride and Prejudice and Zombies* are possible because nineteenth-century texts are in the public domain, available to be reused and remixed freely. This raises interesting questions about authorship. As Aram Sinnreich asks, in reference to remixes of pre-recorded songs, "Who is the author of a mash-up, and who is its audience?" (2010, 8). Similarly, one might ask, who is the author of *Pride and Prejudice and Zombies*: Jane Austen or Grahame-Smith? Andrew J. Salvati understands such literary mash-ups in terms of Sinnreich's (2010) notion of configurable culture. If mash-ups are on the rise, it is partly because the Internet allows for "an unprecedented plasticity" whereby "every cultural artifact can be used by anyone, in any way, to create new cultural artifacts of any kind" (Sinnreich 2010, 73; qtd. in Salvati 2016, 100–1).

Often, where contemporary Gothic mash-up is concerned, this reconfiguration is done for commercial reasons: the intent is to profit from stories that are culturally familiar and marketable. In *Abraham Lincoln, Vampire Hunter*, for example, Grahame-Smith capitalizes on both the popularity of vampire stories and Lincoln to create a "quirky commercial novelty" (Salvati 2016, 112). Crucial to the success of a Gothic mash-up is the recognizability of its sources, whether they are taken from fiction or history. This is seen in multi-source neo-Victorian adaptations like *Penny Dreadful*, in which characters lifted from famous narratives (*Frankenstein, Dracula, The Picture of Dorian Gray*) are reimagined and made to interact. Much of the pleasure of engaging with such works comes from noticing allusions and alterations to the original stories and observing how the story worlds overlap and intersect in the mash-up. Contemporary mash-ups reward (and sometimes frustrate) viewers or readers who are well-versed in the source texts. The mash-ups benefit from the popularity of the sources to the extent that they attract ready-made audiences. In turn, of course, the mash-ups play a role in perpetuating the popularity of the stories they adapt.

The Gothic is especially suited to adaptation and mash-up not only because of its popularity and commerciality as a genre, but also because Gothic texts are always already mash-ups. For this reason, *Gothic Mash-Ups* covers texts from a range of periods instead of focusing on recent mash-ups alone. Appropriative and hybridizing practices are not new to the Gothic, but rather they are among the genre's most defining traits. This aspect of the genre led Xavier Aldana Reyes (2018) (also a contributor to the current volume) to refer to contemporary Gothic fiction as "the fragments of an already atomized type of literature." In an earlier evocation of the Gothic's fragmentary nature, Jerrold E. Hogle (1994) describes the hybridity and fakery of early British Gothic novels like Horace Walpole's *The Castle of Otranto* (1764) with respect to their treatment of history. Hogle argues that novelists like Walpole offered "counterfeit" representations of "fragments of the past" (1994, 23). The early Gothic novels are historical mash-ups. The plots play out against the backdrop of anachronistic, pseudo-Medieval settings that reveal as much about Britain in the late eighteenth century as they do about the European Middle Ages.

If the early Gothic novels mash up the past, they also mash up past texts and genres. De Bruin-Molé argues that the twenty-first-century "Frankenfictions" examined in her recent study are "simply another iteration in a long line of Gothic hybrids" that can be traced back to Walpole's text (2020, 5). Widely considered the "original" Gothic novel, *The Castle of Otranto* is in fact a generic farrago that borrows from chivalric romances, sentimental novels, stage tragedies and comedies, and Augustan satires. Setting a pattern for later Gothic stories, *Otranto* is stylistically and tonally mixed. In the preface to the second edition, Walpole defends his inclusion of comic characters in an ostensibly somber work by citing the precedent of Shakespearean tragedy

([1764] 1998, 10–11). By mixing the serious and the comical, he implicitly challenges the eighteenth-century practice of removing comic scenes from Shakespearean tragedies in the interest of dramatic purity. By extension, he rejects the idea that a work of fiction should elicit a single pure response from readers; instead, when engaged with *The Castle of Otranto*, "the mind [of the reader] is kept up in a constant vicissitude of interesting passions" (to quote the preface to the first edition) (Walpole [1764] 1998, 6). Indeed, Gothic always evokes a mixture of responses, from horror, uneasiness, and surprise to amusement, ironic detachment, and laughter—and this is, at least in part, a function of its stylistic hybridity and characteristic intertextuality. Certainly, the recent hybridizing of Gothic with comedy is not new, as Spooner notes herself (2017, 22). Scholars such as Victor Sage (1994) and Avril Horner and Sue Zlosnik (2005) argue that Gothic texts have long see-sawed between horror and humor, and the sublime and the ridiculous, drawing from comic traditions as well as earlier supernatural fictions.

Gothic is also conducive to mash-up because of its extreme conventionality as a genre, or what Deidre Shauna Lynch calls "the repeatability of this fiction's formulae" (2008, 47). From its beginnings in the late eighteenth century, the Gothic was disparaged for its unoriginality and predictability. The earliest reviewers criticized Gothic novels for being admixtures of already clichéd Gothic scenes thrown in merely to attract readers. The early productions of Walpole and Ann Radcliffe were much imitated, and as the genre rose in popularity, it grew increasingly formulaic. In an 1810 letter, Samuel Taylor Coleridge offers a catalog of early Gothic conventions. He notes,

> I amused myself a day or two ago on reading a Romance in Mrs. Radcliff's [*sic*] style with making out a scheme, which was to serve for all romances a priori—only varying the proportions—A Baron or Baroness ignorant of their Birth, and in some dependent situation—Castle—on a Rock—a Sepulchre—at some distance from the Rock—Deserted Rooms—Underground Passages—Pictures—A ghost, so believed—or—a written record—blood on it! A wonderful Cut throat—&c &c &c. (Coleridge [1810] 1959, 294)

The et ceteras suggest just how imitative Gothic novels had become by the early nineteenth century, at least according to Coleridge. To be sure, even the most ground-breaking nineteenth-century Gothic novels rely on a combination of imitation and invention. Two illustrative examples, one from the beginning of the century and one from the end, are Mary Shelley's *Frankenstein* (1818) and Oscar Wilde's *The Picture of Dorian Gray* (1890). Shelley created her archetypal monster story by rewriting the myth of Prometheus, the legend of Faust, German ghost stories, and her father's earlier Gothic novel, *Caleb Williams* (1794). For his part, Wilde reworks Charles

Robert Maturin's *Melmoth the Wanderer* (1820), itself a version of the Faust story, among other sources that are discussed in chapter 10 of this collection. *Frankenstein* and *Dorian Gray* are intertextual mash-ups no less composite and "stitched together" than Shelley's multipart monster, and they are also among the classic Gothic texts most often adapted and mashed up.

To this day, the Gothic is a paradoxical genre, its shocking subject matters seemingly at odds with a tendency to rely on familiar tropes and formulae. As Lynch puts it, Gothic texts are "compounds of the unknown and the too well-known" (2008, 47). In old Gothic novels and contemporary horror films alike, the mysterious, the supernatural, and the extraordinary are converted into a fictional formula for popular consumption. What this means is that tropes of Gothic literature and horror film can be easily extracted from their original contexts to be reshuffled and reused in "new" mash-up texts.

APPROACHES TO MASH-UP

The contributors to *Gothic Mash-Ups* give "mash-up" a wide interpretation. The term has specific meanings in different contexts, including in the fields of recorded music (see Sinnreich 2010; Navas 2012), digital media (see Sonvilla-Weiss 2010), and web development (see Daniel and Matera 2014). Within the context of modern and contemporary art, Kathleen S. Bartels defines mash-up broadly as "the art of carefully crafted juxtaposition" (2016, 16) comprising many different practices (collage, montage, sampling, remix, etc.). Other definitions are similarly commodious. Bruce Grenville defines mash-up as "the mixing, blending and reconfiguration of existing materials" (2016, 20), while for Salvati, a mash-up is, simply, "an assemblage of found cultural materials" (2016, 102).

For the purpose of this collection, mash-up is an umbrella term that encompasses a range of deliberately appropriative narrative strategies. In a mash-up, the borrowed elements are purposely mixed, but they are still distinguishable. A mash-up is not merely an adaptation or a remake of a previous work: whereas a traditional adaptation or remake is a retelling or re-presentation of an earlier story, mash-up entails crossing or interleaving elements from at least two earlier works or kinds of works to produce a new, intertextual hybrid. In fact, as De Bruin-Molé argues of "Frankenfictions," Gothic mash-ups are "monstrous adaptation[s]" to the extent that they are not faithful to a single source text, nor do they set out to be (2020, 7–8). According to the standards of fidelity criticism, Gothic mash-ups are "BADaptations" (Elliot 2018).

The Gothic mash-ups discussed in this collection include fictional crossovers, two-source or multi-source adaptations, pastiches, parodic metafictions, generic hybrids, and richly intertextual Gothic texts in an array of storytelling media. The chapters explore the relationship between mash-up and other related practices (e.g., adaptation, parody, and remix), while attending to such issues as creativity, originality, authorship, collaboration, intellectual property, fandom, commercialization, and canonicity. The contributors also consider the many ways that Gothic storytellers engage with their sources. Mash-ups can expose tensions or dark undercurrents in the appropriated narratives. Alison Halsall has shown that neo-Victorian mash-ups like *The League of Extraordinary Gentlemen* reveal the "ideological paradoxes that characterize" the Victorian source texts and "project contemporary concerns onto received notions of the nineteenth century" (2015, 252, 253). To give another example of the critical possibilities of popular mash-up, Marie Mulvey-Roberts argues of *Pride and Prejudice and Zombies*: "The zombified mash-ups actualise the horrors lurking in the margins of Austen's novels, particularly slavery and war, at the same time as making ironic concessions to the decorum of Regency society" (2014, 17). As the chapters in the collection show, Gothic source texts are put to various uses in mash-ups. Some mash-ups simply trade on the popular or nostalgic appeal of earlier stories; in others, the sources are parodied, or otherwise critiqued, or used to offer social commentary. Mash-ups can be playful or subversive, celebratory or critical. In every case, however, the mash-up newly contextualizes the source material and is, therefore, an invitation to see it with fresh eyes.

To cover a wide range of Gothic mash-up, the book is organized into three parts: "Film and Television Mash-Ups," "Literary Mash-Ups," and "More Mash-Ups: Comics, Performance, and Games." In part I, "Film and Television Mash-Ups," the contributors discuss twentieth- and twenty-first-century screen mash-ups. In chapter 1, "Do the Monster Mash: Universal's 'Classic Monsters' and the Industrialization of the Gothic Transmedia Franchise," Megen de Bruin-Molé explores Universal Studio monster mash-ups in terms of copyright issues, the economics of industrialization, and transmediatization. The chapter is a useful starting point not only because De Bruin-Molé argues that "Universal monsters become a logical touchstone for present-day mash-up and transmedia culture" (4), but also because many of the subsequent chapters engage with the theories of mash-up presented in her 2020 study, *Gothic Remixed*. Chapter 2, "Adapting Monstrous Creation: *Lisztomania* and *Gothic* as Gothic Mash-Ups," by Kevin M. Flanagan, places two films by Ken Russell within larger conversations about Gothic authorship, adaptation, and intertextuality. Paradoxically, Russell directs stories about Romantic authorship, "originality[,] and individualized expression via the quoting and repurposing of the Gothic mash-up mode" (22), as Flanagan contends. Chapter 3, "Gothic Exploitation: Transnational Appropriation, Hybridity, and Originality in

Continental Horror Cinema, 1957–1983," examines twentieth-century Spanish, Italian, and French horror films through a mash-up lens. Xavier Aldana Reyes makes the compelling argument that filmmakers balanced industry pressures and yet "managed to innovate within a context that fostered recycling and repetition" (38). In chapter 4, Sarah E. Maier and Rachel M. Friars turn to the small screen with "Queer(ly) Mash(ed) Up: Portraits of Neo-Victorian Others in *Penny Dreadful*." The authors shed light on "the various—and mashed-up—implications of *Penny Dreadful*'s queer characters as they explore and refute the social as well as sexual limits of their neo-Victorian society" (57). Finally, in chapter 5, "Horror, Humor, and Satire in *Get Out*," Chesya Burke situates *Get Out* within the context of Black horror mash-ups, offering new insights into how Jordan Peele uses horror, humor, and "a mash-up of intertextual references to [. . .] traditional horror texts" to satirize anti-Black racism in the United States (74).

Part II, "Literary Mash-Ups," begins with Stephanie Russo's "Anne Boleyn, Tudor Vampire," an examination of novels that fictionalize, and Gothicize, the life of Anne Boleyn. Russo argues that the Boleyn-Gothic mash-ups "[heighten] and [make] visible the ideological underpinnings of any Anne Boleyn history fiction" (91). Gothic mash-ups have the potential to disrupt received ideas about history, and yet the Boleyn mash-ups are most interesting because they "reiterate centuries-old stereotypes" about the Tudor queen (104). In a similar vein, L. N. Rosales, in chapter 7 ("The Holmes-Meets-Dracula Mash-Up"), looks at six neo-Victorian crossover fictions in which the world of Sherlock Holmes intersects with that of Count Dracula. Rosales finds that the authors do not challenge the misogyny in the Victorian source texts; instead, they engage in playful but "uncritical imitation of the past, past forms, and past texts" (121). The next chapter also focuses on nineteenth-century literature, but attention is given to nineteenth-century Gothic texts *as* mash-ups, not *in* mash-ups. In "Orgiastic Authorship in *The Picture of Dorian Gray* and *Teleny*," Sandra M. Leonard compares two Wildean works to analyze the author's patchwork approach, collaborative compositional process, and evocation and subversion of Gothic conventions. Oscar Wilde is, she observes, "a master of mash-up" whose texts employ a "range of intertextual styles from subtle influences and parody to plagiaristic cut-and-paste" (123). Kelly Baron rounds out part II with "Rewriting Indigeneity in the Canadian Gothic: Monsters, Mash-Up, and *Monkey Beach*," a discussion of the contemporary Indigenous Gothic novel by Eden Robinson. According to Baron's reading, Robinson's mix of Canadian Gothic tropes and Haisla storytelling methods exposes the true Gothic "monster": "the political conditions of settler colonialism, which continue to impact the Haisla people" (151).

In the first chapter of part III ("More Mash-Ups: Comics, Performance, and Games"), Matthew Costello and Mary Beth Tegan discuss how the Marvel Comic series *Werewolf by Night* mashes up the superhero and Gothic genres. Their chapter—"'The crawling thing within me': Marvel Comics and the Return of the Gothic Body"—explores the hybrid figure of the "Gothic superhero" in terms of twentieth-century ideas about masculinity. Costello and Tegan further suggest that the werewolf, a mutable and composite monster, is an apt metaphor for Gothic mash-up itself. Continuing the focus on comics, Julia Round, in "*Misty*, Mash-Ups, and the Marginalized in British Girls' Comics," describes the "mash-up methods" used in the Gothic comic book series *Misty*. Round reveals that "while *Misty* sometimes used mash-ups and namechecks quite superficially to create an atmosphere of Gothic horror," it also revised Gothic tropes to address the concerns of young female readers (174). In chapter 12, "Mashing Up Magick: Bizarre Magick and the Fuzzy Gothic," Nik Taylor moves beyond print or screen texts to consider how bizarre magick, a subgenre of performance magic, relies on Gothic storytelling and mash-up. Taylor explains how bizarre magicians reworked and combined a broad range of Gothic sources to create "intimate storytelling experiences" (201). Their performances, he argues, are spooky and playful examples of Gothic revival. The final chapters are concerned with games of different kinds. In chapter 13, "Gothic Gaming, Queer Mash-Ups, and *Gone Home*," Ewan Kirkland argues that "[i]n addition to being Gothic, video games have always been mash-ups," which blend multiple storytelling, art, and media forms (210). The chapter uses *Gone Home* to explore the fascinating intersections among "the video game, the Gothic, the mash-up, and the queerness of ludic digital experiences" (206). Finally, in "Hypertext of Horrors: A Post-Mortem of *Evermore: A Choose Your Own Edgar Allan Poe Adventure*," Adam Whybray describes the creation and reception of his own mash-up hypertext game, *Evermore*, in which plotlines taken from over 60 works by Edgar Allan Poe form an interactive "choose-your-own-adventure" story. As Whybray maintains, Poe's own works are "proto-hypertext" mash-ups, and so they lend themselves to this treatment (230). The chapter is an illuminating conclusion to the collection because it gives us Whybray's perspective as a creator of Gothic mash-up. In his "Poe-st Script," for example, he grapples with the criticism that "*Evermore*'s pastiche was not significantly differentiated from the patriarchal and colonialist ideologies underpinning Poe's work, leading the piece to replicate the oppressive dynamics of the material that I was seeking to deconstruct and parody" (238)—a charge that recalls Rosales's criticism of the Dracula-Holmes mash-ups.

The essays collected in *Gothic Mash-Ups* are varied in approach and focus. Expected texts like *Penny Dreadful* and Gothic crossover fictions are analyzed alongside less obvious examples of Gothic mash-up. Covering a mix of texts, formats, periods, and perspectives, the collection is itself a mash-up. The contributors take different approaches, and yet they are all concerned in one way or another with Gothic intertextuality and with the fundamental hybridity and adaptability of the Gothic as a genre. The chapters explore how Gothic storytellers working in a variety of media appropriate, combine, and reimagine previous stories and, by doing so, keep the genre in a continuous state of reinvention.

REFERENCES

Aldana Reyes, Xavier. 2018. "The Contemporary Gothic." In *Oxford Research Encyclopedia of Literature*. Oxford: Oxford University Press. https://doi.org/10.1093/acrefore/9780190201098.013.187.

Bartels, Kathleen S. 2016. "Director's Foreword." In *MashUp: The Birth of Modern Culture*, edited by Daina Augaitis, Bruce Grenville, and Stephanie Rebick, 16–17. London: Black Dog Publishing.

Botting, Fred. 1996. *Gothic*. London and New York: Routledge.

de Bruin-Molé, Megen. 2020. *Gothic Remixed: Monster Mashups and Frankenfictions in 21st-Century Culture*. London: Bloomsbury.

Coleridge, Samuel Taylor. [1810] 1959. "To William Wordsworth." October 1810. In *Collected Letters of Samuel Taylor Coleridge*, vol. 3, edited by Earl Leslie Griggs, 290–6. Oxford: Clarendon.

Daniel, Florian, and Maristella Matera. 2014. *Mashups: Concepts, Models and Architectures*. Berlin: Springer.

Elliott, Kamilla. 2018. "The Theory of *BAD*aptation." In *The Routledge Companion to Adaptation*, edited by Dennis Cutchins, Katja Krebs, and Eckart Voigts, 18–27. London and New York: Routledge.

Grenville, Bruce. 2016. "Introduction." In *MashUp: The Birth of Modern Culture*, edited by Daina Augaitis, Bruce Grenville, and Stephanie Rebick, 18–51. London: Black Dog Publishing.

Halsall, Alison. 2015. "'A Parade of Curiosities': Alan Moore's *The League of Extraordinary Gentlemen* and *Lost Girls* as Neo-Victorian Pastiches." *The Journal of Popular Culture* 48 (2): 252–68.

Hogle, Jerrold E. 1994. "The Ghost of the Counterfeit in the Genesis of the Gothic." In *Gothick Origins and Innovations*, edited by Allan Lloyd Smith and Victor Sage, 23–33. Amsterdam: Rodopi.

Horner, Avril, and Sue Zlosnik. 2005. *Gothic and the Comic Turn*. Houndmills, Basingstoke, Hampshire: Palgrave Macmillan.

Hutcheon, Linda. 2006. *A Theory of Adaptation*. New York and London: Routledge.

Lynch, Deidre Shauna. 2008. "Gothic Fiction." In *The Cambridge Companion to Fiction in the Romantic Period*, edited by Richard Maxwell and Katie Trumpener, 47–63. Cambridge: Cambridge University Press, 2008.

Mulvey-Roberts, Marie. 2014. "Mashing up Jane Austen: *Pride and Prejudice and Zombies* and the Limits of Adaptation." *The Irish Journal of Gothic and Horror Studies* 13 (Summer): 17–37.

Navas, Eduardo, 2012. *Remix Theory: The Aesthetics of Sampling*. New York: Springer Wien New York Press.

Piatti-Farnell, Lorna. 2019. "Introduction." In *Gothic Afterlives: Reincarnations of Horror in Film and Popular Media*, edited by Lorna Piatti-Farnell, 1–9. Lanham, Boulder, New York, and London: Lexington Books.

Sage, Victor. 1994. "Gothic Laughter: Farce and Horror in Five Texts." In *Gothick Origins and Innovations*, edited by Allan Lloyd Smith and Victor Sage, 190–203. Amsterdam: Rodopi.

Salvati, Andrew J. 2016. "History Bites: Mashing Up History and Gothic Fiction in Abraham Lincoln: Vampire Hunter." *Rethinking History* 20 (1): 97–115.

Sinnreich, Aram. 2010. *Mashed Up: Music, Technology, and the Rise of Configurable Culture*. Amherst: University of Massachusetts Press.

Sonvilla-Weiss, Stefan. 2010. "Introduction: Mashups, Remix Practices and the Recombination of Existing Digital Content." In *Mashup Cultures*, edited by Stefan Sonvilla-Weiss, 9–23. Germany, Springer-Verlag/Wien.

Spooner, Catherine. 2017. *Post-Millennial Gothic: Comedy, Romance and the Rise of Happy Gothic*. London: Bloomsbury.

Walpole, Horace. [1764] 1998. *The Castle of Otranto*. Edited by W. S. Lewis. Introduction by E. J. Clery. Oxford and New York: Oxford University Press.

Part I

FILM AND TELEVISION MASH-UPS

Chapter 1

Do the Monster Mash

Universal's "Classic Monsters" and the Industrialization of the Gothic Transmedia Franchise

Megen de Bruin-Molé

The first lesson of mash-up is that nothing is really new. Some have suggested that the Dark Universe—a planned monster mash-up series which effectively began and ended with 2017's *The Mummy*—marked Universal's first failed attempt to join other major studios in launching a tentpole transmedia franchise (see for instance Rivera 2017; Moreno 2020). This assessment of the Dark Universe's motives overlooks 2004's *Van Helsing*, a financially (if not critically) successful film, which had several transmedial extensions and teased potential film sequels. It also ignores *The Fast and the Furious* franchise, which was already a hugely successful transmedia property for Universal by the time of the Dark Universe. More importantly, of course, those who read the Dark Universe as Universal's first, if aborted, transmedia franchise omit the studio's black-and-white monster mash-ups of the 1940s and 1950s, including films such as *Frankenstein Meets the Wolf Man* (1943), *The House of Frankenstein* (1944), and *Abbott and Costello Meet Frankenstein* (1948), in which the studio's monsters "team up" against each other or against famous Universal heroes. Indeed, the repeated attempts at Dark Universe-type franchises only highlight how central Universal's 1930s "Classic Monsters" films have remained for the studio, nearly 100 years after their initial release. Universal's *Dracula* (1931) and *Frankenstein* (1931) form two-thirds of Kamilla Elliott's Gothic "triptych" in film (2008, 24). Xavier Aldana Reyes highlights how Universal films "provide visual models for a number of monsters, such as the vampire, the Frankenstein creature, the mummy and the werewolf, that would have a tremendous impact on the history of the Gothic beyond the screen," becoming in some cases "as significant, if not more so, than the literary sources that inspired them" (2020, 100). But how did these films become the icons they are today?

When we think of the modern digital mash-up, Universal's Classic Monsters of the 1930s may at first be far from our minds. In fact, thinking of Universal's films as monster "mashes" or "mash-ups" is something relatively new. It was only in the 2000s that the term "mash-up" became "widely used" not just in reference to music, but "in conjunction with a variety of other media forms made from extant media" (Borschke 2017, 46). Universal's multi-monster films of the 1940s and 1950s were originally referred to as "Super-Shocker[s]," or later as "monster rall[ies]," rather than mashes (Scott 1944, 5; Weaver, Brunas, and Brunas 2007, loc 1562). Despite recent attempts to historicize it (see Willis 2016; Freeman 2016; Pearson 2017) transmedia is likewise a relatively new term, and as a concept it is reliant on modern media processes of industrialization, consumer culture, and regulation (Freeman 2016, 44). Yet, if we think about Gothic mash-up as a "propensity [. . .] to borrow from earlier texts and make new stories out of older ones" (x), as this edited collection proposes, Universal monsters become a logical touchstone for present-day mash-up and transmedia culture. Not only did most of these films start out as multimedia adaptations or appropriations themselves, they have been reimagined, rebooted, and remixed many times since they first graced the silver screen.

Focusing on Universal Studios' curation and cultivation of the Classic Monsters brand from the 1930s through to the early twenty-first century, then, this chapter gives an overview of the brand's evolution from successful stand-alone horror adaptations to a monster mash comedy franchise, and then to its self-recycling and mash-up in later films, in television, and in off-screen merchandising and entertainment. Through its analysis of this history, the chapter argues that Universal Studios effectively industrialized the monster mash-up. Not only did it set a precedent for how later film franchises would capitalize on mash-up and other recombinant strategies, it offers one of the earliest cinematic examples of configurable or transmedia storytelling in the age of media conglomerates and convergence.

FROM ADAPTATION TO TRANSMEDIA: VARIATIONS ON SAMENESS (1931–1956)

As with most Hollywood films and franchises Universal's Classic Monsters began with an adaptation. From the outset, with *Dracula* (1931), *Frankenstein* (1931), *Murders in the Rue Morgue* (1932), and *The Invisible Man* (1933), Universal seemed set on banking on already familiar and popular authors and texts to do much of the publicity work for its horror titles, relying on the "prestige appeal of their literary, theatrical, or biographical source material" and also emphasizing this appeal in their publicity materials (Hall and Neale 2010, 100). Given this tradition of mining from popular nineteenth-century literature, one might assume that most of Universal's 1930s monster movies fall neatly into one of the most common popular conceptions of adaptation— the conversion of a story from book to film (Leitch 2012, 89; Cartmell and Whelehan 1999). In practice, however, the situation was more complicated. To start, ideas about adaptation, shaped by turn-of-the-century copyright battles, were somewhat different than they are today. Not only were films themselves still understood as a new medium, but cinematic adaptations were being copyrighted in new ways. Because of the way that cinema and photography were perceived to capture reality, early practitioners had a hard time convincing copyright judges that they were even capable of original productions (Decherney 2012, 48). The idea that films could layer original or novel detail onto a familiar story still did not imply that the act of *filming* itself was original. Only the creative work involved in set design, lighting, staging, and so forth was considered original, and this was work already pioneered and copyrighted by the theater industry.

Theater would also play a large role in Universal's horror of the early 1930s. By 1931's *Dracula* and *Frankenstein*, film companies needed to buy the rights to the stories they were producing, but the book-to-film adaptation of these texts was by no means direct. Universal acquired the rights to Stoker's 1897 novel, but also to the Deane and Balderstone stage versions of 1924 and 1927 (Edwards 2014b, 17), and the studio and director made a number of their own revisions and additions to the plot. Mary Shelley's *Frankenstein* (1818) was already in the public domain, but the copyrights to stage versions were likewise acquired for Universal's adaptation. This multi-source borrowing further complicates the idea of direct adaptation—though again, we have not quite arrived at anything that might be termed a remix or mash-up in the strict sense. From *Frankenstein* we can already see the beginnings of a franchise mindset, however, with studio boss Carl Laemmle Jr. allegedly instructing director James Whale to change the film's ending so "the company could deploy the key characters in *Frankenstein*, and the studio-contracted actors associated with them, in subsequent Universal horror films" (Edwards 2014b, 20).

Though we are still far from the modern mash-up, with Laemmle Jr.'s instructions to Whale we already find ourselves one step closer to the contemporary transmedia franchise, in which adaptation rights and IPs are extended far beyond a single film. Rather than attempting to retell a story in a new medium or context, transmedia builds and extends its stories by remixing or recombining different narrative elements (characters, plot points, key ideas, places, or phrases) across multiple platforms and audiences. Henry Jenkins's early definition of transmedia storytelling marks it very broadly as those kinds of stories "that unfold across multiple platforms, with each medium making distinctive contributions to our understanding of the world" (2006, 334). Jenkins's definition also echoes Nate Harrison and Eduardo Navas's assertion that a "defining characteristic of the mashup, whether it is music, image, or software, is that its elements operate together but remain discrete" (2017, 197). We can take Universal's Classic Monsters films as a loose example of this; transmedia storytelling is what allows *Dracula* to exist—and to be enjoyed—separately from *Frankenstein*, but it also allows their titular characters to be systematically and consistently brought together and further developed in other films and media.

In particular, it is important to note the ways in which industrialization in the early twentieth-century United States "marked a turn towards an economics of industrial production that established an industrial means of producing variation on sameness" (Freeman 2016, 46). This kind of production has had a huge impact on arts and popular media more broadly, but is particularly essential to remix, mash-up, and other recombinant modes of creativity. In Hollywood horror, this economics of industrialization has also been closely linked to copyright and its regulation (or lack thereof). As Peter Decherney points out in his history of Hollywood copyright battles, Universal, like other Hollywood corporations, "has, throughout its history, actively worked to standardize its products, to keep things relatively unoriginal. Since the earliest narrative films, the majority of movies have been adapted from literature, drama, cartoons, news stories, or some pre-existing idea" (2012, 59). Most importantly from the perspective of mash-up, with every change in Universal's ownership and management, and most new developments in technology, the studio would also borrow from itself. Despite their iconic status in later Gothic and horror media, then, Universal's monster movies were never "original" in any conventional Romantic sense. Nor did they attempt to present themselves as unique and uncopiable intellectual property at this stage—though as Decherney points out, "Hollywood studios regularly used contracts to protect characters like Rin Tin Tin, Mickey Mouse, and Frankenstein, which provided the bases for ongoing series" (2012, 102).

Universal certainly made full use of its biggest stars and their links to the studio in the 1930s, in particular Boris Karloff and Bela Lugosi (Edwards 2014b, 24). Lugosi's work was mostly for other studios in the early 1930s, but when he did appear in Universal's films the studio regularly referred back to his role in *Dracula*. Karoly Grosz's posters for both *Murders in the Rue Morgue* (1932) and *The Raven* (1935, also starring Boris Karloff, billed simply as "Karloff") respectively advertise Lugosi as "Bela Lugosi (Dracula Himself)" and "Bela (Dracula) Lugosi," reminding audiences of this role and the actor's past affiliation with the studio. Boris Karloff starred in four other Universal movies between 1931's *Frankenstein* and 1935's *Bride of Frankenstein*. Not all were horror films, but two also featured Bela Lugosi. These leading men would continue to appear together in Universal films over the course of their careers.

Beyond the use of Karloff and Lugosi's star value in other films, and the decision to produce a direct sequel to *Frankenstein* in *Bride of Frankenstein* (once again featuring Karloff as the Monster and Colin Clive as Henry Frankenstein), there seems to be little conscious extension or transmediatization in this first Universal horror cycle. We do see the beginnings of an industrialized consumer culture using Universal's then-limited resources, linking back to Matthew Freeman's assertions that "mass distribution gave rise to the business of a number of interconnected licensing practices associated with corporate authorship's managerial function, and in turn transmedia storytelling became corporatised" (2016, 21). Universal's films were advertised in newspapers, on radio, and in other, often unexpected media forms. For instance, Universal owned a baseball team in the early 1930s, which was staffed by various cinema crew members. From 1933 the team was managed by Jack Pierce, head of Universal's makeup department and creator of the Frankenstein's Monster makeup. Notably, to "promote the upcoming release of Universal's *The Bride of Frankenstein*," baseball player and Universal City grip worker Frank Lubin "would come out before games dressed as the monster and perform for the crowd. Taking advantage of Lubin's height, Pierce would dress Lubin in the same make-up and costume as Karloff had worn, including the platform shoes, ragged coat, and bolts in the neck" (Kupfer 2015, 13).

Narratology sometimes tends to overlook this kind of advertising or merchandizing as separate from the "real" story, but we should not underestimate the storytelling power of paratexts. As Jonathan Gray has argued, such paratexts are almost always "more than hypercommercialized cashgrabs," contributing to media storyworlds in many different kinds of ways (2010, 187). How audiences first become aware of a story is a very important part of how they ultimately receive it. Additionally, as a number of critics have pointed out, the difference between transmedia storytelling and transmedia branding is often a very fine one (Jenkins 2010, 944; Ryan 2015, 2). As Carlos A. Scolari puts it, "If transmedia storytelling is a narrative told across multiple media and platforms with the collaboration of users, and a brand is a series of symbolic traits and values expressed by the narrative that identifies one good or service as distinct from the others," transmedia branding is simply "a brand narrative told across multiple media and platforms with the collaboration of users" (2018, 4–5). In the early 1930s Universal's activity was still relatively minimal in terms of this kind of industrialized storyworld development and transmedia tie-ins, however.

Dracula's Daughter, the 1936 sequel to *Dracula*, would not feature Lugosi, and following its release, other Universal horror films were briefly taken out of production altogether. This was due at least in part to the enforcement of the Hays Code and its mission of censorship from 1934 (see *Variety* 1936, 6; Petley 2017, 139). The situation was not helped by the Laemmles's loss of their controlling stake in the studio in the same year. The most recognizable instances of transmedia world-building and mash-up would only begin shortly thereafter.

Tom Weaver, Michael Brunas, and John Brunas define Universal's "classic" horror films as those produced between 1931 and 1946, ending with the merger of Universal and International Pictures (2007, 14). In 1936, however, ten years before this merger, the studio was taken over by Charles Rogers and J. Cheever Cowdin from Standard Capital Corporation, after the Laemmles defaulted on a production loan (Mallory 2009, 14). Michael Mallory suggests that horror was "the first thing swept out the door" in this "New Universal," in favor of more family-friendly fare and "straight dramas" in response to continued Hays Code enforcement (2009, 19). Whatever the reasons for the pause, this hiatus in horror production would be short-lived. The reason for its return—and for the cultural icon that Universal's Classic Monsters would ultimately become—was still not a transmedia story extension, but rather an instance of "remix" or recombinant marketing. In August 1938, Emil Umann, the independent owner of the Regina-Wiltshire Theatre, procured the rights to screen Universal's *Dracula* and *Frankenstein* along with RKO's *Son of Kong* in a four-day triple bill. Tim Concannon of the *Black Mass* cinema exhibition archive writes about how this quickly became a surprisingly lucrative double bill show of *Dracula* and *Frankenstein*, with "Kong Jnr [. . .] dropped after the second day," and the double bill running "continuously at the Regina for 21 hours a day" (Concannon 2020). Umann hired Bela Lugosi, whose career had otherwise stalled, to "make nightly personal appearances" (Brooks and Dello Stritto 2012). *Variety* magazine reported that "Police had to be called to handle the crowds" (*Variety* 1938, 11). Universal quickly realized the value of the horror films they were sitting on, though unfortunately they had lent their prints to Umann for a flat rate and were not reaping the profits on quite the level they wanted. They happily copied Umann's tactics, however, taking their prints back from him after four weeks and setting their own screening campaign in motion, duplicating "the success of the Regina-Wilshire under terms more beneficial to the studio" (Brooks and Dello Stritto 2012). Bela Lugosi even continued making personal appearances as Dracula on tour. The first step toward mashing up Universal's monster was not to create sequels or spin-offs, then, but to re-cement the older films as "originals" and objects of continued relevance and nostalgia. Without this step the later Universal horror films would almost certainly never have come to be.

Once assured of horror's profitability and market, the studio quickly resumed production of new horror titles. In December 1938, columnist Robbin Coons would report that Universal, "scanning its profit books, has lost no time in producing another modern sequel, 'The Son of Frankenstein.' This is proceeding rapidly on eerie sets" (1938, 6). *Son of Frankenstein* would be released in January 1939 to rave reviews, with Boris Karloff back as Frankenstein's Monster and Bela Lugosi as Ygor. As a *Film Daily* advertisement for the studio's next Frankenstein sequel *Ghost of Frankenstein* (1942) noted, the sequel market was kind to Universal, with Frankenstein's monster serving as "Universal's 'Midas' again! Out for more gold!" (*Film Daily* 1942, 3; see figure 1.1). Universal would go on to make far more horror films *after* 1939 than it did before, often at much cheaper production rates. The studio often did this by following the same template they had with Umann, using a method that had already proven successful and adapting or industrializing it so that it could be done more cheaply. In many cases this involved exploiting existing names and intellectual property in ways that at the time were still unregulated. For instance, the makeup artist Jack Pierce was replaced with a cheaper team of artists who could identify and mimic his designs, which belonged to the studio rather than to himself.

Though Universal would introduce a few new monsters in this period, most famously Lon Chaney Jr. as *The Wolf Man* (1941), the films it produced were overwhelmingly sequels and crossovers. The most notable examples are *Frankenstein Meets the Wolf Man* (1943) and the monster rally films we might today call monster mashes: *House of Frankenstein* (1944), *House of Dracula* (1945), and *Abbott and Costello*'s meet-the-monster series of comedy films (beginning with 1948's *Abbott and Costello Meet Frankenstein* and ending with 1955's *Abbott and Costello Meet the Mummy*), which all contain an extensive roster of monsters from past Universal films. *Abbott and Costello Meet Frankenstein* has a closing scene that we might compare with the post-credits sequences of twenty-first-century transmedia like the Marvel Cinematic Universe (MCU). Sitting together in a boat, Abbott and Costello congratulate themselves on surviving the events of the film. "Now that we've seen the last of Dracula, the Wolf Man, and the Monster, there's nobody to frighten us anymore," says Abbott. "Oh that's too bad, I was hoping to get in on the excitement," a mysterious voice intones from over Abbott's shoulder, and an invisible figure lights a cigarette which floats in thin air. "Allow me to introduce myself," the voice continues, scaring the comedy duo out of the boat, "I'm the Invisible Man!" (figure 1.2). Whether or not this was an intentional tease, it would come to fruition in *Abbott and Costello Meet the Invisible Man* (1951). Today such scenes have become a popular way to expand the world of the story, and sometimes to hint at future stories to come.

Figure 1.1   Advertisement for Ghost of Frankenstein, as Featured in the Trade Paper *Film Daily* on February 27, 1942. Image courtesy of the Library of Congress, Motion Picture, Broadcasting and Recorded Sound Division (Location 41027959).

As transmedia productions have become larger and more sophisticated, transmedia has also become understood as operating within a larger interrelated "storyworld," and as the body of scholarship around this kind of media has become more established, there has been a marked shift in focus from how transmedia constructs multipart narratives to a broader concept of branding, storyworlds, and world-building (Fast and Örnebring 2017, 637). Dan Hassler-Forest defines *transmedia world-building* (i.e., the construction of fragmented and "complex fantastic storyworlds") as a process that "takes place *across* media," "involves *audience participation*," and "*defers narrative closure*" (2016, 5; original italics). From a commercial perspective, the deferral of narrative closure means that the intellectual property in question can continue to earn for its parent company, and for that company alone. In Universal's monster rallies, transmedia world-building also reveals that all of these stories are, or at least could take place, in a shared universe: villains, locations, and themes repeatedly return, and familiar characters from different movies appear "all together" on screen (to quote the movie tagline

Figure 1.2 The Invisible Man Reveals Himself at the End of *Abbott and Costello Meet Frankenstein* (1948). Screenshot by the author.

of *House of Frankenstein*). Not only is this a draw for fans hoping to spend more time with their favorite characters, it is also important from a branding perspective. By suggesting that these monsters exist in the same universe, it sets up the possibility for monsters to join or return to the universe in future, but it also begins to establish Universal's world as the "real" home of horror, a universe in which *all* monsters might conceivably live, and against which all stand-alone monster films might be compared. The focus on "worlding" over individual stories or characters also allows the brand to experiment with very different sets of characters, stories, and genres, all while still claiming a certain sameness or integrity—something Universal horror did on many separate occasions as it moved from prestige pictures to horror-comedies, to action thriller and back again.

Universal's B-horror films would become some of the most important for cementing its monstrous legacy. With the end of "prestige" adaptation horror and the Laemmles's descent into debt, Universal's monster mash truly begins, its characters becoming "presold properties that required little marketing" (Edwards 2014b, 25). Crucially, the "monster rally" mash-up period in the 1940s was "hardly seen at the time as one of infertility; commentators believed they were witnessing an unprecedented boom in horror film production" (Edwards 2014a, 164). The monster rallies were acknowledged as low-budget B movies, but nonetheless did much better than expected on the first-run market. Coons, writing about the 1938 Regina double bill, noted that "It seems to have dawned on somebody that what the public wanted, after all, was horror. Confronted with the playfully murderous cavortings of two movie monsters, the public—at least momentarily—could forget about War and Dictators" (Coons 1938, 6). Amid the horrors of WWII, these films would be memorable precisely because they were designed to be ephemeral and entertaining. There is also little sign of franchise fatigue during this period—pre-1936 there were complaints that Universal's *Werewolf of London* (6 May 1935) was released too soon after *Bride of Frankenstein* (April 22, 1935; Universal also released *The Mystery of Edwin Drood* and *The Raven* in the same year), but in general it seemed like audiences could not get enough of horror (Peirse 2013, 173). Universal was happy to oblige, and as a result of cheaper and more industrialized production tactics it was able to saturate the market.

In this period Universal's horror films also struck an important tone somewhere between prestige horror and silly romp, becoming more self-referential and tongue-in-cheek. Of *House of Frankenstein*, A. H. Weiler wrote for *The New York Times* that the film's all-star cast of monsters was like "a baseball team with nine Babe Ruths, only this grisly congress doesn't hit hard; it merely has speed and a change of pace. As such, then, it is bound to garner as many chuckles as it does chills. However, lampoon or no, put this item down as a bargain for the bogie hunters" (Weiler 1944). Writing on Christmas Eve (nine days after *House of Frankenstein* was released in New York), *Harrison's Reports* rather more dubiously commented that the film was "only a mild horror picture, more ludicrous than terrifying. The whole thing is a rehash of the fantastic doings of these characters in previous pictures and, since they do exactly what is expected of them, the spectator is neither shocked nor chilled" (*Harrison's Reports* 1944, 207). One can nevertheless imagine this being read as a positive review by reality-weary, entertainment-seeking consumers in the winter of 1944: a little welcome variation grounded in familiarity and sameness. To contemporary critics this might seem lazy or unoriginal, but it is important to note the creative and critical work being done to actually implement this self-referential tone and style in practice, sustained across multiple interrelated films. As Alison Peirse points out, many 1940s remakes and sequels resorted directly to remix and recombination in recreating classics sets and scenes, in some instances involving "a certain pecuniary consideration when reusing footage and sets," in others involving "a great deal of effort" on behalf of set and production design "to replicate certain moments" for sequels and monster rallies (2013, 25). None of these things were common practice or reliably industrialized by the 1940s, and many studios would destroy or discard materials from past productions, requiring later films to either scrounge around or start from scratch.

ONE (MORE) FOR THE MONEY: THE EARLY CONGLOMERATE ERA (1962–1990)

Universal continued to make Abbott and Costello monster mashes through the mid-1950s, as well as stand-alone creature features such as *Creature from the Black Lagoon* (1954; originally released in 3D) and the 1959 *The Mummy*, starring Christopher Lee and Peter Cushing, in co-production with the British Hammer studios. This film was based on Universal's three 1940s sequels to *The Mummy*: *The Mummy's Hand* (1940), *The Mummy's Tomb* (1942), and *The Mummy's Ghost* (1944). Ultimately, however, Universal's 1950s horror-comedies were less financially successful than its 1940s monster rallies (Edwards 2014a, 167), and it wasn't until the 1960s that Universal horror would really take the popular spotlight again. Just as in the 1930s, this expansion of the universe would involve repetition, mash-up, and parody. In 2009 Michael Mallory suggested that the fact that Universal's horror films are "as popular as ever" so many years after they were first made is "a testament to the scores of actors, writers, directors, producers, composers, designers, special effects and makeup artists, and cameramen who made them" (2009, 19). But if we look to recent history, the brand's success is much more directly due to the use of recombinant branding and transmedia techniques. This, again, can be linked to the growing scale of consumer culture and branding more generally, through which Universal horror continues to historicize its own brand as prestigious and "classic" up to today (Edwards 2014b, 26).

If the 1940s and 1950s saw an expansion and solidification of the Universal monsters storyworld through sequels and cinematic cross-references, in the 1960s it became more fully and consistently transmedial. Through various corporate mergers and distribution deals it also tapped into a much vaster fan base than it could have hoped for through cinema alone. In 1957, for instance, Universal struck a ten-year television deal with Screen Gems for the distribution of 52 old titles. As Decherney points out, this is an important moment in cinema history: "Today, we think of the television industry as a part of Hollywood, which it is. But in the 1950s, the television and film businesses were distinct, and many Hollywood leaders viewed television as a threat rather than an extension of their industry" (2012, 101). Universal would soon discover the many opportunities afforded by television, however. Universal's Screen Gems package was marketed under the name *Shock!* and came complete with a pressbook with tips for transmedia branding through one's local community, radio, or television network. *Mel's Matinee Movie*, hosted by Mel Jass, represents one particularly successful talk show and screening combo. It ran from 1958–1979 and included many Universal titles including *Dracula*, *The Mummy*, and *The Wolf Man*. Stephen Sommers, the director of Universal's *The Mummy* (1999) and *Van Helsing* (2004), writes that the credit for his "introduction to the Universal Monsters goes as much to him [Mel Jass] as to the likes of James Whale and Tod Browning" (2009, 8), and this is undoubtedly true of many other Universal horror fans today.

The 1960s television also saw horror-comedies like *The Munsters* (1964–1966), based on Universal-trademarked characters, as well as similar programs like *Addams Family*. In 1962, Universal underwent yet another takeover, this time becoming part of the Music Corporation of America (MCA), also a major television producer at the time. The MCA had already purchased the Universal lot in 1958, and exerted influence on Universal products from this point. As with previous takeovers and mergers, MCA opened up new possibilities for industrializing branding and remix transmedially across platforms. In 1964, for instance, Universal Studios would launch a series of studio tours, which would soon include appearances by Frankenstein's monster, bringing audiences into the storyworld of its classic monsters. Each of these recombinations and reappearances of Universal's monsters helped to cement them in the minds and hearts of new audiences.

Interestingly, one of the most memorable monster mashes from this period was not produced by Universal at all: Bobby "Boris" Pickett's "monstrously catchy" 1962 parody song "The Monster Mash" (Hunt 2020). In Roger Ebert's 2004 review of *Van Helsing*, he quotes from Pickett's song to summarize the film: "The zombies were having fun / The party had just begun / The guests included Wolf Man / Dracula and his son" (Pickett 1962; Ebert 2004). Ebert jokes how strange it is that such a production "would forget to play 'Monster Mash' over the end credits" (Ebert 2004). The simplest reason is that Universal would have had to pay another corporation to do so—Garpax Records, and not MCA, produced the track. "The Monster Mash" riffs on Universal's monsters but also Dee Dee Sharp's "Mashed Potato Time" (1962) and the related dance craze, the Mashed Potato. Notably, this is also the point at which the word "mash" in music begins to converge with the "monster mash" of the latter twentieth century. In addition to Dee Dee Sharp and the Mashed Potato, Harrison and Navas note that

> mash" can be traced back at least to Jamaican patois from the early 1970s. In the island's reggae and dancehall music, MCs would occasionally proclaim mash it up!" as a way to build energy during performance. To mash," then, was a general call to succeed, to do well, to push the music's vibe" forward, not unlike hip hop MCs shouting put your hands in the air!" (Harrison and Navas 2017, 189)

From the 1960s Universal horror may not have graced the silver screen with the regularity of previous years, but thanks to successful branding and transmedia extension, both in-house and from other sources, its monsters and its universe remained alive and well to fans and audiences across the country.

THE "BIG FOUR": INDUSTRIAL HORROR (1990–2017)

From here, Universal's growth (and that of its horror brand) only intensifies, following familiar patterns. There is also a closer and more intense link between transmedia storytelling and transmedia branding, though the studio never quite returned to the fevered pace of serialized horror production it maintained in the 1940s and 1950s. Ultimately it did not need to—it could simply repackage its existing films and stories to new audiences, but with the affordances of new technologies and corporate synergies making this process even easier than before. In 2011, in an ironic echo of Universal's big four monsters (Dracula, Wolf Man, Frankenstein's Monster, the Mummy), Universal became part of Comcast, one of the "Big Four" of telecommunications conglomerates (America's second-largest after AT&T, followed by The Walt Disney Company and ViacomCBS). Before this, however, it was being steadily absorbed by larger and larger corporations, with further and deeper opportunities for the industrialization of transmedia storytelling and branding. In 1990 Universal was part of a merger between Panasonic (then Matsushita) and several other corporations. Echoing its response to the popularity of television in the mid-twentieth century and TV distribution deal with Screen Gems, between 1991 and 1995 Universal released home video VHS editions of many of its horror films. This was the first time these films were actually packaged together as "Classic Monsters," complete with a newly designed logo. The 1990s also saw a merchandising surge of Universal Monsters material, a postmodern "recycling and re-inventing [of] everything that has already come and gone before," which once again introduced a new audience to the films (Biscotti 2016).

Besides the Classic Monsters and the Dark Universe, Universal made other forays into transmedia storytelling and world-building. In 1999 it released *The Mummy*, directed by Stephen Sommers. *The Mummy* was a campy adventure romp, not a prestige horror film like those of the 1930s, but its mid-range budget of $80 million did mark a change of tactics for Universal, in contrast with its low-budget horror films of the 1940s and 1950s. The risk paid off—*The Mummy* made five times its budget in ticket sales alone, and more in theme park tie-ins and other merchandising. The studio would also release two sequels and an animated series, as well as the spin-off franchise *The Scorpion King* (2002). In 2004 Universal returned to the old "monster rally" format and released *Van Helsing* (a full four years before the MCU's opening installment *Iron Man* in 2008), directed once again by Stephen Sommers and this time with a higher budget. With echoes of 1945's *House of Dracula*, in *Van Helsing* Count Dracula (Richard Roxburgh) seeks to use Frankenstein's Monster (Shuler Hensley) for his own nefarious plans. The film also features werewolves, ghosts, and Jekyll and Hyde, as well as the titular monster hunter Gabriel Van Helsing (Hugh Jackman). As suggested at the beginning of this chapter, *Van Helsing* was intentionally transmedial, boasting an animated prequel (Bridgeman 2004) and a stand-alone comic book extension (Dysart and Alexander 2004). It was a year for cinematic monster mashes more broadly—or more accurately, for monster mash-up, since it is here that the musical terminology of remix began to be used in reviews of Universal's films for the first time. 20th Century Fox's film *The League of Extraordinary Gentlemen*, which premiered just ten months before *Van Helsing*, featured Jekyll and Hyde, a vampire Mina Harker, and a super-healing Dorian Gray, among other monstrous characters from literature. Both films were critically reviled, and *Van Helsing* would not lead to a sequel, though crucially it still made Universal a great deal of money. *Van Helsing* also played into Universal's previous successes with its rebooted *Mummy* franchise and featured numerous Easter eggs and callbacks to classic Universal Monsters films. Notably, in that same year the Classic Monsters series also came to DVD. While it might not have been planned as part of a shared transmedia storyworld in the same sense as the Dark Universe, *Van Helsing* certainly contributed to expectations for monster mash-ups going forward, as well as to a sense of audience engagement and nostalgia for Universal's Classic Monsters.

REVISITING THE DARK UNIVERSE

Given the seemingly easy success of the brand in its previous resurrections, where did Universal's Dark Universe go wrong? To start, it existed in a dramatically different media landscape than Universal's monster rallies of the 1940s or family action blockbusters of the late 1990s. More importantly, however, one could also argue that Universal lost sight of its own brand identity and extensive history in recombinant cinema and "unoriginal" horror. Gone were the low-budget camp releases, replaced by extremely expensive action tentpoles. The 2017's *The Mummy* cost a staggering $350 million to make, which it only just managed to recoup at the box office. Unlike previous waves of mash-up, there was also no fresh re-release of Universal's "Classic Monsters" to establish new audiences and recognition for the history of the brand. Ultimately this meant *The Mummy* was largely reaching out to old fans who already had a long-established "favorite" entry in the Universal Monsters universe, either in the television re-runs of the 1970s and 1980s, or in the campy reboots of the 1990s and 2000s.

Fittingly, then, at the end we come back to the beginning: to adaptation and to low-budget stakes. After the failure of its Dark Universe, Universal struck a co-production deal with Blumhouse for new adaptations of their classic properties. Their investment in this venture was minimal. The first film in this collaboration, *Invisible Man* (2020), cost just $7 million to make. As with Universal's old favorites, however, cheap production and familiar, high-prestige source texts became the key. Only now, Universal's own monster had become the "original" works. *Invisible Man* went on to gross over $142 million worldwide. Unlike *Dracula Untold* or *The Mummy*, *Invisible Man* also had the benefit of a readily available Classic Monsters archive library for fans to discover (or return to). Blu-ray editions were released in 2018, and in 2020 the monsters were streamed for free on the "Fear: The Home of Horror" YouTube channel—a clever way for Universal to establish dominance over the property in the digital streaming market before *Dracula* and other 1931 films enter the public domain in 2027. In practice this will have little impact on the monsters' copyright status, since Universal has kept them trademarked through other productions, but it will leave the film footage itself open to mash-up and parody by fans and adaptors. In the current media climate, this will benefit the studio. The spread of such mash-ups will only add to the Classic Monsters' brand recognition, and Universal can use the opportunity to seem open and generous with its old intellectual property while still maintaining informal authority over it.

As Freeman argues of historical transmedia, Universal's story of monster mash and the industrialization of Gothic remix practices is one of variations on sameness. It also teaches us that we cannot overlook the importance of "unoriginal" production to the world of Gothic and horror more generally. These kinds of practices reduce production costs, potentially allowing for more horror to enter a popular market in which it is often seen as a risky investment with a niche audience (as Aldana Reyes also argues in his chapter in this collection). More importantly, recombinant practices also demonstrate yet again that meaning and value are relative, and that the same text in a new context can produce new readings and perspectives. As Aldana Reyes points out in an earlier publication, we have only come to count Universal's Classic Monster films among the ranks of the Gothic because they are "unoriginal"—because they are adaptations: "Adaptations are crucial to any discussion of Gothic cinema because, whereas the 'Gothic' label can be ambiguous, adaptations of well-known Gothic texts [like *Dracula* and *Frankenstein*] present themselves as de facto Gothic, regardless of their aesthetic treatment" (2020, 12). Here, as always, the repetition of sameness also brings us something new. By the end of the Classic Monsters cycle in the 1950s, sets and locations had become "architectural pastiches of their predecessors embalmed in a Gothic timelessness that renders periodization irrelevant" (Aldana Reyes 2020, 113–14). Audience genre expectations adjusted with them, and today we recognize the Gothic visual mode as one that is not only set in the past, but which haunts our modern era as well. Universal's Classic Monsters teach us that, in many ways, contemporary mash-up, reboot, and transmedia culture is nothing new, and that we will be doing the monster mash well into the future.

REFERENCES

Aldana Reyes, Xavier. 2020. *Gothic Cinema*. Routledge Film Guidebooks. London: Routledge.

Biscotti, Steven. 2016. "Who Remembers The 90's Resurgence of the Universal Monsters?" *Universal Monsters Universe* (blog). 28 July 2016. https://universalmonstersuniverse.com/2016/07/28/who-remembers-the-90s-resurgence-of-the-universal-monsters/.

Borschke, Margie. 2017. *This Is Not a Remix: Piracy, Authenticity and Popular Music*. New York: Bloomsbury Academic.

Bridgeman, Sharon. 2004. *Van Helsing: The London Assignment*. Animation. Universal Pictures.

Brooks, Andi, and Frank Dello Stritto. 2012. "The 1938 Dracula & Frankenstein Double-Bill." *The Bela Lugosi Blog* (blog). 30 January 2012. https://beladraculalugosi.com/the-1938-dracula-frankenstein-double-bill/.

Cartmell, Deborah, and Imelda Whelehan, eds. 1999. *Adaptations: From Text to Screen, Screen to Text*. New York: Routledge.

Concannon, Tim. 2020. "Emil Umann, the Man Who Invented Midnight Movies?" *Black Mass* (blog). 24 August 2020. https://www.blackmassmovies.com/emil-umann-the-man-who-invented-midnight-movies/.

Coons, Robbin. 1938. "Hollywood Sights and Sounds." *Kingston Daily Freeman*, 12 December 1938.

Decherney, Peter. 2012. *Hollywood's Copyright Wars: From Edison to the Internet*. Columbia University Press.

Dysart, Joshua, and Jason Shawn Alexander. 2004. *Van Helsing: From Beneath the Rue Morgue*. Milwaukie, OR: Dark Horse.

Ebert, Roger. 2004. "Van Helsing Movie Review & Film Summary (2004)." *RogerEbert.Com*. 7 May 2004. https://www.rogerebert.com/reviews/van-helsing-2004.

Edwards, Kyle. 2014a. "'Hot Profits Out of Cold Shivers': Horror, the First-Run Market, and the Hollywood Studios, 1938 to 1942." In *Merchants of Menace: The Business of Horror Cinema*, edited by Richard Nowell, 163–85. New York: Bloomsbury.

———. 2014b. "'House of Horrors': Corporate Strategy at Universal Pictures in the 1930s." In *Merchants of Menace: The Business of Horror Cinema*, edited by Richard Nowell, 13–29. New York: Bloomsbury.
Elliott, Kamilla. 2008. "Gothic—Film—Parody." *Adaptation* 1 (1): 24–43.
Fast, Karin, and Henrik Örnebring. 2017. "Transmedia World-Building: *The Shadow* (1931–Present) and *Transformers* (1984–Present)." *International Journal of Cultural Studies* 20 (6): 636–52. https://doi.org/10.1177/1367877915605887.
Film Daily. 1942. "You Can't Keep a Good Monster Down (Advertisement for Ghost of Frankenstein)." *Archive.org*. 27 February 1942.
Freeman, Matthew. 2016. *Historicising Transmedia Storytelling: Early Twentieth-Century Transmedia Story Worlds*. London: Routledge.
Gray, Jonathan. 2010. *Show Sold Separately: Promos, Spoilers, and Other Media Paratexts*. New York: New York University Press.
Hall, Sheldon, and Stephen Neale. 2010. *Epics, Spectacles, and Blockbusters: A Hollywood History*. Contemporary Approaches to Film and Television Series. Detroit, MI: Wayne State University Press.
Harrison, Nate, and Eduardo Navas. 2017. "Mashup." In *Keywords in Remix Studies*, edited by Eduardo Navas, Owen Gallagher, and xtine burrough, 188–201. New York: Routledge.
Harrison's Reports. 1944. "'House of Frankenstein' with Boris Karloff and Lon Chaney." 24 December 1944.
Hassler-Forest, Dan. 2016. *Science Fiction, Fantasy, and Politics: Transmedia World-Building Beyond Capitalism*. London: Rowman & Littlefield.
Hunt, El. 2020. "The Strange Tale of 'Monster Mash,' the Graveyard Smash That Will Never Die.' *NME*. 28 October 2020. https://www.nme.com/features/monster-mash-bobby-pickett-misfits-halloween-2800745.
Jenkins, Henry. 2006. *Convergence Culture: Where Old and New Media Collide*. New York: New York University Press.
———. 2010. "Transmedia Storytelling and Entertainment: An Annotated Syllabus." *Continuum* 24 (6): 943–58. https://doi.org/10.1080/10304312.2010.510599.
Kupfer, Alex. 2015. "Sporting Labor in the Hollywood Studio System: Basketball, Universal Pictures, and the 1936 Berlin Olympics." *Spectator* 35 (2): 10–17.
Leitch, Thomas. 2012. "Adaptation and Intertextuality, or, What Isn't an Adaptation and What Does It Matter?" In *A Companion to Literature, Film, and Adaptation*, edited by Deborah Cartmell, 87–104. Hoboken, NJ: Wiley-Blackwell.
Mallory, Michael. 2009. *Universal Studios Monsters: A Legacy of Horror*. 1st ed. New York: Universe Publishing.
Moreno, EJ. 2020. *The Dark Universe That Never Was: A Short History of Universal's Failed Monster Franchise*. YouTube: Flickering Myth. https://www.youtube.com/watch?v=zDYi4wnWe74.
Pearson, Roberta. 2017. "World-Building Logics and Copyright: The Dark Knight and the Great Detective." In *World Building*, edited by Marta Boni, 109–28. Amsterdam: Amsterdam University Press.

Peirse, Alison. 2013. *After Dracula: The 1930s Horror Film*. London: I. B. Tauris. https://doi.org/10.5040/9780755698202?locatt=label:secondary_bloomsburyCollections.
Petley, Julian. 2017. "Horror and the Censors." In *A Companion to the Horror Film*, edited by Harry M. Benshoff, 130–47. Malden, MA: John Wiley & Sons.
Rivera, Joshua. 2017. "'The Mummy' Franchise's Cinematic Universe Seems to Be Crumbling." *GQ*. 8 November 2017. https://www.gq.com/story/dark-universe-dying-again-lol.
Ryan, Marie-Laure. 2015. "Transmedia Storytelling: Industry Buzzword or New Narrative Experience?" *Storyworlds: A Journal of Narrative Studies* 7 (2): 1–19. https://doi.org/10.5250/storyworlds.7.2.0001.
Scolari, A. Carlos. 2018. "Transmedia Branding: Brands, Narrative Worlds, and the Mcwhopper Peace Agreement." *Semiotica* 2018 (224): 1–17. https://doi.org/10.1515/sem-2016-0216.
Scott, John L. 1944. "Thriller Stars Convene." *Los Angeles Times*, 23 December 1944.
Sommers, Stephen. 2009. "Foreword." In *Universal Studios Monsters: A Legacy of Horror*, edited by Michael Mallory, 1st ed., 8–9. New York: Universe Publishing.
Variety. 1936. "Horror Films Taken off U Sked." 5 May 1936.
———. 1938. "Inside Stuff—Pictures." 10 August 1938.
Weaver, Tom, Michael Brunas, and John Brunas. 2007. *Universal Horrors: The Studio's Classic Films, 1931–1946*. 2nd ed. Jefferson, NC: McFarland & Co.
Weiler, A. H. 1944. "At the Rialto." *The New York Times*. 16 December 1944, sec. Archives. https://www.nytimes.com/1944/12/16/archives/at-the-rialto.html.
Willis, Ika. 2016. "Amateur Mythographies: Fan Fiction and the Myth of Myth." *Transformative Works and Cultures* 21: n. pag.

Chapter 2

Adapting Monstrous Creation

Lisztomania *and* Gothic *as Gothic Mash-Ups*

Kevin M. Flanagan

Two films that combine director Ken Russell's (1927–2011) interest in artists with his forays into fantastic genre cinema are *Lisztomania* (1975), a Warner Brothers production released the same year as the highly profitable rock opera *Tommy* (1975), and *Gothic* (1986), made for Richard Branson's Virgin Vision. *Lisztomania* paints a chameleonic portrait of composer Franz Liszt (1811–1886), providing commentary on his life as distilled through such disparate cultural lenses as comic books, progressive rock, and horror film homage. *Gothic*, by contrast, focuses on a very specific meeting of artists: the 1816 summer gathering at the Villa Diodati that put Percy Shelley, Mary Shelley, Lord Byron, Dr. John Polidori, and Claire Clairmont into conversation with one another and resulted in the ghost story challenge that inspired Mary Shelley's *Frankenstein* (1818) (Mellor 2003, 10). Looked at from one direction, these are both original cinematic properties. For *Lisztomania*, Russell wrote his own screenplay, devising a unique scenario whose pop sensibilities were encouraged by producer David Puttnam, and whose scenes resemble the stand-alone, tonally varied set pieces of recent films *Mahler* (1974) and *Tommy* (Lanza 2007, 181–2). With *Gothic*, Russell directed the script by Stephen Volk, a noted horror author whose reputation also rests on the BBC mock-documentary *Ghostwatch* (1992). Both films share a narrative fascination that aligns with the Romanticist discourse on artistic creation, with its nascent obsession with the idea of individual originality and concurrent exploration of the process of adaptation. Ultimately, each film emerges as a kind of Gothic mash-up or "Frankenfiction," defined by Megen de Bruin-Molé as a subjective recombination of past pieces, properties, or characters (2020, 16–17).

The first academic studies of Ken Russell were keenly interested in his approach to adaptation, with many focusing on his success at filming D. H. Lawrence in *Women in Love* (1969), including much of the first issue of the journal *Literature/Film Quarterly* (Moore 1973, 9–11; Zambrano 1973, 46–54). Joseph A. Gomez's influential book *Ken Russell: The Adaptor as Creator* (1976) uses adaptation as a lens through which to assess Russell's contribution to the cinema, with particular attention paid to *The Devils* (1971), a film based on historical fact, a narrative history by Aldous Huxley, and a play by John Whiting. While most of these early studies consider Russell's fidelity to texts as a primary criterion of success, they nevertheless establish the degree to which Russell worked with the ideas of other artists as the raw material for his films. Many of Russell's feature films are adaptations, but they are not always identified or discussed as such. His biopics are in part holistic accounts of artists but are often explicitly sourced in a single biography or work of remembrance. For instance, *Song of Summer* works from Eric Fenby's book *Delius as I Knew Him* (1936) and uses Fenby's subjective memories to present scenes from the life of Delius as an infirm old man.

Lisztomania and *Gothic* are adaptations of a sort. They use intertextual references from Gothic horror culture to build apparently original commentaries on the act of creation as understood by the Romantic artists they profile. I argue that these two films express this discourse of creative invention through a paradox: originality and individualized expression via the quoting and repurposing of the Gothic mash-up mode. In his writings on textuality, Gérard Genette defines intertextuality as "a relationship of copresence between two texts or among several texts: that is to say, eidetically and typically as the actual presence of one text within another," which he further qualifies as sometimes appearing as quotation, sometimes as plagiarism, and sometimes as allusion (1997, 1–2). Russell's films offer a synthesis of a creative paradigm sourced in accumulated Gothic motifs and the ideas of Romanticism that is filtered through postmodern sensibilities about the promiscuity and movement of texts. More specifically, *Lisztomania* is an unacknowledged adaptation of Mary Shelley's *Frankenstein* (itself a Gothic mash-up of a sort), while *Gothic* is at once partially an unofficial adaptation of on-screen participant John William Polidori's "The Vampyre" (1819) and the story of how Mary Shelley adapted her sense memories and experiences into the eventual writing of *Frankenstein*.

Russell has long been associated with Romanticism. His 1978 Granada television productions on the relationship between William and Dorothy Wordsworth, and on the tumultuous life of Samuel Taylor Coleridge, were gathered together under the name *Clouds of Glory* (the title comes from Wordsworth's 1807 poem *Ode: Intimations of Immortality from Recollections of Early Childhood*, a piece that he shared with Coleridge)

(Sisman 2007, 344–5). Many of Russell's movies as a writer-director (including *Savage Messiah* [1972], *Mahler*, and *Valentino* [1977]) overlay the essentially Romanticist creative problem of the artist striving to produce original, self-actualizing work despite outside pressures on subjects most obviously associated with modernism. Indeed, Russell's self-narrative of success as a filmmaker is one of striving to create personal work despite editorial interference, censorship, or withheld finance (Williams 2013, 351–2; Russell 2001, 1–20, 24). Herbert Read identifies a tension within early Romantic thought that plays out both in Russell's own self-narrative and in the works that he creates, especially *Lisztomania* and *Gothic*: the struggle between the will (the external pressures of the world, realist representation) and the productive wellspring of the imagination. He writes: "The will was seen as always inhibiting or distorting the free play of the imagination, and this 'free play' was identified with the 'real self,'" while "the unconscious, the dream world, became a refuge from an impersonal and harsh materialistic world" (Read 1965, 117).

For Romanticists, the generative power of the internalized, mental world scrapes up against culturally normalizing forces like extant artistic movements, critics, conservative public tastes, and the need to sell art as a capitalist commodity. The desired "free play of the imagination" nevertheless contains a paradox in that the uninhibited mind creates new art through engaging already existing works, ideas, and sentiments. In writing about Russell as an exceptional auteur of "trash" cinema, I. Q. Hunter has described the director as much as a *pasticheur* as a Romanticist prophet: "With Russell trash came to be a stylistic choice, as with dazzling excess, he cut through factitious distinctions between official and popular culture in order to be true to the chaos and tastelessness of the Unconscious, from which creativity—his chief concern—sprang forth" (2013, 153). Nowhere is this more evident than when Russell overlays this mode of creative desire onto already established genre traditions.

In both *Lisztomania* and *Gothic*, two perennial horror figurations—vampiric transference and the creation discourse stemming from Mary Shelley's *Frankenstein*—become possible paradigms and homologous strategies for adaptation in general. In *Lisztomania*, these two tropes have several levels of meaning, ranging from the literal (Wagner becomes Dr. Frankenstein) to the figurative (*Lisztomania* itself, with its assemblage of intertextual references, becomes a Frankenstein's monster of its own). In *Gothic*, there is adaptation of a more traditional kind, such as the Polidori-Byron relationship that mirrors the relationship of Aubrey and Lord Ruthven in Polidori's "The Vampyre," but also justifications for Mary Shelley's inspiration via the other stories and mass hallucinations. Taken together, they are as much typical Ken Russell films as they are engines for creating monstrous bodies.

LISZTOMANIA AND VAMPIRIC TRANSFERENCE

Lisztomania was marketed as a pop-rock biopic of Franz Liszt and his circle—the film's tagline claimed that it "out-Tommy's *Tommy*," with Russell's initial pitch for the project supposedly being that it told the story of "a classical composer who was the Elton John of his day" (Russell 2001, 20)—but there are several sequences that visually and thematically connect the movie to the history of Gothic horror. The first is prompted by Princess Carolyn (Sara Kestelman), who tempts Franz Liszt (Roger Daltrey) to make a demonic pact to secure success in composing. Liszt momentarily resists, but eventually gives in, thereby giving him inordinate energy—phallic and creative—that prompts his series of *Orpheus* symphonic poems. In another, a parasitic Richard Wagner (Paul Nicholas) momentarily transforms into a vampire and bites his former mentor, thereby stealing the teacher's musical prowess. In yet another, a righteous Liszt tracks down Wagner, a Nietzschean superman whose command of music has given him the mad power to create life in his own image. The first part of this sequence shows Wagner and his wife Cosima (Veronica Quilligan) instructing German youth in anti-Semitism in a manner familiar to Nazi propaganda films, with nods to Nietzsche, Jerry Siegel and Joe Shuster's *Superman*, and Russell's own BBC film *Dance of the Seven Veils* (1970), a comic-strip biopic on the life of another German composer, Richard Strauss; the second has Liszt confront Wagner, now a Dr. Frankenstein figure of sorts, who proceeds to showcase his latest creation, a kind of *ur*-Nordic monster, a mechanical Siegfried, played by Yes keyboardist Rick Wakeman. The creature malfunctions, Wagner becomes a vampire once again, and Liszt defeats him with a flamethrower piano. Angered, Cosima stages a reanimation ceremony, where the dead Wagner is brought back to life as a proper Frankenstein's monster (modeled after Karloff) that is dressed as Hitler. Liszt and the women in his life defeat Wagner with a spaceship powered by music. Already in 1975, Russell was in Gothic mashup mode, well before the twenty-first-century flowering.

Attempts at causal description make Russell's *Lisztomania* seem incoherent. It is critically regarded as the precipitous high point of all the director's creative excesses. Joseph Lanza situates the film on a continuum with his success in *Tommy*: "*Lisztomania* continues Russell's harder, more satirical edge, with more lavish sets, more crazed acting, more frenetic plot pacing, and a premise that is simultaneously silly and fantastic" (2007, 180). The film represents a kind of massed attempt at translating thematic tropes from horror literature and culture into productive narrative forces, intertextual frames of reference that organize both the film's semantic elements (its iconography, its carnivalesque sense of history and biography, its extensive quotations of literature, cinema, and music), and its syntactic organization (not just the film's nominal plot, but the general way in which affect and power circulate in this heightened diegesis). While it is easy to dismiss *Lisztomania* as a postmodern mishmash, it can be better understood as an obtuse look at a composer's life in relation to the monstrous imagination of the nineteenth century.

Franz Liszt played piano and composed during the height of Romantic music and was a contemporary of Franz Schubert, Hector Berlioz, and Richard Wagner in music, as well as Byron, George Sand, and Victor Hugo in literature, and Eugène Delacroix in the visual arts. His celebrity caused Heinrich Heine to coin the term "Lisztomania" to explain his virtuosity and the frenzied pleasure of his performances (Heine [1844] 2011). He lived fast and was the center of public scandals, courting the kind of rock star image that Russell holds at the heart of his film (Saffle 2007, 60). As Jacques Barzun notes, Romanticism dealt extensively in imagination, and "it was Romanticist discussion that made the word creation regularly apply to works of art" (2000, 473–4). In *Lisztomania*, Franz Liszt is a worried dreamer whose primary concern is self-expression; he feverishly pursues love and music, often to the detriment of his family and his tacit responsibilities as a creative mentor to a new generation of musicians. Such a man appealed to workaholic Russell, who had previously thematized his own struggles in middle age through his direction of Robert Powell as Gustav Mahler in *Mahler* (Flanagan 2009, xvi).

Lisztomania is an assemblage of scenes and sketches which amount to a biography of Liszt and his contemporary Richard Wagner. The film is suffused with nested dream sequences and fantasies, but a narrative throughline anchored by Liszt's changing fortunes allows it to chart Liszt's rise in popularity, the dissolution of his partnership with Marie d'Agoult (Fiona Lewis), his creative and romantic encounters with Princess Carolyne zu SaynWittgenstein, his decision to become an Abbé, and his escalating dissatisfaction with Richard Wagner, who borrowed his ideas, eventually married his daughter, and espoused a racial philosophy that gelled with the founding tenets of Nazism. *Dance of the Seven Veils* does something similar, imagining the life and music of twentieth-century German composer Richard Strauss, in the process showing his collusion with the Nazi regime, a political gambit that gives him a questionable legacy (Hanke 1984, 39–40). Both resemble comics in their elevation of visual imagery over naturalistic narrative progression, as well as their investigation of the cultural consequences of Nazism on the arts. Both consciously approach, appropriate, and criticize a mode of kitsch that retrospectively seemed foundational to the visual imaginary of Nazism (Huckvale 2012, 111). These films share a thesis with Robert Harbison's controversial *Deliberate Regression* (1980), a book that finds in the cult of Romanticist self-imaging the seeds of fascism: "The furthest excess of Romantic individualism is to recreate a god in the self out of just those parts beyond one's conscious control, so the unconscious and ungovernable is elevated as the true beyond, the highest part of the individual no longer individual" (1980, xv). In *Dance of the Seven Veils*, Strauss chases this godhood until the Nazi regime collapses around him; in *Lisztomania*, Wagner is only prevented from achieving it through Liszt's alliance with his creative muses, and his campy musical spaceship.

At times, *Lisztomania* even approaches sketch comedy, with scenes such as the backstage encounter between Liszt and Wagner containing so many cameos (George Sand! Berlioz!) and historical jokes as to approach the level of the fastest Monty Python gags. Another sequence hallucinates the temptation of Liszt by Princess Carolyn, wherein a giant phallic statue and maypole embody Liszt's creative potential, and Carolyn's threat of a suspiciously sized guillotine visualizes the startling possibility of its failure. This set piece, which gathers the women in Liszt's life into a choreographed musical number, takes place in a cathedral wallpapered by contemporary pop stars imagined as Greek orthodox icons. Elton John, Elvis Presley, Bill Haley, Pete Townshend, and Ringo Starr (who plays The Pope in the film) silently watch over the festivities. The mixing of time, cultural contexts, registers of artistic expression, visual iconography, and film and theatrical genres is indicative of Russell's use of horror intertexts, which are offered not as one-to-one adaptations, but rather as figurations that embody how creativity and imagination work for Romanticist artists.

One sequence of *Lisztomania* offers an especially horrific encounter. Wagner (now a proto-terroristic political activist) flees capture and takes refuge from armed forces. While talking to Liszt, who was otherwise busy composing, Wagner takes advantage of a rare solar eclipse to transform into a vampire and suck away Liszt's creative juices (lest the connection be lost on us, Russell stages this near a piano, such that the two men compose during Wagner's feeding). The visual suggests vampiric faces in Hammer horror films, especially those of a heavily made-up Christopher Lee. But the choice to depict Wagner as a vampire goes beyond the basic explanation of his change in personality and ambitions (that Wagner must syphon creativity from Liszt). There is a weird class politics: poor, revolutionary Wagner steals from new money Liszt in order to become the grand old man of German music. For Thomas Leitch, as for Karl Marx, vampirism is a key type of creative transaction. Marx (1867) bluntly claims that "Capital is dead labour, that, vampire-like, only lives by sucking living labour, and lives the more, the more labour it sucks." Leitch observes, "just as adaptations may be argued to feed like vampires off their source texts, those texts themselves assume the defining characteristic of vampires—the status of undead spirits whose unnaturally prolonged life depends on the sustenance they derive from younger, fresher blood—through the process of adaptation, which allows them to extend their life through a series of updated avatars" (Leitch 2011, 6).

Russell does not just use the figure of the vampire to connect *Lisztomania* to a recent slate of films, but also to put his film into conversation with a whole history of popular mythmaking, from Bram Stoker's venerated *Dracula* (1897) to the oddball *The Satanic Rites of Dracula* (1973, Alan Gibson), thereby highlighting a paradox of creativity in Gothic and Romanticist authorship. On the one hand, single-author originality is put at a premium, but on the other, the radical reinvention of creation myths and canonical stories (Cantor 1984) and the idea of collaborating (Leader 1996) in pursuit of the new are just as valid. This is a thematic impasse that can be traced throughout Russell's career—the tension between individual stardom and team collaboration that differentiates the "real world" and "fantasy" sequences in Russell's adaptation of Sandy Wilson's *The Boy Friend* (1971) comes to mind—but it finds its most explicit realization in *Lisztomania* and *Gothic*, two films that stare down the supposed sources of Romantic creativity.

LITSZTOMANIA AND FRANKENSTEIN

While the spirit of vampirism works for describing Wagner in *Lisztomania*, and likewise explains Russell's symbiotic relationship with past popular culture, it is the film's engagement with Mary Shelley's *Frankenstein* that best explores the method to its madness. *Lisztomania* is a "Frankenstein's monster" of a movie. It creates something new—a transcendent and triumphalist retelling of the life of Franz Liszt—out of a motley collection of parts. Some of the visuals are direct recyclings of previous Russell images. For example, the coffin-piano is a slight variant on Gustav Mahler's coffin-prison from *Mahler*. Others hew extremely close to big sequences in other films, intentionally or not. Princess Carolyn's inflatable, cavernous vagina recalls a similar sequence of a fun house trap in Robert Fuest's *The Final Programme* (1973), while *Lisztomania*'s heavenly chamber concert, where Liszt plays music with the women in his life before stopping the threat of Wagner once and for all, resembles the final scene of *Casino Royale* (1967, Val Guest et al.), in which the seven deputized James Bond characters play harps after the explosion of a nuclear device. David Huckvale notes that *Lisztomania*'s final scenes of the organ-spaceship "resemble the kind of space-age heroics of Gerry Anderson's 1960s TV series *Thunderbirds* and *Captain Scarlet*" in visual execution and in their use of Wagnerian music (2012, 166). Beyond direct and subconscious references, *Lisztomania* uses narrative and iconographic aspects of the biopic, the musical, horror films, silent comedy, and dance to tell its story.

Lisztomania contains several visual Frankenstein monsters. Wagner's Siegfried is conceived in a laboratory and is put together by science and powered by audio recordings of Wagner's philosophy and music. In this brief subplot, Wagner is a mad Dr. Frankenstein character hell-bent on building his perfect creature. *Lisztomania* also joins the illustrious company of texts like Clifford K. Berryman's *Washington Post* cartoon of June 6, 1940, and the cyborg final boss from the PC game *Wolfenstein 3-D* (1992) in imagining a Frankenstein's monster-Hitler hybrid (Hitchcock 2007, 193–4). After Liszt initially defeats Wagner with his flamethrower piano, Cosima resurrects Wagner, now an undead creature who resembles Karloff's monster and Hitler. This is also a nod to *Tommy*, whose "Sally Simpson" sequence features this character (Victoria Russell) entering into an ill-advised marriage to a rock musician (Gary Rich) who dresses in Karloff garb throughout. The trope of the undead Hitler rising from the grave provides a campy forecast to a similarly famous scene from Hans-Jurgen Syberberg's *Hitler: A Film from Germany* (1977), therein used to explore his haunting of German national memory.

But it is *Lisztomania*'s status as an unacknowledged adaptation of *Frankenstein* that most concretely explores its stake in monstrous creation and its bona fides as a Gothic mash-up. The entire narrative arc of the film follows Shelley's book: Liszt is Victor, and his example and success at music "creates" Wagner, a monstrous being who accentuates, mirrors, and ultimately despises his progenitor. Wagner is influenced by/worships Liszt as a musician, adaptor, and creator, Liszt distances himself from Wagner (represented in the film by Liszt's bastardization of Wagner's music in recital), and a monstrous Wagner returns to take his revenge. Like Shelley's *Frankenstein*, the two go after one another in a dogged pursuit of righting perceived wrongs (for Liszt/Victor, the destruction of the failed monster; for Wagner/The Monster, revenge for flawed creation). In the end, Liszt destroys his hideous progeny. Russell clearly does not care that the historical Liszt did not kill an undead Wagner from the afterlife! The director uses the film not as an exercise in historical authenticity, but instead as an incubation chamber for his ideas on art. Russell uses Gothic horror intertexts, and especially *Frankenstein*, to reinvent Liszt and Wagner as mythic beings, ones for whom music, philosophy, sex, and religion were alive, invested with the urgency of the great mysteries of the universe. Like *Frankenstein* and Romanticist thought more generally, *Lisztomania* is about nothing less than the "remaking of man" (Cantor 1984, xvi). That the film achieves this through a Gothic mash-up stew featuring rock stars Roger Daltrey, Rick Wakeman, and Ringo Starr ensures its status as a 1970s curio.

GOTHIC, FRANKENSTEIN, AND GOTHIC MASH-UP

If *Lisztomania* illustrates how the cultural afterlife of *Frankenstein* can resonate in the unlikeliest of places (a pop-rock biopic of a Hungarian composer), then *Gothic* seeks to demonstrate why it has an afterlife in the first place. The 1980s were a strange period for Russell, a decade that contained his biggest film as well as a gradual fall from grace. He directed films for major studios throughout the 1970s, culminating with the big budget *Altered States* (1980) for Warner Brothers. His films of the rest of the decade were either created for television (Melvyn Bragg's *South Bank Show*; *Ken Russell's View of The Planets*, a found-footage documentary cut to Gustav Holst's famous symphony) or for small companies (he directed *Crimes of Passion* [1984] for New World, and made *Salome's Last Dance* [1988], *Lair of the White Worm* [1988], and *The Rainbow* [1989] for Vestron Pictures) (Hillier 1994, 34, 63). *Gothic* was made for Virgin Vision, a company that collapsed in 1986 because of the massive financial loss of the nostalgic pop musical *Absolute Beginners* (Walker 2005, 82), and was distributed by Vestron on VHS. As a package, *Gothic* promises a similar combination of elements as *Lisztomania*: artists behaving badly, music by a contemporary rock star (here Thomas Dolby), a fanciful reconstruction of historical encounters, and Russell's desire to personalize. *Gothic* is the first of a subcycle of films made over subsequent years that revisit the creative maelstrom of that Diodati stay. *Haunted Summer* (1988, Ivan Passer) looks at this time in a manner closer to a conventional costume drama, while *Rowing with the Wind* (1988, Gonzalo Suarez) treads similar ground, albeit with a more visually languid approach.

Gothic sports Russell's favored brand of episodic narration, but condenses a summer's worth of action, intellectual discussion, and private writing into one enchanted evening (Seymour 2000, 153–63). Lord Byron (Gabriel Byrne) and his companion Dr. John Polidori (Timothy Spall) live in exile at the villa on the shores of Lake Geneva and are visited by Percy Bysshe Shelley (Julian Sands), his romantic partner Mary (Natasha Richardson), and Claire Clairmont (Myriam Cyr), Mary's stepsister and Byron's sometimes lover. Over the near-constant consumption of laudanum, the group initiates witty conversation, discusses science, and engages in group sex (Percy alludes to his and Mary's mutual commitment to "free love"). Many of the film's early sequences establish character traits that will later be accentuated, exaggerated, or rendered horrific. For instance, Percy's magnetic attractiveness, his ability to inspire mania in men and women, is shown in a sequence in which young girls chase him in a bout of fevered hysteria, a cult of personality that later causes Polidori to resent Percy for his implied sexual relationship with Byron.

The central narrative of the film is about the effects of the creative generation of narrative ideas prompted by horrific stories: in short, how Romantic genius makes Gothic mash-ups. The group reads a translated book of German ghost stories—the *Fantasmagoriana, ou Recueil de Spectres*—and each listener imagines sights more vivid and graphic than what is on the page

(Seymour 2000, 585). Afterward, Byron produces a skull of a monk discovered at Newstead Abbey, upon which his guests hold a séance. The rest of the film follows gruesome encounters born of the cumulative effects of the substances consumed, the stormy weather, exhaustion, the ghost stories, the creature supposedly raised during the séance, and the painful memories of the group, especially Mary's guilt over her and Percy's stillborn child. *Gothic* contains a rousing climactic sequence, wherein Byron and Percy want to end the madness by holding yet another séance (they also share an on-screen kiss that moves their relationship out of the realm of subtext), Claire is covered in mud and moves like a rat, and Mary takes the initiative by smashing the skull and threatening to stab Byron with one of its jagged fragments. Mary escapes the scene and runs through the labyrinthine recesses of the house, hallucinating images of her dead baby, as well as Byron's designs on the unborn child that he shares with Claire. The spell is broken the next morning, with a sunny picnic during which Byron explains the typical excesses of his summer nights. The film ends with tourists visiting Villa Diodati in the present day, where a skewed fetus lurks under the water, the conceptual germ of Mary Shelley's life and fears. *Gothic* gives several options for the monstrous sources of her *Frankenstein*.

Unlike *Lisztomania*, *Gothic* is *quite obviously* about *Frankenstein*. It shares in *Lisztomania*'s fascination with the process by which artists adapt previous material. This is demonstrated in the sequence during which the group reads from the *Fantasmagoriana*. Russell begins each vignette with characters reading from the book in the film's diegesis, and then switches to voice-over narration as one of the listeners imagines a more horrific variation on what is being read (here, they "make" Gothic mash-ups in real time). In the most literal of these, Percy reads and imagines a contorted woman hanging from a tree. When Mary takes over, she visualizes an armored specter that threatens her and what is presumably her son. The different realities of the film collapse as the specter reveals its face to be covered in worm and maggots, and a sound bridge of Byron screaming prompts a cut into the main narrative space, where Byron discovers a tray of rice topped by leeches (a joke played by Polidori). Claire's reading yields the biggest gap between the page and what is visualized, since her libido motivates the shift from a story in which the specter paralyzes a victim with fear into a scenario where she sexually submits to the specter, who approaches her with a gigantic metal phallus. Each of these shows the primary process of Romantic adaptation: the reception of what has already been thought and said as filtered through the "free play of the imagination."

Gothic occasionally relies on the broad mode of intertextual referentiality used in *Lisztomania*. Some of these moments are motivated by the diegesis and narrative, such as Mary's vision of Henry Fuseli's *The Nightmare* (1781), in which she looks at the painting, closes her eyes, and wakes up, at this point still in the dream, to find herself a part of the image (the impish demon pinning her to the bed). She then wakes up for real to find Claire lying on top of her. Such a reference makes sense in context: Fuseli was Swiss, and his painting fits the mood of the film and creates a cultural shorthand for the historical period in which the film is set. The painting is indicative of both an increasingly popular brand of Gothic morbidity that is occasionally mentioned throughout the film (Byron and Shelley discuss Matthew Lewis's *The Monk* [1796] by name) and of a general Romanticist approach to horror, where elements feared in the unconscious (the dark horse, the demon) overwhelm the body while it sleeps. At one point, Percy and Byron make this explicit, by sharing a sentence that neatly summarizes this aesthetic zeitgeist: "It is an age of dreams and nightmares . . . yes, and we are merely children of the age."

Other potential references straddle the line between homage and coincidence. Joseph Lanza compares the sequence of Percy chased by his admirers to the street stampedes in *A Hard Day's Night* (1964, Richard Lester) (2007, 262). When Polidori appears with a shaved head (first as a hallucination by Byron, when it appears in place of the roasted head of a pig), he bears a remarkable resemblance to Fritz Haarmann (a similarly shorn Kurt Raab) in *Tenderness of Wolves* (1973, Ulli Lommel). Like the represented Polidori, Haarmann is a serial killer with homosexual urges who adopts many the mannerisms of a vampire. *Gothic*'s shock ending, with the dead child submerged in water, thematically resembles the famous end of *Friday the 13th* (1980, Sean S. Cunningham), though that film has the child revive and attack a boat.

LORD BYRON, VAMPIRE

Such references are not nearly as important as the larger, more rigorous way that the film mobilizes horror tropes to reverse-engineer, or retrofit, Mary Shelley's *Frankenstein* for a genre that commonly holds her story as a key founding document. Like *Lisztomania*, *Gothic* is a film in which Gothic horror tropes mingle and hybridize; monstrous and supernatural bodies are constructed through the meeting of real historical events, Gothic motifs, and Romantic invention.

This is most obvious in the film's construction of Byron who, like *Lisztomania*'s Wagner, is portrayed as a charismatic villain whose transgressions overwhelm the genius of his art. Byron shares associations with Wagner: he is given monstrous traits that isolate him from mainstream social life. Characters constantly refer to Byron as a devil, a man given to selfish whims, cruelty, and perversion. This is outwardly (and unfairly) embodied by his limp, often inaccurately called a club foot, but actually "tendon Achilles," which "prevented him from putting his heels to the ground," a condition presented by Gabriel Byrne to emphasize Byron's difference (Jeaffreson 1888, 35). It is most obviously explained by his appetites. In the course of the film's main narration and fantasy sequences, he compels his servant Justine (Pascal King) to wear a mask of his beloved half-sister Augusta; sexually assaults Mary; gulps laudanum by the glass; rapes Claire while she is unconscious; and torments Polidori for his repressed sexuality. Byron is also represented as a werewolf. During the group's post-dinner game of hide and seek, Byron announces himself by howling. He is nocturnal, and his mood swings and demonic urges paint him as something of a shape-shifter.

But Byron is most frequently constructed as a vampire. When he first kisses Claire, he goes straight for her neck. Later, Byron mentions to Percy that the attractiveness of a woman's neck has to do with man's subconscious urge to drink blood from it. Polidori corroborates Byron's makeup and costuming by claiming that Byron "does everything to cultivate a cadaverous image short of sleeping in a coffin." In a sequence partially constructed as a dream, Byron approaches Claire's bed as she fitfully sleeps, apparently unconscious from an earlier experience of terror. Russell and cinematographer Mike Southon construct this as an obvious reference to *Nosferatu* (1922, F. W. Murnau), with Byron's elongated shadow enveloping Claire's body before his actual figure comes into frame. In one of the film's most gruesome moments, Byron suddenly goes from being an immaterial apparition to a carnal force. While Claire remains unconscious, he performs oral sex on her, arising with a mouth ringed with blood. These associations support a general power struggle in the film, whereby Byron "feeds" off the energy, ideas, insecurities, bodily phobias, and sexual desires of those around him. *Gothic* does not want us to see Byron as a solitary genius so much as a social being who fashions poetry out of his tumultuous relationships.

Byron's vampirism is not a causal association thrown together by Russell and Volk, but instead stems from an existing discourse on Byron as a foundational example of the archetype, an image he cultivated himself and that was propagated by his writing and writing inspired by him. According to Kevin Jackson, the Byronic vampire is aristocratic, handsome, charismatic, haughty, seductive, enigmatic, rebellious, melancholic, and doomed (2009, 42). Byron's presence delivers these characteristics, but his relationship with Polidori and *Gothic*'s larger narrative about the creation of horrific stories suggest the film's more specific engagement with "The Vampyre" (1819), the story that Polidori eventually published as a result of that 1816 summer, itself a tale partially inspired by Lord Byron's "Fragment of a Novel," the short piece that best approximates Byron's Villa Diodati ghost story. This "Fragment" is about the approaching death of Augustus Darvell, an aristocratic figure who desires to die in a Turkish graveyard, with the implication that his body can later rise from the dead (Gordon 1904, 446–53). Polidori's "The Vampyre" likewise concerns an aristocratic immortal, but overlays Byron's skeletal outline onto a richer story of a man who preys upon young women. In "The Vampyre," the young narrator Aubrey (clearly a stand-in for Polidori himself) describes his association with Lord Ruthven, an otherworldly man who both resembles Byron and embodies the traits of the Byronic Vampire. Aubrey disapproves of Ruthven's treatment of women in general, but eventually connects Ruthven to the serial murder of women (Polidori [1819] 2001, 65–72). The sense of spiteful torment between Polidori and Byron is expressed in "The Vampyre" as the ultimate insult: Ruthven is killed and then rises from the grave, which causes Aubrey to become fearful and incoherent to the point of insanity, thereby allowing Ruthven to woo and become engaged to Aubrey's sister (whom, by implication, he will eventually consume) (Polidori [1819] 2001). *Gothic* adapts "The Vampyre" not so much as a narrative, but rather as a justification for Polidori and Byron's behaviors. In *Gothic*, Polidori is strangely protective of Mary. The two share a tender scene in the Villa's foyer in what is surely one of the movie's most quiet moments. Polidori is driven mad by Byron's cruelty, his treatment of women in general, and by his continued attraction to this unattainable man; Byron, meanwhile, glides between victims, feeding on them to consolidate his own power.

CONCLUSION

With all these examples of Byron's transgressions, where does Mary Shelley fit into the film? *Gothic* is, after all, framed by the promise of explaining how she created her own novel of monstrosity. Anne K. Mellor argues that the narrative of *Frankenstein* is rooted in Mary Shelley's anxieties about parenthood: having recently lost a daughter at birth, Mary was haunted by "parental abandonment," a structural relationship shared with Victor and his creature (2003, 11). This reading is endorsed in *Gothic*, in which Mary is continuously reminded of her lost child, in literal (her witnessing her own protracted struggle to give birth) and symbolic (her watching as the armored specter stalks her sleeping child) ways. But *Gothic* does not stop there. Russell employs the eclectic approach featured in *Lisztomania*: the mashing up, and attempted reconciliation, of disparate sources that, taken in total, combine to create an original text. Mary is an observer for much of the film, but what she experiences is eventually adapted into *Frankenstein*: the feeling of being stalked by a creature (the spirit summoned in the séance becomes Victor's monster); Percy and Byron's obsession with galvanism and the power of electricity as a means of animating life; physical deformations that signify death (maggots, leeches, animal flesh); paranoia; self-centered, irresponsible parenting (Mary confronts Byron over his disregard for his and Claire's child); and the general confrontation of physical otherness (her disgust at Byron's demonic bearing, as well as the impish monster from her Fuseli dream). Her last lines of dialogue in the film explain the story prompted by the previous evening's mania: "My story is a story of creation, of a creature who is wracked with pain, sorrow, and hunger for revenge. Who haunts his mad creator and his family and his friends . . . to the grave."

Since neither *Lisztomania* nor *Gothic* is a conventional adaptation that exists in a direct relationship to one source text, it is helpful to conceive of their adaptive ambitions as being something other than the faithful recapitulation of a set of sources. What Russell wants to adapt from his nineteenth- and twentieth-century sources approximates what it feels like to be a Romanticist genius, a process he occasions through a focus on how creation and creativity are conceptualized by the Gothic tradition more generally. This aligns with arguments by Chris Dumas and Joan Hawkins who claim that what is important about Russell is not so much the accuracy of what he shows you, so much as the tone, sense of mood, or regime of feeling that he employs. The legibility of content remains important—in his engagement with horror, Russell replicates many iconic moments in the history of the genre—but how these things are put together is what matters. Russell engages in a kind of manic associationism, where ideas, quotations, reference, jokes, and expressions of feeling collide. Dumas aligns *Lisztomania* with a kind of deliberately dissonant filmmaking that baffles conventional academic criticism (2012, 107). Hawkins writes about Russell not just as a challenge to the humanist discourse of high cultural cinema, but as a filmmaker whose works are an art-horror hybrid best understood as tonally unstable, and occasionally radical to the point of playing out like metacritical essays (2014, 506–7).

Both *Lisztomania* and *Gothic* are metacritical film essays about adaptation (in addition to being horror films, biographies, period pieces, and Gothic mash-ups, as well as statements about taste, and windows into the minds of the filmmaking team, especially Russell himself). Each film invites us to view the process of creating new life, ideas, and art out of the textual material in the world around us. These two films help move us away from thinking about Russell primarily as an adaptor of D. H. Lawrence; instead, they align Russell's decades-old work with emerging paradigms in adaptation studies. For Laurence Raw, adaptation is now best understood as a general process by which individuals adjust themselves to new texts and new cultural encounters, wherein textual analysis is most profitable when it looks at interactions across time, location, and creative context (2013, 3). *Lisztomania* and *Gothic* revive a Romanticist discourse about creation, but infuse it with contemporary elements from music, films, popular culture, as well as new approaches to the literary and historical pasts. Both show us that far from being a quiet, sobering activity, such work entails interpersonal struggles and engagements best understood through the tropes and transformations of Gothic horror. Released in the 1970s and 1980s, they anticipate works like Seth Grahame-Smith's *Abraham Lincoln: Vampire Hunter* (2010) or the television series *Penny Dreadful* (2014–2016) by many decades. While the Gothic has always been about the creative reconstitution of old things— Richard Davenport-Hines (1998) spends much of historical survey on the Gothic showing how Gothic Revival architecture brought back ruinous decay and ornamentation in singularly creative ways—Russell's personal goals as a filmmaker align well with an emerging discourse of postmodern sampling in these two films. If *Lisztomania* illustrates how deeply and subconsciously Shelley's *Frankenstein* has entered the cultural landscape, then *Gothic* justifies this place of privilege by demonstrating the pervasiveness of its synthetic imagination.

REFERENCES

Barzun, Jacques. 2000. *From Dawn to Decadence, 1500 to the Present: 500 Years of Western Cultural Life*. New York: Harper.

de Bruin-Molé, Megen. 2020. *Gothic Remixed: Monster Mashups and Frankenfictions of 21st-Century Culture*. New York: Bloomsbury.

Cantor, Paul A. 1984. *Creature and Creator: Myth-Making and English Romanticism*. Cambridge: Cambridge University Press.

Davenport-Hines, Richard. 1998. *Gothic: Four Hundred Years of Excess, Horror, Evil, and Ruin*. New York: North Point Press.

Dumas, Chris. 2012. *Un-American Psycho: Brian DePalma and the Political Invisible*. Bristol: Intellect Books.

Fenby, Eric. 1981. *Delius as I Knew Him*. Cambridge: Cambridge University Press.

Flanagan, Kevin M. 2009. "Introduction." In *Ken Russell: Re-Viewing England's Last Mannerist*, edited by Kevin M. Flanagan, xi–xxv. Lanham, MD: Scarecrow Press.

Genette, Gérard. 1997. *Palimpsests: Literature in the Second Degree*. Lincoln, NB: University of Nebraska Press.

Gomez, Joseph. 1976. *Ken Russell: Adaptor as Creator*. London: Muller Publishing.

Gordon, George (Lord Byron). [1819] 1904. "A Fragment of a Novel by Byron." In *The Works of Lord Byron*, Vol. III, Letters and Journals, edited by Rowland E. Prothero, 446–43. London: John Murray.

Hanke, Ken. 1984. *Ken Russell's Films*. Metuchen, NJ: Scarecrow Press.

Harbison, Robert. 1980. *Deliberate Regression*. New York: Knopf.

Hawkins, Joan. 2014. "'Moody Three': Revisiting Ken Russell's The Devils." In *A Companion to the Horror Film*, edited by Harry M. Benshoff, 501–28. Malden, MA: Wiley.

Heine, Heinrich. [1844] 2011. "Lisztomania" ["The Musical Season of 1844.] *Lapham's Quarterly*, Winter 2011. Accessed 22 Dec 2020. http://www.laphamsquarterly.org/voices-in-time/lisztomania.php?page=all.

Hillier, Jim. 1994. *The New Hollywood*. New York: Continuum Publishing.

Hitchcock, Susan Tyler. 2007. *Frankenstein: A Cultural History*. New York: Norton.

Huckvale, David. 2012. *Visconti and the German Dream: Romanticism, Wagner and the Nazi Catastrophe on Film*. Jefferson, NC: McFarland.

Hunter, I. Q. 2013. *British Trash Cinema*. London: BFI/Palgrave Publishing.

Jackson, Kevin. 2009. *Bite: A Vampire Handbook*. London: Portobello Books.

Jeaffresson, John Cordy. 1888. *The Real Lord Byron: New Views on the Poet's Life*, Vol. 1. London: Hurst and Blackett.

Lanza, Joseph. 2007. *Phallic Frenzy: Ken Russell and His Films*. Chicago: Chicago Review Press.

Leader, Zachary. 1996. *Revision and Romantic Authorship*. New York: Clarendon/Oxford University Press.

Leitch, Thomas. 2011. "Vampire Adaptation." *Journal of Adaptation in Film & Performance* 4 (1): 5–16.

Marx, Karl. 1867. *Capital*, Volume 1, translated by Samuel Moore and Edward Aveling. Accessed 20 Dec 2020. http://www.marxists.org/archive/marx/works/1867-c1/ch10.htm.

Mellor, Ann K. 2003. "Making a 'Monster': An Introduction to *Frankenstein*." In *The Cambridge Companion to Mary Shelley*, edited by Esther Schor, 9–25. New York: Cambridge University Press.

Moore, Harry T. 1973. "D. H. Lawrence and the Flicks." *Literature/Film Quarterly* 1 (1): 3–11.

Polidori, John. [1819] 2001. *The Vampyre: 1819*. New York: Woodstock Books.

Read, Herbert. 1965. *Icon & Idea: The Function of Art in the Development of Human Consciousness*. New York: Schocken Books.

Russell, Ken. 2001. *Directing Film: The Director's Art from Script to Cutting Room*. Dulles, VA: Brassey's.

Saffle, Michael. 2007. "Liszt in the Movies: *Liszt's Rhapsody* as Composer Biopic." *Journal of Popular Film & Television* 35 (2): 58–65.

Seymour, Miranda. 2000. *Mary Shelley*. London: John Murray Publishers.

Shelley, Mary. [1818] 2005. *Frankenstein: The Original 1818 Text*. Edited by D. L. Macdonald and Kathleen Scherf, 2nd ed. Orchard Park, NY: Broadview.

Sisman, Adam. 2007. *The Friendship: Wordsworth and Coleridge*. New York: Viking/Penguin Press.

Walker, Alexander. 2004. *Icons in the Fire: The Rise and Fall of Practically Everyone in the British Film Industry, 1984–2000*. London: Orion Books.

Williams, Linda Ruth. 2013. "Bad Sex and Obscene Undertakings: Ken Russell's *Women in Love*." *Journal of Adaptation in Film and Performance* 6 (3): 341–54.

Zambrano, Ana Laura. 1973. "*Women in Love*: Counterpoint on Film." *Literature/Film Quarterly* 1 (1): 46–54.

Chapter 3

Gothic Exploitation

Transnational Appropriation, Hybridity, and Originality in Continental Horror Cinema, 1957–1983

Xavier Aldana Reyes

The period that runs roughly from 1957, the year *I vampiri* (*The Vampires*) was released to little notice in its native Italy, to 1982, the year the child-friendly monster mash-up *Buenas noches, señor monstruo* (*Good Night, Mr. Monster*) appeared in Spain, is often considered the golden age of European horror.[1] The independent film industries of countries that had contributed only sparingly to the genre until then and were better known for their comedies suddenly exploded in a boom of activity that led to unprecedented record highs. Nearly a quarter of all films made in Spain in 1972 (25 out of 104) belonged to the horror genre (Matellano 2010, 22), a figure that stands in stark contrast to the mere three released in the same country only a decade earlier. There are a number of contextual and financial reasons for this transformation. First, the rise of low-budget indie horror in Britain and the United States, in the shape of Hammer's many successes in the late 1950s and early 1960s and Roger Corman's Poe cycle in the early 1960s, helped change the optics. Horror could be entertained as a relatively safe commercial venture because its "cheapness" made investments easy to recoup. Films such as *La maschera del demonio* (*Black Sunday*, 1960) and *La noche de Walpurgis* (*The Werewolf Versus the Vampire Woman*, 1971) sealed the deal. Their international success signaled that there was serious money to be made and that continental Europe could stand proud as a genre competitor. The existence of tax reliefs and loans, the active encouragement of co-productions, facilitated by the relaxation and modification of existing legislation in the 1960s (Pulido 2012, 36), and the development of distribution deals between Europe and the United States (Heffernan 2004, 136) were all catalysts.

Importantly, a horror cinema that could travel easily and attract different markets became de rigueur.

The stimulation of continental horror in this period needs to be understood within the broader context of the post-war economic forces animating "exploitation" cinema. The growing film industries of Spain, Italy, and France, among others, were interested in capitalizing on any available popular genre (the Western, the *giallo*, and the *peplum*, or sword-and-sandal epic, were of particular interest) and on existing profitable properties, such as individual films, series, or characters (Matellano 2011, 19–29; Di Chiara 2016, 33–4).[2] These countries were also gradually becoming more receptive to foreign models and transgressive material. Even Spain, which remained under Francisco Franco's ultra-conservative dictatorship until the mid-1970s, began to open up under "aperturismo," or the legal loosening of ideological mores partly propounded by tourism and immigration. Continental horror in the 1960s and 1970s, then, can be best conceptualized as one of many competitive genres in demand because it made for recognizable and marketable fare. In turn, the mercantilist ethos behind the influx in horror filmmaking accounts for the look and narrative focus of individual films. It also explains why many of the directors associated with Gothic horror in this period, such as Mario Bava, Jesús Franco, and León Klimovsky, often dabbled in a plurality of genres. The desire to attract large international audiences translated into films that aimed to look "familiar," rather than distinctly national, and that preferred tried-and-tested commodities already in the popular imaginary.[3] The familiarity and previous success of the Gothic aesthetic, which had reigned supreme in the 1930s and continued into the 1940s, as well as that of its main archetypical monsters (Dracula, the Frankenstein Creature, the Wolf Man, the Mummy, Quasimodo), made this subgenre attractive. In other words, it was precisely the worn-out quality of Gothic formulae that made them appealing. This chapter turns to how exploitation cinema managed to innovate within a context that fostered recycling and repetition, and argues that innovation was inherent to the process of remaining artistically unique and solvent in business terms.

MONSTROUS IMITATION AND INNOVATION

Acknowledging that the Gothic was, by the late 1950s, well-established and that droves of filmmakers and producers jumped on the horror bandwagon to make money from it is not tantamount to suggesting that exploitation cinema simply replicated foreign models or had nothing new to offer. In fact, critics have landed on a few traits of the Italian Gothic that are intrinsic to its cultural development in that country. For Roberto Curti (2010, 256–8), the figure of the evil woman—deadly, dual, or neurotic—typical of 1950s and 1960s Italian Gothic horror can be traced back in Italian literature to the nineteenth century. Similarly, writing of *I vampiri* and its successors, Alex Marlow-Mann proposes that Italian Gothic horror films

> revolved around paranoia about death, ageing and the loss of female beauty, resolving themselves in a perverse and fatal attachment to an illusory impermanence. The endless repetition of this narrative over the next decade is, depending on one's point of view, either evidence of the fundamentally imitative nature of the Italian *filone* system or testament to a genuine obsession. (2011, 155)[4]

The motifs Marlow-Mann underscores are especially noticeable in films starring English actor Barbara Steele: *Danza macabra* (*Castle of Blood*, 1964), *I lunghi capelli della morte* (*The Long Hair of Death*, 1964), *Amanti d'oltretomba* (*Nightmare Castle*, 1965), and *Un angelo per Satana* (*An Angel for Satan*, 1966). Steele, who had famously led in the defining *La maschera del demonio* and was contractually bound to Italian cinema for a short period, may have thus inadvertently further entrenched the fatal woman trope with her chilling performance. In the case of Spain, Paul Naschy's ubiquity as actor and screenwriter equally shaped the mode there. Many of his personal obsessions, such as his passion for Universal horror films (Naschy 1997, 37–8), had an impact on the characters and stories he would write. His portrayal of Polish lycanthrope Count Waldemar Daninsky in two of Spain's key Gothic horror films, *La marca del hombre lobo* (*Frankenstein's Bloody Terror*, 1968) and the aforementioned *La noche de Walpurgis*, understood to have kick-started Spanish Gothic horror as a serious international venture, is now iconic (figure 3.1). Although he may not have single-handedly created a market for monster films in Spain, Naschy's investment in this older model of horror is either serendipitous or symbiotic. Whether out of chance or idiosyncrasy, it is clear that countries such as Spain and Italy imprinted the traditional schemata of the Gothic with their own flavor and that these flourishes happened to resonate with the direction of travel of the film industry.

Gritos en la noche (*The Awful Dr. Orlof*, 1962), often credited as an early outlier and main predecessor of the horror genre in Spain (Sala 2010, 49), reveals the complex interplay between influence and originality that takes place when cultural references become imbricated in different national contexts and grow into palimpsests. Aesthetically and thematically, *Gritos en la noche* takes a leaf out of Universal's horror book, with its black-and-white photography, focus on contrasting uses of light, heavy shadows, and imposing castle setting. Its narrative backbone, featuring obsessive surgeon Dr. Orlof (Howard Vernon) and blind henchman Morpho (Ricardo Valle), is lifted from *Frankenstein* (1931) and would have felt at home in any of

Figure 3.1 Monster Mashes Like *La marca del hombre lobo* (*Frankenstein's Bloody Terror*, 1968) Were Simultaneously Imitative and Innovative. Screenshot by the author.

the mad science copycats of the 1930s. Yet its genesis was Hammer's *The Brides of Dracula* (1960), a screening of which the director had recently attended, and the skin-grafting motif belies a further point of reference: Georges Franju's *Les Yeux sans visage* (*Eyes without a Face*, 1960). Its premise of a scientist kidnapping female victims for the purpose of nefarious face transplants is almost replicated. *Gritos en la noche* is a strange combination of Gothic imagery and melodramatic suspense, all spiced up with the director's trademark "eroticism" and "sadism" (Alonso Barahona 2000, 224), evident in the objectification of the captured women. This means that the film necessarily dilutes its Gothic formula somewhat: sensuality is as important as fear, and physical grotesques are replaced with moral monstrosity. Intertextuality becomes more important than following any one specific subgenre. There are traces of Cesare (Conrad Veidt), from *Das Cabinet des Dr. Caligari* (*The Cabinet of Dr. Caligari*, 1922) in Morpho's physique, Dr. Orlof wears a cape reminiscent of that worn by many a filmic Count Dracula, and his very name is an echo of Dr. Orloff (Bela Lugosi), the villain in the noir thriller *The Dark Eyes of London* (1939). Crucially, this kaleidoscope of citations largely hints at the spiritual alignment of the material and does not translate into a staunch commitment to any given archetype and myth. In standard Gothic horror fashion, further sequels followed, as well as other facial horrors, such as *La cara del terror* (*The Face of Terror*, 1962), that watered down the Gothic aspects of the original even more. Such techniques were typical of an emergent horror industry that wanted to monetize profitable trends while also proposing something new. The resulting Gothic horror is defined by both a constant looking backward and a desire to shake things up and push stories and aesthetics into more transgressive territory.

In their vying for attention, many filmmakers decided to exploit existing myths with ready-made audiences that would command international interest. Universal turned monsters into horror's main commodity, and Hammer's revival of them in the form of franchises like *Dracula*'s, which ran throughout the 1960s and into the early 1970s, galvanized them as indexical Gothic horror icons. It is within this context that the veritable explosion of films with "Dracula" in the title needs to be positioned. The direct adaptation *El conde Drácula* (*Count Dracula*, 1970), starring Christopher Lee, is perhaps the most noticeable example, but there were also *La saga de los Drácula* (*The Dracula Saga*, 1973) and *El gran amor del conde Drácula* (*Count Dracula's Great Love*, 1973), as well as comedies such as *Tiempos duros para Drácula* (*Hard Times for Dracula*, 1976) and *El pobrecito Draculín* (*Draculin*, 1977), both of which echoed the earlier Italian *Tempi duri per i vampiri* (*Uncle Was a Vampire*, 1959). The monster mash, once popularized by Universal, made a natural comeback in films such as *Drácula contra Frankenstein* (*Dracula, Prisoner of Frankenstein*, 1972) and, most spectacularly, in *Los monstruos del terror* (*Assignment Terror*, 1970), which included hilariously named creatures like "el monstruo de Farancksalan" (Farancksalan's monster, after Frankenstein's monster) and Tao-Tet (after Imhotep, from the 1932 Universal film *The Mummy*). All these examples betray the capitalist drive of a film industry full of independent filmmakers more interested in dividends than in strict narrative originality. A less cynical attitude might also acknowledge that this type of Gothic horror, as Megen de Bruin-Molé suggests, invites important "questions about authenticity, historicity, appropriation, and the nature of art" (2020, 3), especially because many films borrowed mere shells of characters or the bare bones of dramatic outlines to explore their own, often budget-constrained, scenarios. Their production context and intertextual, heavily referential nature has led to them being overlooked as meaningful national examples of Gothic cinema (Aldana Reyes 2018, 105).

Francesco Di Chiara argues that the genres that blossomed in post-war Italy "should be regarded as productive experiments involving themes, icons and stylistic traits coming from different universes, such as foreign models, distinctly national traits, high art and Italian popular culture" (2016, 33). This is an important point, especially because exploitation cinema is usually disregarded for its lack of material means and the intellectual rigor associated with mainstream, avant-garde, and auteur cinema. It is hardly, if ever, considered a paragon of stylistic experimentation or postmodern hybridization. Yet Di Chiara's argument is easily proven right. *La maschera del demonio* was inspired by "Viy" ("The Viy," 1835), a novella by classical writer Nikolai Gogol, but takes its aesthetic cues from older Gothic horror films in its effective use of chiaroscuro lighting and mise-en-scène. The same applies to the anthology film *I tre volti della paura* (*Black Sabbath*, 1963). Its second segment, "I Wurdulak" ("The Wurdulak"), adapts Alexei Tolstoi's novella "Semya' vurdala'ka" (*The Family of the Vourdalak*, 1884) in a rather sober and colorful fashion, as a Gothic period piece reminiscent of Hammer's vampire films. Yet the first and last segment, "Il telefono" ("The Telephone") and "La goccia d'acqua" ("The Drop of Water"), set in present times, are influenced by the *giallo* and the haunted house film. The varied nature of *I tre volti della paura* offers an indication of how eclectic horror was in the 1960s, as well as how seamlessly national models of filmmaking were woven into international concepts with staying power.

Gothic horror film did not always rely on literary classics either, and sometimes took inspiration from popular pulp culture directly. This is particularly the case with *Il boia scarlatto* (*Bloody Pit of Horror*, 1965), in which Travis Anderson (Mickey Hargitay), a former actor now believing himself to be the reincarnation of the Crimson Executioner, protects his castle from a group of publishers and models working on an impromptu on-site photoshoot (figure 3.2). The crew happens to be preparing some lurid covers involving scantily clad women for a series of novels about the "Skeletrik" character, a masked sadistic villain. The film's cartoony comic-strip look is amplified by self-referential nods that indicate its irreverent, "fun" approach and pay homage to the *fotoromanzi* (photo-novels) and pulp magazines that influenced it. Photonovels had existed in Italy since the 1940s, but they turned to the popular Gothic in the 1960s in the shape of adults-only publications like *Malìa: I fotoromanzi del brivido*. *Malìa* featured Gothic stories about vampires and medieval castles alongside adaptations of popular Italian Gothic horror films such as *L'ultima preda del vampiro* (*The Playgirls and the Vampire*, 1960) and *Metempsyco* (*Tomb of Torture*, 1963). In a thorough appraisal of *Il boia scarlatto*'s contextual sources, Roberto Curti proposes further popular culture referents: "Skeletrik, with the inevitable 'K' in the name and a costume in style, is a nod to Magnus and Bunker's comic book *Kriminal*," and the Crimson Executioner resembles Lee Falk's adventure comic strip *The Phantom*, "one of the main inspirations for the whole wave of Italian superhero films of the mid-to-late Sixties" (2015, 140). At the same time, *Il boia scarlatto* is in dialogue with the Gothic films of Roger Corman in the United States, of Hammer in the United Kingdom, and of Mario Bava in Italy, as is evident from its locale (the impressive Balsorano and Borghese castles) and subject matter. Its mélange of filmic, photonovel-istic, and comic references powerfully illustrates the lack of interest in neatly demarcated generic and media boundaries in continental Gothic horror of the 1960s.

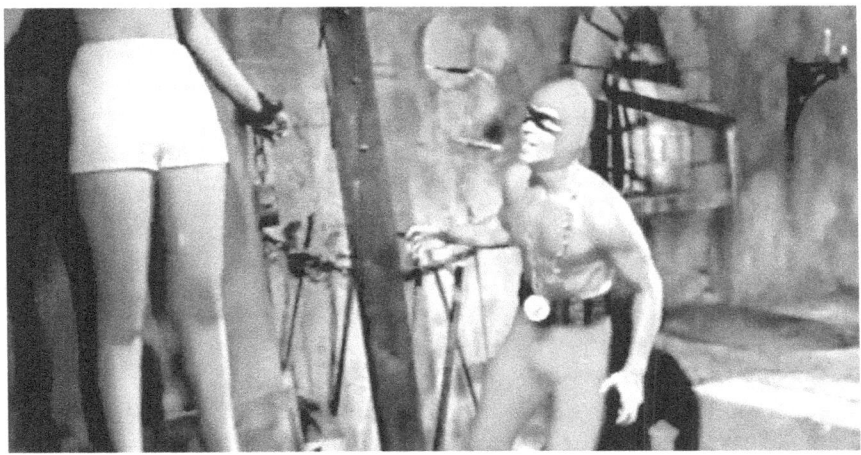

Figure 3.2 Gothic Horror Films Like *Il boia scarlatto* (*Bloody Pit of Horror*, 1965) Were Influenced by Comics and Popular Culture. Screenshot by the author.

GENERIC HYBRIDIZATION AND EROTICISM

The hybridization of genres, multiple aesthetic allegiances, and celebration of "pulp" culture lasted well into the 1970s and are especially obvious in the case of Gothic *gialli*. The *giallo* genre, whose name derives from the yellow covers of the series of popular suspense and crime paperback novels *Il Giallo Mondadori*, designates a type of violent thriller with horror and erotic elements that typically contains a mystery killer whose general attire includes a pair of black gloves (Kannas 2021, 3–4). As developed in famous examples like *L'uccello dalle piume di cristallo* (*The Bird with the Crystal Plumage*, 1970) and *Profondo rosso* (*Deep Red*, 1975), the genre prefers modern settings and privileges suspense and violence. Since *gialli* have been acknowledged as the predecessors of the "slasher" films that would reign in the 1980s (Kerswell 2012, 46–9), when the Gothic aesthetic would wane, it is possible to think of them, alongside the modern supernatural horror film following the critical and box office success of *The Exorcist* (1973), as the new face of modern horror cinema. Yet *gialli* and Gothic horror are closer than one might at first imagine. For starters, the two films credited with having invented the *giallo* as a "cinematic genre" (Koven 2006, 3), *La ragazza che sapeva troppo* (*The Girl Who Knew Too Much*, 1963) and *Sei donne per l'assassino* (*Blood and Black Lace*, 1964), were directed by Bava, and are rough contemporaries of his Gothic offerings *I tre volti della paura* and *La frusta e il corpo* (*The Whip and the Body*, 1963). By the 1970s, the popularity of the *giallo* was such that crossovers started to emerge and change the temporal coordinates of the Gothic, as well as its music and costume design. As Curti puts it, with the arrival of Gothic *gialli*, "Gothic was no longer suspended in a vague and indefinite past; on the contrary, it was heavily characterized geographically and therefore immediately recognizable: here, now, at just a few hours' flight" (2017, 20).

Films such as *Il rosso segno della follia* (Hatchet for the Honeymoon, 1970), *La notte che Evelyn uscì dalla tomba* (*The Night Evelyn Came Out of the Grave*, 1971), *La dama rossa uccide sette volte* (*The Red Queen Kills Seven Times*, 1972), *La morte negli occhi del gatto* (*Seven Deaths in the Cat's Eye*, 1973), and *Tutti defunti... tranne i morti* (*All Deceased... Except the Dead*, 1977) are veritable generic hodgepodges. They still take place in the crumbling castles and ancestral country houses of the Gothic horror film, and exploit a number of the mode's motifs, from uncanny mannequins and tell-tale portraits to black cats and old prophecies, family secrets, and buried treasure. Yet, they simultaneously eschew fantastic monsters in favor of psychotic individuals and vengeful killers, and circle around deadly set pieces with sizable body counts. These aspects belie their *giallo* elements, but also speak to the impact of Alfred Hitchcock's *Psycho* (1960) and the consolidation in the 1960s and 1970s of "'madness' as the prime horror movie expression of insanity" (Tudor 1989, 190). Some of them, such as *La notte che Evelyn uscì dalla tomba* and *La morte negli occhi del gatto*, actually toy with the "explained supernatural," a key element of the Female Gothic, especially the melodramas of the 1940s (Hanson 2007, 63–96; Aldana Reyes 2020a, 126–53), eventually explaining the seemingly impossible (the return of a corpse, a vampire) as human ploys. In other words, although many of the stylistic accoutrements of these new hybrids are Gothic in essence and come from its manifestation as an aesthetic of fear tied to a fantastic past, the remoteness becomes purely geographical, rather than temporal. The isolated and baroque Gothic settings come to connote coterminous ideas in the present: the wealth and privilege of the killer and their aristocratic or otherwise familial connections. They can also resonate with another key aspect: sexual depravity. In *La notte che Evelyn uscì dalla tomba*, the Inquisitorial setting of the late eighteenth-century Gothic novel is transformed into a kinky sex dungeon, the objects of torture flipped into sadomasochistic gameplay.

The broader titillating appeal of cinematic Gothic horror during the golden era of European exploitation is worth further consideration, as it is its most defining trait and one that, as I have argued elsewhere (Aldana Reyes 2020a, 197–9), resonates with the mode's transgressive ethos in literature. The increasingly explicit eroticism that defines continental horror of the 1960s and 1970s, and which would come to an end once the arrival of hardcore films made its thrills redundant, tended to meld terror, violence, and sex.

Although not an unproblematic combination that sometimes could sensationalize violence against women, it is important to bear in mind that continental horror defied high- and low-brow divides and took inspiration from a variety of sources. As Tohill and Tombs put it, the "erotic revolution was also influenced by older cultural movements, drawing power from surrealism, romanticism and the decadent tradition, as well as early 20th century pulp-literature, filmed serials, creaky horror-movies and sexy comic strips" (1995, 5). While directors Renato Polselli, Walerian Borowczyk, and José Ramón Larraz definitely leaned on sexuality and nudity, and films such as *Malabimba* (*Malabimba—The Malicious Whore*, 1979) and *Los ritos sexuales del diablo* (*Black Candles*, 1982) can be best understood as erotic films with horror elements, Gothic horror films are still partly interested in generating fear. This means that the turn to shocking and salacious material generally translated into gratuitous nudity and subliminal sexual messages. The noticeable chest of Gisele Du Grand (Gianna Maria Canale), accentuated by a bare-breasted gryphon statue beside her in a key scene in *I vampiri*, and the nipple quickly flashed in *Il mulino delle donne di pietra* (*Mill of the Stone Women*, 1960) are great examples of the former, and the subtextual necrophilia of *L'orribile segreto del Dr. Hichcock* (*The Horrible Dr. Hichcock*, 1962) and *La residencia* (*The House That Screamed*, 1969) attests to the drive toward more sensational subject matters.

The incipient eroticism of exploitation Gothic horror films is also interesting because it offers an opportunity to observe how production contexts can enhance aspects ingrained in the mode. Horror naturally expresses underlying societal issues—"reflectionist" readings (Hills 2011), or horror as political commentary or exploration of national trauma (Blake 2008; Lowenstein 2008)—and personal auteurist obsessions, but its cinematic specifics have been noticeably dictated by the film industry's economic dimensions, its "logic, strategies and practices" (Nowell 2014, 7). In this way, the predominance of female protagonists in films such as *L'amante del vampiro* (*The Vampire and the Ballerina*, 1960), *Gritos en la noche*, and *Las alegres vampiras de Vögel* (*Vampires of Vogel*, 1975) in the roles of prostitutes and dancers can be understood as motivated by the desire to capitalize on the bodies of beautiful actors. At the same time, this industrial decision had the unexpected effect of advancing the representation of women in Gothic horror. For example, the new heroines of continental horror are modern equivalents of the heroines of the Female Gothic, a politically subversive submode that codifies domestic entrapment and whose main protagonist usually fights a patriarchal antagonist (Wallace and Smith 2009, 2). Although these new women are themselves objectified to varying degrees by their films, their sexually liberated attitudes and fighting spirit endowed the Gothic heroine with a renovated sense of purpose and resourcefulness. By necessity, the films gave women a new sense of narrative centrality. It would be facetious to suggest that all continental Gothic horror films were progressive in their outlook on female plights or that they made female subjectivity their core concern, but it is also hard to think of the self-sufficient androgynous "final girl" or the 1980s slasher without the Gothic horror heroine of 1960s and 1970s exploitation cinema. Industry changes in turn lead to representational ones.

For the purposes of my argument, I have thus far painted exploitation horror's relationship to eroticism in broad strokes. In order to move from the general to the specific and to tackle the issue of auteurism within a heavily commercial context, it is useful to zoom in on a director who consistently contributed to Gothic horror. The filmography of French director Jean Rollin, who began his career as filmmaker with *Le Viol du vampire* (*Rape of the Vampire*, 1968) and continued to produce a constant stream of dreamy, erotic horrors until the early 1980s, stands as one of the great examples of exploitation Gothic horror. On the one hand, films such as *Le Frisson des vampires* (*The Shiver of the Vampires*, 1971), *Requiem pour un vampire* (*Requiem for a Vampire*, 1971), *Lèvres de sang* (*Lips of Blood*, 1975), and *Fascination* (1979) can be read as symptomatic of the period (figure 3.3). Their naked women in revealing diaphanous gowns, morbid and protracted sexual encounters, and interest in sensuality over plot are entirely typical of exploitation cinema. Their fetishistic treatment of the vampire as male fantasy is not wildly different to that in other "sex-vampire" films (Pirie 1977, 98), such as *Les Lèvres rouges* (*Daughters of Darkness*, 1971), *Countess Dracula* (1971), and the various adaptations of Sheridan Le Fanu's *Carmilla* (1871–1872), such as *...Et mourir de plaisir* (*Blood and Roses*, 1960), Hammer's Karnstein trilogy, especially *The Vampire Lovers* (1970), and *La novia ensangrentada* (*The Blood Spattered Bride*, 1972). However, Rollin's cinema can also be read auteuristically. His films have a dreamy, fairy-tale quality to them and are sparse in dialogue, unique qualities that express his vision as a director. For Colin Odell and Michelle Le Blanc, Rollin's melting pot of pulp fiction, sadomasochism, pornography, and "surrealist" elements is precisely what distinguishes him from other filmmakers (2004, 160, 169). Even more relevant to this discussion is their suggestion that Rollin's poetic narrative, style, and editing mean that, despite adopting many supernatural themes that are usually associated with the genre, his cinema may not be considered horror.

The concept of auteurism raises pertinent questions about originality and artistry, especially as directors such as Bava, Franco, Riccardo Freda, Antonio Margheriti, and Ibáñez Serrador have been the subject of individual volumes that pay specific attention to their distinctive qualities. To what extent are exploitation auteurs determined by their production contexts? Should the period-specific circumstances of independent filmmaking, such as low budgets, the imposition of certain erotic material by distributors, or the need to

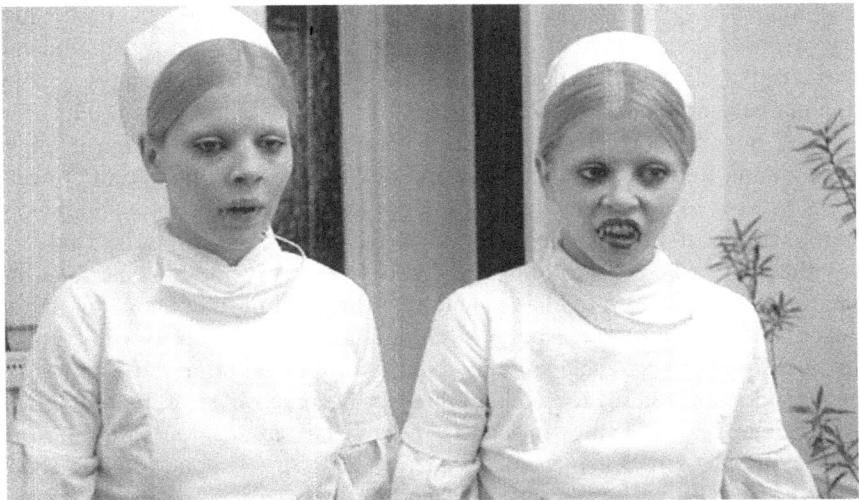

Figure 3.3 Gothic Fever Dreams Like *Lèvres de sang* (*Lips of Blood*, 1975) Illustrate the Tension between Auteurist Vision and Industry Pressures. Screenshot by the author.

work with mixed casts be considered background noise that gets in the way of a given artistic vision? Or is it rather a constituent part? The answers are fraught with ambivalence, and suggest that originality is an inherent part of the creative process even when it operates within the limits of specific material constraints. What seems incontrovertible in the case of Rollin is that eroticism plays a significant role in his cinema, and that the accoutrements of Gothic horror are put to the service of getting across certain images and evocative scenarios. Fantastic creatures like vampires, and atmospheric locales such as derelict castles, crypts, and villas, do not solely terrify, and the nudity and cavorting are more provocative than actually pornographic. These elements come together to form a strange and heady mix of the titillating and the macabre that suggests Rollin was able to create a personal universe by focalizing the formulae of Gothic horror and softcore erotica into a delirious iconography of excess.

CONCLUSION: A FAMILIAR DIFFERENCE

Rollin's example is quite extreme in that prurient aspects often overtake plot development and the elicitation of fear. His films are therefore only representative of the most voyeuristic end of the Gothic horror cinema of the 1960s and 1970s. Even then, a brief discussion of his work is helpful because it foregrounds the issue of innovation. I have mentioned that the co-production-heavy, sectionalized, and international nature of the film industry favored a small number of well-known myths that could be recirculated and adapted idiosyncratically. It is worth noting that creativity is inescapable, and perhaps more important, in crowded markets where individual films need to stick out from other fare in order to attract attention. Although it might be tempting to think that the 1960s and 1970s propitiated a host of copycat films seeking to monetize already successful strands, this is not incompatible with a view that understands each of these iterations as *sui generis*. This is to say that Gothic horror during this period is remarkably varied because of the pressures that forced it to change and hybridize, not despite them. As I have described it, the unstable aspects of Gothic horror are precisely what makes its manifestations valuable. As the ubiquity of the Gothic in the twenty-first century demonstrates, this aesthetic has not become obsolete, but continues to generate new meaning; it persists in carrying out specific cultural work (Aldana Reyes 2019, 401–3; 2020b). This lateral move in our thinking about exploitation Gothic horror involves reading the mode as more than just a process of recycling that returns the same product back to viewers, but as one that comes back ever so slightly changed and more relevant. In short, this is about appraising the films released during the golden age of exploitation cinema not as inferior to mainstream classics or as cheap imitations. It involves rethinking the creative decisions behind *La maschera del demonio*, *La marca del hombre lobo*, and *Gritos en la noche*, among many others, as astonishingly creative in their capacity to merge the international and familiar with the national and unconventional.

It is also vital to underscore that the shape of continental Gothic horror during its golden age—its intertextuality, accessibility, mass appeal, and emphasis on sensation and spectacle—does not run counter to, and is not separate from, possible political intent. While it would be too much of a stretch to suggest that all exploitation cinema attempts to communicate complex messages about, for instance, Francisco Franco's dictatorship in Spain, it is definitely productive to read the Gothic's interest in tyrannical, monstrous figures of the past, often with a religious, occult, or feudal background, such as the knights Templar in *La noche del terror ciego* (*Tombs of the Blind Dead*, 1972), as a commentary on military repression (Lázaro-Reboll 2012, 90). As it happens, many directors who made horror were either skeptical of Spain's government or openly against it, so that exploitation cinema, much as avant-garde cinema, may be understood as an "oppositional" form of artistic expression (Willis 2003, 77). As Ernest Mathijs and Xavier Mendik argue, "[a]lternative European cinema sets itself not just against a mainstream culture, but also against a range of ways of thinking, politically and ideologically" (2004, 4). If it "does not always campaign for politically correct perspectives," it is expedient to think of it as "championing, almost anarchically, a call for liberty"

(Mathijs and Mendik 2004, 5). The same is true of the Gothic mode more broadly, especially when considering how often transgressive artistic material that pushes the boundaries of the acceptable or questions the *status quo* has been censored and suppressed by cultural institutions in countries like Spain (Aldana Reyes 2017, 231–4). The monster mash-ups of Gothic horror, its myriad permutations of licentious scenarios, and frivolous, visceral chills can thus be cast under a different light that understands Gothic hybridity to have emerged as both commercial inevitability and playful engagement with the limits of propriety and censorship.

NOTES

1. Exact periodization of the golden age of exploitation horror varies from one country to another, and is subject to interpretation, but most critics agree that the early 1980s marked the end of a significant period (Shipka 2011; Baschiera and Hunter 2016). In the Spanish context, critics see 1983, the year the Miró decree was introduced, as the death knell for independent Spanish horror cinema (Aguilar 1999; Higueras 2015).

2. As is evident from the case of *Emanuelle nera* (*Black Emanuelle*, 1975), made to cash in on the success of the French film *Emmanuelle* (1974), sometimes simple tweaks to names and characters were enough to circumvent copyright laws.

3. Amando de Ossorio's classic knights Templar are a great example of the industry's reluctance to back up innovation. Rafael Calvo, in his documentary on *Amando de Ossorio: El último templario* (2001), explains that the director initially struggled with producers because the characters were not a well-known myth and that a *Dracula* script would have been preferred.

4. "Filone" (veins, in the original) is the Italian term for what, in this chapter, is being referred to as exploitation cinema.

REFERENCES

Aguilar, Carlos, ed. 1999. *Cine fantástico y de terror español, 1900–1983*. San Sebastián: Donostia Kultura.

Aguirre, Javier, dir. 1973. *El gran amor del conde Drácula (Count Dracula's Great Love)*. Spain: Castilla Films.

Albertini, Bitto, dir. 1975. *Emanuelle nera (Black Emanuelle)*. Italy: Fida Cinematografica.

Aldana Reyes, Xavier. 2017. *Spanish Gothic: National Identity, Collaboration and Cultural Adaptation*. Basingstoke: Palgrave Macmillan.

———. 2018. "Fantaterror: Gothic Monsters in the Golden Age of Spanish B-Movie Horror, 1968–80." In *B-Movie Gothic: International Perspectives*, edited by Justin D. Edwards and Johan Höglund, 95–107. Edinburgh: Edinburgh University Press.

———. 2019. "Gothic and Cinema: The Development of an Aesthetic Filmic Mode." In *The Edinburgh Companion to Gothic and the Arts*, edited by David Punter, 395–405. Edinburgh: Edinburgh University Press.
———. 2020a. *Gothic Cinema*. London and New York: Routledge.
———. 2020b. "Gothic Cinema from the 1970s to Now." In *Gothic Film: An Edinburgh Companion*, edited by Richard J. Hand and Jay McRoy, 77–86. Edinburgh: Edinburgh University Press.
Alonso Barahona, Fernando. 2000. "A modo de historia fílmica nacional: El cine fantástico y de terror en España." In *Las tres caras del terror: Un siglo de cine fantaterrorífico español*, edited by Paul Naschy, 120–267. Madrid: Alberto Santos Editor.
Aranda, Vicente, dir. 1972. *La novia ensangrentada (The Blood Spattered Bride)*. Spain: Morgana Films.
Argento, Dario, dir. 1970. *L'uccello dalle piume di cristallo (The Bird with the Crystal Plumage)*. Italy: Titanus.
———. dir. 1975. *Profondo rosso (Deep Red)*. Italy: Cineriz.
Avati, Pupi, dir. 1977. *Tutti defunti... tranne i morti (All Deceased... Except the Dead)*. Italy: Euro International Film.
Baker, Roy Ward, dir. 1970. *The Vampire Lovers*. UK: MGM-EMI Distributors.
Baschiera, Stefano, and Russ Hunter, eds. 2016. *Italian Horror Cinema*. Edinburgh: Edinburgh University Press.
Bava, Mario, dir. 1960. *La maschera del demonio (Black Sunday)*. Italy: Unidis.
———. dir. 1963. *I tre volti della paura (Black Sabbath)*. Italy: Warner Bros.
———. dir. 1963. *La ragazza che sapeva troppo (The Girl Who Knew Too Much)*. Italy: Warner Bros.
———. dir. 1963. *La frusta e il corpo (The Whip and the Body)*. Italy: Titanus.
———. dir. 1964. *Sei donne per l'assassino (Blood and Black Lace)*. Italy: Unidis.
———. dir. 1970. *Il rosso segno della follia (Hatchet for the Honeymoon)*. Italy: Metro-Goldwyn-Mayer.
Bianchi, Andrea, dir. 1979. *Malabimba (Malabimba – The Malicious Whore)*. Italy: Stefano Film.
Blake, Linnie. 2008. *The Wounds of Nations: Horror Cinema, Historical Trauma and National Identity*. Manchester: Manchester University Press.
Boccacci, Antonio, dir. 1963. *Metempsyco (Tomb of Torture)*. Italy: Filmar.
Caiano, Mario, dir. 1965. *Amanti d'oltretomba (Nightmare Castle)*. Italy: Emmeci.
Calvo, Rafael, dir. 2001. *Amando de Ossorio: El último templario (Amando de Ossorio: The Last Templar)*. Spain: Lorelei Producciones.
Curti, Roberto. 2010. "Fantasmas de amor: El gótico italiano entre la literatura, cine y televisión." In *Pesadillas en la oscuridad: El cine de terror gótico*, edited by Antonio José Navarro, 237–82. Madrid: Valdemar.
———. 2015. *Italian Gothic Horror Films, 1957–1969*. Jefferson, NC: McFarland.
———. 2017. *Italian Gothic Horror Films, 1970–1979*. Jefferson, NC: McFarland.
Darnell, Jorge, dir. 1976. *Tiempos duros para Drácula (Hard Times for Dracula)*. Spain: Aitor Films.
de Bruin-Molé, Megen. 2020. *Gothic Remixed: Monster Mashups and Frankenfictions in 21st-Century Culture*. London and New York: Bloomsbury Academic.

Demicheli, Tulio, dir. 1970. *Los monstruos del terror (Assignment Terror)*. Spain: Castilla Films.
de Ossorio, Amando, dir. 1972. *La noche del terror ciego (Tombs of the Blind Dead)*. Spain: Hispamex.
Di Chiara, Francesco. 2016. "Domestic Films Made for Export: Modes of Production of the 1960s Italian Horror Film." In *Italian Horror Cinema*, edited by Stefano Baschiera and Russ Hunter, 30–44. Edinburgh: Edinburgh University Press.
Ferroni, Giorgio, dir. 1960. *Il mulino delle donne di pietra (Mill of the Stone Women)*. Italy: C. D. C.
Ferry, Isidoro M., and William J. Hole Jr. 1962. *La cara del terror (The Face of Terror)*. UK: Bargate Films.
Fisher, Terence, dir. 1960. *The Brides of Dracula*. UK: Rank Film Distributors.
Fortuny, Juan, dir. 1977. *El pobrecito Draculín (Draculin)*. Spain: Producciones Mezquiriz.
Franco, Jesús, dir. 1962. *Gritos en la noche (The Awful Dr. Orlof)*. Spain: Delta Films.
———. dir. 1970. *El conde Drácula (Count Dracula)*. West Germany: Gloria Film.
———. dir. 1972. *Drácula contra Frankenstein (Dracula, Prisoner of Frankenstein)*. Spain: Chamartín.
Franju, Georges, dir. 1960. *Les Yeux sans visage (Eyes without a Face)*. France: Lux Compagnie Cinématographique de France.
Freda, Riccardo, dir. 1957. *I vampiri (The Vampires)*. Italy: Titanus.
———. dir. 1962. *L'orribile segreto del Dr. Hichcock (The Horrible Dr. Hichcock)*. Italy: Warner Bros.
Freund, Karl, dir. 1932. *The Mummy*. US: Universal Pictures.
Friedkin, William, dir. 1973. *The Exorcist*. US: Warner Bros.
Hanson, Helen. 2007. *Hollywood Heroines: Women in Film Noir and the Female Gothic Film*. London and New York: I. B. Tauris.
Heffernan, Kevin. 2004. *Ghouls, Gimmicks, and Gold: Horror Films and the American Movie Business, 1953–1968*. Durham, NC: Duke University Press.
Higueras, Rubén, ed. 2015. *Cine fantástico y de terror español: De los orígenes a la edad de oro (1912–83)*. Madrid: T&B Editores.
Hills, Matt. 2011. "Cutting into Concepts of 'Reflectionist' Cinema?: The *Saw* Franchise and Puzzles of Post-9/11 Horror." In *Horror after 9/11: World of Fear, Cinema of Terror*, edited by Aviva Briefel and Sam J. Miller, 107–23. Austin, TX: University of Texas Press.
Hitckcock, Alfred, dir. 1960. *Psycho*. US: Paramount Pictures.
Ibáñez Serrador, Narciso, dir. 1969. *La residencia (The House That Screamed)*. Spain: Regia-Arturo González Rodríguez.
Jaeckin, Just, dir. 1974. *Emmanuelle*. France: Para France Films.
Kannas, Alexia. 2021. *Giallo!: Genre, Modernity and Detection in Italian Horror Cinema*. New York: State University of New York Press.
Kerswell, J. A. 2012. *The Slasher Movie Book*. Chicago: Chicago Review Press.
Klimovsky, León, dir. 1971. *La noche de Walpurgis (The Werewolf Versus the Vampire Woman)*. Spain: Hispamex.

———. dir. 1973. *La saga de los Drácula (The Dracula Saga)*. Spain: Calixto Pérez Molpeceres.
Koven, Mikel J. 2006. *La Dolce Morte: Vernacular Cinema and the Italian Giallo Film*. Lanham, MD: Scarecrow Press.
Kümel, Harry. 1971. *Les Lèvres rouges (Daughters of Darkness)*. Belgium: Ciné Vog Films.
Larraz, José Ramón, dir. 1982. *Los ritos sexuales del diablo (Black Candles)*. Spain: La Hispaniola.
Lázaro-Reboll, Antonio. 2012. *Spanish Horror Film*. Edinburgh: Edinburgh University Press.
López Eguiluz, Enrique, dir. 1968. *La marca del hombre lobo (Frankenstein's Bloody Terror)*. Spain: D. C. Films.
Lowenstein, Adam. 2008. *Shocking Representation: Historical Trauma, National Cinema, and the Modern Horror Film*. New York: Columbia University Press.
Margheriti, Antonio, dir. 1964. *Danza macabra (Castle of Blood)*. Italy: Globe Films International.
———. dir. 1964. *I lunghi capelli della morte (The Long Hair of Death)*. Italy: Unidis.
———. dir. 1973. *La morte negli occhi del gatto (Seven Deaths in the Cat's Eye)*. Italy: Jumbo.
Marlow-Mann, Alex. 2011. "Gothic Horror." In *Directory of World Cinema: Italy*, edited by Louis Bayman, 155–6. Bristol: Intellect.
Mastrocinque, Camillo, dir. 1966. *Un angelo per Satana (An Angel for Satan)*. Italy: Discobolo Film.
Matellano, Víctor. 2009. *Spanish Horror*. Madrid: T&B Editores.
———. 2011. *Spanish Exploitation: Sexo, sangre y balas*. Madrid: T&B Editores.
Mathijs, Ernest, and Xavier Mendik. 2004. "Introduction: Making Sense of Extreme Confusion: European Exploitation and Underground Cinema." In *Alternative Europe: Eurotrash and Exploitation Cinema since 1945*, edited by Ernest Mathijs and Xavier Mendik, 1–18. London and New York: Wallflower Press.
Mercero, Antonio, dir. 1982. *Buenas noches, señor monstruo (Good Night, Mr. Monster)*. Spain: José Frade Producciones Cinematográficas.
Miraglia, Emilio, dir. 1971. *La notte che Evelyn uscì dalla tomba (The Night Evelyn Came Out of the Grave)*. Italy: Cineriz.
———. dir. 1972. *La dama rossa uccide sette volte (The Red Queen Kills Seven Times)*. Italy: Cineriz.
Naschy, Paul. 1997. *Memorias de un hombre lobo*. Madrid: Alberto Santos Editor.
Nowell, Richard. 2014. "Introduction: There's Gold in Them Chills." In *Merchants of Menace: The Business of Horror Cinema*, edited by Richard Nowell, 1–10. London and New York: Bloomsbury.
Odell, Colin, and Michelle Le Blanc. 2004. "Jean Rollin: Le sang d'un poète du cinema." In *Alternative Europe: Eurotrash and Exploitation Cinema since 1945*, edited by Ernest Mathijs and Xavier Mendik, 160–71. London and New York: Wallflower Press.
Pérez Tabernero, Julio, dir. 1975. *Las alegres vampiras de Vögel (Vampires of Vogel)*. Spain: Mundial Films.

Pirie, David. 1977. *The Vampire Cinema*. London and New York: Hamlyn.
Polselli, Renato, dir. 1960. *L'amante del vampiro (The Vampire and the Ballerina)*. Italy: Rome International Films.
Pulido, Javier. 2012. *La década de oro del cine de terror español, 1967–1976*. Madrid: T&B Editores.
Pupillo, Domenico Massimo, dir. 1965. *Il boia scarlatto (Bloody Pit of Horror)*. Italy: M. B. S. Cinematografica.
Regnoli, Piero, dir. 1960. *L'ultima preda del vampiro (The Playgirls and the Vampire)*. Italy: Film Selezione.
Rollin, Jean, dir. 1968. *Le Viol du vampire (The Rape of the Vampire)*. France: Les Films ABC.
———. dir. 1971. *Le Frisson des vampires (The Shiver of the Vampires)*. France: Les Films ABC.
———. dir. 1971. *Requiem pour un vampire (Requiem for a Vampire)*. France: Les Films ABC.
———. dir. 1975. *Lèvres de sang (Lips of Blood)*. France: Cinéthèque.
———. dir. 1979. *Fascination*. France: Les Films ABC.
Sala, Ángel. 2010. *Profanando el sueño de los muertos: La historia jamás contada del cine fantástico español*. Pontevedra: Scifiworld.
Sasdy, Peter, dir. 1971. *Countess Dracula*. UK: Rank Film Distributors.
Shipka, Danny. 2011. *Perverse Titillation: The Exploitation Cinema of Italy, Spain and France, 1960–1980*. Jefferson, NC: McFarland.
Steno, dir. 1959. *Tempi duri per i vampiri (Uncle Was a Vampire)*. Italy: Titanus.
Summers, Walter, dir. 1939. *The Dark Eyes of London*. UK: ABPC.
Tohill, Cathal, and Pete Tombs. 1995. *Immoral Tales: Sex and Horror Cinema in Europe, 1956–1984*. London: Titan Books.
Tudor, Andrew. 1989. *Monsters and Mad Scientists: A Cultural History of the Horror Movie*. Oxford and Cambridge, MA: Blackwell.
Vadim, Roger, dir. 1960. *...Et mourir de plaisir (Blood and Roses)*. France: Paramount Pictures.
Wallace, Diana, and Andrew Smith. 2009. "Introduction: Defining the Female Gothic." In *The Female Gothic: New Directions*, edited by Diana Wallace and Andrew Smith, 1–12. Basingstoke: Palgrave Macmillan.
Whale, James, dir. 1931. *Frankenstein*. US: Universal Pictures.
Wiene, Robert, dir. 1920. *Das Cabinet des Dr. Caligari (The Cabinet of Dr. Caligari)*. Germany: Decla-Bioscop.
Willis, Andrew. 2003. "Spanish Horror and the Flight from 'Art' Cinema, 1967–73." In *Defining Cult Movies: The Cultural Politics of Oppositional Taste*, edited by Mark Jancovich, Antonio Lázaro-Reboll, Julian Stringer, and Andy Willis, 71–83. Manchester: Manchester University Press.

Chapter 4

Queer(ly) Mash(ed) Up

Portraits of Neo-Victorian Others in Penny Dreadful

Sarah E. Maier and Rachel M. Friars

Neo-Victorian literature occurs at an interstice between the past and the present, where a desire to understand past texts can help to articulate what is of interest to our postmodern narratives. Many neo-Victorian texts are humorous combinations of traditional and modern-day understandings of popular Victorian fictions. That said, Victorian *ur*-texts which emanate tropes of male power have recently been "mashed up" to create space for the liminal or silenced women and other potentially othered characters in neo-Victorian versions of these stories in John Logan's transmedia series, *Penny Dreadful* (2014–2016). Logan has called *Penny Dreadful* "his nineteenth-century novel, with each episode a chapter in the on-going tale" (qtd. in Gosling 2015, 6). The series is a mash-up of Gothic texts and modes under an original Gothic storyline; it is a remix, or what Megen de Bruin-Molé names "Frankenfiction" or "monstrous adaptation" (2020, 1, 7). Monsters, as Rosie Braidotti reminds us, are "the bodily incarnation of difference from the basic human norm" (1997, 62)—monsters are, definitionally, queer. For that reason, and others, *Penny Dreadful* is rife with queer potential. It luxuriates in the "in-betweenness" of those individuals who live liminal existences, caught between past and present, nightmare and dream, alienation and society. The characters of *Penny Dreadful* are never fully realized in either end point of multiple dichotomies. They exist otherwise along a continuum of queerness from the norm, be it in relation to heteronormative binaries or expectations of female behavior.

The uneasy, angst-ridden, and complex series contains an occult collection of characters. Victor Frankenstein, his Creature, and Justine from Mary Shelley's *Frankenstein* (1818); Dr. Henry Jekyll and his friend (later Sir

Edward Hyde) from Robert Louis Stevenson's *The Strange Case of Dr. Jekyll and Mr. Hyde* (1886); Dorian Gray from Oscar Wilde's *The Picture of Dorian Gray* (1890); and Mina Murray/Harker, her father Sir Malcolm Murray, Dr. Abraham Van Helsing, and Dracula from Bram Stoker's *Dracula* (1897) are among those drawn together. Benjamin Poore sees the series not as a penny dreadful but as a "De(Re)composing" adaptation (2016, 72) with the appropriate recombination of creaturely queer parts to create a neo-Gothic narrative. To a mindful reader, Marie-Luise Kohlke's warning is essential; she encourages a critical awareness that "presentism may produce unintentional misreadings of the past in so far as individuals remain unaware of (or in self-denial about) the extent to which their modern mindsets infiltrate, inform, and possibly distort their assessments of another age and its cultural produces, discourses, and ideologies" (2018, 4). To that end, our reading tracks how the neo-Gothic series uses the original texts and their characters to create a meditation on literary narratives that focus on the boundaries between accepted society and a queered world that exists otherwise.

Two violations take place with this conjoining of old and new; first, new characters are created who support and challenge the canonical ones. Second, the movement and interaction of all the characters beyond their own literary worlds into the urbane, occult word around them upends the canon, the timelines, and the expectations of how such literature works. Rosemary Jackson describes the "uneasy assimilation" of the Gothic in nineteenth-century texts: within the main, realistic text there exists "another non-realistic one, camouflaged and concealed but constantly present" (qtd. in Finegan 2017, 222). *Penny Dreadful* uses this space to juxtapose the Victorian against the neo-Victorian and neo-Gothic narratives, making the narrative a kind of uncanny haunting of the present. Logan melds storylines in a convincing manner to lead us forward in the trials and tribulations of, and surrounding, the beautiful Vanessa Ives (played by Eva Green), who is the "most mysterious thing in London" (Logan 2014, 1.4.51:02).

David Halperin writes that "queer is by definition whatever is at odds with the normal, the legitimate, the dominant" (1997, 62). Similarly, the Gothic, with its tendency toward the subversive, transgressive "recasting" of the acceptable boundaries of the home, family, and body, directly opposes moral stratification (Botting 1996, 7). Ardele Haefele-Thomas writes that "'Gothic' and 'queer' are aligned in that they both transgressed boundaries and occupied liminal spaces, and in so doing, they each consistently interrogate ideas of what is 'respectable' and what is 'normal'" (2012, 2). With its "multi-layered hybrid form," *Penny Dreadful* deploys this queer interrogation of sexual and social boundaries through an adaptation of the Gothic *ur*-texts. By (re)placing the characters into a Gothic storyline alongside new characters such as Vanessa and Ethan Chandler (played by Josh Harnett), each adapted character moves into queer conversation/collision with other characters to expose the subversive queer plots of the original Victorian texts. As Paulina Palmer writes, "the ability of Gothic to transgress, in both the 'itinerant' and 'unorthodox' senses of the term, is partially apparent in its encounter with queer" because both "uncover and bring to light reference to 'perverse' sexualities and genders in texts previously interpreted in a predominantly heteronormative context" (2012, 11). *Penny Dreadful*'s mash-up is facilitated by queer catalysts in the form of iconic characters who form networks of homosexual interaction via traditional Gothic tropes, linking both the original tropes of the source texts and the new, essentially queer, plot in which they have been adapted. Giving most attention to Dorian Gray (played by Reeve Carney) and Vanessa Ives, this chapter explores the various—and mashed-up—implications of *Penny Dreadful*'s queer characters as they explore and refute the social as well as sexual limits of their neo-Victorian society.

DETACHED (IN)DIFFERENCE: DORIAN GRAY

Unlike the multitude of characters that *Penny Dreadful* lifts from their various *ur*-texts, such as Dracula or Frankenstein, Dorian Gray and his portrait (a character in its own right) are the only adapted figures from Wilde's original 1890 novel. "A young man of extraordinary personal beauty" (Wilde [1890] 2017, 9), the charismatic Dorian gains immortality through his mysterious portrait; however, the portrait also bears the weight of Dorian's debauchery and sin. Wilde's original novel (pre-bowdlerization) is a homosexual one; Basil and Lord Henry fall in love with Dorian's beauty and charm. In *Penny Dreadful*, the characters who surround Dorian (Basil, Lord Henry, Sybil) are absent, and Dorian arrives in the series temporally and adaptively distant from his original plot. While the other characters follow a version of their nineteenth-century storylines—Victor Frankenstein (played by Harry Treadaway) contends with his Creature, Dracula is hunted by men who seek to save the woman in their lives—Dorian, by virtue of his amorality, exists without a plot which directly ties him to the action of the series. He moves throughout the narrative as a transitory character who meddles in the plots or subplots of other characters and mashes them up through the sexual networks he creates. He is involved with both adapted and original characters alike to the point where Lourdes Monterrubio-Ibáñez contends that the "immutability of Dorian Gray acquires different meanings regarding the characters to whom he relates" (2020, 17). He is alternately Vanessa's confidant, Ethan's lover, Brona/Lily (played by Billie Piper) Frankenstein's evil partner, or Victor's co-conspirator. Wherever Dorian's place in the plot, his presence queers the narrative, and through his adaptive transferability, he serves as the queer connecting force between characters and *ur*-texts.

Because "transmedia characters" can be "as much cultural as textual" (Albertsen 2019, 244) Dorian's portrayal signals a (post)modern adaptability that the other characters lack. Like his original counterpart in Wilde's novel, Dorian is "always searching for new sensations" and is devoted to "a new Hedonism"; indeed, Lord Henry suggests that Dorian "might be its visible symbol" (Wilde [1890] 2017, 29). Dorian's status as the only sustained, long-term immortal character casts him as both out of time and, here, out of the text(s). Aside from his queer sexuality which connects him to other characters, Dorian presents a recognizable modernity that sets him apart from the other characters.

In the series, Dorian's physicality signals his queer and modern potential. His style of dress signals his transgression and others him from the series' characters. In Wilde's original text Lord Henry comments that "the costume of the nineteenth century is detestable"; "It is so sombre, so depressing" compared to "Sin," which "is the only real colour-element left in modern life" (Wilde [1890] 2017, 34). Dorian's specific articles of clothing are rarely described in Wilde's novel, but he is framed as "exquisitely dressed" (173), in a "necktie" (162), "scarf-pin" (162), or "an elaborate dressing-gown of silk-embroidered cashmere wool" (96), and often his "mode of dressing, and the particular styles that from time to time he affected, had their marked influence on the young exquisites of the Mayfair balls and Pall Mall club windows, who copied him in everything that he did" (Wilde [1890] 2017, 130). *Penny Dreadful* follows Wilde's critique of nineteenth-century fashion through Dorian as it modernizes his stylishness. To capitalize on the visual medium, Dorian is often pictured in a confusion of traditional and modern clothing: leather pants, loose collars, unbuttoned jackets, missing waistcoats, or shirtless altogether, all of which serve as queer indicators of his indifference to tradition. His hair remains long and boyish throughout the series, and his appearance generally eschews the mores of Victorian society. In contrast to Sir Malcolm Murray (played by Sir Timothy Dalton) with his Victorian high collars and starched suits, only traded out for his colonial explorer clothing, Dorian's clothing signals a resistance to cultural structure and socially acceptable gender performance, overall a gesture toward modernity. Just as he is not confined by plot, he resists confinement to any given temporal code. In every scene, his modern and queer potential are signaled to the viewer through his clothing—or lack thereof. This symbolic lack of restraint emphasizes Dorian's queer potential in the mash-up; unlike the other characters, Dorian seems to engage with his queerness with an "outness" that we recognize. While characters like Ethan have a more complicated relationship with their potential bisexuality, Dorian's clothing signals to the viewer—and the other characters—that his body is queerly othered in the mashed time between Victorian and neo-Victorian worlds.

As an out queer character with temporal and plot-based transferability, Dorian's queerness links the Gothic mash-up together through sexual/textual connection. In her discussion of the work of Romantic poetry in *Penny Dreadful*, Nina Farizova writes that the "main characters of *Penny Dreadful* form a kind of sexual network in which many of the members, without knowing, share partners with other members in the most fanciful combinations"; there is no doubt that Dorian is "the irresistible pansexual sinner" who is "the centre of this network" (2020, 188). The queer implications of these sexual/textual networks are particularly crucial in the context of the Gothic mash-up. Dorian has sexual encounters with Vanessa, Ethan, and Brona/Lily. Vanessa and Ethan are in love, and Brona is Ethan's consumptive sexual partner, while the reborn, bride-like Lily is Victor's sex partner. Each primary character in the mash-up is connected through Dorian. Dorian effectively serves as the queer catalyst for the series, and his sexual networks generate dramatic irony that signals the queerness of voyeuristically, decadently watching the series. Only Dorian and the audience—also temporally disconnected from the series' plots—are privy to the transgressions of the whole.

Dorian's presence in the text as a (post)modern, transgressive queer body creates space for other queer individuals, those who are different in mind or body from social convention. Because Dorian has no plot, only his Hedonistic pursuits, the series is able to place him in various queer subplots. Dorian meets Angelique (played by Jonny Beauchamp), a transwoman and a sex worker who has "no last name" (2.2.20:47) and presents a mysterious identity from the outset. The woman boasts "boldness" and a desire "to shock" (2.2.20:30). While she "tries to stop [herself]" she "can't" (2.2.20:35), and the series indicates that Angelique's pursuit of pleasure is in line with Dorian's own. Her banter with Dorian intrigues him, as does her gender ambiguity. Both characters maintain a capacity for queer transformation—Dorian with his portrait, and Angelique with her gender. They have each removed themselves from their designated social, temporal, and sexual contexts to exist otherwise.

Dorian's subplot with Angelique creates queer space in the mash-up. Dorian's character facilitates queer visibility in the series by integrating Angelique into the Victorian city and its glittering society (a gaming hall in 2.3, the opera in 2.5, and the ball in 2.6). Although she is "raising a few eyebrows," Dorian encourages her to "let them stare" because "provocation is food and drink to [him]" (2.3.27:54). When Angelique is recognized at the opera and called a "little freak" (2.5.40:40) by the hypocritical men (perhaps former clients) who accost her, they accuse Dorian of liking "that kind of thing" (2.5.40:47). In response, Dorian kisses Angelique's hand, a gendered gesture of affection that unnerves the men and causes one of them to spit on her (2.5.40:56). Like Dorian's attraction to Sybil in Wilde's novel, here Dorian is entranced by feminine performance and the roles played by Angelique. Dorian rejects Sybil when she refuses to continue to mash her life into various characters on stage (Wilde [1890] 2017, 89–90]), just as he rejects Angelique's attempt to return to performing masculinity, insisting "that's not what you are" (2.5.44:13), objectifying rather than embracing her potential fluidity. When Angelique accuses him of preferring "the freak" (2.5.44:16), he replies "Do you think I don't understand what it is to be different?" (2.5.44:56).

Angelique shares the history of her own queer life with Dorian: "From the moment I was born I was not as I was meant to be. No one spoke of it. My parents ignored me as best they could. So, I came to London and created Angelique, leaving me fit for no trade but whoring, and myself fit for nothing but degradation and ridicule" (2.5.44:15). Angelique's honesty in the portraited ballroom—itself a complex and out-of-time space where many queer characters converge and, potentially, observe—creates a queer visibility facilitated by Dorian's character. "In this house we celebrate the unusual" (2.6.5:58), he explains to Angelique, "let them gape at our uniqueness" (2.6.6:21). The brashness of Wilde's Dorian transfers to *Penny Dreadful* where his neo-Victorian character creates queer space in which queer bodies emerge and openly infiltrate the Victorian Gothic setting.

Dorian also facilitates queer transgression and subversion through his rescue of Justine (played by Jessica Barden) in yet another subplot that mashes up the characters of Wilde's, Shelley's, and Logan's originals. "Justine" invokes Shelley's character who is unjustly hanged and the Marquis de Sade's character who is the victim of sexual sadism. Here, Dorian and Lily infiltrate a kind of dungeon-like space (3.2) wherein men have paid to watch while Justine is to be tortured and killed at the hands of a masked executioner—a mash-up between Gothic literature, neo-Victorian narratives, and modern depravity in a kind of live snuff film. Saved by Dorian and Lily, Justine is "a feral animal raised on the streets, forced to [her] knees when [she] was a girl" (3.2.35:12). In their ambition to recruit "Whores and fallen women" (3.3.46:53) to their cause of "Power. [. . .] Revolution. Freedom" (3.3.47:14), the two libertines indoctrinate Justine into their strange, violent religion/army. The problem with this militant plot, Kohlke writes, is its various "presentist over-simplifications" such as the belief that "all Victorian prostitutes were abused victims of patriarchy" and that "all Victorian men used/abused prostitutes. Hence, all men are equally guilty and deserving of punishment" (2018, 7). Justine's vengeful presence in the series, as indoctrinated by Lily and Dorian, forces a limited, one-dimensionality onto her character in contrast to the mash-up's other complex and various storylines.

Like Angelique, Justine recounts her traumatic history in the portraited ballroom. "He bought me when I was twelve. He used me as his pet whore for a time. Like a monkey on a chain. When I got older he grew tired of me and whored me out. Set me up on a platform and let them fuck me ten at a time. Gave me to the sailors and the Chinks and the Lascars, finally" (3.3.40:52). Just as Dorian promises Angelique that she is "not fighting alone" (2.5.45:22), he offers Justine an opportunity to defy the people who have abused her and live freely. Dorian presents Justine with the man who bought and abused her (3.3); she stabs the man to death and the three—Dorian, Justine, and Lily—engage in a blood-soaked threesome to consummate their involvement. The transgressive and amoral nature of the Gothic visually depicts queer sexuality in a scene which reads as a dark baptism.

Although Lily refers to Dorian as "an exceptional creature [. . .] unlike all others" (3.3.12:47), Angelique and Justine encounter versions of Dorian's self that reveal both a limited capacity for emotion and an inability to transcend the *ennui* of his immortality. When Angelique discovers his "secret" (2.7.36:36) by entering the stone room where the portrait is kept, he reveals his true self to her on the canvas and asks if she can accept him as he is. Although she insists that she can, presumably as he has accepted her queerness, he replies "I don't think you can" (2.7.38:09) and poisons her. Similarly, Justine asks, "How many women have you paid to debase?" (3.6.11:27–40); in return, he warns: "Listen, child. I can toss you out like the baggage you are whenever it pleases me. And don't think for one moment your tiresome Sapphic escapades shock me. You think you're bold? You think you know sin? You're still learning the language. I wrote the bloody book" (3.7.24:28).

In his relationships with all women except Vanessa, Dorian is "simultaneously the rescuer and violator, liberator and sexual exploiter, avenging angel and the Ripper's double" (Kohlke 2018, 10). He reinforces patriarchal boundaries, demonstrating his reliance on his biological sex, when he kills Angelique and Justine. Although Angelique is paralleled with Wilde's Sybil who kills herself (Wilde 2017 [1890], 100–1) under performance pressure, Justine's neck is snapped; her difference—her queerness from the false portraits of idealization which surround them as if watching from the walls—is punished. It is clear Dorian's acts eliminate the transgendered and queered feminine in his own interest.

Dorian's devotion to the queer others in *Penny Dreadful* in conjunction with his killing of them represents his emotional detachment and amorality. Physically and morally stagnant, "Dorian's immortality precludes identity ambivalence and turns him into an immutable identity, with no possibility of evolution" (Monterrubio-Ibáñez 2020, 24). Dorian's inability to evolve culminates in his final conversation with Lily, the other immortal character who refuses Dorian's philosophy that "Passion will undo the best of us and leads only to tragedy. It's ever thus for those who care so deeply" (3.9.15:22). Lily comes as an adaptation of an adaptation—the bride demanded and, in this case, given to Victor's first-born Creature. Brona's rebirth as Lily awakens Victor's physical desire; he exhibits caring companionship for his second-born gentle Creature and consummates his desire for Lily before releasing her to Dorian. Ultimately, she rejects "An eternity without passion," one "Without affection" (3.9.17:30) and chooses to leave Dorian with his portraits, telling him "I hope they watch over you" (3.9.18:21). Victor's female Creature abandons Dorian in his home, finally isolating him from the rest of the mash-up characters. Although his character's temporal mutability enables him to create several queer sexual connections as well as link adapted characters to make space for new, queer bodies, Dorian's fate in the series is to remain unchanged and without significance.

A WOMAN OF QUEER VISION(S): VANESSA, THE CUT-WIFE, AND DR. SEWARD

Penny Dreadful gives us a new perspective on Wilde's Dorian, a perspective based on the "what ifs" of a queer life fully lived; it also provides a new character who brings together, or remixes, a gathering of female traits found in Gothic novels: a damsel in distress, one hunted by dark forces, who is sexually desirable yet unattainable but chastely devoted to one man. If Dorian's lack of passion defines his queerness, then the newly created Vanessa Ives is his counterpart. In addition to her conventional traits, she is an aristocratically powerful but abject, heterosexual but queer, woman whose dark destiny leads her via occult occurrences to the edge of madness. She is not a victim; she is a powerful warrior against the combined forces of Dracula and his followers. Vanessa stands for women, and women stand at her back to shift the power of patriarchy.

The fragmentation, disruption, and transgressiveness of the narrative structure resemble its protagonist; Vanessa is, in all ways, queered from the perceived ideal of womanhood. William Hughes and Andrew Smith argue that to "be queer is to be different, yet it is also to be unavoidably associated with the non-queer, the normative which, though it implicitly represses through the mechanisms of conformist culture, may yet serve as the catalyst to liberation. The two states exist in reciprocal tension. If the queer is to be regarded as the abjected demon of the non-queer, then the reverse may also apply" (2009, 3–4). *Penny Dreadful* exists not within a social, heteronormative context but within the realm of queer Gothicism and "Horror London" (Louttit 2016, 3). The first episode opens on September 22, 1891, a time tainted by the murders effected by "Jack the Ripper"; the mood is set: late

Victorian London becomes a confluent space, "the meeting point of the spiritual perils and horrors of the alienated urban characters" (Akilli and Oz 2016, 16) of the time. Logan reminds us that the nineteenth century brought us monsters—from Victor Frankenstein and his Creature, Jekyll and his Hyde, and Count Dracula with his dual personas—to terrify nonconformists while at the same time pointing the reader to society's many flaws, particularly in relation to women's vulnerability. In *Penny Dreadful*, Vanessa is a composite—a Gothic mash-up—of the many expectations of woman; she has a self-contained nature, but she is unconstrained by social niceties. She does, however, understand what society requires of her and acts accordingly, which allows her female agency but results "in a monstrous representation" (Schäfer 2016, 44) of Victorian woman.

Vanessa's singularity leads to her having a non-heteronormative, non-blood relation family of choice, which includes Sir Malcolm as the father figure; his manservant Sembene (played by Danny Sapani) who is mostly silent but wise and caring; and Ethan, a self-exiled American sharpshooter (who recalls Quincy Morris). Her understanding of Ethan's hidden complexity is that he is a "man who's been accustomed to wealth but has given himself to excess [. . .] a man more complicated than he likes to appear" (2014, 1.1.9:20). Their recognition of dual queerness—his complex sexuality and her occult persona—leads Vanessa to acknowledge, "this is not who you are" (1.1.25:40). Neither of them cares about social conventions. There is much confusion about how to categorize, and thereby deal with, Vanessa's queer abilities. Ethan's protective relationship with Vanessa exemplifies the ultimate in-betweenness of both characters who are in, but not of, the Victorian world. Unable to explain, Ethan must take it, ironically, on faith that they seek common answers even though each holds back a secret.

Vanessa's queer nature is affirmed at a *fin-de-siècle* séance given by Mr. Ferdinand Lyle (played by Simon Russell Beale). The homosexual but normatively/heterosexually married scholar demands social intercourse to observe Vanessa and Ethan, perhaps to see how they perform under pressure. The desire of Mr. Lyle to watch confirms that the decadent social life of the upper ten is a performance and that "those around us may be harbouring mysterious inner lives" (Louttit 2016, 8). All three characters are queer(ed) in the narrative, but for entirely different reasons. Vanessa is separated in kind and intention from the late-Victorian fraudulent spiritualists/mediums. In an extreme example of the transformation she suffers, Vanessa's body is used to ventriloquize several voices, which accuse Sir Malcolm of failing his family and Vanessa of betraying Mina (1.2.30:19). Jill Galvan convincingly argues that "Portraits of female media commonly return to two allegedly feminine traits: sensitivity or sympathy, often imagined as the product of women's delicate nervous systems; and an easy reversion to automatism, or a state of unconsciousness [. . .] by subtracting her intellectually from the path of communication" for maximum "manipulability" (2010, 12, 13). Vanessa's physical metamorphosis in erotic demeanor as well as disconcerting appearance leaves no one in doubt that something substantial occurred even if they are uncertain what it was: trance, seizure, or madness. She is, in fact, highly intellectual and is an integral part of the experience rather than merely a passive receptor of it.

The question of what follows in *Penny Dreadful* becomes whether evil possesses Vanessa or if there another explanation, either earthly or otherwise, for her non-normative nature. She may be spiritually overtaken, physically ill, or, in another scenario, the reincarnated embodiment of the Egyptian goddess Amunet pursued by Amun-ra, her past beloved (here embodied in Lucifer's fallen brother, Dracula, who walks in the light as Dr. Alexander Sweet [played by Christian Camargo]). Vanessa, significantly, begins to manifest her abilities after her betrayal of Mina (played by Olivia Llewellyn). In a flashback, the beginning of her psychological trauma becomes clear when, after lying asleep with Mina, and kissing her while she sleeps, she gets up and seduces Mina's fiancé. Caught *in flagrante*, Vanessa looks straight into the eyes of her friend, an act which suggests the queer but forbidden love they share should be what is valued, not this man. Vanessa does not desire the man but Mina.

The life-altering event leaves both friends vulnerable to evil. Mina is taken by evil, and Vanessa manifests the symptoms of madness. As a Roman Catholic, Vanessa prays desperately for deliverance from God and receives no answer. The families are horrified by the young woman's improper, cruel, and willful behavior. Vanessa is ironically castigated by her own mother who then must watch as her child descends into an unnamed illness, now in/validated as hysteric. In a crucial episode, Vanessa writes "an endless ribbon of words" (1.5.3:25) in hundreds of letters to Mina, a salve for her mind after the passing of what she has believed is an illness but had felt like a "demon inside" (1.5.11:55) to her. Her lesbian desire, its castigation, and her invalidation combine as she retreats into herself; quickly, her weakness is sensed by Dracula/Amun-ra, and he fills the void in her spirit.

Like other/ed women of the nineteenth century, Vanessa is placed under the care of Dr. Christopher Banning (played by Frank McCusker) at his "Clinic for Women," a less threatening name than asylum. Once they arrive, and despite her mother's protestations to the doctor that Vanessa was not suffering from "exertions; she was being tormented" (1.5.29:00), their initial interaction is revealing. Dr. Banning runs through the reasons for Vanessa's catatonia and possibilities of epileptic seizures but lands his immediate diagnosis on the female malady. He claims "Hysteria of a psychosexual nature can be treated. The treatments involve narcotics and escalating hydrotherapy. Cold water reduces circulation to the brain and thereby the metabolism and motor activity [. . .] mental trauma will cease" (1.29:10). The doctors do not even consider the intentionality of Vanessa's actions but assume she must be ill; her non-heteronormative desire is for Mina, a desire that is, by definition, inverted and therefore queer.

In *Penny Dreadful*, the connection between Mina and Vanessa parallels the friendship between Mina and Lucy in Stoker's novel; however, in this case, Vanessa is visibly fraught at the thought of Mina's social acquiescence to be married, a disruption to their queer bond of intense, if not sexual, female companionship. Vanessa must, necessarily, be seen as ill, and a "cure" must be found for her. Victorian women who preferred the company of women were "inverts," or "women [who] differ [. . .] from the normal, or average, woman in that they are not repelled or disgusted by [. . .] advances from persons of their own sex" (Ellis [1900] 1915, 133). In other words, they were women who, rather than participate in patriarchal culture, chose a necessarily mad way of life. The mash-up between *Dracula* and the intrusive new character allows for a change in perception of those outside normative heterosexual behaviors. Unlike Stoker's Mina, whose New-Woman-ness is still contained by her normative relationship with Jonathan Harker, Logan's Vanessa, like Dorian, exists otherwise, outside normal boundaries of acceptability; and their queerness leads to their isolation.

As a case study in medical mismanagement and severe abuse of women for their differences, Vanessa undergoes a variety of "treatments," all of which fit into the assumption that she suffers from "hysteria." There is an occult infection of Vanessa's mind and body, one categorized by Banning as hysteria but exposed as misogynistic by this neo-Victorian narrative. Vanessa suffers; she is forced into ice baths, strapped down to beds and chairs, drugged into passivity, hosed down while tied to a wall like a fallen Christ, shorn of her glorious raven hair, and isolated in an always-lit padded cell while forced to wear a bit in her mouth (1.5), all of which reflect not only the horrors of the Victorian asylum but its sadistic exploitation of women in "a spectacle of punishment upon the deviant female body" (Buckley 2020, 367).

Vanessa's physical manifestations confound the medical and scientific men who read medical journals of the mid- to late nineteenth century such as *The Lancet* and *The British Medical Journal*. Such professionally authorized opinions were highly critical of any understanding of spiritualism; rather, unable to prove the phenomenon, they "asserted that spiritualism could have no intrinsic interest for 'educated and intelligent people'" (Owen 1990, 142). The only interest any idea of spiritualism or possession could possibly hold was "beyond the scope of orthodox scientific inquiry'" (Owen 1990, 143) and in the realm of parapsychology or parascience both of which are often embodied in the Gothic. Maintaining the tension between science and the unexplained, Vanessa is crucial "since the Victorian period witnessed such fierce scientific, intellectual and theological debates over the boundaries between science and Spiritualism, science and pseudo-science" (Noakes 2004, 24). What is missed in the scientific dissection of Vanessa is the potentiality to create a larger queer space for Vanessa's emotional grounding in her relationship with Mina.

There is no doubt that Vanessa and the men surrounding her are intellectual—one an aristocratic adventurer, one a medical doctor, one a scholar working at the British Museum, and one a world-wise American—so it must be possible for there to be intelligent believers in the *demimonde* who find that conventional explanatory theories are inadequate. On more than one occasion Vanessa feels she has a "thing inside" like an "animal scratching to get out" (1.7.23:17), and the series is a litany of attacks on Vanessa and those persons for whom she cares. To "solve" Vanessa as a kind of Freudian case study, self-exploration can only occur in a trusting space—one she finds with the Cut-Wife of Ballentree Moor.

Watching the series, we find there are often gaps which seem to leave unsettled the question of how the troubled girl-child Vanessa becomes the self-possessed, determined, impeccable woman who combats evil. In a flashback episode in the second series, it is revealed that Vanessa, after the death of her mother, leaves home to seek out the Cut-Wife, Joan Clayton (played by Patti LuPone), a woman—a witch (another staple of Gothic womanhood)—who lives isolated on the moors. Hated but needed by women and men for her skills, she is reviled for her difference. Joan knows that "They despise me. So it is always for those who do for women" (2015 2.3.33:40). To win entry and an extensive education in the ways of the earth and of her gifts, Vanessa must show fortitude and strength, waiting outside in a storm until Joan asks her if she is like the other girls who have come for abortions. Vanessa responds, "I am like no others" (2.3.7:35), a queer manifesto Joan immediately identifies as truthful.

Vanessa asks Joan to help her discover "Why I am like I am . . . Cursed. Cursed to see things not of this world" (2.3.11:30). Vanessa has admitted previously, "I see things sometimes. I am affected by forces beyond our world" (1.3.28:02). The difficulty is with her desire to understand its draw upon her being and her mind. Recalling Julia Kristeva's power of horror, for Vanessa there "looms, within abjection, one of those violent, dark revolts of being, directed against a threat that seems to emanate from an exorbitant outside or inside, ejected beyond the scope of the possible, the tolerable, the thinkable" (2018, 68). Vanessa is hauntingly drawn to, but simultaneously horrified by, the power she holds. She refuses to "agree to the [. . .] rules of the game"; rather, from a "place of banishment" with Joan, Vanessa is an active participant because the "abject does not cease challenging [the] master" (Kristeva 2018, 68) who seeks to subsume her.

Joan's perceptiveness in seeing Vanessa's need to reassert her subjectivity in order to deny abjection allows for a powerful coming together of two strong women, each considered queer by society. Joan understands Vanessa like no other might and allows her to enter with the admonition to "leave everything you were outside this door. Bring everything you are" (2015, 2.3.9:00). She then teaches Vanessa about the ways to survive in nature, about the abilities they share. A daywalker like Vanessa, Joan has cartomancy and clairvoyance, longevity and apotropaic abilities, and Vanessa comes to share these under her mentor's demanding tutelage, which she learns to control as means of protection. The mentor emphasizes the need for self-protection from evil in this world and the other. The story of Joan Clayton is complex; from the time she gave shelter to Oliver Cromwell in 1644 and he made a gift of the land, she has lived upon it away from her sister (whom we find is the witch, Evelyn Poole) and her sister's coven. Ironically, Cromwell was a Protestant believer, and Joan was branded in the past for her powers and occult wiccan beliefs; in addition, in this present, she is burned to death by a mob of villagers doing "God's work" (2.3.39:10). At the same time, Vanessa is branded with an inverted cross. Anticipating her own death, Joan gives Vanessa the land so she will always have safety outside of society.

After Joan's death, Vanessa's return to London underscores her determination to embrace herself as a queer woman, an intention that is facilitated by the urban, industrialized, alienating setting, which "allows for an examination of the monstrous identities of the characters" with "bodies that appear normal and yet house the non-human" (Rocha 2016, 35). The layering of the city matches the palimpsestic nature of Vanessa's visions, the complexities of Ethan's manifestations, and, later, the intrinsic intensity of Kaetenay's spirit visions. These men, considered overtly masculine and, unlike Vanessa, not openly different/queer, believe in her, but after an extreme recurrence of the fight between herself and her spirit, even Vanessa questions her own sanity. She asks Sir Malcolm, "Is this what it is to go mad? Your darkest fears made manifest before your eyes?" which he immediately and authoritatively dismisses as ridiculous with "You're not a neurotic Vanessa" (2.2.3:50). If medical science cannot explain the phenomenon that is Vanessa Ives, then there must be other means of discursively situating the many kinds of visions she experiences. Sir Malcolm, the father figure of this family of choice, is confronted with the "most controversial aspect of Spiritualism [which] was [. . .] undoubtedly the interpretation of such manifestations" (Noakes 2004, 27), especially in relation to what he knows are Vanessa's Catholic beliefs. Ultimately, Sir Malcolm does not need to believe in God but just to see Vanessa as a daughter of choice in devastating need of help.

Vanessa's moment of contemplation parallels the series' "meditative approach to the subject" (Manea 2016, 42) of her traumatic, but perhaps blessed, life. One scientific woman—Dr. Florence Seward (alienist/psychologist, also played by Patti LuPone)—joins her woman-centered, rational studies to the paranormal activities of the side of light. Dr. Seward is the strongest example of a character who ushers the various adapted *ur*-texts together. She is the antithesis of Stoker's Seward, a drug addict who is a part of the triangle of homosocial men (Quincy Morris and Sir Arthur Holmwood) who are in love with Lucy, but like the other Seward, Renfield plays a significant part on behalf of Dracula, and she records all sessions on wax. Contributing to Dr. Seward's mashed-upness is her relation to Joan Clayton. LuPone's double roles as both the Cut-Wife and Dr. Seward emphasize that both strong women focus on female need without concern for patriarchal approval. Dr. Seward is both re-gendered and, perhaps, asexual; her clothes and hair are indicative of male tropes of the gentleman, and her forceful attitude is imbued with appropriated masculine assertiveness. Unorthodox and unapologetic, Dr. Seward offers her strength and knowledge to Vanessa as both a survivor and investigator of women's traumas, and like the Cut-Wife, as a friend and mentor. They discover that Dr. Seward's ancestor was Joan Clayton, a not-insignificant coincidence, and that Dr. Seward is an expatriate New Yorker who has killed her abusive husband.

Both Vanessa and Dr. Seward are strongly intellectual and aware of the evil of the world; their first interaction contrasts starkly with the one Vanessa had at the Banning Clinic. Dr Seward is direct: "I am not your friend, your Priest, or your husband. I'm your Doctor [. . .] Do you understand that you are ill? Not bad, not unworthy, just ill? Do you understand that?" (2016, 3.1.33:00). Dr. Seward rebuts Vanessa's doubts and verbal distancing of politeness with a demand for absolute honesty because "there are no emotions unwelcome in this room" (3.1.34.37). The physical space of the alienist's office is significant; it is a professional, safe space where Vanessa will be seen, not dismissed and wherein she is expected, not dissuaded, from speaking her truth. Dr. Seward ends their first session with a detailed list of how she sees Vanessa—unhappy, isolated, unworthy, and having lost something very important; she is full of self-blame and does not eat; she avoids mirrors and sunlight (as if she were a vampire); she sees that Vanessa is an unconventional woman who is drawn to dark, complicated, impossible men but is unhappy alone (3.1.36:00). Of course, all of these descriptors are accurate, and Vanessa agrees to return and to be hypnotized, remarking to Dr. Seward, "You need interesting people to collect" (3.1.35:00). Dr. Seward tells her they can awaken her memory to see when her first encounter with evil had occurred, but that Vanessa will have full free will and must allow it, "like a dream" (3.3.49:00), to overtake her conscious mind.

Dr. Seward does not seem to believe it is a coincidence that the moment in Vanessa's past when she feels deserted by God and in confrontation with

Lucifer is during her imprisonment at the asylum. It is made excruciatingly clear, via her caretaker (who, in another conflation of texts, later becomes Victor's Creature), that if she would only perform passive femininity—in other words, conform—society would willfully, and blindly, set her free. Vanessa's mind retreats into her time at the asylum, and she unpacks the many secrets of how evil came to her while she was being "cured" by a medical science that invalidated her selfhood.

Vowing to Vanessa "I am not leaving you for anything in this world" (3.4.23:00), Dr. Seward acknowledges Vanessa's overwhelmingly traumatic past but stands firm that Vanessa must go straight through it to heal (3.4.22:45). Logan is clear that it "was important to me not to create a victim" but a character who has a choice in being "the manifestation of what it is to be a monster" (qtd. in Gosling 2015, 123, 125). To demonstrate how a family in late-Victorian London would seek out comfort for such a person as Vanessa, Logan decided that she should be taken to "a medical clinic where, instead, they put her through what are, from our [neo-Victorian] perspective, barbaric procedures, to try to heal her—without realizing that what needs to be healed is something deeply ingrained within her and is as much supernatural as psychological" (qtd. in Gosling 126–7)—or, more interestingly, the intersectional nexus between both and her sexual nature. Dr. Seward is the opposite of Dr. Banning; he believes Vanessa can be cured by physical punishment including trepanning, while she accepts, fully and without question, Vanessa's queer otherness. Dr. Seward knows that the dualisms must be embraced; she stands with Vanessa to physically battle the evil that threatens to consume her client, now friend.

Penny Dreadful is a significant intertextual mash-up for Gothic studies. The characters have backstories and fictional biographies that intersect. Adapted characters escape the pages of their own narratives to mix with characters who "may have been" at the same time, and "may have known" each other well enough to recognize their queer narrative bonds across texts and time. Dorian Gray represents the early man of difference, one who exists in the shadows of Victorian representation, while Vanessa Ives and Dr. Seward represent queer women partners who work to empower women and fight dark patriarchal forces that seek to medicalize or marry them. As a result of its mash-up of old and new stories, Logan's *Penny Dreadful* gives narrative and physical space to queer potentialities only whispered at in traditional Gothic texts.

REFERENCES

Akilli, Sinan, and Seda Oz. 2016. "'No More Let Life Divide...': Victorian Metropolitan Confluence in *Penny Dreadful*." *Critical Survey* 28 (1): 15–29.

Albertsen, Anita Nell Bech. 2019. "Palimpsest Characters in Transfictional Storytelling: On Migrating Penny Dreadful Characters from Television to Comic Books." *Continuum* 33 (2): 242–57.
Botting, Fred. 1996. *Gothic: The New Critical Idiom*. Oxford: Routledge.
Braidotti, Rosi. 1997. "Mothers, Monsters, and Machines." In *Writing on the Body: Female Embodiment and Feminist Theory*, edited by Katie Conboy, Nadia Medina, and Sarah Stanbury, 59–79. New York: Columbia University Press.
de Bruin-Molé, Megen. 2020. *Gothic Remixed: Monster Mashups and Frankenfictions in 21st-Century Culture*. London: Bloomsbury Academic.
Buckley, Chloé Germaine. 2020. "A Tale of Two Women: The Female Grotesque in Showtime's *Penny Dreadful*." *Feminist Media Studies* 20 (3): 361–80.
Ellis, Havelock. [1900] 1915. *Studies in the Psychology of Sex: Sexual Inversion*. London: F. A. Davis Company.
Farizova, Nina. 2020. "Romantic Poetry and the TV Series Form: The Rhyme of John Logan's *Penny Dreadful*." *Adaptation: The Journal of Literature on Screen Studies* 13 (2): 176–93.
Finegan, Samuel. 2017. "'...Touched by the Back Hand of God': Outcasts, Monstrous Love and Queer Fellowship in *Penny Dreadful*." *Australasian Journal of Popular Culture* 6 (2): 219–30.
Galvan, Jill. 2010. *The Sympathetic Medium: Feminine Channeling, the Occult, and Communication Technologies, 1859–1919*. New York: Cornell University Press.
Gosling, Sharon. 2015. *The Art and Making of Penny Dreadful*. London: Titan Books.
Haefele-Thomas, Ardele. 2015. *Queer Others in Victorian Gothic: Transgressing Monstrosity*. Wales: University of Wales Press.
Halperin, David. 1997. *Saint Foucault: Towards a Gay Hagiography*. Oxford: Oxford University Press.
Hughes, William, and Andrew Smith. 2009. "Introduction: Queering the Gothic." In *Queering the Gothic*, edited by William Hughes and Andrew Smith, 1–10. Manchester: Manchester University Press, 2009.
Kohlke, Marie-Luise. 2018. "The Lures of Neo-Victorianism Presentism (with a Feminist Case Study of *Penny Dreadful*)." *Literature Compass* 15 (1): 1–14.
Kristeva, Julia. 2018. "Approaching Abjection." In *Powers of Horror: An Essay on Abjection*. In *Classic Readings on Monster Theory: Demonstrare*, edited by Asa Mittman and Marcus Hensel, 68–75. York: Arc Humanities Press.
Logan, John, creator. 2014–2016. *Penny Dreadful*. Showtime (US) and Sky Atlantic (UK).
Louttit, Chris. 2016. "Victorian London Redux: Adapting the Gothic Metropolis." *Critical Survey* 28 (1): 2–14.
Manea, Dragos. 2016. "A Wolf's Eye View of London: *Dracula, Penny Dreadful* and the Logic of Repetition." *Critical Survey* 28 (1): 40–50.
Monterrubio-Ibáñez, Lourdes. 2020. "'Penny Dreadful' (2014–2016). Postmodern Mythology and Ontology of Otherness." *Communication & Society* 33 (1): 15–28.
Noakes, Richard. 2004. "Spiritualism, Science and the Supernatural in Mid-Victorian Britain." In *The Victorian Supernatural*, edited by Nicola Bown et al., 23–43. Cambridge: Cambridge University Press.

Owen, Alex. 1990. *The Darkened Room: Women, Power and Spiritualism in Late Victorian England*. Philadelphia: University of Pennsylvania Press.
Palmer, Paulina. 1990. *The Queer Uncanny*. Cardiff: University of Wales Press.
Poore, Benjamin. 2016. "The Transformed Beast: *Penny Dreadful*, Adaptation, and the Gothic." *Victoriographies* 6 (1): 62–81.
Rocha, Lauren. 2016. "Angel in the House, Devil in the City: Explorations of Gender in *Dracula* and *Penny Dreadful*." *Critical Survey* 28 (1): 30–9.
Wilde, Oscar. [1890] 2017. *The Picture of Dorian Gray*. London: Arcturus.

Chapter 5

Horror, Humor, and Satire in *Get Out*

Chesya Burke

Many years ago, my sister died. She was a track star and had an undiagnosed heart condition. She died while running track after school one day. At the hospital, moments after she passed, my family was naturally distraught, so I did what just comes naturally for us, and many people within the Black diaspora. I cracked a dark joke: "Well, she told y'all she hated running, now didn't she." My family burst out laughing, although they had been inconsolably crying only seconds before. However, the doctors and nurses were mortified.

In many ways, this story highlights how Black communities often mash up humor and horror as a "coping mechanism to get through dark times," as scholar Kinitra Brooks once explained to me when we were discussing *Get Out*. As such, dark humor and satire are about addressing tense or difficult situations, not by ignoring them, but by bringing attention to the horror right in front of you, particularly for marginalized communities who have few outlets to process pain and injustice. According to Jonathan Greenberg, satire "exposes frauds, debunks ideals, binds communities, starts arguments, evokes unconscious fantasies [. . . .] [It] does not just identify vice and folly but aims to reform or punish them" (Greenberg 2018, i, 13). Similarly, Nicholas Diehl contends: "Satire is traditionally thought of a literary mode with a moral purpose; the satirist writes with a sense of moral vocation and with a concern for the public interest" (2013, 312). To simplify it further, according to Oxford Dictionary, satire, "use[es] humor, irony, exaggeration, or ridicule to expose and criticize people's stupidity or vices, particularly in the context of contemporary politics and other topical issues."

Scholars have long debated what does and does not constitute satire, specifically juxtaposing it to dark humor. Greenberg defines "Black Humor"[1] as joking about suffering, cruelty, and death [. . . .] It is, in Breton's words, "the mortal enemy of sentimentality," and offends middlebrow, middle-class sensibility in order to critique it [. . . .] He cites [. . .] comedians W. C. Fields and the Marx Brothers, and crowns Jonathan Swift as "the true initiator" of the mode. For Breton, as for many after him, black humor eschews the narrow moralism of satire, embracing instead its perversity and violence; in the words of comic novelist Bruce Jay Friedman, black humor explores "darker waters out beyond satire." (2018, 61)

My intent is not to argue the differences between satire and dark humor but instead to find the site where the two intersect—a space for subversive social commentary. As an example of the use of dark humor to satirize injustice, I point to one of the most famous satirical essays ever written, *A Modest Proposal for Preventing the Children of Poor People From being a Burthen to Their Parents or Country, and For making them Beneficial to the Publick*, commonly referred to as *A Modest Proposal* (1729). In the essay, Jonathan Swift argues that poor Irish children are a plague on society, and to ease the economic burden, the rich should simply eat them. Of course, the essay is deeply ironic; the point of the horrific proposal is to mock the callous and cruel treatment of the poor, particular the Irish, by the rich. *A Modest Proposal* is an example of how horror and humor can be mixed to call out the hypocrisy of a ruling class.

In the same vein as *A Modest Proposal*, the 2017 horror hit *Get Out* by Jordan Peele uses satire to highlight the hypocrisy of white, middle-class moderates. The film follows Chris (Daniel Kaluuya), a Black man, visiting his white girlfriend's family, who totally "by the way, would have voted for Obama for a third term if [they] could have" (*Get Out*). Chris eventually learns that his girlfriend, Rose (Allison Williams), has set him up to be bodily enslaved to her white community. The film is a satirical allegory on the ways white progressives use microaggression to deny and reinforce racism, causing physical harm to Black bodies. While horror often "mashes up" the horrific with satire to ease the tensions of fear, in this chapter I will argue that Jordan Peele uses horror and humor as Swift does: to expose the violence perpetrated by the ruling class. In Swift's time, this meant challenging classism and British imperialism, and in Peele's it means challenging white supremacy. Using a mash-up of intertextual references to such traditional horror texts as *The Shining* (1980), *The Stepford Wives* (1972), and *Night of the Living Dead* (1968), *Get Out* mixes horror and satire to critique racial relations within the United States. While I will not directly juxtapose Peele with Swift in this chapter, it is important to acknowledge the long-standing tradition of using satire and dark humor to address horrific injustices.

MASHING UP HORROR, HUMOR, AND RACE

The most common mash-up in the horror genre is the combination of horror and humor, or horror and satire. Avril Horner and Sue Zlosnik state "that the comic within the Gothic foregrounds a self-reflexivity and dialectic impulse intrinsic to the modern subject" (2014, 4). This makes sense because horror and the Gothic are often personal and deal with heavy, dark topics that are relevant to contemporary audiences. Because these works force audiences to deeply self-reflect, viewers often need the break in tension that comic relief offers. Furthermore, over-the-top plotlines and characters in states of extreme distress often leave audiences both horrified and forced to laugh at the absurdity of it all. Films such as *Young Frankenstein* (1974), *An American Werewolf in London* (1981), and *Fright Night* (1985) mash up traditional scary monsters (vampires, werewolves, and Frankenstein and his creature) with overtly comedic elements; however, these films do not offer any real critique of the social or political conversations that were happening at the time. A more recent film, *The Cabin in the Woods* (2011), follows five college students, each representing a horror trope (the jock, the intellectual, the stoner, the slut, and, of course, the virgin), to parody the entire genre. In the film, the coeds are lured to the cabin by an underground organization that has made a pact with the Underworld to sacrifice the five to the monsters of tradition, which include zombies, clowns, a Merman, and The Reanimated. The group must die to keep the world and humans safe from these dangerous creatures. The film hinges on the convention that the virgin must survive until everyone else has died, and then she can either live or die—it doesn't matter according to tradition. Like *Shaun of the Dead* (2004) before it, *The Cabin in the Woods* offers a critique of a genre which is often accused of being stale and clichéd. What neither film does, however, is provide astute social commentary when it comes to race. In fact, *Cabin* deliberately skirts the opportunity. One of the most notable tropes of horror is "the first Black man." Many will recognize this character as one who may be the "jock," "clown," or "brute" but who is traditionally known to die first. In *Horror Noire: Blacks in American Horror Films from 1890s to Present*, Robin R. Means Coleman locates the emergence of the trope in horror movies made in the wake of the Blacksploitation films of the 1970s:

> As this short-lived era of on-screen afro-enlightenment faded into oblivion it seems that the doors of mainstream horror began to creak open, but just enough to lead a few more token Negroes to the slaughter [. . . and] in the 1980s [. . .] Hollywood entered into its "Kill a Nigga" phase [. . . .] During this period, it seemed that if a Black character was allowed on the screen he or she was dead by the time the credits rolled [. . . .] Not only were the vast majority of Black

characters killed off during this period, but they were often the first to die. (2011, xiii)

"The first Black man" is conspicuously absent from *The Cabin in the Woods*. Jesse Williams plays the character of the jock, but he is missing all identifying racial markers. His race is not mentioned, and the film does not play up the racial aspect in the same way that it does misogyny (the virgin must survive until the end because she is good and pure). A racially mixed actor, Williams can easily pass for white. This is significant because not only is Williams racially non-descript, but he does not die first, and to ignore the trope of the Black man in horror movies is to disregard the obvious racial problems in the genre itself. If the point of the film is to satirize the genre and critique the problematic aspects of horror, then race should have been forefront. Because the film does not take up the issue of race, it falls short of its promise as a "smart, witty" (Lyttelton 2012) commentary on the genre and instead simply recreates the racial problems found in horror films. As such, Black horror audiences are left pretty much as they have been throughout the history of horror films: with little to no representation at best and dying to protect white characters at worst.

Black horror mash-ups like *Blacula* (1972), *J. D.'s Revenge* (1976), and *Bones* (2001), on the other hand, address the elephant in the room: race and systemic injustice. These films not only mash up horror and comedy, but they also center race to offer cautionary tales about the dangers both within and outside the Black community. Another film that stands out is *Tales from the Hood* (1995). A mash-up of *Boyz n the Hood* (1991) and *Tales from the Crypt* (1989–1996), it is a satirical horror comedy that addresses racial bias in the United States. According to one early assessment, *Tales from the Hood* "both fails to be the witty satire that it was promoted as being and the serious scarefest it actually aspires to be" (Dequina 1995). In hindsight, however, the film is both a witty satire and terrifying in its prediction of race relations in the United States. In the post-Trump, post-insurrection, post-QAnon and Proud Boys ("Stand back and stand by.") era, it becomes clear that the film was both ahead of its time and that it is a "lesson" for those who would not learn from the history of anti-Black terror.

Hood is an anthology film, which follows four different, independent stories. One of them, "KKK Comeuppance," shows how it is a prescient satire of U.S. politics and racial dynamics. The story follows a white supremacist, Duke Metger (Corbin Bernsen), who is running for elected office. A man who calls Black people "nigras" and refers to Black protestors a "minstrel show," he purchases an old plantation where enslaved people were murdered by the slave master to keep from setting them free after the Civil War—and he purchases the house because this history "adds to [the] southern charm"

(*Hood*). The souls of the wronged still roam the land and were put into dolls by "an old voodoo woman" whose spirit is still residing in the house. After being stalked and hunted by of one of the spirit dolls, the white supremacist begins beating the mural of the Black "voodoo" woman with the American flag, and the image begins to bleed (an evocation of the way Black bodies are abused in the United States). Eventually he tries to cover himself in the flag as the dolls attack him, and the old woman materializes from the mural into reality to watch the death of the representation of white supremacy. The film follows the classic revenge ghost stories of traditional horror. It is both "angry and optimistic" as poet W. H. Auden observes of satire in general (1966, xi). Surely Duke Metger's views and behavior toward the Black community are infuriating, but despite all appearances *Tales from the Hood* is also hopeful. Not only does telling this story in the form of a fable suggest that a lesson can be learned, but the story ends by eliminating the evil that is white supremacy. The "lesson" is society's to learn.

American horror has a long and racist history. In the beginning, Black people were played by whites in blackface—*The Birth of a Nation* (1915) being an early example. Since then, the genre has ignored Black people completely, murdered Black people first, and written them as submissive, willingly dying so that white characters survive. Naturally this works to maintain the status quo of white, racial dominance, whether intended or not. Black horror satire, however, critiques the system, as Jonathan Crane states, to show that the "[the monsters] are [white people], and [we] never know when [whites] will act as monsters" (1994, 8).

JORDAN PEELE, RACE, AND HORROR MASH-UPS

In many ways, Jordan Peele's career is a continuous mash-up. He wears the hat of actor, comedian, and filmmaker. While he is known for the popular Comedy Central sketch comedy series, *Key & Peele*, he is best recognized for directing *Get Out* and *Us*, in which he mashes up comedy, horror, and satire, like many of his Black directorial predecessors. In interviews throughout his career, Peele has said that he takes most of his influences from horror and comedy greats. His horror influences include such films as *Night of the Living Dead, Candyman, Rosemary's Baby*, and *The Shining*. While as a comedian, some of his influences are Richard Pryor, Dave Chappelle, and Steve Martin. What we can understand from this mix of influences is that Peele takes inspiration from an array of sources, and as such, the mash-ups within his films are natural and endemic.

Take for instance one of the skits from his comedy sketch show with fellow actor and comedian, Keegan-Michael Key. Called *Alien Imposters*, the short film follows two Black men (played by Key and Peele themselves) who are trying to survive an alien apocalypse in which the aliens are disguised as human beings. While it would be impossible for most people to know if someone is alien or human within this apocalypse, the two use racism to their benefit. When the pair run into white people, they ask them a series of questions to find out if the person has been indoctrinated with racist ideologies. Obviously, the point is if they are not racist, then they are also likely not to be human. The first person they run into is a white man, a "hillbilly" type, wearing a confederate hat and a mullet. The man stops them claiming to offer help: "Hey! Hey guys! Oh, thank god! We've started a community of survivors. Y'all come live with us." Immediately Peele guns him down as yellow blood explodes from his chest and he turns back into alien form as his dead body hits the ground. When asked by Key's character how he knew the man was an alien, Peele responds, "Come on. Redneck wants us to move into his community. Us?" It's important for viewers to challenge their own ideologies while engaging with this thought-provoking piece. One thing of note is that the alien species could conceptualize human speech and its nuances (using "y'all" appropriately), but the construction of bias based on race is outside their reasoning. While the sketch is ironic, it reflects the real concerns that Black people face within society—that racism is an integral part of everyday society.

The one person the two men choose to bring along is a white woman, Emily, who says that "[her] best friend is Black" and that she "love[s] JAY Z, and [that her] favorite movie is *Think Like a Man*." With her stereotypical "white girl" name, Emily has clearly been socialized to behave stereotypically toward Black people and in doing so her life is spared. The gag here is that similar to Black people and racism, white women understand sexism so well that they can turn it on its head and use it to survive, just as Key and Peele are doing. But this method of detection can also identify a fellow Black person, as the pair soon run into a Black man who upon being asked what he thinks about "the police" replies that he "loves their third album." Of course, this is something a being who has studied the society—but not understood it—would say, so they shoot the alien dead.

The joke of course is that racism isn't rational and that creatures intelligent enough to develop the technology to travel to another universe would not understand the simplicity and ignorance of racism. The satire lies in the fact that Black survival is contingent on understanding white supremacy; the exaggerated storyline works to expose society's bigotry against Black bodies while giving audience members the opportunity to laugh at the ridiculousness it all—both the skit and our own existence in a racist (and sexist) society.

Peele continues to critique race through satire in *Get Out*. In the film, there is one non-Black person at the auction trying to purchase Chris's Black body.

An unnamed character, he is an Asian man who has chosen to uphold the racial status quo, bidding on the Black man. He asks Chris if he thinks being Black in America has more advantages or disadvantages. This character is interesting as it introduces the idea that white supremacy can be upheld by non-white people and that other racial minorities can hold anti-Black views. However, when looking at this Asian man's question to Chris, it also suggests that he is trying to get a "racial leg up," betting that being Black in this country is "better" than being Asian. Here Peele's satire is at its best because this is absurd. Although Asians are often seen as the "model minority," scholars Bic Ngo and Stacey J. Lee assert that "the model minority stereotype is used to silence and contain Asian Americans even as it silences other racial groups" (2007, 416). While this model is often viewed as having accomplished the American Dream, it often comes with loss of cultural identity as Asians are forced to assimilate, and this does not even account for the recent anti-Asian violence during the Trump era. However, in this moment the perceptive viewer is forced to ask themselves, "Is being Black better than being Asian?" followed immediately by the realization that simply to ponder this question is to have to admit to a racial hierarchy. The joke here is not on Chris but instead it is on the society that maintains this injustice so that minorities are constantly fighting each other. The point of satire is to criticize people's stupidity, and in this scene we all discover how stupid we must be to allow this ridiculous system to stand. We come to understand our own culpability in this system and though we know we are not the Armitages, we cannot fully ignore our own complicity.

Like Black horror creators before him, Peele has successfully mashed up horror with comedy and satire by focusing on the intersections of race, gender, and class, and like those before him, his satire is effective in critiquing this society so as to shine a spotlight on the injustices that exist around Black and marginalized bodies.

GET OUT: INTERTEXTUAL MASH-UP

Not only is *Get Out* a horror/satire hybrid, but it is also a mash-up of intertextual references, specifically in the way Peele deliberately invokes a mix of horror films to strengthen his satirical social commentary. While there are many intertextual references in the film, the ones I will focus on are to *The Shining*, *The Stepford Wives*, and *Night of the Living Dead*.

Get Out opens with a Black man, Andre (LaKeith Stanfield), walking at night in a white American suburb. He is on edge because he "sticks out like a sore thumb," signaling immediately that while white people would consider this neighborhood benign and even a paradise, Black people are always unsafe in spaces constructed for whiteness. Andre jokingly compares this white paradise to "a fucking hedge maze," just before he is kidnapped, and the audience later discovers his body has been sold to the highest bidder, while his mind has been taken over by that very whiteness he has always feared. Andre's remark is a pointed allusion to the hedge maze in Kubrick's adaptation of King's *The Shining*, which follows a family that moves to an isolated hotel so that the father can work as a caretaker but also have the freedom to work on his novel. In the book and subsequent adaptation, the hotel is haunted, and the father goes mad trying to kill his family. Through the allusion to the hedge maze Peele invites the viewer to look for the links between *Get Out* and *The Shining*, and numerous links can be found, including the Armitages's house being isolated like the Overlook Hotel, and the visuals around the drive sequences in both films.

However, the most notable link for the purpose of this discussion concerns race and the handling of racial history in both films. The Overlook Hotel in *The Shining* is built on "Indian burial ground" and there are hints that the settlers killed off the Indigenous population to build the structure. Native American references permeate the film, highlighting white violence against minority bodies. This theme is never more apparent than with the only Black character, Dick Hallorann (Scatman Crothers). Hallorann is a traditional "magical negro" character, in that he is, as Matthew Hughey states, "a stock character" that is "lower class, uneducated [and] Black, who possesses supernatural or magical powers" (2009, 544). Hallorann uses his powers to aid the young white protagonist, Danny, and is promptly murdered by the father, Jack. At one point a ghost of the house warns Jack that "a nigger cook" is coming to save Danny, as Jack repeats the word. To the film's credit, it seems to make a clear connection between evil and racism. Malevolent ghosts and corrupted whites willingly use the derogatory word in the same way they are willing to kill innocent women and children. (Jack is manipulated into trying to kill his family, but the film has already set him up as abusive to his son and wife, and the first owners of the hotel killed off Natives.)

The Shining certainly offers satirical commentary on the white American nuclear family through its portrayal of alcoholism, domestic abuse, and isolation. It shows the dark side of white America, just as Peele does in *Get Out*. A moment of humor in *Get Out* that plays on the white American nuclear family is at dinner when Rose's brother is commenting on Chris's "genetic makeup" and her mother deflects by cheerfully announcing she has a "carrot cake!" A moment of comic relief that breaks up the tension, it also highlights the racial disparities in the house, as hidden away in the kitchen, Chris had just seen the Black maid staring at him emotionlessly, holding that very same cake. The Armitages position themselves as good employers to their Black staff and are seen as upstanding, good people. They have the perfect appearances of a father, mother, and two loving children, a boy and a girl. More importantly, they would never call Black people by the "n" word, after all, they would have voted for Obama for a third time if given the opportunity. They are, by all accounts, liberal. As such, Peele's film suggests that racism does not function in the expected way—with the angry white racist saying the "n" word and trying to murder Black people, as seen in *The Shining*—but racism is instead often more insidious. It is built within the fabric of the American household and reflects what scholars call the "white epistemologies of ignorance," whereby white people often downplay "overt racism" in favor of "subtle" forms of racism (Combs 2018, 38). This effectively works because it allows white people to engage in not so obvious forms of racism without taking ownership of the harm they cause. It is when white people use systemic white supremacy, but maintain innocence because they haven't, for instance, used the "n" word.

Peele's allusions to *The Shining* firmly situate his film within the tradition of satirical horror, playing not only on the tropes of the nuclear family, but also on the horror that happens when one finds themselves outside the reach of the American Dream. In the film, Chris's only access to that dream is through his art, but the Armitages show clearly how white people can play on Black people's dreams to exploit them. The message to Chris from the Armitages—and from white people to Black people, which Peele illustrates—is that no matter how hard you try or how talented you are, you are still simply seen as that word that no one is willing to say anymore, but that still has a lingering impact on Black bodies in this country.

Even more so than *The Shining*, the 1975 film *The Stepford Wives* (an adaptation of the satirical thriller by Ira Levin) is in many ways a model for *Get Out*. *The Stepford Wives* follows Joanna (Katharine Ross), an amateur photographer (like Chris) and a supporter of "women's lib," who moves to Stepford with her husband and children. Soon Joanna realizes that the women in the area are "changing" and becoming more domestic, much to their husbands' delight and her dismay. Joanna learns too late that the men in Stepford are replacing their wives with more perfect, robot versions of them. By the end, Joanna is murdered and replaced by the robotic version of herself. *The Stepford Wives* is a satirical commentary on the patriarchy, and I argue, on the upper-middle-class white society that isolates itself away from the "lower classes," while engaging in harmful, abusive behaviors, with the consent of authorities—in this case, the police.

Throughout the film, Joanna's husband, along with the men in the town, "gaslight" her, trying to convince her that her very real fears are all in her head. At one point her husband persuades her to go a psychologist, because she is "going crazy," when he knows that everything she says is true (*The Stepford Wives*). While Joanna is, like Chris from *Get Out*, strong-willed and knows that something is very wrong, rationality tells her—like Chris—that her suspicions cannot be true. Gaslighting—a term made popular by the 1944 film *Gaslight* about a husband who works to drive his wife insane by controlling her reality—is the psychological manipulation of people which forces them to question their own sanity. When it comes to race, Angelique M. Davis and Rose Ernst state that

> racial gaslighting offers a way to understand how white supremacy is sustained over time. We define racial gaslighting as the political, social, economic and cultural process that perpetuates and normalizes a white supremacist reality through pathologizing those who resist. Just as racial formation rests on the creation of racial projects, racial gaslighting, as a process, relies on the production of particular narratives. (2019, 763)

In both *The Stepford Wives* and *Get Out* the characters conspire to create a narrative that presents the world as normal and even acceptable, purposefully to hide the very real danger they are creating for the protagonists. When Joanna's children are taken, she knows that she cannot contact the police because they are part of the system. Set in the current political sphere of Black Lives Matter and police brutality, Chris likewise knows that the police are not safe for him. In the final scene, Chris and the audience brace themselves at the police lights and sirens because there is often no safety in the authorities for Black people. The Armitages, having created a space for Chris that they know is not safe, like the male characters in *The Stepford Wives*, proceed to gaslight him into not trusting his own instincts. Chris, like Joanna, flounders through this unreliably narrated world, with no roadmap.

By the end of *The Stepford Wives* Joanna is murdered and her robot happily shops for groceries, signaling to the viewer that the patriarchy has won. Peele, however, offers a different ending for his character. Chris defeats white supremacy—if just for the moment. In an interview for *Vanity Fair*, Peele said that he recognized that "[t]he ending needed to transform into something that gives us a hero, that gives us an escape, that gives us a positive feeling" (Desta 2019). To invoke Greenberg's definition of satire, Peele seems to use this opportunity to "bind" not only the horror "community," but the Black community who needed to see hope despite all the madness (Greenberg 2018, iv). Chris does not die because for him to do so would be to suggest that white supremacy has won, and that his (and by extension, the Black community's) fight is in vain. *The Stepford Wives* uses horror to satirize sexism; *Get Out* to satirize racism. If a fictional character can't escape white supremacy, what chance does anyone else have? As such, while it might have been realistic, Chris's death would not have offered hope to the Black community. Instead, Peele changed the narrative that would have had Chis die because of the oppression committed against his body, providing, if not a happy ending, one where Blackness defeats enslavement of the body and mind.

The final film I discuss, *Night of the Living Dead* (*NotLD*), is a classic horror mash-up. A 1968 film with a Black hero, it arguably satirizes white racism, despite the director, George A. Romero, not initially understanding the racial importance of the film. A zombie film, *NotLD* follows the Black man who is locked in an abandoned farmhouse with fellow white survivors. Throughout the night, not only is Ben (Duane Jones) forced to fend off zombies, but he must fight against his white housemates as well. Ben clearly understands the precarious position that he is in but does not fall victim to the American apartheid system of the time, choosing instead to take charge so that they can all survive.

There is no intentional humor in *NotLD*—unless you count the opening scene with the brother trying to scare his sister in the cemetery or Barbara's melodrama—but it is a strong social commentary on race relations within this country. The connections between the films are clear. Both Ben and Chris are Black men, and both spend the night trying to fight off white people. In the case of *NotLD*, Ben must fight off both living and dead white people. Chris, I argue, fends off the worst kind of zombie: the living, breathing one. Likewise, at one point in both films, the Black male protagonists are forced to attack white women to save themselves and received backlash from white audiences.

While Mikal J. Gaines argues that *Get Out*'s "greatest theoretical contribution may very well be how it further elaborates upon older conceptions of black ontology, epistemology, and survival" and discusses the film in relation to Du Bois's double consciousness (2020, 160), there is little commentary on *Get Out* as a zombie film. This is because zombies have mostly been conceptualized as brain eaters, and thus *Get Out* does not stand out as your classic zombie film. However, the history of zombies begins in Haiti in the seventeenth century under brutal French rule and enslavement. Originally, zombies represented the fear of losing control over oneself and body, as enslaved Black people had little control over either. This is the central premise of *Get Out*. The Armitages want to create a brain-dead, zombified being so that they can control him. In fact, *Get Out* clearly follows older zombie films such as *White Zombie* (1932), *I Walked with a Zombie* (1943), and many others. The difference is that in each of these prior films the protagonists are white, and whiteness is being corrupted by the dark forces of black magic, and more importantly, Blackness.

So, it is easy to see how *Get Out* fits within the zombie canon. However, I want to complicate this. While Chris clearly would have become a zombie if the Armitages and their white community had their way, I posit that the white people, themselves, represent the zombies within the film. While zombies are often the reanimated dead, another view sees them as mindless, often disease-infected beings with one goal—to devour brains. Moreover, the idea that people become zombies by mindlessly engaging in any task has permeated American culture for as long as we can remember. Mark Deuze says that "intense and immersive media use can be seen as turning us into helpless [devotees], slaves to machines—zombies," and indeed this can be said of any activity that takes away people's ability to reason and productively engage with the world around them (2014, 278). While the Armitages are not the walking dead, they are effectively ideological zombies, slaves to the ideology of white supremacy.

In the scene in *Get Out* that resembles the slave auction block, a supersized picture of Chris appears under the gazebo while white people silently bid on him, hoping to consume his brain. Historically, however, white people would bid on actual Black bodies at auction blocks, as enslaved people were examined, their "arms," "strength," and "teeth inspected." Cayla McNally argues that an important theme in *Get Out* is "scientific racism, [which is] part of a longstanding process to portray racial difference as biological in order to uphold uneven power structures" (2020, 212). White supremacy is built around the idea of genetic difference existing between racial groups, and while white supremacists believe that white people are mentally superior to Black people, they also often believe that Black people are more adept at physical labor. In the film, white people become zombies to the extent that they intensely immerse themselves in long outdated interpretations of race, turning into helpless devotees, slaves to white supremacy.

In Chris's picture on the auction block, he is stoic faced; he does not smile or show any teeth, leaving the bidders unable to fill the historical role. As such, the group creates another opportunity to complete the historical steps of the auction—the complete examination of the body before purchase. Those steps of inspecting the aforementioned "arms," "strength," and "teeth" to fulfill the mindless task of white supremacy happen just prior to the auction, as is customary. Before the group auctions off Chris's body, the Armitages have a mock-party that serves as the customary "viewing," where his arms, strength, and teeth are examined. The history around Black enslaved bodies positions them as chattel, the property of white supremacy. Importantly, when Rose walks Chris in, she tells him to "smile," to show "teeth." She takes him around, showing him off to those who seek to purchase him. At one point a woman, Lisa Deets, sizes up his arms, asking, "So, is it true? Is it better?" This is a clear reference to his sexual prowess. Not only is she checking his strength by feeling muscles in his arms, but this plays on the stereotype of the "buck," as Black men were historically used for breeding. Likewise, Gordon Greene asking about his golf swing is also about Chris's agility, strength, and physical capabilities—again based on racial stereotypes.

Completely and thoughtlessly indoctrinated into the ideology of white supremacy, white people within *Get Out* reject conscious and critical thought, willingly becoming thoughtless monsters in the process. At the mock-party scene, this is signaled by the fact that when Chris walks up the stairs, just out of view, they all stop as if single-minded, no rationality, and no individuality. The moment is at once humorous and horrific. White people in *Get Out*, in essence, become like the hoard that chases Ben, attempting to devour his brain.

Following more traditional ideas of masters manipulating their brain-dead subjects and zombifying them, the Armitages seek to control Chris's mind and turn him into a zombie; in reality, however, they are enslaved to the ideologies of white supremacy to the point that they have lost the ability to reason and productively engage with the world—in a satirical reversal, they become the mindless zombies. White zombies seek Ben's brain in *NotLD*; in *Get Out*, Chris is surrounded by ideological zombies that want to control his mind. In the end, both heroes manage to fend off the zombies all night. Whereas Ben, in an ironic twist, is killed by the police sheriff's posse in the morning, Chris manages to survive his zombies. Horrific and darkly satirical, both films ultimately reveal that the true monsters are the racist living, not the (un)dead. While both end on a grim note, there is a moment of comedy at the end of *Get Out* when Rod (Lil Rel Howery), Chris's friend, emerges from the police car—much to Chris's and the audience's relief. Before they drive away Rod deadpans, "I mean, I told you not to go in that house" (*Get Out*). The relief we all experience in that moment relies on the humor Black people use to protect themselves and that white people refuse to acknowledge. Wholly white spaces are too often not safe for Black bodies. Rod's warning to Chris is told by way of a joke, not because the situation is funny, but as that vital "coping mechanism to get through dark times."

CONCLUSION

Jonathan Swift said that "satire is a sort of glass, wherein beholders do generally discover everybody's face but their own; which is the chief reason for the kind of reception it meets in the world, and that so few are offended with it" ([1704] 2008, 104). When interviewed on *Late Night with Seth Meyers*, Allison Williams, who played Rose, said that people come up to her trying to justify the character. They claim Rose "was hypnotized . . . or a victim . . . and"; she admits, "it is a hundred percent of white people that say that" (Williams 2017). She must explain to them that Rose is "just evil, she's just bad," and even then, they do not want to accept it (Williams 2017). The reason that many white people refuse to accept that white women can be harmful is because white supremacy allows for a type of cognitive dissonance that positions white women as victims and never perpetrators. In discussing *Get Out*, Robert LaRue argues that within white supremacy "race always retains a certain malleability in its application, so that it becomes able to expand and contract as needed in order to perform various tasks" (2020, 175). White supremacy re-envisions reality to protect white people against perceived harm, even and especially when it comes to Black people. This defense of Rose is because, in many ways, white people likely see themselves in her privilege, and they need to rationalize her behavior. Perhaps, to return to Swift, what white people wrestle with when it comes to satire in the film is seeing the ways in which white supremacy functions against Black bodies within our society—it is not that they are white supremacists per se, but that when oppression is systemic, people within that system do not see the reflection within the glass.

Peele not only sees the glass but writes himself, as a Black man, into it to critique the status quo, particularly white supremacy. His mash-up of horror and humor is the film version of the "dark joke" that I told my family in that hospital room: sad but seeking hope through the horror that we live in our everyday lives. He uses references that are readily obtainable for the audience and themes from traditional horror films to tackle issues around race and injustice. Peele recognizes that there is power in depicting the horrors of white supremacy, satire in the absurdity of it all, and in the way that even liberal ideologies often function to support systemic injustices. *Get Out* does not allow audiences to maintain the fictions that we have built around racial harmony in this country or around the globe. It shines Swift's looking glass up to us and does not allow us to turn away. It mashes up horror and humor with reality to mock and ridicule us, hopeful that we will recognize our own stupidity.

NOTE

1. For the purposes of this chapter, I will refer to Black Humor as Dark Humor. There are a few reasons for this, but most importantly it is because using Black to represent "bad" or something negative is inherently biased and anti-Black. I do not want to make any even tangential connections between Blackness and negativity.

REFERENCES

Auden, W. H. 1966. "Introduction." In *Selected Poetry and Prose of George Gordon Lord Byron*, edited by W. H. Auden, xi. New York: New American Library.
Coleman, Robin R. Means. 2011. *Horror Noire: Blacks in American Horror Films from 1890s to Present*. New York: Routledge.

Combs, Barbara Harris. 2018. "Everyday Racism is Still Racism: The Role of Place in Theorizing Continuing Racism in Modern US Society." *Phylon (1960–)* 55, (1 & 2), 38–59.
Crane, Jonathan Lake. 1994. *Terror and Everyday Life: Singular Moments in the History of the Horror Film*. Sage Publications.
Davis, Angelique M., and Rose Ernst. 2019. "Racial Gaslighting." *Politics, Groups, and Identities* 7 (4): 761–74.
Dequina, Michael. 1995. "Tales from the Hood." *The Movie Report Archive, Volume 1* (#11–16). http://themoviereport.com/movierpt1.html#taleshood.
Desta, Yohana. 2017. "Jordan Peele's *Get Out* Almost Had an Impossibly Bleak Ending." *Vanity Fair*, March 3, 2017.
Deuze, Mark. 2014. "Living as a Zombie in Media is the Only Way to Survive." *Journal of the Fantastic in the Arts* 25 (2/3) (91): 278–94.
Diehl, Nicholas. 2013. "Satire, Analogy, and Moral Philosophy." *The Journal of Aesthetics and Art Criticism* 71 (4): 311–21.
Forbes, Bryan, dir. 1975. *The Stepford Wives*. Columbia Pictures.
Gaines, Mikal J. 2020. "Staying Woke in Sunken Places, or the Wages of Double Consciousness." In *Jordan Peele's Get Out: Political Horror*, edited by Dawn Keetley, 160–73. Ohio State University Press.
Greenberg, Jonathan. 2018. *The Cambridge Introduction to Satire*. Cambridge University Press.
Horner, Avril, and Sue Zlosnik. 2014. *Gothic and the Comic Turn*. Palgrave Macmillan.
Hughey, Matthew W. 2009. "Cinethetic Racism: White Redemption and Black Stereotypes in 'Magical Negro' Films." *Social Problems* 56 (3): 543–77.
Kubrick, Stanley, dir. 1980. *The Shining*. Warner Bros.
LaRue, Robert. 2020. "Holding onto Hulk Hogan: Contending with the Rape of the Black Male Psyche." In *Jordan Peele's Get out: Political Horror*, edited by Dawn Keetley, 174–86. Ohio State University Press.
Lyttelton, Oliver. 2012. "'The Cabin in The Woods' is A Smart, Witty Blast for Genre Fans." *IndieWire*, April 11, 2012.
McNally, Cayla. 2020. "Scientific Racism and the Politics of Looking." In *Jordan Peele's Get Out: Political Horror*, edited by Dawn Keetley, 212–22. Ohio State University Press.
Ngo, Bic, and Stacey J. Lee. 2007. "Complicating the Image of Model Minority Success: A Review of Southeast Asian American Education." *Review of Educational Research* 77 (4): 415–53.
Peele, Jordan, dir. 2017. *Get Out*. Universal Pictures Home Entertainment.
Romero, George A., dir. *Night of the Living Dead*. Image Ten, 1968.
Swift, Jonathan. [1704] 2008. Preface to *The Battle of the Books*. In *A Tale of a Tub and Other Works*, edited by Angus Ross and David Woolley, 104. Oxford: Oxford University Press.
Williams, Allison. 2017. "Allison Williams Reveals What White People Ask Her About *Get Out*." Interview by Seth Meyers, *Late Night with Seth Meyers*, NBC TV, December 1, 2017.

Part II

LITERARY MASH-UPS

Chapter 6

Anne Boleyn, Tudor Vampire

Stephanie Russo

The story of Anne Boleyn reads like a Gothic novel: woman catches the eye of the king so powerfully that he discards his first wife and breaks from the Catholic Church, only to later lock that same woman up in a tower and execute her on trumped-up charges of adultery. Contemporary Gothic mash-ups such as A. E. Moorat's *Henry VIII: Wolfman* (2010), Cinsearae S.'s *Boleyn: Tudor Vampire* (2010), Kate Pearce's *Blood of the Rose* (2010), Lucy Weston's *The Secret History of Elizabeth Tudor: Vampire Slayer* (2011), and Jonathon East's *The Conjured Vengeance of Anne Boleyn* (2015) incorporate Gothic monsters such as werewolves, vampires, and zombies into the well-trodden tale of Henry VIII and Anne Boleyn. However, these texts differ radically in their presentation of Anne Boleyn. Anne can be variously martyr or whore, victim or shrew, object or agent, vampire, witch, or ghost—a neat reflection of the complexities and contradictions of her literary afterlife. The assumption of some Gothic mash-ups is that Anne's execution was an historic injustice that still requires resolution, whereas others replicate sexist stereotypes of Anne as a power-hungry shrew who seduces Henry in order to satisfy her own ambitions. Still others parody the well-known story of Henry and his executed wives by rendering Henry's villainy literal: he is, in fact, an actual monster. The Gothic mash-up, then, heightens and makes visible the ideological underpinnings of any Anne Boleyn history fiction.

From the moment that Henry VIII turned his sexual attentions onto her, Anne Boleyn has been a popular subject for novelists, poets, playwrights, and screenwriters alike. Commencing with Sir Thomas Wyatt's poetry about Anne, in which she appears as the perfect untouchable Petrarchan mistress, to Natalie Dormer's sexy, intelligent Anne in the Showtime series *The Tudors* (2007–2010), writers have been drawn to Anne's story, which is both extremely well-known and yet somehow unknowable and endlessly confusing (Russo 2020a). Jerome de Groot has written of the appeal of Anne Boleyn historical fiction in the twentieth and twenty-first centuries, writing that Anne allowed novelists to consider subjects such as

> female agency; the dynamic between personal relationships and how this is manifested in the public sphere; martyrdom; women's cruelty to women in her hatred of Katherine of Aragon; religious fanaticism; [and] the struggles of women in the early modern period. (2009, 71)

While fictions about Anne Boleyn have always been popular, the rise of e-books and self-publishing in the twenty-first century has led to a further expansion in the volume of material written about her, as I have documented (Russo 2020a). While twentieth-century fiction about Anne Boleyn is largely confined to the pages of the woman's historical novel, Anne Boleyn transgeneric fiction is now increasingly popular. Transgeneric fictions about Anne Boleyn include time travel novels, counterfactual historical novels, novels in which Anne is reimagined as a contemporary woman and, of course, Gothic mash-ups. While such transgeneric fictions might seem strange or unlikely, Anne's story has always shown the capacity to reflect the interests of a changing world. As Katherine West Scheil has argued, too, speculative biographical fiction has the power to "destabiliz[e] prevailing narratives" and "encourag[e] communities of readers to rethink the certainty of various biographical premises" (2018, 193). Gothic mash-ups perform a similar rhetorical maneuver, prompting readers to reflect upon the familiar contours of Anne's story and reimagine them. What is perhaps surprising, however, is that while Anne Boleyn Gothic mash-ups ask readers to speculate about history, they ultimately reinforce existing ways of thinking about Anne Boleyn.

THE GOTHIC MASH-UP

The contemporary Gothic mash-up was inaugurated with the publication of Seth Grahame-Smith's novel *Pride and Prejudice and Zombies* in 2009. A slew of similar texts have appeared since, such as Amanda Grange's *Mr. Darcy: Vampire* (2009), Ben H. Winters's *Sense and Sensibility and Sea Monsters* (2009), and Vera Nazarian's *Mansfield Park and Mummies* (2009), to name only a few representative examples. Grahame-Smith followed up on the success of *Pride and Prejudice and Zombies*, which was adapted into a film in 2016, with 2010's *Abraham Lincoln: Vampire Hunter*. While the initial set of Gothic mash-ups remixed classic literature with the zombie novel, Grahame-Smith's *Abraham Lincoln: Vampire Hunter* and A. E. Moorat's *Queen Victoria: Demon Hunter* (2009) have no set source text but instead translate historical narratives into Gothic mash-ups. While Grahame-Smith's text is presented as a history book uncovering the truth of Abraham Lincoln's involvement in pursuing vampires, Moorat's *Queen Victoria: Demon Hunter* is a parodic historical novel, featuring many of the elements that one might expect in a historical fiction about Queen Victoria, such as details about her domestic life, blended with a narrative about demon hunting.

The Gothic mash-up, then, has the potential to move beyond its association with canonical novels; it can remix a wide variety of fiction and non-fictional forms for a range of ideological purposes. As Megen de Bruin-Molé has recently written, Gothic mash-ups, or Frankenfictions, are "also a kind of monstrous historical fiction: monstrous because they deal even more freely with the 'facts' of the past than most fictional historiographies" (2020, 8). The Gothic mash-up is always a form of historical fiction, and one that reflects the Gothic's prevailing interest in the past: "the Gothic, in other words, is a genre already well suited to discussions of the ethics and aesthetics of historical appropriation" (de Bruin-Molé 2020, 6). These fictions also reflect the postmodern impulse toward drawing attention to the constructedness of any form of historical writing—what Linda Hutcheon would call historiographic metafiction (Hutcheon 1989).

Scholarship on the publishing phenomenon that is the Gothic mash-up has stressed the parodic, disruptive potential of the genre. Miriam Borham-Puyal writes that Gothic mash-ups of canonical texts "blend two different narratives and even historical contexts, appropriating the idealised past and its paradigmatic texts, stripping them of their aura and bringing them closer to a wider reading public" (2019, 1315). The Gothic mash-up can bring high cultural products into the mass-market sphere, demystifying and democratizing these novels for a new reading audience. In the case of a Gothic mash-up of a historical narrative, the same effects can be seen; the Gothic mash-up can have the effect of making the past seem more familiar or accessible than the standard historical account. Marie Mulvey-Roberts reads *Pride and Prejudice and Zombies* through the prism of parody and describes the Gothic mash-up as a kind of colonization of the source text: "The original has not been wiped out, nor written over in the sense of a palimpsest, but inserted into a new contextual framework" (2014, 21). The Gothic mash-up brings past and present into conversation with each other quite explicitly. Andrew J. Salvati also argues that the "playful references and exaggerations of mash-ups and parodies can allow us to see old material afresh, defamiliarizing received knowledge and assumptions in order to reveal latent elements within, and connections between texts" (2016, 98–9). He argues that Grahame-Smith's *Abraham Lincoln: Vampire Hunter*, in particular, "ironically references the processes and codes of formal historiography only to turn them against themselves, opening them up for the kind of scrutiny and critical reflection that

[Linda] Hutcheon has associated with postmodern parody" (Salvati 2016, 102).

What is curious about Anne Boleyn Gothic mash-ups is that they do not capitalize on the potential of the form to provide an alternative reading of the familiar history of Henry VIII's second and most infamous wife. Even when the novel is overtly parodic, such as in the case of Moorat's *Henry VIII: Wolfman*, the Anne Boleyn Gothic mash-up rarely provides new ways of thinking about Anne Boleyn, the Tudor past, or history more generally. Instead, these novels display a conservatism in their telling of Anne's story that seems out-of-step with the radical potential of the form. De Bruin-Molé has drawn attention to the fact that the Gothic mash-up is not always a progressive form and can, in fact, be conservative (de Bruin-Molé 2020, 12). Indeed, the incorporation of Gothic elements into Anne Boleyn's narrative has a long history, with Gothic novels featuring Anne first appearing in the early nineteenth century. The Gothic mash-up, then, despite its patina of innovation and newness, in fact returns us to characteristically nineteenth-century ways of writing about Anne Boleyn, perhaps a reflection of the form's embeddedness in neo-Victorianism.

GOTHIC ANNES

The Gothic novel has always been a form of historical fiction, from the publication of Horace Walpole's genre-inaugurating *The Castle of Otranto*, with its camp medievalist fakery, in 1764. The Gothic is characteristically engaged in the process of remixing past and present, and so the Gothic mash-up is "simply another iteration in a long line of Gothic hybrids" (de Bruin-Molé 2020, 5). The story of Anne Boleyn already features tropes associated with the Gothic: illicit sex, imprisonment in the Tower, and a violent death. Folklore about Anne's restless ghost has also continued to proliferate since her execution. Therefore, Gothic mash-ups of that story are rather less surprising a phenomenon than they might at first appear and, in fact, reflect a nineteenth-century propensity to accrue Gothic apparatus around the familiar historic narrative of Anne's rise and fall. The addition of supernatural elements into Anne's story is a phenomenon that stretches back to Francis Lathom's novel *Mystic Events* (1830) and William Harrison Ainsworth's *Windsor Castle* (1842). *Mystic Events* incorporates several supernatural occurrences into its narrative. The novel centers on the fictional knight Leolin, who obtains Anne's love through the mechanism of an enchanted love apple. Leolin eventually discovers that his friend the Count de Beaumarchis, who gave him the apple, is in fact his father, an alchemist who has used his abilities to mask his real age. The novel, however, is only tangentially interested in Anne, focusing far more on the sexual exploits of her brother George. Anne is represented in the novel in a characteristically nineteenth-century manner as passive victim of the machinations of men (Russo 2020a).

William Harrison Ainsworth has long been associated with a growing fascination in the Victorian period with Tudor horror. Tudor horror narratives were stories of violence, imprisonment, and terror set within the landscape of the Tower of London. One of Ainsworth's most popular novels was his 1840 *The Tower*, about the life and death of Lady Jane Grey, another of the Tower's most infamous victims. Billie Melman argues that Ainsworth, "exploited the prison and scaffold lore [. . .] and articulated this lore into an organizing image of Tudor history" (2011, 49). *Windsor Castle* moves away from the Tower to the castle of its title, but again links nostalgia for the physical remains of the past with the Tudor horror iconography of the scaffold. Again, a supernatural story is overlain over Anne's narrative, with the story of the demonic ghost Herne the Hunter juxtaposed with the story of Henry's pursuit of Anne. *Windsor Castle* is far darker and more traditionally Gothic than *Mystic Events*, and provides a model for the demonic Annes that would emerge in twenty-first-century Gothic mash-ups. Anne's eyes have an "irresistible witchery," but she is ultimately little more than a flirt who sacrifices love to ambition (Ainsworth [1842], 34). However, if Anne is bewitching, then Henry is so tyrannical that even Herne is disgusted by him, telling him that, "I know you have no proof of [Anne's] guilt, and that in your heart of hearts you believe her innocent. But you destroy her because you would wed Jane Seymour!" (Ainsworth [1842], 404). Henry is so tyrannous that he disgusts even a demonic being; again, this novel functions as a forerunner for those mash-ups that turn Henry into a literal monster.

The novels of both Lathom and Ainsworth are manifestations of popular Tudor horror, in which the period is represented as a Gothic landscape and characterized by equal parts romance and terror. Even after the historical novel shifted to a more realist mode in the later nineteenth century, however, Anne's story continued to be associated with Gothic horror and/or supernatural tales. The Anne that appears in M. P. Shiel's *Cold Steel* (1899) is not a literal Gothic monster but is as vicious a villain as any Gothic novel could ever produce. The novel is almost incomprehensible in its complexity, but largely involves Anne traversing the country in pursuit of the (fictional) Laura Ford, who has captured the attention of Henry. Anne plans to force Laura to have sex with Henry, so that he can quench his desire and subsequently tire of her. Shiel's Anne is so forceful that even her (fictional) illegitimate half-brother Sidney is terrified of her. Anne is described as monstrous: "spittle speckled her lip, her dishevelled visage showing like a chaos of sunset flushed" (Shiel [1899] 1929, 201). Anne thinks nothing of murdering whoever gets in her way and is quite capable of arranging for the rape of another woman. Shiel's *Cold Steel* thus anticipates the vampiric Annes of the Gothic mash-up.

The incorporation of Gothic elements into Anne's narrative that we see in nineteenth-century historical novels is also a feature of twenty-first-century writing about Anne Boleyn. The Gothic mash-up about Anne can be understood as a natural extension of a long tradition of "Gothicizing" Anne's story. Folklore about sightings of Anne's ghost has also been circulating for centuries (Russo 2020b). These stories often take as their premise the belief that Anne still has unfinished business in the world of the living; revenge upon her husband or her successor, Jane Seymour, for instance. The gaps in Anne's narrative make her the ideal fit for a ghost story: as Elmar Schenkel writes, the unknown is "the new black bo[x] which we are filling with our ghostly imagination" (2016, 11). In novels such as Zoe Bramley's *The Boleyn Necklace: A Tudor Ghost Story* (2016), Anne is a particularly vengeful ghost who taunts Jane Seymour to death. In R. B. Swan's *The Tower of London* (2014), the Tower is imagined as a kind of collective meeting point for historical ghosts who seek revenge upon those who wronged them, including the Princes in the Tower, Mary Queen of Scots, and Anne Boleyn. The conviction that Anne Boleyn's death is a crime that still requires restitution is expanded upon in the twenty-first-century Gothic mash-up, in which Anne is finally given tangible means of obtaining that revenge.

ANNE BOLEYN: UNDEAD AVENGER

The contemporary Anne Boleyn Gothic mash-up essentially takes two primary forms: the Gothic revenge narrative or the monstrous-Anne narrative. These two forms reflect and replicate the martyr/whore dichotomy that has long been associated with Anne Boleyn: Anne is either the passive victim and martyr, or the femme fatale that tore the Catholic Church apart with her sex appeal. The Gothic revenge narrative does not quite represent Anne as a passive victim, but gives her supernatural power in order to allow her to obtain revenge over Henry and all those others from his court that she deems to have wronged her in some fashion. This type of Gothic mash-up presumes that she lacked historic agency in life. By necessity, the Gothic revenge narrative begins with Anne's death. This narrative thus also has close ties to the ghost narrative. As Owen Davies writes, the ghost returning to the world of the living to correct a legal injustice was a popular one in the early modern period (2007, 5). What is distinctive about Anne Boleyn Gothic mash-ups is that they go one step further than the ghost narrative by transforming Anne into a monster whose power to cause harm to those who have wronged her goes beyond her ability to simply "haunt." Anne Boleyn, Undead Avenger, has the power to commit actual violence against—and kill—those she deems responsible for her spectacular fall from power.

Cinsearae S.'s *Boleyn: Tudor Vampire* takes as its premise that Anne has been turned into a vampire when she curses God at her execution. Vampire Anne then spends the rest of the novel devising ways to torture Henry: "I wanted my revenge and, damn it all to hell, I *would* have it!" (Cinsearae 2010, 16). The novel, in common with ghost narratives about Anne, imagines Anne as a woman who is owed posthumous vengeance. One of Anne's first actions is to revive the men who were executed with her, and she soon employs a zombie version of her brother, George Boleyn, and a ghostly Mark Smeaton—one of the men who was executed for adultery with her—as emissaries for her posthumous vengeance. Anne sets about confronting all those she blames for her own demise, including her father, who is represented as power-hungry and craven: "It was YOU who pushed me to get into the king's good graces! YOU who wanted more power!" (Cinsearae 2010, 27). On the whole, however, Vampire Anne's revenge is largely confined to the kinds of rather benign hauntings we usually associate with ghosts: she arranges for the ghostly Mark Smeaton to play his violin, has flowers affixed to Jane Seymour's door, and writes the words *Henry, see your sins* on a door in pig's blood (Cinsearae 2010, 45). Even Anne seems rather dissatisfied with her own efforts, noting that, "Once I *had* exacted my vengeance, what then?" (Cinsearae 2010, 45).

Boleyn: Tudor Vampire takes a basically sympathetic view of Anne, despite her new status as a vampire. Anne regrets her rise to power and has largely been the passive victim of other people's ambitions. If she is in a state of furious anger throughout most of the novel, Cinsearae S. evidently believes she is largely justified in that anger. The novel thus suggests that Anne is owed posthumous restitution for the ways in which she was used and exploited by men, including her father, Thomas Cromwell, and Henry. The novel does, however, demonstrate a wariness about the mechanisms through which Anne tries to achieve that justice. Anne's revenge plot becomes increasingly convoluted and culminates in a scene in which she confronts Henry directly for his crimes and prophesies the rise of her daughter: "The Boleyns *will* rise to power one day" (Cinsearae 2010, 141–2). She is prevented from killing Henry, however, by Thomas Wyatt, who "kills" undead Anne. *Boleyn: Tudor Vampire*'s vision of vampirism aligns with folkloric representations of the vampire as a being who comes back from the dead in order to obtain direct revenge upon the person that brought about their death. Alan Dundes argues that "if there is guilt on the part of the living as having caused that death [. . .] then it is possible that through projective inversion that the lost object (the deceased loved one) will return to take revenge by means of sucking or biting" (1998, 167–8). Having been prevented from doing just that, there is nothing left for Anne to do but to die once again. It is somewhat disturbing, however, that Anne, whose life has been largely dictated by the men around her, is once again prevented from acting by a man. Even in the afterlife, Anne is always acted upon by men.

By the end of *Boleyn: Tudor Vampire*, Anne has resolved all her rage, even if her desire to kill Henry has been thwarted. Her reward is to be reconciled with her family in the afterlife: "All quarrels and disputes had been reconciled" (Cinsearae 2010, 146). Having had the chance to assert her innocence directly to Henry, all her desire for revenge dissipates and she can move on to the next stage of her afterlife. The only substantive difference between *Boleyn: Tudor Vampire* and Anne Boleyn ghost narratives is that, as a vampire, Anne has the power to actually kill Henry; she has a concrete existence in the world that allows her to be far more threatening than a mere ghost. That Anne ultimately fails to kill her husband and take her fullest revenge is represented as a signifier of her innate goodness, despite her desire for vengeance.

Boleyn: Tudor Vampire, in common with the earliest Gothic novels, imagines the past as a time of mindless violence and superstition. Anne reflects that "these were still dark, dark, ages we lived in. I had hoped humankind had gotten past the silly notions of sorcery and superstition, but I realized such things would never be wiped from the minds of uneducated, simple people" (Cinsearae 2010, 6). Despite Anne's disdain for the superstition of the citizenry, the novel is set within a world where vampirism is possible, and thus would seem to affirm the superstitions that Anne decries: as De Bruin-Molé writes, the Gothic novel suggests "how history itself is both uncomfortably real and increasingly distant or surreal" (2020, 139). The end of the novel, however, suggests that Anne has been folded back into a Christian universe and is now in heaven. The very fact that Anne becomes a vampire *because* she has cursed God on the scaffold suggests an underlying Christian ethos to this rather strange novel. In a key moment in the novel's epilogue, Anne forgives her father for his exploitation of her, remarking that, "that's all I wanted to hear, father" (Cinsearae 2010, 146). Instead of the catharsis of killing Henry, the novel gives her the far more benign catharsis of forgiving her father. Somewhat surprisingly, for a novel which so overtly capitalizes on the popularity of the Gothic mash-up, *Boleyn: Tudor Vampire* is actually a deeply moral tale about the consequences of one's actions and the importance of forgiveness and repentance. While the beginning of the novel could be read as a parody, with an enraged Anne Boleyn becoming an all-powerful vampire, the end of the novel instead becomes a Christian parable about suffering, forgiveness, and mercy.

Another novel in which Anne is given the chance to wreak posthumous vengeance is far less interested in assessing the morality of revenge. Jonathon East's 2015 novel *The Conjured Vengeance of Anne Boleyn* sees Anne rise from her grave 500 years after her death to swear that, "I shall remain in the shadows of this world, unseen by its people, for as long as I have on Earth. Until I choose to reap my conjured vengeance upon them" (East 2015, 310). She then immediately kills a descendant of Lady Worcester, one of the ladies-in-waiting who had betrayed her. Clearly, East's Anne is far more malignant than that found in *Boleyn: Tudor Vampire*. However, most of the novel takes place *before* Anne Boleyn has the chance to rise from the dead, and thus largely leaves her vengeance unfulfilled and unseen. The fact that we are not allowed to see Anne prosecute her vengeance means that we are can never really glean any insight into whether Anne becomes a crazed monster or simply eliminates those she blames for having had a hand in her demise. We are also given little information about Anne's mortal life. *The Conjured Vengeance of Anne Boleyn* has more parodic force than *Boleyn: Tudor Vampire*, in that the evil Anne Boleyn is far more obviously an exaggerated monster. However, the short amount of time that we have with Undead Avenger Anne means that any broader implications of the novel's representation of Anne Boleyn are lost. *The Conjured Vengeance of Anne Boleyn* does, however, anticipate the second strand of the Anne Boleyn Gothic mash-up.

ANNE BOLEYN: EVIL BITCH MONSTER OF DEATH

While the ideological assumption of the Undead Avenger narrative is that Anne is owed restitution for the betrayals she suffered in life, other Gothic mash-ups replicate all the most negative stereotypes that have accrued around Anne Boleyn for centuries. There is nothing new about representations of Anne Boleyn as a malignant, borderline evil woman. For Catholic polemicists in the sixteenth century, Anne was virtually the embodiment of evil. In Nicholas Sander's 1573 *Rise and Growth of the Anglican Schism*, Anne is portrayed as nothing short of monstrous: she has a large goiter on her chin, a sixth finger, and, most startlingly and implausibly, she is actually Henry's daughter through an extramarital affair he had with her mother, Elizabeth (Sander 1877). More recently, Anne has regularly been portrayed as the archetypal "other woman": the dangerous femme fatale who plots her way to the crown using her sex appeal. It is frequently assumed in many historical fictions of the twentieth century, in particular, that Anne was "vengeful, near hysterical [. . .] and power mad" (Burstein 2007, 3). In the second half of the century, the villainous Anne became a mainstay of historical fiction in novels such as Jane Lane's *Sow the Tempest* (2001) and Joanna Dessau's *All or Nothing* (1997). The villainous Anne is a career woman who has sacrificed love and sexuality at the altar of her ambition, only to regret it or be undone by her lack of appropriate feminine softness and submissiveness

(Russo 2020a). The monstrous-Anne narrative, then, like the Gothic avenger narrative, only makes literal what was already latent in fictions about Anne Boleyn.

In Kate Pearce's 2011 novel *Blood of the Rose*, Anne is a vampire who is using Henry to obtain power. Anne wants to turn the king into a vampire after their marriage, and is working on behalf of the Vampire Council, a shadowy organization that plans to undermine the peace of the kingdom. That basic plot—the woman who uses her sex appeal to gain power through a man—is the basis of centuries of writing about Anne Boleyn. What Pearce does is simply to take this narrative one step further: she makes Anne an actual monster. In fact, in this novel it is the entire Boleyn family who has turned to the side of evil: "It is whispered that the family has turned to the Dark Arts to ensure their rise to power" (Pearce 2011, 26).

In a clear homage to *Buffy the Vampire Slayer*, *Blood of the Rose* centers on the attempts of the vampire slayer Rosalind Llewellyn to prevent evil vampire Anne taking over control of England. Rosalind is quick to realize that Anne is a centuries-old vampire, and that Henry's sexual interest in her is a serious problem both for himself and for the nation. In *Blood of the Rose*, Anne is depicted as having a supernatural hold over Henry: "It's as if she has bewitched him" (Pearce 2011, 46). Pearce is here self-consciously drawing upon Anne's popular association with witchcraft, and the long-standing—mistaken—belief that she was charged with witchcraft in her own time. Anne is twice referenced in *The Chilling Adventures of Sabrina* (Netflix, 2018–2020) as a witchy ancestor from whom Sabrina and her coven are descended. Roland Hui has shown that these legends arose in the twentieth century, and largely from the pages of historical fiction. He writes that "Anne Boleyn as a sorceress is in fact a relatively recent concept—a twentieth- and twenty-first century perception developed by modern writers and historians, and perpetuated in popular culture" (Hui 2018, 98). While *Blood of the Rose* does not portray Anne as a witch per se, her vampirism does give her power to entrance and entrap the witless Henry, who does not realize "she is after the crown" (Pearce 2011, 50).

Rosalind the Vampire Slayer spends most of the novel plotting to bring about Anne's downfall, only to come to a compromise with Anne, with the help of the Druids. The Druids will provide Anne with a fertility drug, and Anne will give up on her plot to turn the king into a vampire. Anne agrees, and while it is prophesied that Anne will break the bargain, the book ends before she can do so. Anne requires assistance with fertility because female vampires cannot procreate easily, a supernatural explanation for Anne's struggle to bear a healthy child after Elizabeth. The abnormal body of the female vampire is not capable of healthy reproduction, reflecting the ability of the vampire to represent a perversion of the nuclear family (Benefiel

2004). Again, there is also an echo of other Anne Boleyn fictions here. In Philippa Wiat's *The Heir of Allington* (1973), for instance, Anne cannot conceive a child with Henry VIII because their love is not authentic. When she sleeps with the poet Sir Thomas Wyatt, however, she immediately conceives Elizabeth; the emotional authenticity of that bond is generative, whereas her relationship with Henry is not (Wiat 1973). In both *Blood of the Rose* and more conventional historical fictions, Anne and Henry's relationship is not a healthy or a normal one, and so cannot be the basis of the family that Henry craves.

Blood of the Rose is quite an unusual Gothic mash-up, as its incorporation of Gothic elements into the story of Anne Boleyn and Henry VIII lacks any sense of the parodic or the burlesque. *Blood of the Rose* is the second in the Tudor Vampire Chronicles series, a series of Gothic novels that capitalizes on the success of sexy vampire novels such as the *Twilight* series. The book is much more interested in dramatizing Rosalind's relationship with Christopher Ellis, who has vampire blood, and thus should be Rosalind's enemy, than it is with Anne Boleyn. Again, a slayer in love with a (part) vampire recalls *Buffy the Vampire Slayer* and Buffy's relationships with Angel and Spike, who are both vampires. Christopher, as with his *Buffy* forebears, is reflective of a new breed of sympathetic vampires, what Milly Williamson calls the "morally ambiguous, sympathetic vampir[e] who lure[s] audiences with the pathos of their predicament and their painful awareness of outsiderdom" (Williamson 2005). Anne, however, as the monstrous woman, never gets this kind of sympathetic light turned onto her. Anne is useful insofar as her reputation as an ambitious femme fatale sets her up as a foil for Rosalind, but the novel asks no questions about her historical reputation, and merely replicates the same assumptions that have long animated writing about Anne. Like the earliest Gothic novels about Anne, *Blood of the Rose* is, in fact, not very interested in Anne at all. The Tudor period is only useful to Pearce because it offers a suitably historic Gothic landscape to situate the narrative within, and the novel has very little to say about Tudor history or even the form of the mash-up itself.

Unlike *Blood of the Rose*, which takes itself seriously as a Gothic novel, A. E. Moorat's *Henry VIII: Wolfman* clearly takes a light-hearted approach to its subject matter, announcing itself on the back cover as "Wolf Hall, With Bite." The novel's tagline is "Divorced, Beheaded, Died, Mauled, Savaged, Survived": a humorous play on the "Divorced, Beheaded, Died, Divorced, Beheaded, Survived" rhyme taught to schoolchildren attempting to memorize the fate of Henry's wives. The novel's premise is simple: What if Henry VIII, infamous historical monster, was an actual monster? The novel opens with Henry about to go on the hunt: "It was his time for the month and Henry was getting hungry" (Moorat 2010, 3). As Moorat explains in the historical note, "the action sticks very closely to real-life history and characters," but, he admits, somewhat unnecessarily, "I've taken some enormous liberties with it" (2010, 407). While the most obvious liberty is the fact that werewolves and emissaries of the Devil exist as a part of this world—and have recently brokered a peace deal with humanity—the novel does cleave closely to the established historical record, reflecting a generic convention of the Gothic mash-up to incorporate as much of the source text as possible.

Both Anne and Henry have become werewolves in *Henry VIII: Wolfman*, although Anne chooses to become one while Henry is accidentally bitten during an attack of the wolfen on Catherine of Aragon and her newly born son (lost to history as he is eaten by werewolves on the day of his birth). However, while Anne is a relentless and largely thoughtless killer, Moorat makes Werewolf-Henry an unusually thoughtful werewolf. Werewolf-Henry does kill Jane Seymour in a moment of temporary madness, but he never entirely loses touch with his capacity to reason. However, Werewolf-Anne is simply a crazed monster. She almost immediately joins an attempt by the werewolves to take over the kingdom and becomes involved in a lesbian attraction to—if not relationship with—the female head of the werewolves, Aisha (Moorat 2010, 365). Anne and Henry's marriage falls apart not because she is a werewolf, but because she is deeply unpleasant entirely aside from her wolfish nature: "Anne has shown quite a vindictive side to herself in her treatment of Thomas" (Moorat 2010, 342). In *Henry VIII: Wolfman*, as in history, Anne is accused of being the prime mover against Sir Thomas More; it is not her monstrousness, but her humanity, that is at issue.

Despite the inclusion of Gothic monsters, the Anne Boleyn of *Henry VIII: Wolfman* is familiar to anybody who has read even a smattering of Anne Boleyn historical fiction. Wolsey summarizes Anne as "not as pretty as Mary, very ambitious, and—oh—a Lutheran" (Moorat 2010, 230). This summation is characteristic of most Anne Boleyn fiction of the twentieth century (Russo 2020a). Anne embraces her supernatural powers in the novel because they provide her another opportunity to obtain the power that she craves. Werewolf-Anne is far more dangerous than Werewolf-Henry, despite Henry's superior political power. Henry elects to rid himself of the curse of the wolfen, although he ultimately fails to do so, while Anne revels in the power: "soon our kind will rule" (Moorat 2010, 385). Her execution is greeted by a universal sigh of relief, and she is quickly dispatched precisely as history tells us she was: "Queen Anne had been executed for high treason" (Moorat 2010, 399). Henry marries Jane Seymour, who is represented as everything Anne is not: kind, blonde, and devoted to ridding England of the threat of the wolfen. Again, with the exception of her role in fighting werewolves, this portrayal of Jane Seymour is so familiar as to be clichéd.

As Karen Lindsey writes, Seymour is "Snow White to Ann Boleyn's wicked witch" (1995, 118–19).

One might argue that *Henry VIII: Wolfman* is parodying stereotypes associated with Henry, Anne, and Jane, and overplaying these stereotypes for comedic effect. In this reading, Moorat is aware that Anne Boleyn is usually portrayed as a power-hungry social climber, and makes her an actual monster as a way of comically exaggerating these qualities. In this reading, the novel reflects the fact that the Gothic mash-up is "not meant to be read as authentic or to be taken seriously" while at the same time "embody[ing] very real and serious anxieties" (de Bruin-Molé 2020, 139). In this case, the anxieties the novel represents are those associated with the powerful, ambitious woman. However, there is little to no attempt to challenge these tropes or play these exaggerations for laughs. While the novel treats aspects of Henry's transformation into a wolf comedically, Anne actually does prove to be a threat to the stability of England, and the novel's casual disinterest in how the rest of her story plays out does not suggest that Moorat has any interest in interrogating preconceptions about Anne, or making a broader statement about how society views ambitious women. While he does mine the well-known story of Henry VIII and his six wives for its comedic potential, the novel simply adds a patina of the supernatural over that narrative without asking more searching questions or exposing it to any kind of critique.

ELIZABETH TUDOR: VAMPIRE SLAYER

It is somewhat fitting that the only Gothic mash-up to deviate from the martyr/whore dichotomy that plays itself out in other mash-ups focuses on Anne's daughter, Elizabeth I. The tradition of representing Elizabeth's accession to the throne as Anne's posthumous triumph stretches back to Elizabeth's own time (Russo 2020a). Lucy Weston's *The Secret History of Elizabeth Tudor, Vampire Slayer* (2011)—another novel that clearly takes its cue from *Buffy the Vampire Slayer*—opens when Elizabeth, about to be crowned queen, is told that she has inherited the power of the vampire slayer through her mother. The name Lucy Weston is a pseudonym, and a reference to the character of Lucy Westenra in Bram Stoker's *Dracula*. The novel thus remixes Tudor history with both *Buffy the Vampire Slayer* and the *ur*-vampire text. Anne is a descendant of the legendary Arthurian figure Morgaine, who has been locked in battle for a thousand years with Arthur's vampiric son, Mordred. The novel is largely interested in Elizabeth learning to use her powers as the slayer, but also presents Anne, through flashbacks, as a savvy and intelligent woman who has passed on a legacy of female power to her daughter. Anne has also left a letter for her daughter in which she asserts that she has used her powers to arrange for Elizabeth's protection, and prophesies her glorious victory and reign: "Queen Regnant, protector of this realm, victorious over the demonic forces that, should you falter, will rule to the end of time" (Weston 2011, 150).

The Secret History of Elizabeth Tudor, Vampire Slayer is unique among Gothic mash-ups as it gives us an Anne who is neither martyr nor whore, undead avenger nor evil bitch monster of death. Instead, Anne is agentic and powerful in her own right. Her powers are not tied to her status as victim, and she uses them to protect England, not seek to destroy it. The novel also suggests a hidden legacy of female power that lies just underneath the patina of patriarchal society. The novel thus reflects the growing turn toward representations of a third-wave feminist Anne, which have become popular in the wake of Natalie Dormer's performance as Anne in *The Tudors* and the enthusiastic online fandom it inspired. As Susan Bordo writes, this Anne "resists definition as either flirt or 'brain,' 'feminine' or feisty, mother or career woman, sexpot or 'one of the guys,' saint or sinner" (2014, 255).

That *The Secret History of Elizabeth Tudor, Vampire Slayer* is the only Gothic mash-up to elude the martyr/whore dichotomy that characterizes other novels in the genre is somewhat surprising. The form has the potential to radically disrupt our understanding of history and yet these novels only reiterate centuries-old stereotypes. It is, potentially, the focus on Elizabeth in this novel that accounts for the novel's representation of Anne; Anne and her role as a vampire slayer are only ever of marginal interest in the novel, and we never actually get to witness Anne fighting vampires. She is always simply the dead woman. Elizabeth I is one of history's most powerful women and remains one of the paradigmatic figures to think through the operation and mechanism of female power. Anne Boleyn, by way of contrast, has always been variously the victim or the sinner in Gothic novels. Even the Gothic mash-up, with all its associations with parody, disruption, novelty, and modernity, cannot quite find a way to rescue Anne Boleyn.

REFERENCES

Ainsworth, W. H. [1842] n.d. *Windsor Castle*. London: Collins Clear-Type Press.

Benefiel, Candace R. 2004. "Blood Relations: The Gothic Perversion of the Nuclear Family in Anne Rice's Interview with the Vampire." *The Journal of Popular Culture* 38 (2): 261–73.

Bordo, Susan. 2014. *The Creation of Anne Boleyn: A New Look at England's Most Notorious Queen*. Boston: Mariner Books.

Borham-Puyal, Miriam. 2019. "New Adventures in Old Texts: Gender Roles and Cultural Canons in Twenty-First-Century Mash-Ups." *Journal of Popular Culture* 51 (6): 1312–31.

Bramley, Zoe. 2016. *The Boleyn Necklace: A Tudor Ghost Story*. Kindle.
de Bruin-Molé, Megen. 2020. *Gothic Remixed: Monster Mashups and Frankenfictions in 21st-Century Culture*. London: Bloomsbury.
Cinsearae, S. 2010. *Boleyn: Tudor Vampire*. Printed by the author.
Davies, Owen. 2007. *The Haunted: A Social History of Ghosts*. Basingstoke: Palgrave Macmillan.
Dessau, Joanna. 1997. *All or Nothing: The Life-Story of Anne Boleyn*. Leicester: Ulverscroft.
Dundes, Alan. 1998. "The Vampire as Bloodthirsty Revenant: A Psychoanalytic Post Mortem." In *The Vampire: A Casebook*, edited by Alan Dundes, 159–78. Maidson: University of Wisconsin Press.
East, Jonathon. 2015. *The Conjured Vengeance of Anne Boleyn*. Kindle.
de Groot, Jerome. 2009. *The Historical Novel*. London: Routledge.
Hui, Roland. 2018. "Anne of the Wicked Ways: Perceptions of Anne Boleyn as a Witch in History and in Popular Culture." *Parergon: Journal of the Australian and New Zealand Association for Medieval and Early Modern Studies* 35 (1): 97–118.
Hutcheon, Linda. 1989. "Historiographic Metafiction: Parody and the Intertextuality of History." In *Intertextuality and Contemporary American Fiction*, edited by P. O'Donnell and Robert Con Davis, 3–32. Baltimore: Johns Hopkins University Press.
Lane, Jane. 2001. *Sow the Tempest*. London: House of Stratus.
Lathom, Francis. 1830. *Mystic Events, or, The Vision of the Tapestry: A Romantic Legend of the Days of Anne Boleyn*. Volume IV. London: A. K. Newman & Co.
Lindsey, Karen. 1995. *Divorced, Beheaded, Survived: A Feminist Reinterpretation of the Wives of Henry VIII*. Reading: Addison-Wesley.
Melman, Billie. 2011. "The Pleasures of Tudor Horror: Popular Histories, Modernity and Sensationalism in the Long Nineteenth Century." In *Tudorism: Historical Imagination and the Appropriation of the Sixteenth Century*, edited by Tatiana C. String and Marcus Bull, 37–56. Oxford: Oxford University Press.
Moorat, A. E. 2010. *Henry VIII: Wolfman*. London: Hodder & Stoughton.
Mulvey-Roberts, Marie. 2014. "Mashing up Jane Austen: *Pride and Prejudice and Zombies* and the Limits of Adaptation." *The Irish Journal of Gothic and Horror Studies* 13 (Summer): 17–37.
Pearce, Kate. 2011. *Blood of the Rose*. New York: Signet Eclipse.
Russo, Stephanie. 2020a. *The Afterlife of Anne Boleyn: Representations of Anne Boleyn in Fiction and on the Screen*. Palgrave Macmillan.
———. 2020b. "At the Border of Life and Death: The Ghost of Anne Boleyn." *Parergon: Journal of the Australian and New Zealand Association for Medieval and Early Modern Studies* 37 (2): 125–49.
Salvati, Andrew J. 2016. "History Bites: Mashing up History and Gothic Fiction in Abraham Lincoln: Vampire Hunter." *Rethinking History* 20 (1): 97–115.
Sander, Nicholas. 1877. *Rise and Growth of the Anglican Schism*. Edited by David Lewis. London: Burns and Oates.
Scheil, Katherine West. 2018. *Imagining Shakespeare's Wife: The Afterlife of Anne Hathaway*. Cambridge: Cambridge University Press.

Schenkel, Elmar. 2016. "Preface: Ghosts—or the (Nearly) Invisible." In *Ghosts—or the (Nearly) Invisible: Spectral Phenomena in Literature and the Media*, edited by Maria Fleischhack and Elmer Schenkel, 11–12. Frankfurt: Peter Lang.

Shiel, M. P. [1899] 1929. *Cold Steel*. London: Victor Gollancz.

Swan, R. B. 2014. *The Tower of London*. Kindle.

Weston, Lucy. 2011. *The Secret History of Elizabeth Tudor, Vampire Slayer*. New York: Gallery Books.

Wiat, Philippa. 1973. *The Heir of Allington*. London: Robert Hale.

Williamson, Milly. 2005. *The Lure of the Vampire: Gender, Fiction, and Fandom from Bram Stoker to Buffy*. London: Wallflower.

Chapter 7

The Holmes-Meets-Dracula Mash-Up

L. N. Rosales

Sherlock Holmes is a lasting Victorian cultural referent who has maintained the status of household name for over 100 years. Holmes's long life is partly due to the enduring power of Sir Arthur Conan Doyle's immensely popular short stories and novels; however, Holmes's longevity has been assisted by numerous stage, radio, television, and film adaptations—not to mention a century's worth of rewritings and pastiches. The legendary detective is not alone in his continuance from nineteenth-century culture to our own. Count Dracula, too, is one of the most frequently adapted characters in the last century; his association with the Gothic is persistent and pervasive through decades upon decades of popular media. When Sherlockian pastiche authors bring the detective face-to-face with the vampire, the result is a mash-up of two genres, and two of the genres' best-known characters. What is the result of combining the two narrative worlds? In this chapter, I examine six different Sherlockian pastiches that feature Dracula, and I analyze the effects of their mashed-up nature. Despite the potential for neo-Victorian rewritings to "fill in the blanks or right the wrongs of history" (de Bruin-Molé 2020, 35), I contend that these six texts, as representative of the Holmes-meets-Dracula mash-up, merely repeat the past, rather than take the opportunity to revise it. By simultaneously highlighting the authors' commitment to emulating their chosen modes and each text's appalling treatment of women, I show that to mash up Sherlock Holmes with Dracula is to forfeit pretensions to creating critical pastiche. Instead, these texts are doomed to repeat; they sacrifice critical awareness for pastiche accuracy.

A QUESTION OF TERMS

The Sherlock Holmes fan community is robust and long-lived. Over the last 140 years, it has developed its own traditions and terminology. The earliest Sherlock Holmes rewritings were stories published in *Tit-Bits*, sister magazine to the *Strand* (itself home to the original Holmes stories); in 1883, *Tit-Bits* hosted a Sherlock Holmes story-writing competition, reportedly receiving over 22,000 entries (McClellan 2017, 6.1). Late nineteenth-century authors such as Mark Twain and J. M. Barrie wrote parodies involving Sherlock Holmes as well, though the draconian enforcement of copyright laws by the Conan Doyle estate sought to put a stop to the unauthorized use of Holmes in the mid-twentieth century (Nyqvist 2017, 1.1). However, as leadership of the estate changed, so, too, did that level of vigilance, and from the 1980s to today there has been an enormous boom in published stories and novels that are set in the Sherlock Holmes universe.

Within the Sherlock Holmes fandom, these texts have long been referred to as "pastiches." The traditional definition of a literary pastiche is a text written in the style of another—another text, another author, another genre, and so on. Though there continues to be debate (see Redmond 2015; Thomas 2015) in the community regarding the extent to which this label may or may not apply to online fan fiction, it is frequently used for published texts featuring Sherlock Holmes even if they do not strictly adhere to the stylistic precedents of Conan Doyle's canon (Nyqvist 2017, 1.2). However, outside the Sherlockian realm, the phrase is loaded in a different way. Fredric Jameson famously condemns pastiche as "speech in a dead language" (1991, 17). In his view, to imitate past literary styles is to lack innovation. Scholars of neo-Victorian studies are less concerned about innovation than they are about subversion; critics such as Ann Heilmann and Mark Llewellyn demand that historical fiction critically engage with the past in its attempts to represent it (2010, 4). Otherwise, historical fiction can problematically romanticize the past without acknowledging that its flaws are in fact flaws. In other words, pure repetition (for Jameson, pastiche) is ineffective, not to mention problematic.

Writing about parody, Linda Hutcheon highlights the significance of "repetition that includes difference," that difference being the place where self-conscious, critical work can take place (1985, 37). Jameson, too, recognizes the "ulterior motives" of parody, praising the "satiric impulse" which has unfortunately been "amputated" from pastiche (1991, 17). Though the Sherlockian community has not adopted the "parody" label for the many rewritings within its purview, some scholars have argued that there is potential in some of these texts to engage critically with the Sherlock Holmes oeuvre, as well as its late Victorian and Edwardian time periods.

In her 2017 article, Sanna Nyqvist contends, "By rewriting their source texts, as it were, from within, pastiches reveal the limitations and potential of the originals, as well as the cultural context that forms them" (1.5). Even the most austere, finely tuned "repetitions" of Doyle's style and the Holmesian universe, she avers, "bear traces of radical subversion" (2017, 1.5). This subversion occurs in the differences—however small—displayed in the text, coinciding with both Hutcheon's conception of parody and the neo-Victorian requirement of critical self-consciousness. It is important to note, however, that within the fandom these texts are still referred to as "pastiches."

The six novels I discuss in this chapter fall under the Sherlockian pastiche label, according to fandom tradition; yet due to the nature of these texts, which each to some extent adapt and/or rewrite both the universe of Sherlock Holmes and that of Bram Stoker's *Dracula* (1897), there are a number of other relevant terms. Holmes/Dracula pastiches are an example of Matt Hills's "counterfictions," or "alternate story stories" as Sándor Klapcsik calls them, which is to say that such texts intertextually weave together other known fictional worlds (Klapcsik 2018, 70). Significantly, Klapcsik contends that counterfictional works "frequently have a critical stance—they do not only borrow but also subvert previous narrative worlds and worldviews" (2018, 71). Such endeavors are similar to crossover fan fiction, in which characters from different fictional worlds are thrown together—this is done playfully, rather than critically, however. Unfortunately, I argue, the texts I examine likewise fail to show any evidence of critique or subversion; instead, they perpetuate the failings of the originals, and indeed seem to highlight a misogyny beyond the levels of that which was inherent of the period.

Megen de Bruin-Molé's recent work on "Frankenfictions," which exist "at the intersection between mashup, remix, adaptation, and appropriation," introduces further terms that might also apply to texts that place Sherlock Holmes and Dracula side-by-side (2020, 3). De Bruin-Molé's definition of "mashups" is particularly relevant. Quoting from Stefan Sonvilla-Weiss's 2010 essay collection *Mashup Cultures*, De Bruin-Molé suggests that "mashup" refers to texts that are assembled of multiple source materials without the "original format" being changed beyond recognition; this is, De Bruin-Molé adds, "a tenuous concept where narrative is concerned" (2020, 22). The texts I describe below vary in their "loyalty" to *Dracula*, so far as characters and plot are concerned; they adhere more closely to the Sherlock Holmes universe. But, for example, is it too much of a departure for Sherlock Holmes to be related to Dracula? For Dr. Watson to become a vampire? If the "format" is still sprinkled with those familiar details which make the Sherlock Holmes universe instantly recognizable to fans (Holmes's residence at 221B Baker Street; his landlady's being called "Mrs. Hudson"; Dr. Watson's objections to Holmes's use of cocaine, and so on), are such forays acceptable enough that the texts may be deemed mash-ups, as defined above?

Given the lack of critical subversion in the texts I examine, De Bruin-Molé's description of "Frankenfiction" may be most apt here, and closest to my definition of "mash-up":

> Frankenfiction delights in fakery for the sake of spectacle and pleasure, and for [. . .] sheer enjoyment [. . . .] This performance need not always derive from a didactic will to mock or critique the past. Often Frankenfiction chooses past objects and stories not to make a *historical* point about them, but because it likes what they make possible in the present, or simply because they have become familiar enough that they can be effortlessly recycled in a camp parody of our own nostalgia-obsessed culture. (2020, 11)

Many Sherlockian pastiches are written precisely for "spectacle and pleasure." Throughout the canon, Watson and Holmes both refer to various cases that are not fit for public consumption, and a plethora of pastiche writers have put pen to paper to fill in those canonical blanks. But other writers have simply pondered, "What if?" What if, for example, Sherlock Holmes met Sigmund Freud, another infamous cocaine user? Nicholas Meyer ponders this question in *The Seven-Per-cent Solution* (1974), emulating Doyle to such an extent that he even includes continuity errors to better resemble the original stories (Boström 2017, 367). Imitating Dr. Watson's narration style is a hallmark of the pastiche writers, who frequently preface their novels with detailed explanations of how this "new manuscript" from Dr. Watson's bank box or Holmes's personal items made its way into their hands; occasionally, authors even go so far as to pronounce Dr. Watson the true author on the book cover, calling themselves "editor"—an example of just the kind of playful "fakery" that De Bruin-Molé describes.

THE MASH-UPS

There are many mash-ups that place Holmes face-to-face with Dr. Jekyll and Mr. Hyde (from Robert Louis Stevenson's eponymous 1886 novella), Victor Frankenstein and his "monster" (à la Mary Shelley's 1818 novel), and the Martians from H. G. Wells's 1897 novel *The War of the Worlds*. Pastiche writers have also placed Holmes in conversation with historical personages, from Karl Marx to, as previously mentioned, Sigmund Freud. A staggering number of pastiches have set Holmes on the historically unsolved case of Jack the Ripper. Although it would be a stretch to suggest that there is a tradition, per se, of Sherlockian pastiches that feature

Dracula, there is still a striking preponderance of such texts—more than I can address in this chapter, certainly. Below I describe six representative mash-ups: *Sherlock Holmes vs. Dracula: The Adventure of the Sanguinary Count* (1978); *The Holmes-Dracula File* (1978); *Séance for a Vampire* (1994); *The Tangled Skein* (1992); *Sherlock Holmes and the Plague of Dracula* (1997); and *Sherlock Holmes and Count Dracula: The Adventure of the Solitary Grave* (2014). A larger study might take into account such graphic novels as Ian Edginton and Davide Fabbri's *Victorian Undead II: Sherlock Holmes VS Dracula* (2011) and Martin Powell and Seppo Makinen's *Scarlet in Gaslight: An Adventure in Terror* (1988), or novels in which Holmes is more of a tertiary figure, such as Kim Newman's *Anno Dracula* (1992) or Michael Geare and Michael Corby's *Dracula's Diary* (1982).

The first two pastiches featuring Holmes and Dracula were both published in 1978: Loren Estleman's *Sherlock Holmes VS Dracula: Adventure of the Sanguinary Count* and Fred Saberhagen's *The Holmes-Dracula File*. Recently republished (2012) as part of "The Further Adventures of Sherlock Holmes" series from Titan Books, Estleman's *Sherlock Holmes VS Dracula* tries to align events of *Dracula* with the universe of Sherlock Holmes. Holmes is consulted by a journalist in Whitby regarding a strange ship that has run ashore absent of any crew save for the corpse of the captain lashed to the wheel. The captain appears to have died from blood loss, but he has no wounds other than two small punctures on his neck. This same ship is featured in *Dracula*, but the official forces call off Holmes and Watson's investigation before the two narratives can quite intersect. It is not until the appearance of the "bloofer lady" (the nickname for the vampirized Lucy Westenra in *Dracula*) on Hampstead Heath that the tales merge; when Holmes and Watson stake out the Heath, they follow the trail back to her tomb, where they find the quartet of men from *Dracula* hammering a wooden stake into her chest. As for Dracula himself, Watson describes his visit to 221B: "I became convinced that to open the door to this creature was to invite all the terrors of the primordial night to invade the sanctity of our Baker Street digs [. . . .] All my instincts screamed for me to slam the door upon this vile apparition, to cast it back into the blackness whence it came" (Estleman 2012, 103). The focus in *Sherlock Holmes VS Dracula* appears to be on the diabolical otherness of Dracula. Even when he knows he has been defeated, he gambles his capture to demand of Watson why he follows Holmes's directives without question and at great risk to his own life. When Watson responds, flabbergasted, that it is out of loyalty and friendship, the vampire cannot grasp the concepts. Estleman's narrative sees Holmes and Watson tracking Dracula's coffins of Transylvanian earth throughout London and uncovering his hiding places on multiple occasions. When Dracula's threats fail to deter them, he kidnaps Dr. Watson's wife, Mary. In the end, however, they rescue Mary and, as in the canon, Professor Van Helsing and company put an end to Dracula.

Also published in 1978, Saberhagen's *The Holmes-Dracula File* is the second book in his Dracula series. Saberhagen's series develops Dracula's character extensively, giving him an ethical code and a keen sense of honor and duty. There are two narrative threads: first, that of an old man—later revealed to be Count Dracula—who has been kidnapped, bludgeoned, and used in a nebulous scientific experiment; second, that of Sherlock Holmes and Dr. Watson, who are approached by a young woman whose fiancé, a medical researcher, went missing in Sumatra but has reportedly reappeared in London. After Dracula escapes and vows to wreak vengeance upon his captors, his path intersects with Holmes and Watson's as they appear to be in pursuit of the same villains. As the plot thickens and they dig deeper into the case, Watson's narration takes careful note of Holmes's emotional state. When he asks Watson what he knows of vampires, he seems to be overexcited and near collapse. Dracula's sporadic narrative control gives him the opportunity to cast himself as a much more sympathetic character. He explains in a footnote, "[you] know only the stories told by my enemies and their dupes, from my breathing days in the 15th century, through the 19th when Van Helsing concocted his lurid lies [. . .] in my breathing days, as Prince of Wallachia, I was accused by some of being *too scrupulously honest*" (Saberhagen 1978, 107). It is also worth noting that in this text, Dracula is related to Sherlock Holmes. The detective, therefore, at no point needs to be convinced that vampires exist; he has known it nearly his entire life.

Interestingly, in the eighth installment in Saberhagen's Dracula series, *Séance for a Vampire* (1994), Holmes and Dracula meet again. This novel sees Holmes and Watson investigating a brother-sister duo of mediums who have brought a wealthy family into contact with their drowned daughter. When they sit in on the séance, however, chaos ensues: the skeptical father becomes a believer when he touches his daughter's solid hand; her fiancé instead believes her to still be alive but kidnapped and under duress; the medium brother is killed when a tremendous boulder is hurled at him from apparently nowhere; and Holmes himself disappears into thin air. After Holmes fails to reappear, Dr. Watson takes the only course that occurs to him—he enlists the aid of Holmes's cousin, Count Dracula. Like Estleman's *Sherlock Holmes VS Dracula*, *Séance for a Vampire* was republished in "The Further Adventures of Sherlock Holmes" series (Titan Books, 2010).

The next significant mash-up, David Stuart Davies's *The Tangled Skein* (1992), is set shortly after the events of *The Hound of the Baskervilles*, itself the most canonically Gothic of the Holmes oeuvre. Holmes finds that Jack Stapleton—the antagonist of *The Hound of the Baskervilles*, who was thought dead—is alive, and Holmes pursues him for revenge. The assassination plot merges with the vampire narrative when the woman warning Holmes about Stapleton ends up dead on Hampstead Heath, ostensibly the victim of a "phantom lady" who has been luring children thence and wounding them on the neck. Holmes and Watson stake out the Heath in pursuit, and they are nearly overcome by the hypnotic powers and superhuman strength of the lady—but, fortunately, Professor Van Helsing comes to their rescue with a crucifix. Once they discover the identity of the "phantom lady" and neutralize her vampiric corpse, Van Helsing explains that Count Dracula is the vampire responsible for bringing the disease to Britain (Davies [1992] 2006, 72). Watson confesses in his narration, "I had never heard the name before, and yet the very mention of it seemed to waken in me some dread indefinable fear" (Davies [1992] 2006, 75). Ironically, that *un*known will take Holmes and Watson into *known* territory—back to the moors of Devonshire, the setting of *The Hound of the Baskervilles*. Here, Holmes tracks Dracula to a girls' school, where he thwarts the vampire's attempt to convert one of the pupils into his next bride.

Stephen Seitz's *Sherlock Holmes and the Plague of Dracula* (1997) differs in its portrayal of Dracula and vampirism in that Holmes and Watson maintain throughout that there is no such thing as a vampire. Famously, in the canon, Holmes admonishes Watson, "How often have I said to you that when you have eliminated the impossible, whatever remains, *however improbable*, must be the truth?" (Doyle [1890] 2001, 60). Some pastiches clearly interpret this philosophy as though Holmes would therefore be willing to consider the possibility of vampires with evidence before him. However, Seitz's narrative positions Holmes as considering actual vampirism as "the impossible" and that which "remains, however improbable" to be such stagecraft as fake fangs filled with belladonna extract, sleight of hand, theatrical makeup, and the power of fear and superstition. The connection to Stoker's *Dracula* is established immediately, as Holmes and Watson are consulted by Mina Murray, who worries that her fiancé Jonathan Harker has come to harm in Transylvania, and they pursue his trail to Castle Dracula.

Despite both Holmes and Watson's steadfast belief in science and dismissal of such "backward superstitions" as vampires and the power of the crucifix, they do have a harrowing experience at the castle. Dracula himself is absent, and they think the estate abandoned until they encounter three women. Readers of *Dracula* will undoubtedly remember Jonathan Harker's encounter with these same three women—he reports, "There was something about them that made me uneasy, some longing and at the same time deadly fear. I felt in my heart a wicked, burning desire that they would kiss me" (Stoker [1897] 1997, 42). And indeed, in highly sexual language, he further describes his "agony of delightful anticipation" as one of them comes to her knees and bends over him with "a deliberate voluptuousness" before bringing her teeth to his neck (Stoker [1897] 1997, 42). In that novel, Dracula interrupts the charged moment before the woman can actually bite Harker. However, in this pastiche, Sherlock Holmes is not so lucky. Watson encounters them first, and though he is hypnotized by their beauty, he remembers a crucifix given to him by a villager and thrusts it at the women. They recoil, but at that very moment Holmes emerges from his bath in nothing but a dressing gown. Swiftly, the women swarm the detective, pushing him into a bedroom and slamming the door behind them. Watson writes to his wife, "You know well Holmes' indifferences to the charms of the fairer sex, but from the lascivious sounds from behind the door, I could tell he was succumbing" (Seitz 2012, 49). Here, as in *Dracula*, the women's bloodlust is infused with sexual overtones. The sexual nature of vampires in this tradition has long been acknowledged by scholars; as Sarah Sceats notes, "in the Victorian period penetration by biting and the exchange of blood—with ecstatic responses—allowed the coded but explicit representation of erotic activity" (2001, 108).

Watson climbs out of a window and, from the outside walls of the castle, breaks into the bedroom to witness a kind of blood orgy:

> The ghastly sight will be with me to my dying day. Holmes lay on the bed, impotent and semi-conscious. The women were arrayed around him like vultures dividing up prey. Fresh bright arterial blood dripped from the harpies' lips, and one was sucking at a fresh wound opened on Holmes' chest when I landed.
>
> I faced the blonde, who was leaning over Holmes when she saw me. She had exposed her breast, which was bleeding freely, and when I saw the dark spots around Holmes' mouth, I realized with a shock that she had made him drink, too. (Seitz 2012, 51)

Poor Holmes is helpless in the most sexual of terms ("impotent"), but he has taken blood from the breast of one of the women—an uncanny perversion of mother's milk, or even a suggestion of the breastmilk kink. Watson drives the women away, and Holmes falls into a delirious fever. They manage to escape and return to London, still convinced, despite their experience, that there is a rational explanation for all that occurred, one which does not involve actual vampires. Though Holmes's teeth appear to morph into fangs, this phenomenon is short-lived. As he casts a reflection in mirrors and does not feel compelled to drink blood, the matter seems closed.

In Seitz's pastiche, Holmes's nemesis James Moriarty is depicted as working with Dracula to cause a major British banking crisis; however, Holmes foils this plot. This ruination of Moriarty's plans is the fuel that drives him to pursue Holmes, as in the events of "The Final Problem." The final chunk of this pastiche seeks to tell the reader "what really happened" between the canonical stories of "The Final Problem" (in which Holmes dies) and "The Adventure of the Empty House" (in which Holmes reveals himself to Watson as having never been dead). Though for a time events may seem to symbolize the triumph of the supernatural over the rational, the novel does not end on such a note. Watson ultimately concludes, "Now the darkness of superstition has been put aside in place of a plausible scientific theory" (Seitz 2012, 166). The pastiche does not compromise in the assertion of the scientific over the superstitious, making it perhaps the most in line with the spirit of the original stories.

In Christian Klaver's *Sherlock Holmes and Count Dracula: The Adventure of the Solitary Grave* (2014), Dracula is not even the enemy. In fact, he comes to Holmes and Watson for assistance. He is looking for his wife—Mina. The discrepancy that his marriage causes with Stoker's canonical work goes unexplained, as this pastiche uproots one or two characters from *Dracula*, rather than attempting to reconcile the events of that text with the Holmesian universe. Dracula may not be the prime antagonist of the narrative, but the villain is a vampire. James Moriarty, it transpires, has survived the tumble down the Reichenbach Falls because he was already undead. He is on a quest to create an army of vampires, and part of his quarry includes Watson's wife, Mary. Watson finds her inexplicably in a side street of East London, scantily clad, and she turns him into a vampire as well. In what Dracula himself will later tell him is a truly remarkable persistence of his moral fiber, Watson refuses to drink any human blood during his transition. When he awakes again at 221B Baker Street, Holmes does not bat an eye:

> He brought the tea service to my bedside. Though a hunger consumed me, the thought of this once comforting ritual now caused a wave of nausea inside of me, until the aroma of something I *did* need came to me.
>
> "Holmes!" I cried when I divined his strange joke. "Really, this has gone too far. I cannot go on with this charade as if nothing has happened to me!"
>
> "Tut, tut," he said, pouring out the warm red fluid into a tea cup in front of me. "Of course you can't. But I also know that you need sustenance to survive, and is the consumption of flesh that every good British citizen partakes in really more cultured than this? Oh, I admit this is certainly very outré, to say the least, but I see no reason why you should have to descend to the level of a beast. And this has come from the butcher's shop, the same as my breakfast sausage and from the same source, I am sure."
>
> My objections rose in my throat, but they were momentarily forgotten when Holmes set the tea cup of warm blood in front of me. It was the sheerest

mockery in my mind to pour it from one of Mrs. Hudson's best tea pots. My hand shook as I picked it up and I felt a wave of deep emotion for this man who had done this for me, even though he acted as if it were nothing more uncommon than our usual breakfast. (Klaver 2014, 39)

On the one hand, this scene is one of comical irreverence. Dr. Watson drinking pig's blood from the landlady's best china! It checks the pastiche box for Sherlockian playfulness, but it is also Gothic because every aspect of this moment is uncanny. Watson feels sick to his stomach because the ritual of teatime is at once familiar and newly made strange. Holmes points out that the diet of "every good British citizen" already contains "flesh"—but how many omnivorous humans consider their roast beef sandwiches, their hot dogs, their chicken alfredo, or their fish 'n' chips in those terms? Moreover, Holmes acts as though nothing has changed, when obviously a significant change has occurred. He attempts to normalize that which is anything but. We may find this comical, but our chuckles are covering up our discomfort.

CRITICAL POSSIBILITIES

The pastiches that I feature in this chapter do not exhibit critical differences from either *Dracula* or the Sherlock Holmes canon. In fact, these texts repeat those aspects of both canons that would most benefit from a counterfictional rewrite: namely, their treatment of women. Within the Sherlock Holmes oeuvre, the detective makes it clear that he has very little use for women. The somewhat recurring female characters of the canon—an ambiguous number of Mrs. Watsons and 221B's long-suffering landlady, Mrs. Hudson—make the most minor of appearances. Though Watson in his narration is often sympathetic to the female clients when they appear (not to mention appreciative of their good looks), once they have apprised Holmes of their needs, they do not frequently reappear. Jasmine Yong Hall notes, "As the text focuses on the male-male conflict, the female client fades into the background" (1991, 300). Irene Adler of "A Scandal in Bohemia" is canonically the one woman who outsmarts Sherlock Holmes, famously earning his admiration. But even she triply loses her potential mastery over the narrative. As Pascale Krumm points out, Irene Adler's marriage midway through "A Scandal in Bohemia" in a religious ceremony to a lawyer "changes her status from harlot to housewife"; she "acquires legitimacy in the eyes of God and Men and as such, she is no longer a threat to society" (1996, 200). In case the absorption of Irene Adler into the most patriarchal of institutions is not enough, however, the narrative also sends her out of England—*and*, in addition, casts her as the "late" Irene Adler (Doyle [1891] 2008, 5). The one potentially empowered woman of the entire Holmes oeuvre is domesticated, then banished from England, and then subtly pronounced dead for good measure.

The women in *Dracula* are not treated much better. The three vampiric women who inhabit Castle Dracula and attack Jonathan Harker are portrayed as frenzied hypersexual beings, as I described above. They are evil, and their sexuality is tied directly to their villainy. Lucy Westenra is depicted as "the noblest heart that God has made"—three men propose to her in the same day, and she is so noble that she weeps when she turns two of them down (Stoker [1897] 1997, 62). However, after she becomes a vampire, those same three men will unite with Professor Van Helsing to violently destroy her. As a vampire, her voice is "voluptuous," her "sweetness was turned to adamantine, heartless cruelty, and the purity to voluptuous wantonness," and her smile both "voluptuous" and "wanton" (146, 187, 188). It is with a "voluptuous grace" that she calls to her former fiancé, "My arms are hungry for you. Come, and we can rest together. Come, my husband, come!" (188). The men are appalled by her behavior; her overt, aggressive sexuality is conflated with her evilness, just like Dracula's three brides. Ultimately, that fiancé hammers a wooden stake into her chest while she lets loose blood-curdling screams, before Van Helsing will saw off her head. Mina Murray, the remaining female character in *Dracula*, eagerly learns shorthand specifically to be of use to her new husband, and she writes parodically of the "New Women" and their scandalous sexual forwardness in her diary (55, 87). When Dracula forces her to drink his blood, the men become galvanized with an almost religious fervor to restore her purity. To ensure that we believe they have achieved just that, the final "Note" in the text is an afterward from Jonathan, her husband, proclaiming that she is now the mother of their baby boy, cheerfully announcing her fate as socially approved domestic bliss.

The pastiches repeat these late-Victorian portrayals of women, neglecting the opportunity presented by mid-twentieth century's women's liberation and decades of ground-breaking feminist theory to counter this aspect of either canon. I have already shown how the portrayal of the three vampire women in Castle Dracula in *The Plague of Dracula* is identical to Stoker's: the women are aggressively sexual and (thus) evil. Lucy Westenra suffers the same phallic wooden stake fate in *Sherlock Holmes VS Dracula* and *The Plague of Dracula*—the only two pastiches I analyze in which she appears. In the former, Watson describes, "the memory of my beloved wife forbids it, and yet I am bound by the demands of truth to record that I was suddenly filled with a hellish desire to be kissed by those lips and to take in my arms the sensuous figure which was only too visible beneath the gossamer material of her white gown" (Estleman 2012, 67). His desire to be kissed by her is "hellish"—condemnation indeed!—and he seems to blame her for being so scantily clad that her gown leaves nothing to the imagination. Though Watson feels ashamed of his erotic pull toward Lucy due to what he feels is owed to his wife, that shame seems to spur his anger toward the vampire rather than to cause him to censure himself.

Speaking of Watson's wife, Mary Watson does appear in a number of these pastiches. In the above-mentioned text, she is abducted by Dracula as an incentive to keep Holmes and Watson from pursuing him. According to a neighbor, she fainted as Dracula took her away. She is next seen as a "limp form in [. . .] white night dress," then "motionless [. . .] very frail indeed, like a baby bird," and "small and fragile" in her hospital bed, before lastly appearing in the conclusion as knitting Holmes's Christmas present (Estleman 2012, 160, 165–6, 172, 182). As I have already mentioned, in *Sherlock Holmes and Count Dracula: The Adventure of the Solitary Grave*, Vampire Moriarty turns Mary Watson into a vampire. Dr. Watson is surprised to see her in an East London alley; he knows something is wrong, but this does not stop his observation that she is wearing "no more than a wisp of clothing" (Klaver 2014, 31). He continues, "I tore off my coat and flung it around her, but she seemed to have no interest in this, but only clung to me in a wanton manner I found most unlike the woman I had known these past years" (31–2). Just as with Lucy Westenra's and Dracula's concubines, the vampire Mary Watson is "wanton." Watson explicitly informs the reader that that kind of behavior is uncharacteristic of his wife, passing judgment utterly irrelevant to the plot. She bites Watson and converts him into a vampire; however, once he escapes from the opium den, Mary disappears from the narrative just like one of Holmes's canonical female clients. Having been utilized to move along the plot, there is no longer a need for her.

Once again, in *Sherlock Holmes and the Plague of Dracula*, Mary Watson is victimized by a vampire. Count Dracula seduces her while Watson and Holmes search for Jonathan Harker in Transylvania; when Watson finds her at the country home of her old friend, she is belligerent and ill, accusing him of preferring Holmes's company to hers. Of Dracula, she professes, "You can't keep me from him! [. . . .] He loves me! He was there when I needed him! Where were you?" (Seitz 2012, 64). Her complaints are presented as the ravings of a woman not herself; to add to the picture, she scratches him at the eye socket with the brute force of her nails and presses into the woods in a thin nightdress. Though they rescue her from Count Dracula, Watson must beg Holmes to agree not to pursue the vampire, for the sake of his wife. She later persists in what Watson refers to as her "delusion" that Watson would rather spend his time with Holmes; she even believes that Holmes had intended her to die so Watson could move back into 221B. Belittling her feelings, Watson exasperatedly recounts, "If she had a clear and complete memory of that night I'm sure she would feel the same way that I did—gratitude and relief . . . that I took a wolf bite myself on her behalf seems to matter little" (Seitz 2012, 115). However, whatever her accusations, Mary Watson disappears from the narrative when she returns to the country and allows Watson to pursue the rest of the narrative unhindered by her grievances, or even her presence.

Perhaps the most disturbing vampire victim is a young schoolgirl in Devonshire in *The Tangled Skein*. Though Holmes and Watson labor to rescue her from the slow conversion into a full vampire, Dracula's confederates manage to trick them, and she is captured. Her exaggerated adoration of Dracula depicted in the following scenes is most troubling. She drinks blood from a cut on his chest "with murmurs of delight," unoffended when he suddenly and aggressively jerks her head away (Davies [1992] 2006, 157). Indeed, she thanks him with adulation. When Holmes shoots Dracula in the hand with a silver bullet and he staggers away from the girl, Watson describes the ensuing scene:

> The girl whimpered at his side, making desperate attempts to embrace him. As these entreaties grew more demanding, Dracula turned on her with a roar of fury. "Away with you," he commanded, spitting the words into her face. This harsh rejection brought hysterical shrieks from the girl, and she threw herself on her knees and clung even tighter to the Count. Tears streamed down her cheeks as she gazed up at Dracula, pleading with him to let her stay by his side.
>
> With a snarl of rage, he grasped the girl with his uninjured hand and cast her from him. Such was the force of his action that she was flung straight against the wall by the fireplace. There was a sharp crack as her head hit the stonework and, to my horror, I saw the girl fall and tumble sideways into the fireplace. As she collapsed on to the burning logs, the voracious yellow tongues lapped hungrily about her, speedily setting her dress alight. The garment seemed to explode into flames. Pain wrenched the girl into a dazed consciousness and, with choking gasps of terror, she tried desperately to drag herself from the fire. I started to the girl's aid, but halted in my tracks as I recollected what she had become. I watched numbly as, her eyes wide in torment, she writhed helplessly, the blaze enveloping her whole body. The sizzling roar drowned her feeble screams, as she was consumed by the tenacious flames. (Davies [1992] 2006, 160–1)

Dracula's excessively violent spurning of his recent convert may seem to reflect most poorly on him, but the elaborate detail of her death scene is unnecessary. It is not enough that she cracks her skull on the stonework of the fireplace, but an entire paragraph details her being burned alive. Though Watson describes the flames as "lapping hungrily" about the poor girl, the overly descriptive depiction of her gasps, her screams, her writhing, seems to suggest a hunger, certainly—the hunger for violence against women that is consistent in vampire narratives. This scene serves no purpose, as far as the plot is concerned. It seems that the girl is being used simply as a prop, whose gruesome death contributes to the tone of horror that Watson is working to establish.

Women continue to be used to move the plot forward and they lack development in these mash-ups, though poor Catherine Hunter, described above, remains the most disturbing example. In *The Holmes-Dracula File*, the character of Sally emerges early on as a sympathetic woman with a disfiguring birthmark whom Dracula manipulates into, but subsequently honors for, helping him. However, she is ultimately trampled by horses and dies a quiet death at a hospital off-stage. The woman who brings the case of her missing fiancé to Holmes is, like many of their female clients, described appreciatively by Watson. He notes, "Few visitors more lovely can ever have crossed our threshold" (Sabergagen 1978, 30). The woman makes sporadic appearances throughout the remainder of the narrative, seemingly for the sole purpose of reminding the reader that, though there be vampires afoot, there is another thread as well.

In *Séance for a Vampire*, the villain is a vampire who has purposely turned the daughter of a family in order to send her back to them via mediums to obtain information about a long-lost treasure. Before her death, Louisa Altamount was engaged to be married, and the novel shows her escaping from her captor to find her fiancé, Martin. The narrative is filtered through Dracula before it reaches the reader; he illustrates the scene as told to him by the conflicted fiancé. As he depicts it:

> The woman who had come to him last night [. . .] was no substitute for Louisa Altamount, but rather Louisa Altamount transformed. The girl to whom he, Martin Armstrong, had once proposed marriage had not become a ghost—but certainly the young woman who had wantoned in his bed last night was not the same one who had accepted his proposal of holy matrimony. Last night's . . . last night's *whore* (in the privacy of his own thought, he could try how that word sounded, when applied to his betrothed) . . . that woman could not be identified with the sunlit figure in a summer dress who last month had smiled at him so lovingly just before the rowboat tipped. (Saberhagen 2010, 206)

It is unclear whether these words are Martin's or Dracula's, creating a layer of unreliability to the narration, which is itself another Gothic trope. That which makes these women no longer exactly themselves is a newly displayed sexuality—that "wanton" behavior, those "voluptuous" movements so oft repeated throughout these pastiches, which disgust the male narrators. Louisa Altamount's body will later be found in an abandoned garden shed, impaled unceremoniously by a rusty iron pitchfork.

CONCLUSION

The Holmes-Dracula pastiches are perhaps condemned to repetition. Detective fiction broadly, and Holmes stories more specifically, are of a certain formula; to add *Dracula* and therefore also the betroped Gothic mode to the mix is to create so many character, plot, and detail requirements that is becomes almost impossible for such a text to expend energy in any other direction than in meeting those requirements. The mash-ups cannot simultaneously emulate and innovate. If the writer's foremost determination is to create a text that, in style, characterization, and other details, could conceivably have come from the original canon but for being locked in a bank's strong box or lost among a man's disorganized effects, then the very purpose is not to deviate or subvert. Kate Mitchell rhetorically asks of neo-Victorian texts, "Can these novels recreate the past in a meaningful way or are they playing nineteenth-century dress-up?" (2010, 3). In the case of the Holmes-Dracula mash-ups, the entire point is to play "dress-up"—Victorian dress-up, Sherlock Holmes dress-up, Dracula dress-up, Gothic dress-up. The uncritical imitation of the past, past forms, and past texts leads to the precise problematics predicted by scholars regarding pastiche and historical fiction. The writers may succeed in their goals of emulation and play, but as I have demonstrated, in these six particular texts, the female characters—victimized, discarded, undeveloped—suffer for it.

REFERENCES

Boström, Mattias. 2017. *From Holmes to Sherlock*. New York: The Mysterious Press.

de Bruin-Molé, Megen. 2020. *Gothic Remixed: Monster Mashups and Frankenfictions in 21st-Century Culture*. London: Bloomsbury.

Cottom, Daniel. 2012. "Sherlock Holmes Meets Dracula." *ELH* 79 (3): 537–67.

Davies, David Stuart. [1992] 2006. *The Tangled Skein*. Ware, Hertfordshire: Wordsworth.

Doyle, Sir Arthur Conan. [1891] 2008. "A Scandal in Bohemia." In *The Adventures of Sherlock Holmes*, edited by Richard Lancelyn Green, 5–29. Oxford: Oxford World's Classics.

———. [1890] 2001. *The Sign of the Four*. Peterborough, ON: Broadview.

Edginton, Ian, and Davide Fabbri. 2011. *Victorian Undead II: Sherlock Holmes VS Dracula*. DC Comics.

Estleman, Loren D. 2012. *Sherlock Holmes VS. Dracula*. London: Titan Books.

Geare, Michael, and Michael Corby. 1982. *Dracula's Diary*. New York: Beaufort Books.

Hall, Jasmine Yong. 1991. "Ordering the Sensational: Sherlock Holmes and the Female Gothic." *Studies in Short Fiction* 28 (3): 295–303.

Heilmann, Ann, and Mark Llewellyn. 2010. *Neo-Victorianism: The Victorians in the 21st-Century 1999–2009*. Houndmills, Basingstoke, Hampshire: Palgrave.

Hills, Matt. 2003. "Counterfictions in the Work of Kim Newman: Rewriting Gothic SF as 'Alternate-Story Stories." *Science Fiction Studies* 30 (3): 436–55.

Humphreys, Anne. 2002. "The Afterlife of the Victorian Novel: Novels about Novels." In *A Companion to the Victorian Novel*, edited by Patrick Brantlinger and William B. Thesing, 442–57. Blackwell Publishing.

Hutcheon, Linda. 1985. *A Theory of Parody: The Teachings of Twentieth-Century Art Forms*. New York: Methuen.

Jameson, Fredric. 1991. *Postmodernism, or, the Cultural Logic of Late Capitalism*. Durham: Duke University Press.

Klapcsik, Sándor. 2018. "Shadows of the Fantastic Over Baker Street: Counterfictionality in Recent Rewritings of the Sherlock Holmes Saga." In *Crime and Detection in Contemporary Culture*, edited by Martina Vránová, Zénó Vernyik, and Dávid Palatinus, 68–80. Americana eBooks.

Klaver, Christian. 2014. *Sherlock Holmes and Count Dracula: The Adventure of the Solitary Grave*. Amazon Publishing.

Krumm, Pascale. 1996. "'A Scandal in Bohemia' and Sherlock Holmes' Ultimate Mystery Solved." *English Literature in Transition, 1880–1920* 39 (2): 193–203.

McClellan, Ann K. 2017. "*Tit-Bits*, New Journalism, and Early Sherlock Holmes Fandom." *Transformative Works and Cultures* 23. https://doi.org/10.3983/twc.2017.0816.

Mitchell, Kate. 2010. *History and Cultural Memory in Neo-Victorian Fiction: Victorian Afterimages*. Houndmills, Basingstoke, Hampshire: Palgrave.

Newman, Kim. 1992. *Anno Dracula*. New York: Carroll & Graf.

Nyqvist, Sanna. 2017. "Authorship and Authenticity in Sherlock Holmes Pastiches." *Transformative Works and Cultures* 23. http://dx.doi.org/10.3983/twc.2017.0834.

Powell, Martin, and Seppo Makinen. 1988. *Scarlet in Gaslight: An Adventure in Terror*. Newbury Park, CA: Eternity Comics.

Redmond, Chris. 2015. "You Say Fanfic, I Say Pastiche - Is There a Difference?" *I Hear of Sherlock Everywhere*, March 9, 2015, www.ihearofsherlock.com/2015/03/you-say-fanfic-i-say-pastiche-is-there.html#.YKHsS7VKjIX.

Saberhagen, Fred. 1978. *The Holmes-Dracula File*. New York: Ace Books.

———. 2010. *Séance for a Vampire*. London: Titan Books.

Sceats, Sarah. 2001. "Oral Sex: Vampiric Transgression and the Writing of Angela Carter." *Tulsa Studies in Women's Literature* 20 (1): 107–21.

Seitz, Stephen. [1997] 2012. *Sherlock Holmes and the Plague of Dracula*. London: MX Publishing.

Stoker, Bram. [1897] 1997. *Dracula*. New York: W. W. Norton.

Thomas, Amy. 2015. "Pastiche vs Fanfiction: The Debate That Wouldn't Die." *The Baker Street Babes*, March 10, 2015, bakerstreetbabes.com/pastiche-vs-fanfiction-the-debate-that-wouldnt-die/.

Chapter 8

Orgiastic Authorship in *The Picture of Dorian Gray* and *Teleny*

Sandra M. Leonard

Oscar Wilde was a master of the mash-up. His poetry, lectures, essays, short stories, and novel make use of a wide range of intertextual styles from subtle influences and parody to plagiaristic cut-and-paste. Wilde's magpie style has frequently been the target of criticism, as was the case when the Oxford Union refused his *Poems* on the grounds that they were written "not by their putative father at all, but by a number of better-known and more deservedly reputed authors" (Elton qtd. in Ellmann 1988, 146). However, this same style has also been greatly admired. Paul K. Saint-Amour, while cautious to avoid over-attributing motive, reads Wilde's work as "celebrations of literary appropriation" (2003, 95), and in her study on Wilde's philosophy of plagiarism, Florina Tufescu unreservedly praises Wilde's "selective genius" in source use (2011, 141). Wilde himself seemed proud of his intertextual techniques, at one time reportedly boasting, "Of course I plagiarise. It is the privilege of the appreciative man" (qtd. in Beerbohm 1965, 36).

Partly because of Wilde's unorthodox use of sources, followers and fans have felt free to appropriate from the master by likewise manipulating attributions, to the extent of misattributing texts to Wilde himself. In his recent study of Wilde forgeries ranging from letters and poems to whole plays, Gregory Mackie explores several Wilde fakes that he reads as "fan fiction"; according to Mackie, the forgers are participating in a community with "an abiding interest in Oscar Wilde that was so intensive that they enlarged his literary legacy with fresh legends, outlandish fantasies, and textual fabrications" (2019, 123). Because Wilde's own artistic practices and philosophies encourage deception as "the proper aim of Art" ([1891] 2003, 1092), Mackie believes that many of these creative forgers see themselves as having "Wildean authorization" (2019, 146). I would argue that *Teleny* (1893), a homoerotic Gothic and Decadent mash-up that was likely collaboratively written during Wilde's lifetime and is widely attributed to Wilde, is yet another illustration of Mackie's interpretation of forgery as fan fiction. In this chapter, I draw a parallel between Wilde's own appropriations in *The Picture of Dorian Gray* (1890) and those in *Teleny*, asserting that *Teleny* is an important work in consideration of Gothic mash-ups in that it illustrates not only a wide-ranging appropriation of Gothic motifs but also a collaborative palimpsest of the author's legacy. I read *Teleny* specifically as a revision of Wilde's novel *The Picture of Dorian Gray*—itself a mash-up of Gothic motifs—and *Teleny* as a fictive culmination, an act of orgiastic authorship.

COMPOSITE COMPOSITION IN *THE PICTURE OF DORIAN GRAY*

To begin the conversation on *Teleny* as a palimpsest of *Dorian Gray*, I would like to explore some of the ways that *Dorian Gray* is itself a mash-up. Written in 1889–1890 and first published in the July 1890 issue of *Lippincott's Monthly Magazine*, *The Picture of Dorian Gray* tells the story of a wealthy young man who mysteriously exchanges the transience of his youth for immortality. While he stays young and handsome, his portrait suffers the ravages of time and moral decay in his stead. Freed from consequences and under the influence of an older man who encourages him to yield to his temptations, Dorian engages in hedonistic pleasures that result in his moral corruption. After causing the suicide of his lover and killing his friend, Dorian stabs his own portrait, simultaneously breaking the curse and killing himself. Within this Gothic story, so many plot and stylistic elements can be traced to other sources that, in many ways, it cannot truly be called original. Thus, to understand the text fully one must recognize its composition as a mash-up of Gothic plot elements, aesthetic philosophy, and Decadent description in service of themes addressing the nature of individual identity and influence.

One sense in which *The Picture of Dorian Gray* is a mash-up is in terms of genre. Though the central elements of the story are undoubtedly Gothic, involving a Faustian pact as well as the moral decay and duality of the main character, the novel is thematically and stylistically composite. As Nils Clausson notes in his study on *Dorian Gray* as Gothic novel, when the novel was first published, there was a good deal of confusion on whether to read it as a Decadent text in the tradition of "yellow" French novels, a romance, or a parable (2003, 340). A review in the *Daily Chronicle* called the novel, "a tale spawned from the leprous literature of the French *Décadents* — a poisonous book, the atmosphere of which is heavy with the mephitic odours of moral and spiritual putrefaction" (qtd. in Hart-Davis 1962, 263, n.1). This and other reviews made allusions to the fact that the novel hinted at homosexual relationships that were then legal in France but not in England. In response, Wilde deflected on the issue of sexuality and instead further complicated the text's genre by calling it "an essay on decorative art. It reacts against the crude brutality of plain realism. It is poisonous if you like, but you cannot deny that it is also perfect, and perfection is what we artists aim at" (Letter to the Editor of the *Daily Chronicle* [1890] 1962, 264). Wilde elaborated on this response in the preface to the book version of *Dorian Gray*: "The moral life of man forms part of the subject-matter of the artist, but the morality of art consists in the perfect use of an imperfect medium" ([1891] 2003, 17). At least part of the "imperfect medium" of *Dorian Gray* is its identity as a mash-up of Gothic and French Decadent genres, both of which Wilde signals as well as diverges from, particularly in the sources that he draws from.

One Gothic source that inspired *Dorian Gray* is *Melmoth the Wanderer*, written in 1820 by Charles Robert Maturin, Wilde's great-uncle. In exile in France after his release from prison, Wilde took the name "Sebastian Melmoth" in partial reference to Maturin's accursed character. Explaining his new moniker in a letter, he justified his choice with his lasting fascination with the novel, describing it as "though imperfect, a pioneer" (Wilde [1900] 1962, 813). While Wilde recognized flaws in his great-uncle's novel, his own text reuses and revises some of its most distinctive elements. In the novel, which is composed of layered and fragmented narratives, the mysterious Melmoth is cursed with unnaturally long life until he can find a way to swap places with another willing soul. Like Dorian, Melmoth struggles with his immortality and attempts to ameliorate his condition through the influence of others. Both also become the lovers of unworldly women: while Dorian targets an actress Sibyl Vane who only lives within her art on stage, Melmoth tempts the childlike castaway, Immalee. Both seductions ultimately bring about the deaths of these women. By the end of *Dorian Gray*, Dorian becomes a tempter figure to rival Melmoth, with rumors flying that he "sold himself to the devil for a pretty face" (Wilde [1891] 2003, 139).

The most significant difference between Melmoth and Dorian is in their contrasting attitudes. For most of *Dorian Gray*, Dorian embraces his longevity as a gift, while Melmoth knows he is cursed. At the end of *Melmoth*, having failed to find someone with whom to exchange his damnation, he is outwardly and inwardly wracked with pain and horror: "His hairs were white as snow, his mouth had fallen in, the muscles of his face were relaxed and withered—he was the very image of hoary decrepit debility" (Maturin [1820] 1989, 540). In contrast, in *Dorian Gray*, it is the portrait that bears witness to Dorian's crimes, while Dorian himself wears his perpetually youthful guise and maintains a sociopathic indifference to his wrongdoings even as he attempts to engage in introspection: "His sin? He shrugged his shoulders" (Wilde [1890] 2003, 158). It is only after Dorian attempts to kill his conscience by stabbing the portrait through the heart and dies, that his body wears the evidence of his guilt and becomes, much like Melmoth, "withered, wrinkled, and loathsome of visage" (Wilde [1890] 2003, 159). However, this tragic conclusion was not enough of a condemnation for critics who noted that Dorian's punishment was not fully realized and that the novel itself was full of coded references to male sexual relationships and seemingly indulgent descriptions of Dorian's collections of aesthetic objects.

More so than Melmoth, Dorian's attitude resembles that of Joris-Karl Huysmans's Des Esseintes, the protagonist of his 1884 Decadent novel *À Rebours*, often translated into English as *Against Nature* or *Against the Grain*. Though the novel lacks the shared plot of supernaturally extended life, Des Esseintes nevertheless operates under a sort of personal geas to explore the limits of sensual pleasure. Absent the moral guilt of Melmoth, Des Esseintes seeks out elaborate aesthetic experiences, such as having meals of flowers and, most famously, bejeweling a tortoise. Like Des Esseintes, Dorian pursues "sensations that would be at once new and delightful, and possess that element of strangeness that is so essential to romance" by reveling in the aesthetics of Catholic ritual, musing upon art objects, studying perfume, and collecting precious gemstones (Wilde [1891] 2003, 100). Beyond these similarities, *À Rebours* seems to have a special status as not only influential to the novel, but appearing within it. Notably, Dorian does his aesthetic experiments under the influence of a "poisonous book" that has been widely interpreted to be *À Rebours* (Cevasco 2001, 67–91). In *Dorian Gray*, this book is described as "a novel without a plot, and with only one character, being, indeed, simply a psychological study of a certain young Parisian, who spent his life trying to realise in the nineteenth century all the passions and modes of thought that belonged to every century except his own" (Wilde [1891] 2003, 96). This description seems to fit exactly what makes Huysmans's novel so distinctive.

Though published versions of *Dorian Gray* never mention the title of Dorian's "poisonous book," and the descriptions of setting and chapters in this novel do not entirely correspond to *À Rebours*, many continue to believe that Wilde's descriptions of the book's style, plotless narration, and the Decadent goals of the protagonist amount to an obvious allusion. During his first trial in a series that would end with his two-year imprisonment for gross indecency, Wilde was cross-examined by Edward Carson about *À Rebours* in order to connect *Dorian Gray* with this "sodomitical" novel. Though *Dorian Gray* had not been explicit about male relationships, *À Rebours* had, making one such encounter another of Des Esseintes's transgressive sensual experiences. In addition to questioning what could possibly make a *novel* "sodomitical," Wilde defensively clarified that, though Huysmans's novel had given him some initial ideas, he had made conceptual alterations and "imagined it as being grander than it was" (qtd. in Holland [1895] 2003, 98, 97).

The fact that Wilde describes Dorian's unnamed novel as "poisonous" prefigured these criticisms against *Dorian Gray* as well as those in the *Daily Chronicle* and the accusations against Wilde himself. In contrast to the description in the *Daily Chronicle* in which poison is a metaphor for the immorality derived from Decadent literature, when Wilde describes this novel as well as his own as "poisonous" (but "also perfect") it is with reference to influence itself. Lord Henry warns Dorian early in the novel, "All influence is immoral [. . . .] He does not think his natural thoughts, or burn with his natural passions. His virtues are not real to him. His sins, if there are such things as sins, are borrowed. He becomes an echo of some one else's music" (Wilde [1891] 2003, 28). Dorian is "poisoned by a book" not because it contains morally corrupting ideas, but rather because he falls so entirely under its spell that "the whole book seemed to him to contain the story of his own life, written before he had lived it" (Wilde [1891] 2003, 97). Wilde ironically reinforces the theme of influence as immoral throughout *Dorian Gray*, having Sibyl Vane, Dorian's love interest, take her own life as her only act of self-determination. Wilde's acts of intertextuality are also ironic metatextual references to an overarching theme of influence as both vital and fatal to artistic production.

Notably, in the chapter in which Dorian becomes fascinated with this poisonous book, Wilde engages in a mode of performative plagiarism, copying verbatim passages from museum catalogs when describing Dorian's own illicit art collections (Leonard 2018). After a passage that seems to allude to the experiments in perfume in *À Rebours*, Wilde embarks on a series of passages that describe exotic instruments, jewels, and embroideries, all of which borrow directly from source material. This is yet another form of mash-up within the novel that critics took issue with at the time of its publication. The British humor magazine *Punch* noted: "The luxuriously elaborate details of his 'artistic hedonism' are too suggestive of the South Kensington Museum and aesthetic Encyclopedias" ("Our Booking Office" 25). These passages act as a culmination of source use, a masterly mash-up that symbolizes Dorian's subsummation into his influences with indirect reference to the Decadent experiments of Des Esseintes.

What critics often fail to recognize is that, by incorporating allusions to Huysmans in his own novel, Wilde is not merely drawing on *any* Decadent novel to suit his purposes; instead, he has deliberately chosen a text that is itself about the fraught nature of influence. Des Esseintes sets up aesthetic experiments with the aim of losing himself within their influences. Cutting himself off from society, he stages elaborate sensory experiences that would "transport him to some unfamiliar world, point the way to new possibilities, and shake up his nervous system by means of erudite fancies, complicated nightmares, suave and sinister visions" (Huysmans [1884] 2003, 50). Though

Des Esseintes is often successful in subjecting himself to these weird and wonderful sensations and does so without any seeming guilt, he is also harmed by the richness of these experiences. He grows ill, anemic, and hypersensitive, and he is eventually forced to abandon his project when he can no longer eat or sleep, all consequences that Dorian might have faced had he not switched fates with his portrait.

In many ways, Dorian is a revision of Des Esseintes: he is a man who can overcome human limitations to endure the rich sensory passions that Des Esseintes could not. Unlike Des Esseintes who, in the end, has no choice but to quit his aesthetic experiments and can no longer enjoy them, Dorian's appetite is bottomless; he is able to truly "abandon himself" to these passions one moment and walk away with "curious indifference" the next (Wilde [1891] 2003, 100). Perhaps this is partly what Wilde meant by imagining the novel "as being grander than it was" (Holland [1895] 2003, 97). While Des Esseintes is physically compromised by his influences, Dorian's fall is unhindered by physical limitations and therefore Dorian is capable of being wholly spiritually subsumed.

The echoes between the two novels do not stop with the protagonists, as *The Picture of Dorian Gray* can be also read as responding to the thematic elements of *À Rebours*. Des Esseintes's aesthetic is one of artificiality, "the distinctive mark of human genius" (Huysmans [1884] 2003, 22). He focuses on artwork or nature manipulated by man such as flowers bred to resemble artificial ones. Dorian, too, collects art and puts on bizarre aesthetic performances, but, more than that, he is conflated with art itself. Not only is the "real Dorian" said to be the one painted in the picture, Dorian is also encouraged by Lord Henry to cultivate himself as living art. Lord Henry urges Dorian to "give form to every feeling, expression to every thought, reality to every dream" in order that he may "realise [his] nature perfectly" (Wilde [1891] 2003, 28). In a similar manner, Des Esseintes curates his aesthetic experiences, transforming his authentic experiences into false copies. Huysmans describes Des Esseintes's practice of hanging his bedroom with mirrors so that "mirror echoed mirror, and every wall reflected an endless succession" ([1884] 2003, 11). What Des Esseintes mirrors in this infinite recursion is his own pain by hanging a cricket as a reminder of his childhood loneliness, and this repetition intensifies his feelings. Similarly, Dorian grows obsessed with his portrait, calling it "the most magical of mirrors" and using it to track the progress of his growing corruption (Wilde [1891] 2003, 84). In both cases, recursion is an intensifying and destructive force, but in making Dorian's repeated image a portrait, Wilde's novel revises and arguably improves upon Huysmans's aesthetic of artificiality.

By borrowing so heavily from *À Rebours* as well as alluding to the novel within his own, Wilde situates himself within a tradition of appropriation.

Like Dorian, Des Esseintes is also deeply affected by books, particularly the Decadent Roman erotic and sometimes farcical fiction, *Satyricon*, which Des Esseintes describes as a "story with no plot or action in it" (Huysmans [1884] 2003, 30). Wilde mirrors Huysmans's description and transforms it to describe Dorian's book as "a novel without a plot" ([1891] 2003, 96), effectively turning Huysmans's description of an exterior book back in upon itself. Des Esseintes's "fascination" with the "splendidly wrought style" of this plotless book is then reflective of *À Rebours* itself (Huysmans [1884] 2003, 31). Wilde's reuse of Huysmans's text along with the appearance of the text within his own, acts as a type of mirroring, reinforcing the Gothic double motif in *Dorian Gray*. Like Dorian's soul trapped in his portrait, Huysmans's text is also mirrored and encapsulated by Wilde. Because Huysmans's text also reuses another which describes itself, the effect is one of recursion, a *mise en abyme*, a copy of an image within itself (Eells 2016, 67).

Wilde may have used *À Rebours* as a model because Huysmans's text seems to invite it through its multiple references to mirrors and copies, lengthy descriptions of other works of art, and a protagonist overcome with the influence of those works. Thus, when Wilde has Dorian pick up the plotless book which might be *À Rebours*, and Dorian is influenced by this book just as Des Esseintes is influenced by the plotless *Satyricon*, this action becomes a tacit acknowledgment as well as a recursive self-reference. Like the mirrors in Des Esseintes's bedroom that "reflected an endless succession" (Huysmans [1884] 2003, 11), a copy of a copy is an intensified experience that multiplies the effect, but it is also a degraded experience as copies deteriorate in quality. Hence, Dorian is an intensified and degraded version of Des Esseintes, one who can achieve Decadent goals that Des Esseintes cannot, but who also comes to a Gothic end resembling the fallen Melmoth.

THE DIFFERENT HANDS OF *TELENY*

Oscar Wilde and *Dorian Gray* have been associated with *Teleny* since its publication in 1893. In his initial prospectus, publisher Leonard Smithers names no author but seems to suggest Wilde by calling the writer of *Teleny* "a man of great imagination," implying that he would be well known to the English public, and remarking that the novel contains "scenes which surpass in freedom the *wildest* licence" (qtd. in Caleb 2010, xxi; emphasis mine). Despite the fact that Wilde was not known to write pornographic material (Stratford 2016, 115–18), later editions of *Teleny* included Wilde's name on the cover, as well as an account by Charles Hirsch, who claimed that Wilde had a hand in *Teleny*'s production.

At first glance, the plot of *Teleny* bears very little resemblance to *Dorian Gray*. First published in 1893, *Teleny* recounts Camille Des Grieux meeting and beginning a relationship with the Hungarian pianist, René Teleny. Even before formally meeting, the two have a psychic connection through Teleny's piano playing, and later this connection grows into a passionate love affair. The narration, which is presented as a dialogue between Des Grieux and an unnamed man, takes twists and turns into Des Grieux's past sexual experiences and fantasies before reprising the love story and culminating in Des Grieux witnessing a homosexual orgy. Des Grieux and Teleny's relationship ends in tragedy after Des Grieux finds his mother having sex with Teleny, and Teleny kills himself. In addition to the differences in plot, there are many thematic and stylistic differences between *Dorian Gray* and *Teleny*. Though a homosexual romance is central to *Teleny*, *Dorian Gray* only ambiguously alludes to such relationships. Dorian has no mother figure to act as a sexual rival, and there is no psychic connection between Dorian any other person. *Teleny*'s dialogue structure also contrasts with *Dorian Gray*'s third-person narration.

However, the starkest difference between *Dorian Gray* and *Teleny* is the lack of unity in the latter. Though *Dorian Gray* might be understood as a sometimes-plagiaristic mash-up of aesthetic essay, Decadent experiment, and Gothic novel, these elements are thematically unified for Wilde's purposes. In his dialogue on aesthetic philosophy, "The Critic as Artist," Wilde makes it clear that a mash-up of source materials and various genres can still make for a unified work so long as an individual artist exerts masterful control: "For there is no art where there is no style, and no style where there is no unity, and unity is of the individual. No doubt Homer had old ballads and stories to deal with, as Shakespeare had chronicles and plays and novels from which to work, but they were merely his rough material" ([1891] 2003, 1119). Wilde's aesthetic philosophy relies on the centrality and strength of a singular personality who can embrace influence, remain anonymous, or even write under an assumed name, but still unify the artistic production. In contrast, portions of *Teleny* seem to draw from very different perspectives and knowledges. At one point there are numerous Biblical references and sophisticated theological discussion that are absent in other sections. While sometimes there are Decadent listings of furnishings, at other times the style is sparse and action oriented. While at some points sexual embrace is touching and tender, at other points there is rape and abuse.

Teleny's purported origins may account for these inconsistencies and variations. Writing in 1934, about 40 years after *Teleny*'s initial publication, Hirsch claimed that in 1890 Oscar Wilde left a sealed notebook at his shop, and that, upon presenting Wilde's calling card, various young men would take the notebook for a short time and then return it. On one occasion, Hirsch opened the package to discover a mash-up manuscript. In his note Hirsch reflected, "What a curious mixture of various handwritings, of erased parts, omitted, corrected or added pages by different hands!" ([1934] 2010, 172). From this, Hirsch concluded that it was a collaboration between Wilde and several others. However, because the original manuscript has never been found and there is no record of Wilde ever acknowledging (nor disavowing) the work, literary critics and biographers have generally treated this story and Wilde's association with *Teleny* as spurious. Despite scholarly consensus, the book continues its popular association with Wilde and is still often printed with his name on the cover (Stratford 2016, 109–12).

Regardless of Wilde's actual involvement in the novel and its significant differences from *Dorian Gray*, the impression of Wilde's personality on the text is unmistakable, and readers who have perceived a kinship between these novels have picked up on subtle cues that signal the work as mash-up re-creation and revision of *Dorian Gray* and its sources. Throughout, there are lines in *Teleny* that echo Wilde's turns of phrase and philosophy of transgression. For instance, Teleny calls sin "the only thing worth living for" ([1893] 2010, 53), in comparison with Lord Henry who says in *Dorian Gray* that "Sin is the only real colour-element left in modern life" (Wilde [1891] 2003, 35). At another point, Des Grieux muses in a Wildean manner that, "It is the sinner and not the saint that needs a Savior, an intercessor, and a priest" ([1893] 2010, 136). Wilde uses similar phrasing and perspective after Dorian writes a too-late apology to Sibyl Vane: "It is the confession, not the priest, that gives us absolution" ([1891 2003 77–8). Descriptions of white heliotrope scent, majolica, fans, lace, gemstones, and other aesthetic details are also common to both Wilde's works and *Teleny*, and these Decadent details recall the derivative mash-up cataloging in *Dorian Gray*.

Though not as overt as the poisonous book exchanging hands in *Dorian Gray*, *Teleny* also subtly hints at its indebtedness to a multiplicity of efforts, and this speaks to the theme of influence in *Dorian Gray*. Shortly after meeting, Teleny and Des Grieux remark on their uncanny connection as "an uninterrupted current" ([1893] 2010, 18). Robert Gray and Christopher Keep read this "uninterrupted current" as alluding to the novel's intertextuality: "the productive passing of desire from one individual to another in the text, as well as the promiscuity of identifications and liaisons that characterize its narrative development" (2017). Furthermore, the dialogic style of the novel "serves as a model for its communal or collective authorship" (Gray and Keep 2017). The interlocutor sometimes interrupts to ask questions that lead the narrative in different directions, making the storytelling a collaborative exercise that also has sexual overtones since it becomes clear that the speakers share a sexual history. Similarly, much as Hirsch remarks on *Teleny*'s production as "a curious mixture [. . .] by different hands," *Teleny* contains a passage in which Des Grieux, being psychically pleasured by Teleny, muses on individual personalities as expressed through their hands:

> Some hands are coy, others paddle you indecently; the grip of some is hypocritical, and not what it pretends to be; there is the velvety, the unctuous, the priestly, the humbug's hand; the open palm of the spendthrift, the usurer's tight-fisted claw. There is, moreover, the magnetic hand, which seems to have a secret affinity for your own; its simple touch thrills your whole nervous system, and fills you with delight. ([1893] 2010, 10)

These hands, all of different qualities and characteristics, are unified in passionate production, metaphorically echoing the novel's supposed method of creation. This model of intertextual influence and imitation as a joyous production is a revision of the philosophy in *Dorian Gray* about influence leading to a degeneration of self and art.

In much the same way that *Dorian Gray* was a revision of some elements of *À Rebours*, *Teleny* is a revision of *Dorian Gray*. Music provides one such point of comparison between the two novels that illustrates their contrasting views on imitation in art. Both Teleny and Dorian Gray are pianists, but the way they practice their art is entirely different. To Dorian, playing piano is an imitative act; he excels at it by learning written sheet music, and he is mentioned playing particular composers (Wilde [1891] 2003, 26). Dorian is so good an imitator that he uses music as a mask to hide his emotions, which is befitting of Wilde's aesthetic philosophy presented in his Preface to *Dorian Gray*: "to reveal art and conceal the artist is art's aim" ([1891] 2003, 17). To demonstrate this, when Dorian is in agony, Wilde has Lord Henry misinterpret Dorian's practiced playing as joyful and ironically remark, "What a blessing it is that there is one art left to us that is not imitative!" (Wilde [1891] 2003, 154). Teleny, on the other hand, genuinely expresses his soul through music. Though Teleny is also playing written compositions, the composer is unnamed; instead, the music is described by its cultural character in terms that might also describe Teleny, which has the effect of uniting the artist and music ([1893] 2010, 5). His artistic self-expression is so sincere that Des Grieux claims Teleny is "the very personification of his entrancing music" ([1893] 2010, 6). Teleny's piano playing is what establishes his psychic link with Des Grieux, causing him to have a series of erotic visions through their "uninterrupted current." Later, when Teleny loses his connection with Des Grieux, his playing suffers and reflects his emotional state ([1893] 2010, 80–1). In *Teleny*, influence and art go hand in hand, and, unlike in *Dorian Gray* and *À Rebours*, this influence is not an overpowering artificiality that leads to degeneration of the self. Rather than merely being "an echo of someone else's music," *Teleny*'s philosophy of art is rooted in sincere expression that embraces influence as a positive force. This authentic connection of music is a departure from *Dorian Gray* not only in aesthetic philosophy, but also in that it adds a major Gothic supernatural element not in Wilde's story. While both novels have elements of Gothic horror, *Teleny* centers its supernatural elements not around the relationship between art and a human being, but around the authentic connection of two human beings.

This human connection achieved by means of the supernatural is an answer to the jaded artificiality in *Dorian Gray* that also manifests in *Teleny*'s reuse of the motif of mirrors. Whereas *Dorian Gray* in some ways furthers the theme of recursivity in *À Rebours*, *Teleny* advances that theme to its breaking point and replaces the suspicion of mimesis as degradation with a connection of true equals. In *Dorian Gray*, Dorian is doubled with his portrait, which represents his soul, and his relationship with the portrait evolves over the course of the narrative. There is an erotic overtone to this doubling as he kisses his own portrait "in boyish mockery of Narcissus" (Wilde [1891] 2003, 84). Though this portrait is a copy of Dorian, the nature of its magic is in its uneven distribution, with agency unshared by the party that bears the consequences. Though Dorian is doubled in his image, ultimately the portrait and his physical being are asymmetrical. Des Grieux and Teleny, however, are presented as equal beings with independent agency and personalities that nevertheless share an uncanny bond and resemblance. Their love for one another is not based on domination or dependency but upon mutual "sympathy" as Teleny describes his first psychic recognition of Des Grieux being that of a "sympathetic listener" who shares his emotions and understanding ([1893] 2010, 11–12). When they first recognize their mutual love for one another, it is on a bridge that suggests a mirror-like meeting: "The river, like a silvery thoroughfare, parted the town in two" ([1893] 2010, 87), and when they embrace for the first time, it is by touching foreheads and exchanging breath as if in mirrored reflection of one another ([1893] 2010, 89). In a self-aware manner, the two comment upon their resemblance and tease the reader with an expectation of the usual Gothic conclusion, remarking "Who knows—you are, perhaps, my *Doppelgänger*? Then, woe to one of us! [. . . .] In our country they say that a man must never meet his alter ego, it brings misfortune to one or to both" ([1893] 2010, 114). By the end of the novel, their meeting results in Teleny's death, but it is out of sacrifice for his love rather than an attempt at an impossible separation, as is the case in *Dorian Gray*.

Though the mirroring motif in *Dorian Gray* is strengthened by the relationship between Teleny and Des Grieux, it also represents the most significant way in which *Teleny* revises and overwrites *Dorian Gray*. *Teleny* is an explicit homosexual love story with detailed pornographic depictions of homosexual acts. Dorian is mentioned as corrupting young men; however, the closest the novel gets to plainly expressing same-sex desire is in the scene in which Basil tells Dorian his "secret": when he had painted Dorian's portrait he had been "dominated" by his influence (Wilde [1891] 2003, 89). This scene provides an illustration of how *Teleny* makes explicit that which *Dorian Gray* only suggests. To describe his artistic and emotional process, Basil mentions how he painted Dorian in a number of poses, many of which are allusions to male sexual relationships including one where, "crowned with heavy lotus-blossoms [Dorian] had sat on the prow of Adrian's barge, gazing across the green turbid Nile" (Wilde [1891] 2003, 89). This scene casts Dorian in the role of Antinous, a young companion often understood to be a slave and the lover of the Roman Emperor Hadrian (Westernized as "Adrian"). During a trip down the Nile, Antinous was found dead, possibly the result of suicide or ritual sacrifice for his lover (Opper 2008, 174). Basil's scene captures a moment before Antinous's death on the Nile. In Wilde's allusion, the object of desire as well as the foreshadowing of Dorian's death are merely implied and would only be understood by those knowledgeable in the Classics. In *Teleny*, this brief scene is rewritten in a more explicit manner when Des Grieux shares a series of erotic visions including this one: "I saw a barren land, the sun-lit sands of Egypt, wet by the sluggish Nile; where Adrian stood wailing, forlorn, disconsolate for he had lost for ever the lad he loved so well" ([1893] 2010, 6). In this revision, the romantic nature of the relationship as well as its tragic end is foregrounded rather than alluded to. Throughout the remainder of the novel, the motif of Antinous becomes a touchstone for the lovers, with Des Grieux giving Teleny a ring with a cameo of Antinous's face and remarking that they both resemble him ([1893] 2010, 114). Furthermore, this scene is an inverse of Basil's portrait. Whereas Basil displays the beloved Dorian/Antinous looking out to his lover, *Teleny*'s scene takes on the perspective of Adrian, the lover weeping for his beloved. If we extend this scene as a metaphor of the representative roles of the two texts, Wilde's takes on the traditional pederastic role of the beloved (*eromenos*), whereas *Teleny* plays the role of the older, more experienced lover (*erastes*). This role fits the more explicitly sexual nature of *Teleny*, but also positions itself as usurping the other's authority, not merely parodying or appropriating but also revising the nature of the text.

Teleny makes use of this position of authority to revise a major aspect of how homosexuality is understood in *Dorian Gray*. Inasmuch as *Dorian Gray* does suggest homosexual relationships, it does so with the attachment of sin and unnaturalness. Basil's obsession with Dorian is the subject of pity and shame, with Dorian reflecting that he "felt sorry" for his friend after his confession of secret obsession (Wilde [1891] 2003, 91). When Basil remarks on Dorian's bad reputation, he asks why relationships with young men are "so fatal" (Wilde [1891] 2003, 112). This attitude toward homosexuality is akin to that shown in *À Rebours*. In a scene that was referred to in the first of

Wilde's trials, Des Esseintes is approached by a young man with whom he begins a relationship that, like his other aesthetic sensory experiments, leaves him overstimulated and enervated. Des Esseintes reports that the relationship lasted several months, but that he "could not think of it now without a shudder," his satisfaction a perverse guilt stemming from the transgression in breaking social, religious, and—in his view—natural law ([1884] 2003, 102). Similarly, that Dorian sees his actions as immoral and is punished for them at the end of the narrative is a moralistic move that Wilde would call "the only error in the book" (To the Editor of the *St. James Gazette*, June 26, 1890, 259). Due to Wilde's personal history as a closeted but ultimately unapologetic gay man who was persecuted for his sexuality, his portrayal of homosexuality in any sort of negative light in his art has often been understood to be his own mask (Ellmann 1988, 322).

Teleny, however, wholly overturns the view of homosexuality as "against nature." In explaining his lack of sexual experience with women, Des Grieux claims: "I was predisposed to love men and not women, and without knowing it I had always struggled against the inclinations of my nature" ([1893] 2010, 28). After his first night with Teleny, rather than feeling shame, enervation, or—as his interlocutor suggested—"seedy," Des Grieux feels unreservedly joyful: "I was blithe, merry, happy. Teleny was my lover; I was his. Far from being ashamed of my crime, I felt that I should like to proclaim it to the world" ([1893] 2010, 106–7). Des Grieux's homosexuality is not a perversion or secret sin, but simply the inclination of his nature. Whereas any hint of homosexual love is inherently transgressive in *Dorian Gray*, *Teleny* treats the subject without any such pretense and in so doing offers a form of rehabilitation, a palimpsestic rewriting of *Dorian Gray* as an openly homosexual love story.

Not only does *Teleny* cast Des Grieux's homosexuality as resulting from natural inclination, it acknowledges homosexuality as an identity shared with a community of others. Dorian Gray and the models on which he is based—Melmoth and Des Esseintes—have no community of peers in their respective texts. They do not truly connect with their lovers or friends. Even Lord Henry, who might be said to be Dorian's closest friend, is not aware of Dorian's secret and, by the end of the narrative, is under a complete misapprehension of his character. However, in *Teleny* there is a community of sympathetic others that represent a model of collaborative authorship. This is demonstrated in his invitation to a symposium where Des Grieux is initiated into homosexual society by a literal unmasking, having his identity known to other homosexual men of society, joining in a pact of mutual acknowledgment and tacit secrecy. The symposium quickly becomes an orgy, a "pandemonium of lewdness," which culminates in a carnal spectacle involving five men ([1893] 2010, 130). The orgasm that results is described as "an electric shock" shared with everyone in the room, which produces a shared voice: "'They enjoy, they enjoy!' was the cry, uttered from every lip" ([1893] 2010, 132). In *Teleny*, the orgasm is not an individual experience, but one shared with other like-minded individuals. The joining of voices in this orgasmic scene is a demonstration of the collaborative authorial experience as a sensual act of simultaneous fulfillment.

Contrary to Wilde's stated view on aesthetic beauty, in *Teleny* unity is not of the individual. It is of a group of sympathetic minds that can maintain their individuality while joining in a collaboration. Inasmuch as *Dorian Gray* is read into this novel, *Teleny* dramatically revises Wilde's aesthetic of unity of the individual in its theme as well as in its very method of production as written by many hands. Additionally, it does so by putting on a mask that appropriates Wilde's identity, which, at first glance, might seem manipulative or contrary to Wilde's aesthetic. However, I believe that ultimately we should not read this as an act of misappropriation, but true sympathy. Wilde, after all, was an appropriator of appropriated texts, the "appreciative man" who mashed-up Gothic tropes and Decadent fiction to produce his "perfect" text. In doing so, he furthered the aesthetic philosophy of his sources, giving potency to Des Esseintes and revealing Melmoth's soul. *Teleny* is indeed a departure from Wilde's aesthetics, but it also drives them to their logical conclusions. In providing further recursion in an erotic symmetrical relationship, containing a portrayal of homosexuality that was extremely transgressive, and making use of the collaboration of a group of authors that remain masked to this day, *Teleny* rewrites Wilde with that sense of "Wildean authorization" common to his truest appropriators. Furthermore, *Teleny* is a revision of our view of Oscar Wilde, not as a lone author, misunderstood and ultimately ostracized by his community, but a fantasy of Wilde un-masked and belonging to a group of authors such that his voice could be blended with theirs in mutual pleasure. Far from being a sign of its aesthetic failure, *Teleny*'s status as mash-up reinforces and heightens these crucial themes and enables its participation in the plagiaristic tradition of *Dorian Gray*.

REFERENCES

Beerbohm, Max. 1965. *Letters to Reggie Turner*. Edited by Rupert Hart-Davis. Philadelphia: J. B. Lippincott.

Caleb, Amanda. 2010. "Introduction." In *Teleny or The Reverse of the Medal*, edited by Amanda Caleb, vii–xxv. Kansas City, MO: Valancourt Books.

Cevasco, G. A. 2001. *The Breviary of the Decadence: J.-K. Huysmans's A Rebours and English Literature*. New York: AMS Press.

Clausson, Nils. 2003. "'Culture and Corruption': Paterian Self-Development versus Gothic Degeneration in Oscar Wilde's *The Picture of Dorian Gray*." *Papers on Language and Literature* 39 (4): 339–64.

Eells, Emily. 2016. "'La consolation des arts': *The Picture of Dorian Gray* and Anglo-French Cultural Exchange." *Études anglaises* 69 (1): 62–75.

Ellmann, Richard. 1988. *Oscar Wilde*. New York: Knopf.

Gray, Robert, and Christopher Keep. 2017. "'An Uninterrupted Current:' Homoeroticism and Collaborative Authorship in *Teleny*." In *The Oscholars: Special Teleny Issue*, edited by John McRae. *Oscholars*. https://oscholars-oscholars.com/special-issues/teleny-revisited/.

Hart-Davis, Rupert, ed. 1962. *The Letters of Oscar Wilde*. New York: Harcourt.

Holland, Merlin, ed. [1895] 2004. *The Real Trial of Oscar Wilde*. New York: HarperCollins.

Huysmans, Joris-Karl. [1884] 2003. *Against Nature (A Rebours)*. Translated by Robert Baldick. New York: Penguin.

Leonard, Sandra M. 2019. "Borrowed Sins: Oscar Wilde's Aesthetic Plagiarisms in *The Picture of Dorian Gray*." *JNT: Journal of Narrative Theory* 49 (2): 137–68.

Mackie, Gregory. 2019. *Beautiful Untrue Things: Forging Oscar Wilde's Extraordinary Afterlife*. Toronto: University of Toronto Press.

Maturin, Charles. [1820] 1989. *Melmoth the Wanderer*. New York: Oxford University Press.

Opper, Thorsten. 2008. *Hadrian: Empire and Conflict*. United States: Harvard University Press.

"Our Booking Office." 1890. *Punch* (14 December, 1890): 25.

Saint-Amour, Paul K. 2003. *The Copywrights: Intellectual Property and the Literary Imagination*. Ithaca: Cornell University Press.

Stratford, John. 2016. "Teleny—Wilde or Not?" *The Wildean* 48 (January 2016): 104–21.

Teleny or The Reverse of the Medal. [1893] 2010. Edited by Amanda Caleb. Kansas City, MO: Valancourt Books.

Tufescu, Florina. 2011. *Oscar Wilde's Plagiarism: The Triumph of Art over Ego*. Dublin: Irish Academic Press.

Wilde, Oscar. [1891] 2003. "The Critic as Artist." In *Complete Works of Oscar Wilde*, edited by Merlin Holland, 1108–55. London: Collins.

———. [1890] 1962. Letter to the Editor of the *Daily Chronicle*, June 30, 1890, in *The Letters of Oscar Wilde*, edited by Hart-Davis, Rupert, 263–64. New York: Harcourt.

———. [1890] 1962. Letter to the Editor of the *St. James Gazette*, June 26, 1890, in *The Letters of Oscar Wilde*, edited by Hart-Davis, Rupert, 258–59. New York: Harcourt.

———. [1900] 1962. Letter to Louis Wilkinson, January 4, 1900, in *The Letters of Oscar Wilde*, edited by Hart-Davis, Rupert, 813. New York: Harcourt.

———. [1891] 2003. "The Picture of Dorian Gray." In *Complete Works of Oscar Wilde*, edited by Merlin Holland, 18–159. London: Collins.

Chapter 9

Rewriting Indigeneity in the Canadian Gothic

Monsters, Mash-Up, and Monkey Beach

Kelly Baron

In an interview on *Monkey Beach* (2000), Eden Robinson commented on her decision to destroy the second draft of her acclaimed novel: it was "too moody, too Gothic. The only ones who liked it were [her] German publishers" (qtd. in Hunter 2000). The next draft would be published to critical acclaim, but, interestingly, it did not stray from the Gothic origins Robinson intended to discard. A review from Joan Thomas described the novel as a "glorious Northern Gothic," while another reviewer, Warren Cariou, suggested that Robinson used "the trappings of a contemporary Gothic novel" in the style of Stephen King (qtd. in Andrews 2001, 1). In an early article on the novel, Jennifer Andrews agrees with these reviews, noting that Robinson retained many of the thematic conventions of the Gothic novel while making the genre her own "by setting her text in the First Nations Haisla community located on the British Columbia coastline" (2001, 1). *Monkey Beach* follows the story of Lisamarie Hill, a young Haisla woman whose brother, Jimmy, has been lost at sea somewhere off the British Columbia coastline near the isolated Monkey Beach, known for its B'gwus, or Sasquatch, sightings. The Sasquatch, also called Bigfoot, is a massive, ape-like creature from North American folklore. In Haisla storytelling, the B'gwus are similar in size and stature to Bigfoot. They are viewed as misunderstood or made strange by their isolation and are known for sneaking into nearby villages to steal the women of their fancy. As Lisamarie searches for her brother, she reflects on their youth together, one which was filled with monsters such as the B'gwus due to her connections with the spirit realm. The remote settings, tormented heroes, and dreamscapes that are characteristic of many early Gothic texts are present in Robinson's novel. And while I agree with Andrews's assessment that Robinson made the Gothic her own by including Indigenous settings and protagonists, it is important to note that Robinson's text is part of a larger body of Indigenous Gothic works in Canada. Consider, for example, Nathan Niigan Noodin Adler's *Wrist* (2016), the protagonist of which is a descendent of the Wiindigo, an Ojibway monster with an insatiable appetite for human flesh, and Cherie Dimaline's best-selling *The Marrow Thieves* (2017), a YA novel with the Indigenous protagonists running for their lives from Recruiters, settlers who hunt Indigenous peoples for their bone marrow. In film, we see this trend appearing in movies such as Jeff Barnaby's *Blood Quantum* (2019), which details a zombie uprising to which the residents of the Red Crow Indian Reservation in Quebec are immune as a function of their Indigenous heritage. In theater, similar themes appear even earlier in Drew Hayden Taylor's "A Contemporary Gothic Indian Vampire Story" (1992), which he later adapted into a novel, *The Night Wanderer: A Native Gothic Novel* (2007).

While incorporating Indigenous settings, storytelling, and characters into Gothic works is not an isolated phenomenon in Canada, books such as *Monkey Beach* are important precisely because they invert and subvert the Canadian Gothic tradition of incorporating Indigeneity as the monstrous Other. David Gaertner remarks that "Indigenous peoples and communities are often the objects of repression and return in the North American Gothic," resulting in their being subjected to the dehumanizing effects of repression in Gothic works, such as in John Richardson's *Wacousta* (1832), or as seen in the treatment of Coyote in Sheila Watson's *The Double Hook* (1959), for example (Gaertner 2015, 49). Such a treatment is well-founded in early scholarship on the Canadian Gothic. In 1977, Margaret Atwood wrote her now-canonical essay on Canadian monsters, in which she notes that in the Canadian Gothic tradition, settler writers have frequently mined First Nations and Inuit storytelling as a resource for their monsters, resulting in Indigenous peoples being positioned as the monstrous Other "represent[ing] forces outside and [. . .] opposed to the human protagonist" ([1977] 1982, 101–2). One year earlier, Margot Northey wrote *The Haunted Wilderness: The Gothic and Grotesque in Canadian Fiction*, a monograph which remains one of the "most substantial stud[ies] of the significance of the 'Gothic' in a distinctly Canadian context" (Andrews 2001, 1). Northey does not linger on the role of Indigenous peoples and storytelling in the Gothic; however, in her chapter on *Wacousta*, she writes that the novel is haunted by Indigenous peoples, "the irrational children of nature, who at times appear as Gothic embodiments of inscrutable demonism," advancing a view of Indigenous peoples being the monstrous Other in Canadian Gothic texts (1976, 23). These works of early scholarship, and the early Canadian Gothic novels they analyze, depend on a binary of settler hero versus Indigenous monster.

More recent analyses of the use of the Gothic in contemporary Canadian literature posit a divide between Canadian and Indigenous Gothic. While the European model of the Gothic was characterized by its use of medieval settings, namely isolated, possibly haunted castles, such locales do not exist in Canada. As a result, the Canadian Gothic is instead characterized by a "haunted wilderness," a term initially developed by Margot Northey but reinvigorated by Justin Edwards's recent monograph, *Gothic Canada: Reading the Spectre of a National Literature* (2005). As Edwards writes, the Canadian settler is depicted as "struggling against the threatening forests or the harshness of the prairies," a conclusion he reaches by analyzing the famously frightening depiction of the natural landscape in Susanna Moodie's 1852 account of early settler life, *Roughing it in the Bush* (Edwards 2005, xxviii). Moodie describes Canada as a "terrifying" land "only fit for wild beasts" (qtd. in Edwards 2005, xxviii). Not only is the Canadian landscape a "place of fear," argues Edwards, but Canadian writers also use Gothic language as a tool for othering all those who are not white and European (2005, xxviii). In discussing Maria Campbell's *Halfbreed* (1973), for example, he remarks that the positioning of Indigenous peoples in Canadian literature as "bloodthirsty savage[s]" fulfills a necessary goal of settler colonialism by "justifying land acquisition and displacement," allowing European settlers to "pretend that the land was void of humanness and thus appropriate it without guilt or shame" (2005, 112). Others come to similar conclusions on the Canadian Gothic. Cari Carpenter remarks that the field of Canadian literature is "imagined as springing from an initially uninhabited, dangerous wilderness" before she transitions to consider how the Indigenous Gothic differs in its treatment of the natural landscape and its understanding of evil (2017, 50). The Indigenous Gothic offers a more nuanced treatment of the land—what Carpenter refers to as an "unceasing attachment to a homeland"—and presents a more complicated notion of evil (2017, 51). Specifically, in Indigenous Gothic texts, monsters are often "objects of sympathy" by virtue of their association with the natural and the spiritual world, and the antagonists of the texts are, instead, the "colonizing forces" (Carpenter 2017, 50). As Michelle Burnham notes in her chapter "Is there an Indigenous Gothic?", the villains of Indigenous Gothic "take on such forms as consumer capitalism, acquisitive hyperindividualism, or historical amnesia" (2013, 229).

In *Monkey Beach*, Robinson engages in a mash-up of settler and Indigenous Gothic tropes. She develops a terrifying, isolated natural setting, one reminiscent of the "haunted wilderness" so often associated with the Canadian Gothic, but she maintains the Indigenous consideration afforded to monsters. At first, the B'gwus are depicted in terrifying childhood stories, but the B'gwus become naturalized by the end of the novel, ensuring that Robinson's monsters are also a mash-up of European and Haisla storytelling.

As a result, Robinson reclaims the B'gwus from the settler understanding of the Sasquatch or Bigfoot. Robinson's focus on reclaiming the monstrous is, I propose, an inversion of Megen de Bruin-Molé's formulation of how the Gothic has been remixed in recent years. Whereas De Bruin-Molé takes as her focus of study the "Frankenfictions" that "resurrect old texts and narratives specifically to feed a pervasive, commercial desire for the monstrous," asking what it means that "our historical monsters have moved from the margins to the mainstream" (2020, 3), Robinson, through reclaiming the Sasquatch as the B'gwus, explores how settler monsters have their roots in Indigenous storytelling. What does it mean that the monsters that settlers have renamed and reappropriated into modern mainstream stories originate in Indigenous oral traditions? And, more important for this chapter: What happens when those monsters are no longer the antagonists of our Gothic novels and instead become an element of nature living undisturbed alongside us? Robinson draws from Haisla storytelling to remove the monster from its role as Gothic antagonist. The antagonist lurking behind the trauma and Gothic scenes of her text is more insidious because it does not have its roots in the supernatural or the fantastic; instead, the true monster is settler colonialism, the legacies of which find their way into Lisamarie's familial life. In this chapter, I analyze how Robinson mashes up the Gothic to reclaim Indigenous stories and rewrite Indigeneity in contemporary Gothic narratives. I achieve this through three parts: first, I discuss *Monkey Beach* as an Indigenous Gothic text; second, I consider how Robinson's depiction of the B'gwus is a Gothic mash-up of Indigenous and settler monsters; and third, I reflect on what such a mash-up can achieve in an Indigenous Gothic novel. Ultimately, I argue that Robinson contributes to a rewriting of the Canadian Gothic tradition, calling attention to the collective, intergenerational trauma inherent in Indigenous experiences in Canada.

MONKEY BEACH AS INDIGENOUS GOTHIC

A number of scholars have commented on the Gothic features of Robinson's novel. Andrews, for example, works from Elizabeth MacAndrew's *The Gothic Tradition in Fiction* (1979) to explain the key elements of Gothic fiction found in *Monkey Beach*. As Andrews explains, Gothic fiction was intended to draw in the readers emotionally, evoking a response of either terror or horror, defined by Ann Radcliffe as "evil in the environment rather than in humankind" and "evil as inherent in people," respectively (qtd. in Andrews 2001, 3). In order to convey such evil to the readers, Gothic novels include elements that have become characteristic of the genre: "dream landscapes and figures of the subconscious imagination" and "beings—mad monks, vampires, and demons—and settings—forbidden cliffs and glowering buildings, stormy seas and the dizzying abyss" (MacAndrew qtd. in Andrews 2001, 3). The Canadian equivalent of the traditional European Gothic setting is, of course, the isolated natural Canadian landscape—Northey's "haunted wilderness"—along with its harsh weather conditions, which are well-established in *Monkey Beach*. Robinson begins the novel with Lisamarie hearing a foreboding message in Haisla from the crows outside her window, telling her to look at the bottom of the ocean for her brother, Jimmy, who is lost at sea. In the scenes that follow, we learn of Lisamarie's ability to dream about the deaths and misfortunes of her loved ones before they happen. But beyond the dreamscapes of Lisamarie's youth, the coastal setting is irresistibly Gothic. The eponymous Monkey Beach is a secluded location accessible only by boat. Its isolation is quite clear in Robinson's text; Lisamarie, in a moment of second-person narration, addresses the reader directly:

> If your finger is on Prince Rupert or Terrace, you are too far north [. . . .] To get to Kitamaat, run your finger northeast, right up to the Douglas Channel, a 140-kilometer-long deep-sea channel, to its mouth [. . . .] Near the head of the Douglas, you'll find Kitamaat Village, with its seven hundred Haisla people tucked in between the mountains and the ocean. At the end of the village is our house. Our kitchen looks out onto the water. Somewhere in the seas between here and Namu—a six-hour boat ride south of Kitamaat—my brother is lost. (2001, 5)

The level of detail needed to communicate where Kitamaat Village is located guarantees that it is immediately recognizable as a small-town location, even without the reference to the population of 700. Describing the remote village as "tucked in between the mountains and the ocean" ensures that the landscape provides a literal barrier between Kitamaat and the rest of British Columbia, isolating the village from the rest of the province. After Lisamarie decides to steal her father's speedboat to go searching for her brother, the weather further reinforces the Canadian Gothic nature of the setting. She describes the weather as "cold" for the middle of August; the "waves hitting the bow send constant shudders through the speedboat" (Robinson 2001, 155). As her journey progresses, she describes the rain as "easing," although she notes that the "weather is inspiring [her] gloomy turn of thoughts" (Robinson 2001, 162, 165). When she finally reaches Monkey Beach in the novel's final section, "The Land of the Dead," her visit on the beach is accompanied by visions of her dead relatives: her uncle Mick, her Ba-ba-oo, her Ma-ma-oo, along with visions of Jimmy's death at sea. The titular setting is one that is isolated, dreary, and accompanied by the dead, ensuring that it fits with the genre requirements for the Canadian Gothic.

Beyond these characteristic genre requirements, there are other ways in which Robinson's novel is distinctly Gothic. MacAndrew notes that over the last three centuries of Gothic texts, there has been a shift in interest from "the origins of evil [. . .] to ambiguous presentations that questioned the nature of evil itself" (qtd. in Andrews 2001, 4). This shift to questioning the nature of evil applies well to the Indigenous Gothic, and to Robinson's novel. There is no clear villain in *Monkey Beach*; by the end of the novel, we learn that Jimmy likely took up the position on the *Queen of the North*, the boat he was working on when he went missing, to go after his girlfriend Karaoke's uncle Josh, who raped her. But in Robinson's earlier collection of short stories, *Traplines*, she provides us with more insight into Jimmy's girlfriend and her uncle. At the end of *Monkey Beach*, Lisamarie finds a card in Jimmy's jacket made by Karaoke, with a picture of her uncle Josh's head pasted onto a picture of a priest, a card which first appears in *Traplines*. The inscription, "Dear Joshua, I remember every day we spent together. How are you? I miss you terribly. Please write. Your friend in Christ, Archibald," is clarified in *Traplines* as a direct reference to Josh's abuse in the residential school system (Robinson 2001, 365). The card, although initially confusing to Lisamarie, is Karaoke's method of reminding Josh that he is now a perpetrator of the sexual abuse to which he had previously fallen victim. While his abuse in the residential school system in no way absolves Josh of rape, it does complicate his past; as Andrews notes, it was colonization through the residential school system that led to "the sexual abuse of children, both by the colonizer (Archibald) and eventually by the colonized (Josh)" (2001, 13).

As an inquiry into the ambiguous nature of evil, Robinson's text denies her readers any easy answer to who is responsible for Jimmy's death. The epigraph to the novel, a Haisla proverb, is fitting: "it is possible to retaliate against an enemy, but impossible to retaliate against storms" (Robinson 2001). While Andrews reads the epigraph literally, suggesting that it "overtly acknowledges the power and danger of the natural world" (2001, 10), a reading which is well-aligned with the genre tropes of the Canadian Gothic, I read the proverb as an inquiry into the nature of evil. The storms are a metaphor for the legacies of colonialism, which, for the Haisla of the Kitamaat Village, include the "forced relocation of Aboriginal people by the government of Canada pursuant to the *Indian Act*; the loss of traditional land and water rights; the pollution of the environment [. . .], and, perhaps even more insidiously, the psychological and emotional damage to Aboriginal children in residential schools" (Castriciano 2006, 802). What this means is that Robinson develops her setting to locate her work within the tradition of Canadian Gothic, but she then challenges that tradition by presenting settler colonialism as the source of evil. For Marie Mulvey-Roberts, "the designation 'mash-up' has destructive connotations, while its intrinsic hybridisation partakes of the monstrous" (2014, 33). Robinson's mash-up of Canadian and Indigenous Gothic shows the true haunting of the Canadian landscape: the enduring legacies of settler colonialism suffered by Indigenous peoples. The storm that Robinson begins her novel with is not of the natural world, but instead it symbolizes the impact of settler society on Indigenous peoples—a mundane, insidious form of evil that accompanies the everyday experience of living in Canada.

DO THE MONSTER MASH(UP): HAISLA B'GWUS AND SETTLER SASQUATCH

Robinson's mash-up of Canadian and Indigenous Gothic elements goes beyond the development of the isolated northern setting and inquiry into the nature of evil to extend into her characterization of the B'gwus. Robinson does not recycle the settler stories of the Sasquatch or Bigfoot in her novel. Rather, I propose, her monsters are distinctly Haisla, and she incorporates the settler signifier of Sasquatch, and the fear and violence associated with it, only to contextualize the B'gwus for her non-Indigenous readers. As a settler scholar writing on a Haisla novel, my goal is not to speak for or interpret the Haisla stories of the B'gwus that Robinson incorporates into her novel; instead, in the spirit of the recommendations from Gregory Younging's *Elements of Indigenous Style* (2018), my goal is to let Robinson speak for herself by quoting from her lectures on *Monkey Beach*, titled *The Sasquatch at Home: Traditional Protocols and Modern Storytelling*, given as part of the Henry Kreisel lecture series in Edmonton in 2011. Her final of the three lectures is the most explicit in detailing her interest in writing about the B'gwus, although her first lecture is also pertinent because it deals with Robinson's mediation of "Haisla culture and the pervasive presence of popular culture," as Andrews writes (2001, 12–13), and sheds light on her use of Haisla sources in *Monkey Beach*. In the first lecture, Robinson describes learning about nusa, or the "traditional way of teaching children nuyem, or Haisla protocols" (2011, 43) through a trip to Graceland with her mother. Her mother, an avid Elvis fan, chose Graceland as the one place in the world where she would go if she could visit anywhere. In her lecture, Robinson describes her mother slowly going through the four Elvis museums and his mansion, telling Robinson stories about Elvis and his family in each room. Robinson explains, "in each story was everything she valued and loved and wanted me to carry with me," an experience she then refers to as nusa (2011, 12). As Rob Appleford notes, *Monkey Beach* is full of popular culture references; "Dynasty, Elvis, Air Supply, and supermarket tabloids" are but a few examples (2005, 88). In her novel, then, Robinson mashes up not only Canadian and Indigenous

Gothic tropes, but also popular and Haisla culture—a mash-up that reflects Robinson's life experiences, as her story about Graceland illustrates.

I read Robinson's mash-up *Monkey Beach* as a similar endeavor in nusa. She knew she "couldn't use any of the clan stories—these are owned by either individuals or families and require permission and a feast in order to be published. Informal stories that were in the public domain, such as stories told to teach children our nuyem, could be published—unless they had information people felt uncomfortable sharing with outsiders, such as spiritual or ceremonial content" (Robinson 2011, 31). As a result, much of her novel is inflected with her father's stories of the B'gwus. As her father taught her, B'gwus meant "Wild Man of the Woods"; he thought they "might not be ape-like creatures at all, but exiles who had been banned from their villages and had gone to live where they wouldn't be harassed and that it was loneliness and isolation that made them so strange" (Robinson 2011, 36). The B'gwus, or the Bekwis, are the best-known monsters of the Haisla territory; the Haisla Stewardship Areas describes them as "large, hairy creatures," which were "reported occasionally in the Q'waq'waksiyas shoreline area just above Bishop Bay, and for that reason it is known as Monkey Beach" (qtd. in Robinson 2011, 29). The chronology in their naming is made clear in the Stewardship documents: "these Bekwis have come to be called Sasquatches or 'stick men' elsewhere" (qtd. in Robinson 2011, 29). As I will argue, the similarities between Robinson's father's stories and the stories she shares in *Monkey Beach* present the novel's monster as distinctly Haisla. But it is worth noting, as Appleford writes, that the monster now known as Sasquatch is a "co-opted sign in settler culture" (2005, 88). As Robinson describes late in the novel, the B'gwus is "the focus of countless papers, debates and conferences," and his image is "even used to sell beer" (2001, 317). For Appleford, the B'gwus becomes yet "another example of popular culture to be catalogued with the myriad other examples in the novel" (2005, 88). What this means is that Robinson mashes up her father's stories of the B'gwus with settler signifiers of the Sasquatch. She reclaims the B'gwus from settler culture by showing that the commercialization of the Sasquatch is far more recent than the Haisla stories of the monster.

The stories Robinson shares from her father in her lecture focus on a man named Billy Hall, who had the last known encounter with the B'gwus in Miskusa, across from Kemano, in 1918. As Robinson tells the story, Hall "shot and killed [a B'gwus] by mistake, thinking it was a bear" before "escaping from the other B'gwus," resulting in Hall gaining special powers (2011, 35). He later had a mask carved to mark the event, and her father also had a B'gwus mask, similar to Hall's. Her father had known Hall when he was a child, and the result was that he had "an insatiable curiosity about Sasquatches for the rest of his life," seeking out elders to learn more stories about the B'gwus and commit them to memory (Robinson 2011, 36). Robinson describes her father as being "delighted" when she told him she would be writing about Monkey Beach, and "more enthusiastic than [she] was to get [her] to the sites he knew so well" (2011, 36). The care that Robinson's father had for these Haisla monsters comes through in Robinson's retelling of her father's stories in *Monkey Beach*, resulting in the reclamation of the B'gwus in Robinson's novel. And the stories she tells of the B'gwus in the novel are, very clearly, a retelling of the stories she heard from her father. She echoes her father's definition of B'gwus as the "wild man of the woods" in *Monkey Beach*, and the central B'gwus story in the novel is one that has clear similarities to the stories Robinson grew up with about Billy Hall (2001, 7). In Robinson's retelling, Jimmy's favorite story was about two trappers in the mountains near Monkey Beach; one of the trappers "heard something big moving in the bushes ahead of him" and after catching a glimpse of light brown fur, "thought it was a grizzly" (2001, 7). While the setup of the story parallels that of Billy Hall's, there is a difference in why the B'gwus was shot: in Billy Hall's story, he continued thinking it was a grizzly, while in Robinson's retelling, she adds a level of awareness, violence, and grief. The trapper encounters 20 monstrous B'gwus: "they were tall, with thick brown hair on their chests, arms and legs"; their "heads were shaped oddly, very large and slanted back sharply from the brow" (Robinson 2001, 7). When one growled at the trapper, the trapper "panicked and bolted back into the bushes, and they began to chase him" (Robinson 2001, 7). Eventually, the trapper is cornered at the foot of a cliff, and he chooses to shoot the leader of the B'gwus to escape. The other B'gwus "let out howls of grief," and the trapper ran (Robinson 2001, 8). In the morning, he finds his partner, dead, at the crossroads where they separated, and the B'gwus begin howling all around him, providing an auditory display of retribution for killing one of their own. That trapper, like Billy Hall, had an artist carve him a mask to commemorate the event, and Jimmy and Lisamarie's father, much like Robinson's, had a copy of the mask (Robinson 2001, 9).

Jimmy loves that B'gwus story because of its gruesome nature, and because of how his father performs the story for him: he howls when the B'gwus is meant to howl, he puts on his copy of the B'gwus mask, and chases Jimmy and Lisamarie around the living room after telling the story (Robinson 2001, 9). But Ma-ma-oo disapproved of their father's gruesome retelling of the B'gwus tale; she would interrupt his "gory descriptions" with "that's not how it happened," pressing her lips together "until they were bloodless" before leaving the room (Robinson 2001, 8). Her version of the same story was notably "less gruesome, with no one getting shot and the first trapper just seeing the B'gwus crossing a glacier, getting scared and running back to the camp" (Robinson 2001, 9). The two competing B'gwus stories represent, I believe, the different reputations of the Haisla B'gwus and settler Sasquatches. Ma-ma-oo dislikes how her son performs violence as entertainment for his children, because the B'gwus are, in her mind, an element of the natural world which incite fear due to a lack of understanding, rather than their own violence. In Lisamarie's father's story, the B'gwus are aggressive and violent Gothic monsters who chase the first trapper and kill the second, more akin to the popular understanding of the Sasquatch in settler society.

Reading these stories in conjunction with Lisamarie's own sightings of the B'gwus provides further credence to Ma-ma-oo's version of the tale, which aligns with the beliefs of Robinson's father; namely, that the B'gwus might be village exiles made strange by isolation and loneliness. Lisamarie has two B'gwus sightings in the novel, one as a child, and one as an adult. Her first sighting is when her family goes to Monkey Beach at Jimmy's request, and she catches a "glimpse of a tall man, covered in brown fur," who gives her a "wide, friendly smile, but he had too many teeth and they were all pointed" (Robinson 2001, 16). After she sees him briefly, he "backed into the shadows, then stepped behind a cedar tree and vanished" (Robinson 2001, 16). Her second sighting has the B'gwus "snarl[ing]" at her, but only after she almost hit him with her car (Robinson 2001, 315). Without the threat of violence, the B'gwus appears friendly, but prefers to stay hidden, out of sight from the humans who live around them. This reading also accords with the stories from Robinson's brother and father. In Robinson's lecture series, one of the final stories she tells of the B'gwus and Monkey Beach begins with an anecdote from her brother, who told her "about a white man who brought gorillas to the Douglas Channel and they escaped, and terrorized people until the winter killed them off" (2011, 38). When she asks her father if that was the reason behind the naming of Monkey Beach, he clarifies that the name is not due to settler interference or violence. As he tells her, "the Haisla name is Awamusdis, the beach of plenty," explaining that there are three kinds of clams and two kinds of cockles that can be found on the beach, cockles being the favorite food of the B'gwus (qtd. in Robinson 2011, 38). He then tells her another story of the B'gwus, in which they steal the cockles gathered by some Haisla campers while they are sleeping; when the campers wake up, they find their "shells sucked clean," along with "large and strange" footprints heading to the woods (qtd. in Robinson 2011, 38). His message is clear: the B'gwus are not associated with violence in Haisla storytelling, but rather they are reclusive creatures who live peacefully at Monkey Beach. Lisamarie's sightings of the B'gwus, along with Ma-ma-oo's story, reclaim the B'gwus from settler lore to accord with the peaceful depiction of the B'gwus taught to Robinson by her father.

A RECLAMATION OF THE MONSTROUS

In her work on Frankenfictions, De Bruin-Molé writes,

> traditional monster narratives normally serve a conservative function—after all, in most classic fictions the monster is destroyed and order restored—because the "monsters" are usually the heroes of Frankenfiction, their punishment is often deferred [. . . .] The monsters of Frankenfiction occupy an uneasy position, never fully embracing otherness, but also never becoming fully subsumed under the conservative authority of mainstream popular culture. (2020, 11)

Such an articulation of the monstrous corresponds well with Robinson's text, a novel that is filled with monsters occupying positions of otherness without becoming the traditional Gothic antagonists. Lisamarie, the protagonist of the novel, exists in a liminal place between the mundane and the monstrous realms due to her ability to interact with the spiritual world. Andrews writes that Lisamarie complicates "the usual Gothic pairing of dark villain and perfect heroine"; instead, she is a "protagonist who reflects on the nature and origin of evil through her relationship to the spirit world and [her] subconscious continually haunts her, forcing her to negotiate her supernatural connections and desire to be ordinary" (2001, 12). Indeed, Lisamarie's fascination with monsters stems from a young age, when she searched for the B'gwus with her brother at Monkey Beach on a childhood trip with her family. Later, she writes a school paper on the T'sonoqua, an elusive female monster in the Haisla tradition, who, in Andrews's words, "reflects [Lisamarie's] own marginalized yet crucial status within the community" (2001, 18). As a young Haisla woman in a settler society, Lisamarie holds a marginalized position, which is further exacerbated by her own liminal positioning between the mundane and spiritual world. Such a positioning is metaphorized well by viewing Lisamarie as the T'sonoqua. As Andrews notes, T'sonoqua "offers an alternative to the commercial fame of the male Sasquatch" (2001, 18); she is, as Robinson describes, "a dim memory," with "no conferences debating her existence," remembered only "in scattered campfires" (Robinson 2001, 337). Scattered campfires are significant here; in the final scenes of *Monkey Beach*, when Lisamarie has made her way to Monkey Beach and is speaking with her deceased ancestors, they are sitting around a campfire, encouraging her to rejoin the realm of the living as she demands that the spirit world show her what has happened to her brother.

Andrews is not the only scholar to see the monstrous in Lisamarie; Appleford also writes about the commonalities between her character and that of the Haisla monster (2005, 90). Importantly, "Monster" was the childhood nickname that her uncle gave her after a playground scuffle ended in the emergency room (Robinson 2001, 67). Although Lisamarie has always been torn between the supernatural and the real, literally seeing ghosts and monsters throughout her life, she becomes a supernatural figure herself by the end of the novel. Whether it be through her childhood nickname or through her association with the T'sonoqua, Lisamarie holds a liminal position between protagonist and monster, contributing to Robinson's redefinition of the monster from Other to natural. Destabilizing the binary of monster and hero helps to unsettle our reading of *Monkey Beach* as a Canadian Gothic novel, showing the impact of Robinson's mash-up. The many monsters of *Monkey Beach*—the B'gwus, the T'sonoqua, even Lisamarie—are not the villains of the story. Rather than being given a singular, monstrous villain responsible for all the violence and trauma in the novel, readers are invited to attend to the insidious details of settler colonialism that accompany much of the narrative: Josh's abuse in the residential school system; Lisamarie's aunt and uncle being sent to residential schools; and her uncle Mick's participation in the A.I.M. movement are all obvious examples of the impacts of Canada's political system (Robinson 2001, 365, 59, 141). The impacts continue to be felt in Lisamarie's generation, as evidenced when she is taken to the principal's office in grade school for refusing to read aloud from a history book that claimed that the Indigenous peoples of northwest British Columbia had killed and eaten people as religious sacrifices, or through her descriptions of the period of first contact between settlers and Indigenous peoples, what Lisamarie characterizes as the "great dying," when "whole families were buried in one plot" (Robinson 2001, 68, 82, 82). Robinson quietly includes these references to settler colonialism in her novel about monsters and death, and their full significance is only understood after it becomes apparent that the B'gwus is not the perpetrator of Lisamarie's familial trauma. The true monster is settler colonialism. The titular Monkey Beach is important not because it is home to the monsters responsible for Jimmy's disappearance and presumed death, but because it is a spiritual home for Lisamarie, where she can speak to the dead in order to better understand the causes behind her family's loss, causes which can be identified as the enduring legacy of settler colonialism and the residential school system in Canada.

REWRITING THE GOTHIC IN CANADA: CONCLUSIONS

Monkey Beach, with its haunted landscape and revised understanding of monstrosity, is a mash-up of Canadian and Indigenous Gothic. By writing the landscape as dreary and isolated from the rest of Canada, Robinson works within the tradition of the Canadian Gothic, in which the haunted

European castle is replaced with the haunted Canadian wilderness. This is, perhaps, why so many early reviewers were able to identify *Monkey Beach* as a Gothic novel, even after Robinson rewrote the second draft because, as she noted, it was "too moody, too Gothic" (qtd. in Hunter 2000). However, Robinson's presentation of the monstrous is more akin to Indigenous Gothic texts. Her monsters are not the antagonists of her novel: they are instead natural elements of the landscape who live alongside—and, in some cases, are conflated with—her Haisla protagonists. As a result, Robinson provides no easy answers to explain the suffering of her characters; instead of giving us the expected Gothic monster, she redirects attention to the only common element uniting the Gothic and traumatic scenes in her novel: the political conditions of settler colonialism, which continue to impact the Haisla people.

It is useful, at this point, to consider De Bruin-Molé's insight regarding the "transgressive *potential*" of Gothic mash-ups (2020, 201; emphasis in original), which can provoke us to question our previous readings of Gothic texts. Robinson's mash-up, by aligning with the Canadian Gothic tradition of presenting a "haunted wilderness" as the general environment of the novel, invites us to reconsider our readings of earlier Canadian Gothic texts. Rather than reading for the tired binary of settler hero versus Indigenous monster, we can read these books to better understand the colonial conditions that produced them. Because Robinson rewrites the traditional monster as a natural element, the legacies of the past—the political conditions that have resulted in the contemporary evils affecting Indigenous peoples—become the true villains. Here, De Bruin-Molé's argument regarding monster narratives holds true: monster stories are important "because the fantastical and the 'real' often bleed into each other" (2020, 8). It is not up to us, as readers, to decide if the B'gwus is real or supernatural, but this much we know to be true: those of us who remain silent in the face of settler colonialism, who allow its historical legacies to continue, deserve the label of villain in Robinson's story.

REFERENCES

Andrews, Jennifer. 2001. "Native Canadian Gothic Refigured: Reading Eden Robinson's Monkey Beach." *Essays on Canadian Writing* 73: 1–24. ProQuest.

———. 2009. "Rethinking the Canadian Gothic: Reading Eden Robinson's *Monkey Beach*." In *Unsettled Remains: Canadian Literature and the Postcolonial Gothic*, edited by Gerry Turcotte and Cynthia Sugars, 205–27. Waterloo: Wilfrid Laurier University Press.

Appleford, Rob. 2005. "'Close, Very Close, a *b'gwus* Howls': The Contingency of Execution in Eden Robinson's *Monkey Beach*." *Canadian Literature* 184 (Spring 2005): 85–101.

Atwood, Margaret. [1977] 1982. "Canadian Monsters: Some Aspects of the Supernatural in Canadian Fiction." In *Second Words: Selected Critical Prose 1960–1982*, 229–53. Toronto: House of Anansi Press.

de Bruin-Molé, Megen. 2020. *Gothic Remixed: Monster Mashups and Frankenfictions in 21st-Century Culture*. London: Bloomsbury Academic.

Burnham, Michelle. 2013. "Is there an Indigenous Gothic?" In *A Companion to American Gothic*, edited by Charles L. Crow, 225–37. Hoboken: Wiley-Blackwell.

Carpenter, Cari. 2017. "Pauline Johnson's 'As It Was in the Beginning' and Drew Hayden Taylor's *The Night Wanderer*: The Gothic Tradition in Canadian Indigenous Literature." *International Journal of Canadian Studies* 56: 47–66. Project Muse.

Castriciano, Jodey. 2006. "Learning to Talk with Ghosts: Canadian Gothic and the Poetics of Haunting in Eden Robinson's *Monkey Beach*." *University of Toronto Quarterly* 75 (2): 801–13. Project Muse.

Edwards, Justin D. 2005. *Gothic Canada: Reading the Spectre of a National Literature*. Edmonton: University of Alberta Press.

Gaertner, David. 2015. "'Something in Between': *Monkey Beach* and the Haisla Return of the Return of the Repressed." *Canadian Literature* 225 (Summer): 47–63. ProQuest.

Hunter, Jennifer. 2000. "Growing Up with Elvis and Sasquatch." *Maclean's*, 20 March 2000. https://archive.macleans.ca/article/2000/3/20/growing-up-with-elvis-and-Sasquatch.

Mulvey-Roberts, Marie. 2014. "Mashing up Jane Austen: *Pride and Prejudice and Zombies* and the Limits of Adaptation." *The Irish Journal of Gothic and Horror Studies* 13 (Summer): 17–37.

Northey, Margot. 1976. *The Haunted Wilderness: The Gothic and Grotesque in Canadian Fiction*. Toronto: University of Toronto Press.

Robinson, Eden. 2001. *Monkey Beach*. Toronto: Vintage Canada.

———. 2011. *The Sasquatch at Home: Traditional Protocols & Modern Storytelling*. Edmonton: The University of Alberta Press.

Younging, Gregory. 2018. *Elements of Indigenous Style: A Guide for Writing By and About Indigenous Peoples*. Edmonton: Brush Education.

Part III

MORE MASH-UPS

COMICS, PERFORMANCE, AND GAMES

Chapter 10

"The crawling thing within me"

Marvel Comics and the Return of the Gothic Body

Matthew Costello and Mary Beth Tegan

The self-censoring Comics Code, established in 1954 to preempt congressional regulation of comic books, banned unequivocally any "scenes dealing with, or instruments associated with, walking dead, torture, vampires and vampirism, ghouls, cannibalism, and werewolfism." The 1971 revision of the Code replaced the categorical prohibition with one defined by canon, permitting creatures of "classic," "high-calibre" Romantic and *fin-de-siècle* literature written by "respected authors whose works are read in schools around the world." Over the next several years Marvel Comics supplied a steady stream of Gothic bodies. These creature-centric comics melded *fin-de-siècle* Gothic monsters with the superhero form, creating a hybrid Gothic superhero that emerged from and reflected the cultural identity crisis of the 1970s. Abject *and* transhuman, the late twentieth-century Gothic superhero allowed readers to engage in a critical encounter with contemporary notions of masculinity. The first such Gothic superhero, Werewolf by Night, is a particularly rich example and therefore the focus of this chapter. Created by Gerry Conway and Mike Ploog (from an idea by Roy Thomas), *Werewolf by Night* (*WBN*) premiered in February 1972 as a three-issue feature in *Marvel Spotlight* (hereafter, *MS*), and achieved its own title by September, running for 43 issues and 5 "Giant-Sized" issues through January 1977. *Werewolf* was followed by *Tomb of Dracula*, in April 1972, and *Ghost Rider* (appearing first in *MS* 5, October 1972); *Adventure into Fear* 10 (October 1972) introduced Man-Thing; *The Monster of Frankenstein* debuted in January 1973, and Son of Satan in *MS* 12 (October 1973). The resurgence of Gothic bodies in early 1970s comics coincided with widespread protest against government foreign policy and the Vietnam War, environmental and anti-nuclear activism, youth resistance to institutionalized authority, and, most notably, the rise of identity politics in the civil rights movements of the 1960s and 1970s. The revision of the Code, replacing a categorical prohibition of Gothic creatures with a murkier borderline depending on "quality" and canon, exposes the medium's struggle to respond to a national identity crisis.

Emerging in an era of national confidence as the United States sought to defeat the Nazis, superheroes of the mid-century were mythic paragons of virtue, fighting with extraordinary powers "far beyond those of mortal men." With the defeat of the Axis powers and the obvious moral threat they posed, superheroes fell from favor; by the mid-1950s almost all superhero titles had been cancelled, replaced by crime and horror books that offered a "macabre and perverse vision of the heart of consensus America" (Costello 2009, 6). The Cold War consensus vanquished these more subversive narratives with U.S. Senate hearings into the comic book industry and the censorship of the self-imposed Comics Code paving the way for a superhero resurgence in the late 1950s. Seeking to capitalize on the renewed popularity of superheroes, Marvel debuted a new type of transhuman hero with the Fantastic Four in 1961. More humanized, with foibles and contradictions, these new heroes were less mythic but more relatable. Often cast as anti-heroes, some, like Spider-Man or the Hulk, were mistaken for villains. Their superhuman powers were gained at great personal cost—Spider-Man is culpable in the death of his beloved Uncle Ben, Bruce Banner gains strength but turns into the green-skinned Hulk, Matt Murdock is blinded but gains power as Daredevil.

The humanized anti-heroes of the 1960s, though popular, could not keep pace with the many challenges to the mid-century ideal of a nation defined by freedom, progress, and virtue. By the early 1970s, superheroes no longer had clear missions and morals, and their powers were insufficient to right society's wrongs. Iron Man's alter ego Tony Stark transforms his munitions firm to focus instead on "peace industries," a disengagement from the military-industrial complex and a tacit criticism of the Cold War ideology supporting it. Captain America becomes less concerned with external threats to America such as communists or Nazis than with internal ones such as organized crime, racism, and fascism, eventually quitting in the wake of Watergate's exposure of corrupt American leadership (*Captain America and the Falcon* 176, 1974). Green Lantern embarks upon a quest to find America after being confronted with his failures to address racial inequality (*Green Lantern* 76, 1970). The Teen Titans hang up their costumes after failing to save the life of a Nobel Peace Prize winner (*Teen Titans* 25, 1970). Even Spider-Man's power is not enough to save the life of his girlfriend (*Amazing Spider-man* 121, 1973). Lacking the moral certainty defining America's Cold War consensus and impotent in the face of contemporary problems, the 1970s transhuman superhero appeared to be exhausted (Lang and Trimble 1988; Pustz 2012).

The comics' tacit acknowledgment of their superheroes' outdated and morally suspect sense of purpose is given a postmodern twist in the metacommentary of Jack Russell, the reluctant star of *Werewolf by Night*. Reflecting on his lunar-enhanced, superhuman powers, Jack proclaims, "I'm not some idiot superhero like Spiderman or Daredevil—And frankly, I don't *ever* want to be one" (*WBN* 12:5). Raised in the shadow of Hollywood, Jack betrays a self-conscious sense of his own belatedness and the "has-been" quality of his narrative, renouncing the exhausted script of his pop-cultural precursors. Though groomed to take his place among the Los Angeles elite, Jack reaches his majority possessed by a "hysterical" feeling he attributes to becoming a "full-fledged hunk of draft-bait" (*MS* 2:4), in essence, the pawn of more powerful men. Rather than inheriting a stable position as a white, upper-class male, Jack suffers the trauma of the duality of his cursed identity. "Something was *crawling* within me, raging to be *released*, my mind felt dull and *hazy* ... the crawling thing within me *welled up*—and my vision suddenly *blurred*! Everything went *scarlet* ..." (*MS* 2:1).

The Werewolf by Night, whose traumatized body is both abject and transhuman, may perhaps be best understood as a figure of generic hybridization: the "Gothic superhero." Not only does his series incorporate three centuries' worth of Gothic matter, including ancestral castles, family secrets, and supernatural life forms, but he can be viewed as a cursed Romantic hero resurrected for the sociopolitical crises of the late twentieth century. Jack's struggle with his dual identity forms the primary plot of the series as he seeks to understand his family history, the nature of his "blood curse," and how to control his alter ego—all within the context of late twentieth-century challenges to white, middle-class manhood and the institutions that support it.

AFFECTIVE FORMS: READING THE GRAPHIC, READING THE GOTHIC

Despite obvious differences in their textual features and genealogies, the graphic narrative and Gothic novel are strangely compatible. Julia Round (2014) suggests that formally, comics share much with the Gothic. Like the confused time and uneven pacing of the Gothic novel, comics freeze action within a panel structure, fracturing time and space. Both deploy multiple perspectives, with the comic's editorial text boxes, solid word balloons, and jagged thought balloons functioning like the Gothic novel's embedded first-person narratives. The comic's nonrepresentational art strikes an artificial, highly saturated note, establishing an "aesthetics of excess" in its rendering of character and action (Round 2014, 59). This mood compares to the world of the Gothic in which "setting swells with nightmarish presence or recedes into sublime distance, but [. . .] is rarely handled with the subtlety [. . .] novel readers take for granted" (Haggerty 1989, 21). Characterized by "fragmentation and instability" (Haggerty 1989, 3), both forms elicit a strong affective response from readers, though the body horror of the Gothic novel is more suggestive than graphic (Aldana Reyes 2020, 394). Comic fans must interpret action in the space between the panels (the gutter) while both media require active readers to grapple with textual inconsistencies and "braid" discrete narrative threads. The shared formal elements identified by Round—fractured temporality, an aesthetics of

Figure 10.1 Fracturing Time and Space. Gerry Conway (writer) and Mike Ploog (artist). "Werewolf by Night!" *Marvel Spotlight* 3 (May 1972). New York: Marvel Entertainment. Marvel Comics™; copyright © Marvel Comics Group, all rights reserved.

excess, and textual indeterminacy—are necessary to achieve the "primary aim" of the Gothic, which "is the emotional and psychological involvement of the reader" (Haggerty 18).

The sympathy between Gothic and graphic narratives is evident in figure 10.1, a half-page panel from the werewolf's second appearance. Commencing his quest to unearth his past, Jack is captured by the sorceress, Andrea, whose tall, lithe figure is extended by her white-striped beehive à la Elsa Lanchester in *The Bride of Frankenstein* (1935). Andrea seeks the Darkhold, the spell-book of Jack's dead, cursed father. She is aided by her husband, a weak creature whose features are dominated by his pince-nez, and Kraig, a hulking, malformed servant with a metal hand. Kraig's abjection is reflected in the spelling of his name: the K substituted for C evokes rocky, barren landscapes and makes a common name something threatening, yet not quite other. Having escaped Andrea's prison, the werewolf battles Kraig on a craggy hilltop. Figure 10.1 presents the sequences in one formless panel, fracturing the flow of time and space as it "frames" three different perspectives. Kraig's shadowed threatening face dominates the upper left, his lone eye peering out at the reader. The image of lightning striking Kraig's raised metal hand fills a third of the panel from the right top. A silhouette of Andrea on a hill in the lower left suggests she oversees the action, while in the bottom right the werewolf rises as he absorbs all these images—apparently yet impossibly—simultaneously. Gothic elements—the celluloid sorceress, the cursed book, the abhuman servant, the sublimely lit hillside in a lightning storm—fracture reality, while the simultaneous presentation of sequential events fractures time, an act of "formal insurgency" that enables the subjective confusion of the Gothic encounter (Haggerty 3).

The stylized art and interplay of image and word demonstrate Round's aesthetics of excess, while the monster's terrifying gaze forcibly disrupts space and time and compels the reader to engage the text in affective relation. The reader's eye is drawn in multiple directions—the iconic film image, Kraig's eye, his towering figure, looming over the werewolf who shares for a moment our perspective. This threatening identification is relieved by the bottom right panel, which repositions werewolf and reader and produces an affective change. Witnessing the wolf's experience from a greater distance, the reader responds with greater objectivity and terror turns to pity. The fracturing of time, space, and perspective is wedded to a fracturing of identities, as the narration blurs the lines between man and beast, imperiled character and implicated reader. Jack refers to himself as "I" when registering his perceptions—"I felt my muscles," "I found myself"—but he ascribes his physical attributes to the wolf—"My wolf's teeth." This indeterminacy makes Jack's quest for identity a mirror for the cultural identity crises from which *Werewolf by Night* emerges, while the reader's rapidly shifting identifications effect their own subjective destabilizations.

I, WEREWOLF: THE MULTIPLICITY AND ABJECTION OF THE GOTHIC SUPERHERO

Marvel writer/editor Roy Thomas originally conceived *Werewolf by Night* as a story called "I, Werewolf," a title in which the cleaving of subject and object is more easily apprehended. While the later title evokes the hero's hybrid nature implicitly (by day he is *not* a werewolf), the original presents a more fluid subjectivity, with the comma establishing the contiguity between the enunciating subject and his other. Thomas insisted the story be told in the first person (Thomas 1974). Rare in superhero comics, the first-person narration works with other formal structures to emphasize the identification of Jack with his wolf-man persona. Consider the paired images in figure 10.2. The first presents the werewolf charging toward the reader and almost breaching the panel. "Why am I *here?*" he asks himself as the "dark dream" begins to slip, and he finds himself "waking" as Jack Russell in the second image, following immediately on the next page. This transformation is the first in the series, and it is notable that the first "I" we meet is the werewolf, who poses

Figure 10.2 Mirror Images. Gerry Conway (writer) Mike Ploog (artist). "Werewolf by Night." *Marvel Spotlight* 2 (February 1971): 3–4. New York: Marvel Entertainment. Marvel Comics™; copyright © Marvel Comics Group, all rights reserved.

the existential question that drives the series *before* his human counterpart. The images mirror one another; the werewolf and Jack are similarly posed, though the wolf's ferocity is met by Jack's terror. There is also the continuity between the text boxes, as the fragmentary sentence of the first is completed in the second, establishing a grammatical link between the fantastic "dream" sequence and the hero's "real" awakening. This confusion is heightened by the first-person narration of man and wolf-man, who assert their subjectivity almost simultaneously, effectively collapsing the binary of real/unreal.

Thomas specifically envisioned "a quasi-human werewolf of the classic cinematic mold with the kind of continuity which has made a certain Amazing Spider-Man a household word" (1974). The hybridity of the wolf is reinforced throughout the series as when, in defining the family "blood curse," Jack's mother warns it will cause him "to become a man-like beast" (*MS* 2, 18). The Werewolf by Night is neither completely inhuman nor completely human; described as feral, savage, and monstrous, the wolf-*man* is also partially clothed and walks as a post-Darwinian biped. Akin to the mutable Gothic bodies Kelly Hurley analyzes in British *fin-de-siècle* fiction—the "slug-men [. . .] beetle-women [. . .] fungus-people" (1996, 4)—the body of the wolf-man is "without integrity or stability," a form "rent within by [its] own heterogeneity and always in the process of becoming-Other" (1996, 9). As Jack's mutable body transforms, it is generally portrayed as an emergence from within, a "splitting" of the male body that parallels physically the lexical "splitting" of the signifier "wolf-man."

"Rent from within," Jack endures the "process of becoming-Other" on a monthly basis, a cyclical transformation in which the "the boundary between subject and object is shaken" (Kristeva 1982, 141). Jack narrates the "splitting" of his self: "Always it seemed as though my body became split in two—one half thirsting, urgent to get out—pushing out and through, until the pain became too great and I blacked out" (*WBN* 4:8). He acknowledges the "half" that urgently "pushes out and through," but once the transformation is complete, he denies the tie between himself and his alter ego. Often referring to the werewolf in the third person, Jack characterizes his second "half" as a completely alien entity. This transformation is portrayed visually across or within panels as physical stages of transformation. In "Eclipse of Evil" (*WBN* 25), the four-panel transformation scene is presented entirely in the first person: "spikes driven into my skull [. . .], my veins [. . .] my skin," but once complete the narration changes to the third person, as "the werewolf was free . . ." (16). Kristeva has described the process by which the "subject finds that the impossible constitutes its very *being*" as a recognition of its own "abjection" (1982, 5), and in Jack's painful rending, the werewolf is cast as the abject which "simultaneously beseeches and pulverizes the subject" (1982, 5).

But if Jack defines the werewolf as other, the text generally does not. Despite its portrayal as "savage and mindless," the werewolf's thoughts, often rational and task-oriented, belie the extent of his savagery, suggesting no clear dichotomy between human and grotesque. Aside from the description of Jack's physical transformation, there is also the first-person narratorial "voice" that suggests the werewolf's abjection is not the complete othering of his nineteenth-century predecessors. Jack may suggest the werewolf is a mindless, feral beast, but the werewolf is no mere collection of savage instincts. The werewolf's thoughts are often practical, reasoned considerations of his situation, where he identifies potential threats and strategies for achieving his goal, which is typically to evade danger and find a forest where he can hunt and move freely. And while Jack and his friends fear the threat the werewolf poses to innocents, and managing his feral savagery is a central plot device, on only three occasions are innocents actually injured: in the first two pages of his first appearance (*MS* 2), and twice when he harms his friend Buck (*WBN* 22 and 31). Most of the werewolf's actions are confrontations with supervillains, evil corporate committees, and supernatural threats, aligning him with the transhuman superheroes more frequently found in the Marvel pantheon.

Xavier Aldana Reyes argues that the shape-shifting of transhuman superheroes is generally positive, distinguishing their metamorphoses from the body horror of grotesque transformations, which are always unwanted (2020, 393). But Thomas's werewolf is at once transhuman *and* abhuman. The transhuman aspect of the werewolf's identity, a form of hybridity distinct from that of the wolf-man, is evidenced by the three markers—dual identity, a recognizable costume, and a pro-social mission—that Peter Coogan identifies as requisite for superhero status (2005, 30–60). Jack seeks to conceal his transformations from his friends and family, constituting a sort of secret identity. As shown in the preceding images, when Jack transforms into the wolf he sprouts bristly brown hair, rends his shirt, and splits his green trousers, a graphic transformation echoing the Hulk's. The dramatic bodily change and the torn green pants—worn always on the nights of the full moon—function as an instantly recognizable costume, while Jack's newly hirsute hide marks the onslaught of a monstrosity that is simultaneously heroic. Jack, though, rejects heroic identification ("I'm not some idiot superhero"), and his episodic narrative consists largely of searching for a cure for his lycanthropy, preventing his wolfish self from harming others, and protecting his sister from the same curse. Only when Jack fully inhabits his wolf identity does he *act* as a superhero. The werewolf's abject monstrosity is countered by his enhanced strength, speed, and flexibility, powers that allow him to stand at the border of the natural and the supernatural. Thus, the Gothic superhero's transformation manifests enhanced abilities that are used to protect humanity from the supernatural threats posed by entities ignored by science and reason, powered by lore and magic. Melding the grotesque "abhuman" and the heroic transhuman, the Gothic superhero defies rigid taxonomies.

As abject quasi-human hybrid, Werewolf by Night stands in critical relation to the world around him. Jarlath Killeen observes that the Gothic is a "kind of literary 'emergency,' mobilized to prevent the final loss of old forms and models of life linked to the pre-modern past, while also allowing its readers to grope their way towards accepting the new mode of life in modernity" (2009, 11–12). In his critical function, the werewolf differs from the Gothic bodies examined by Hurley, presented always as degenerate forms of humanity that threaten the proper social order. Noting the "escalation of the werewolf's monstrosity" from its Romantic-era origins (2002, 14), Chantal Bourgoult du Coudray attributes its grotesque changefulness to the projections of late-Victorian, middle-class Britons, who struggled to maintain an identity uncorrupted by "working class degeneracy, colonial insurrection and racial atavism, [. . .] and the bestial heritage" of post-Darwinian humanity (2002, 7). The cultural work performed by the werewolf and other late nineteenth-century Gothic bodies reinforces the status quo, preserving the established social hierarchies. In contrast, the 1790s origin of the Werewolf by Night's curse situates him within the earlier, subversive Gothic form that cast a critical eye upon society by fragmenting the knowing subject (Haggerty 3). Because Jack's transformation is an abjection rather than an othering, the werewolf functions to disrupt cultural binaries such as human/inhuman, civilized/uncivilized, and moral/immoral, revealing to society "that it *is* none other than the abject" (Kristeva 1982, 5).

"Repelled" by the "city stench" of Los Angeles, the Werewolf by Night consistently betrays an aversion to, or "embodied horror" of, the human characters he meets—a case of mutual abjection. Observing that "abjection is connected to repression," Aldana Reyes observes that it "can help reveal the subjective underpinnings of the social dehumanisation, be it governmental (systemic) or personal (a phobia or fear), of certain communities to the point where some lives may be perceived to be less important than others" (2020, 395). In the Gothic superhero's quest for a stable identity, he encounters a series of characters representing idealized forms of patriarchal power through interpolated tales. The mutual abjection of these iterative encounters and the use of the Hollywood dream factory as backdrop allow *Werewolf by Night* to challenge notions of masculinity, patriarchy, even heroism itself, revealing their artificiality and exhaustion amid the cultural identity crises of the 1970s.

PATRIARCHAL RUINS: IDENTITY, MASCULINITY, AND HOLLYWOOD HEROISM

Jack Russell's eighteenth birthday *should* secure him the privileges of an aristocratic background—wealth, status, and patrimonial entitlement. Yet upon reaching manhood he inherits nothing but a curse from his dead father and the knowledge that his sense of family history is dangerously incomplete. Amid his first lunar cycle, his dying mother explains to him that his father, Baron Gregory Russof, was cursed as a werewolf, a legacy that Jack, and possibly his sister Lissa, is doomed to inherit. Jack remembers his father as a kind, gentle man (*Tomb of Dracula* 18:2; 11), but his mother challenges his memory: "Did you know your father for what he was? A course [sic] rough man? A strong man—a fine man?" (*MS* 2:16). He will also soon discover that the stepfather he loathes, Phillip Russell, is his paternal uncle, another unsettling disclosure that forces him to reconsider their relationship, his lineage, and his own identity (*WBN* 12:19). Jack's ignorance about the men in his family is a constant theme. When he first meets writer Buck Cowan, Buck asks him, "Didn't you know kid? The man who sired you was a well-known European warlock?" (*MS* 4:3). Jack's ignorance is linked with his misplaced anger at his stepfather, and his confusion about his relationships with both underscores his identity crisis. The question "Did you know your father?" thus becomes an interrogation of his place within the Russof/Russell family, of his legitimacy within larger patriarchal structures, and of his epistemological ground. Lacking a comprehensible past to define his present, Jack begins an exhumation of his family's secrets while attempting to conceal his own.

Jack's identity quest is in many ways a classic Gothic plot, dependent upon found manuscripts (the Darkhold or Book of Sins), mysterious helpers, and a return to his family seats. In his first foray, he travels with Cowan to the "Island of the Damned," where the hereditary Baltic castle bequeathed to him has been transported stone by stone and reassembled off the Monterey Coast. Jack's birthright has quite literally been reduced to ruins, stolen from him by his trustee stepfather (who sells the property to protect the family secrets) and sold to Miles Blackgar, a mad scientist who is building an abhuman army with the help of his Gorgon daughter. Jack discovers there the Darkhold manuscript coveted by the sorceress Andrea (figure 10.1, *MS* 3) and once belonging to his father, the Baron. Having vanquished the Blackgars and recovered the Darkhold, Jack and Cowan turn next to Father Joquez, a former classics scholar who can translate the Latin manuscript for them. Father Joquez is now a parish priest who organizes farmworkers—a nod to the political realities of 1970s California. But his role as translator of the "unnatural" Darkhold concludes abruptly when he is possessed by the spirit of Aelfric, the Mad Monk contained within the manuscript (*WBN* 3:2). Aelfric's history is the first of many interpolated occult tales, framed intriguingly here through the werewolf's consciousness. The werewolf hears "spoken only in my mind . . . *his* words . . . and his memories" (*WBN* 3:7), an indication of his highly receptive and unstable subjectivity. Jack's Gothic identity quest continues intermittently throughout the series, taking him twice to the Transylvanian family manor, where the werewolf encounters Dracula, and Jack discovers a diary belonging to the ancestor first stricken with the family curse, courtesy of a female werewolf he rescued from Dracula's castle in 1795.

The origin of the family curse is elsewhere identified as the Book of Sins compiled by the Mad Monk, but this account links Jack's identity quest with late eighteenth-century challenges to long-standing structures of power and an *unmanly* form of embodied experience. Du Coudray has highlighted the "obvious parallel" between the lunar cycle of the werewolf and the monthly menstrual "curse" of women (2003, 64). Though associated with "renewal and fertility," the cycles of women are also demonized, and the werewolf's transitions are no less ambivalent. Introduced as a mama's boy who is close with his sister, Lissa, Jack is strongly aligned (and allied) with women throughout the series. Topaz, a love interest who is initially used by her adopted father Taboo to control the werewolf, is drawn to his "soul" and refuses to harm him (*WBN* 14:6). She grows close to Jack and his family and becomes a series regular, preventing Jack from doing harm in his lunar cycles with her mind-bending powers. As his inter-subjective connection with Topaz suggests, Jack's identification with women is strong. Yet his mother has long kept a dangerous secret from him, Lissa will become a were-demon who battles his alter ego, and his grandmother, a gypsy, tries to kill him before recognizing the werewolf as her grandson. Ambiguous "helpers" all, the women in Jack's life support his quest for self-knowledge while simultaneously reinforcing the insecurity of his gender identity.

Jack's masculinity is undermined even more at home by an absent father, a judgmental stepfather, and the family's nefarious chauffeur, Grant. The last is particularly threatening to Jack's manhood; he angrily tells his sister "I know he could lick me—probably kill me with his bare hands . . . but one of these days . . ." (*MS* 2:5). His impotence in the face of more powerful men is suggested visually, for Jack is depicted with defined pectorals but a very slim waist—a stark contrast to the barrel chested, muscular villains he meets. As the werewolf, itself lithe and wiry, he is often attacked by gangs of men, such as bikers (*MS* 3) or truckers (*WBN* 6), stereotypical hypermasculine foils to his more changeable gender identity. The desiccated notion of masculinity Jack confronts is linked often to the artificiality of his Hollywood setting. Handsome Jack not only sports with screenwriters and actresses, but also works periodically as a stunt man. The celluloid confusion of fact and fiction is evident in the first appearance of the werewolf, which is framed by this "old folk poem" (*MS* 2). "Even a man who is pure of heart and says his prayers by night, may become a wolf when the wolfbane blooms and the moon is full and bright." In actuality, the lines should be attributed to the 1941 film *The Wolfman*, as they are spoken by the gypsy woman Maleva portrayed by Maria Ouspenskaya. Priest notes that much of contemporary werewolf lore derives from Universal studios, and Roy Thomas (1974) notes that his idea for the bipedal Werewolf by Night is not related to actual werewolf lore. And Jack himself will refer to his transformation as "doing my Lon Chaney routine," referencing Lon Chaney, Jr. who played the cursed Lawrence Talbot in the same film. Trapped as much by the detritus of popular culture as his ruinous paternal legacy, Jack is arguably most free when he enters his dreaded lunar cycle.

Jack's quest for a cure follows the episodic formula of the comics medium in a series of interpolated tales, many of which involve confrontations with hypermasculine characters. Jack's own crisis of masculinity is directly linked to the narrative crisis of the superhero genre in the werewolf's confrontation with the Hangman (*WBN* 11–12), a brutal and murderous vigilante, whose morality is defined by 1940s Hollywood cinema. Here the connection between the abject human and an exhausted version of Hollywood masculinity is explicit. As a boy in the 1930s and 1940s, the Hangman absorbed a notion of morality defined by cinematic males from Tom Mix to Humphrey Bogart to John Wayne. His role models did not lead him to moral behavior, but to such excessively vicious and brutal acts that he was court-martialed for murdering Nazis. Rather than reform, he doubles down on his warped view of heroism, becoming a vigilante who sees himself as a hero, but who is, in fact, an abject human.

Figure 10.3 depicts the Hangman's history. In the first panel the boy is surrounded by his film idols, and is then shown as an adult, moving through a series of violent acts, his court-martial, and his rejection by legitimate protectors. In the last panel the adult shares space with the image of the brutal vigilante he becomes. Artist Gil Kane braids the images of Hollywood male icons with the vigilante, suggesting the abject Hangman is a direct product of outdated Hollywood notions of masculinity. More than any other portrayal of bankrupt mid-century masculinities, the story of the Hangman is a meditation on the identity crisis of the superhero genre itself. The Hangman perceives himself to be a superhero—he claims to be protecting innocents from evil while he engages in kidnapping, torture, and murder. Where the Hangman asserts his own superheroism, Jack rejects the role as "idiotic"—an echo of his generation's cynicism.

The werewolf's adventures bring him into contact with other Hollywood types representing a cartoonish and dangerous manhood including Atlas, a disfigured matinee idol seeking revenge on all associated with his disfiguration (*WBN* 22–23). In "The Danger Game" (*WBN* 4), the werewolf is hunted by Joshua Kane, a multi-millionaire movie producer and big-game hunter. Kane's rippling muscles and hypermasculinity contrast with wiry Jack. Ironically, Kane is defeated not by the werewolf itself, but by his own fears and the furniture of film fantasy. His home is a shrine to a movie production of the *Most Dangerous Game* (first filmed in 1931), including props, script, sets with the film title, and even a clack board. Overwhelmed by all

Figure 10.3 Celluloid Heroes and the Exhausted Masculinity. Marv Wolfman (writer), Gil Kane (penciler), and Tom Sutton (inker). "Comes the Hangman." *Werewolf by Night* 11 (November 1973). New York: Marvel Entertainment. Marvel Comics™; copyright © Marvel Comics Group, all rights reserved.

his movie paraphernalia, Kane mistakes a movie-prop bear for the werewolf and suffers a fear-induced attack. The very objects that prop up his self-image prove to be his undoing as his subjectivity collapses in the face of agential things. Grant, the boorish chauffeur, suffers a similar fate when he realizes in the heat of battle that the wolf-man is not costumed (*MS* 2). Practiced in the make-believe of Hollywood manliness, Grant initially assumes the werewolf is masked, just another, extreme, example of masculine posturing. But when confronted with the wolfman's abject reality, his aggression gives way to hysteria. Terror exposes the unreality of Grant's and Kane's masculine identities; confronted with the performative nature of their gender, they collapse into themselves, consumed by the hollow core.

This void at the center of their masculinity may explain why so many powerful men covet the brute, supernatural force possessed by Jack's alter ego. While Joshua Kane wants to harness the wolf's power for personal gain, Kane's brother seeks an assassin in the wolf (*WBN* 5). Cephalos in *WBN* 2 tries to extract the wolf's energy to prevent his own death, while the sorcerer Taboo attempts to use his energy to animate the corpse of his son (*WBN* 13–14). The mystic Rihya (*WBN* 6–7) seeks the werewolf's energy to charge a supernatural gem called the Bloodstone in hopes of obtaining a great treasure. To that end, he drugs and kidnaps Jack for his carnival's "fantasmagorical exhibition" where his lunar transformation will be ogled by craven spectators alongside other "curiosities," much like the carnival "curiosities" in Todd Browning's 1932 film *Freaks*. Trapped within his cage, "the beast's simple mind *reeled* in confusion: who *were* these strange humans who stood sniggering and jeering before him?" (*WBN* 6:15). It is the humans who are "strange" in this carnivalesque confrontation, an inversion of the abject that is punctuated by the alignment of our perspective with the werewolf's. When he grabs the barker by the neck, the spectators flee, "reacting with mankind's customary concern for the welfare of one's fellow man" (*WBN* 6:16). Notably, the most humane treatment Jack and the werewolf receive is offered by the carnival's giant, Elmo, another abhuman. Elmo is accused by the vicious lion tamer Mige of playing "wet-nurse" to Jack, whom he tries to soothe through an embedded tale concerning Rihya's quest to find the supernatural "outcast" who can evoke the bloodstone's power. All of the carnival's "curiosities" have been promised a portion of the wealth the stone will unearth, but when Elmo sees Rihya prepare to sacrifice the werewolf, he rebels, giving up his own life to save Jack's. Throughout the werewolf's adventures he will encounter brutal humans and humane brutes, a clear comment on his own character and on the culture held up for critique.

The werewolf is also sought by establishment men, including the police, whose Lt. Hackett is a particularly brutal and violent pursuer who seeks to become a werewolf himself. "The Committee" is a recurring group of Los Angeles power-players, who want to harness the power of the wolf for various nefarious reasons, including use of the werewolf's blood to give themselves superhuman powers (*WBN* 17–20). The members of the Committee are depicted in business suits, representing corporate power, and they meet monthly to discuss reviving "the flagging economy by any means possible, legal or criminal" (*WBN* 10). Their first plot depends on using the wolf to create a wave of terror they believe will enhance consumer purchases (*WBN* 10). In this he will join a legion of "trained freaks [. . .] encrusted with slime and moss reeking of dried wine and other fouler smells" (*WBN* 10:7) who are led by the whistle of former sound engineer Sarnak. They are dispatched to wreak chaos in Century City, where a young boy clutching his comics cries, "Wow! If only Thor or Spidey were here—*they'd* show 'em!" Alas, there are no superheroes in sight, and the police are ineffectual. Throughout the mayhem that ensues the Committee keeps its hands clean, relying on others to do their dirty work.

In *WBN* 32–33, the Committee hires the mercenary Moon Knight to capture the wolf to serve as their assassin. Yet in their final appearance, Moon Knight turns on the Committee to free the imprisoned werewolf. Moon Knight's rebellion is spurred by the recognition of the noble wolf's superiority to the men who subject him. Jack's sister Lissa scolds Moon Knight, accusing him of "selling [Jack] to filthy men who'll turn him into the murderer he's always feared he would become . . . the murderer he's always fought to avoid—even when it tore his soul in two." Staring at the werewolf in the cage, Moon Knight muses, "Just a beast [. . .] But at least a cleaner and more honest beast than you slimy slugs [. . .] a beast who fights only to be free" (*WBN* 33:15). Comparing the cleanliness of the bestial werewolf to the filth of the dapper Committee members, Moon Knight is seeing the abject reality of the categorical breakdown in the modern world. The capitalists who control the economy are dirty, filthy, grotesque, while the hirsute and wild werewolf is clean and honest. The episodic adventures of Jack and his abject alter ego, driven by their crisis of identity, present a sequence of mirrors for the broader cultural crises of the late twentieth century. The patriarchal figures who claim to protect and serve society are exposed as nothing but a series of conmen, grotesque caricatures of mid-century masculinity. And the very superheroes dominating this art form are defined as "idiots," appear as murderous vigilantes, or are altogether absent when needed.

IDENTITY RECOVERED AND EFFACED: THE DEATH OF THE GOTHIC SUPERHERO

Once Jack's past is exhumed and his sister made safe, he embarks on a new adventure that leads him away from the hybriding that rendered his abjection such a powerful critical lens. At this point in the series, he loses his Gothic edge, becoming a more conventional superhero with control over his powers. Charged by the mystical Three-Who-Are-All to stop Dr. Glitternight from unleashing a cosmic force that will destroy the universe, Jack partners with mystical super-sorcerer Brother Voodoo. Imbued with the spirit of Brother Voodoo's brother, Jack gains control over the wolf, the agency to change at will, and the ability to speak in wolf form. Upon defeating Glitternight and saving the universe, Jack becomes a pure superhero, while the wolf becomes little more than a powerful costume donned at will. Where Jack had once denied his own heroism, he now embraces it, and the rejection he met repeatedly as the werewolf is replaced by commendation. Lt. Northrup, the police officer who had long been investigating Jack tells him, "I've seen you act selflessly like a hero, and more of a hero than I've ever been" (*WBN* 41). Jack's next adventure (*WBN* 42–43) takes him to New York, where he teams up with Iron Man to defeat a supervillain called the Masked Marauder and his agent the Tri-Animan, and Jack observes, "As the werewolf I'm usually considered a monster, but this time I was on the side of a good-guy . . . Iron Man" (*WBN* 43:1). The two share a joke about what a policeman calls Jack's "effective costume," and Iron Man affirms the costume protects "his true identity" (*WBN* 43:17). No longer a Gothic hybrid, Jack has become defined as a transhuman superhero among other superheroes, even spending the night at Avengers mansion.

When Jack accepts his role as superhero and gains control over the wolf, he is no longer abject. He has adopted a defined identity; he no longer cries out. The wolf is now merely Jack in another form, not another aspect of Jack's being. Jack has, in fact, become just another "idiot superhero," stuck battling supervillains in an exhausted form. Rather than exposing problematic cultural categories through his liminal identity, Jack has been fixed in one of those categories. "It's been good meeting and teaming up with you," Iron Man tells him. "Same here, Iron Man. Maybe we can do it again sometime" (*WBN* 43:18). This will be the last solo adventure of Jack Russell, as the book is cancelled after issue 43. The Werewolf by Night now will only appear as a guest in other superhero books alongside Spider Woman, Spider-man, Ghost Rider, and Moon Knight (now a super*hero*), and the Gothic superhero becomes a mere bit player.

The Gothic superhero emerged to address the twin crises of American culture and the superhero genre. The adventures of a wolf-man—a hybrid created by splitting rather than the othering of complete abjection—allowed for an inversion of the abject relation and a critique of institutional structures of domination. *Werewolf by Night* offered a critical encounter with masculinity, patriarchy, and the exhaustion of popular idealizations of America. The tensions in the wolf-man as Gothic superhero created a fertile space for reflection as readers followed Jack Russell's quest to find his own past and future, encountering interpolated tales of abject humanity along the way. Jack's curse became a crying out for all who dwelled on the borders of increasingly ambiguous identity categories, his violent encounters, a mirror for the painful crises of 1970s America.

REFERENCES

Aldana Reyes, Xavier. 2020. "Abjection and Body Horror." In *The Palgrave Handbook of Contemporary Gothic*, edited by C. Bloom, 393–410. London: Palgrave Macmillan.

Conway, Gerry (w), and Mike Ploog (a). 1972. "Werewolf by Night." *Marvel Spotlight* 2 (Feb. 1972). Marvel Comics.

———. 1972. "Werewolf by Night." *Marvel Spotlight* 4 (June 1972). Marvel Comics.

Conway, Gerry (w), Mike Ploog (p), and Frank Bolle (i). 1973. "The Danger Game." *Werewolf by Night* 4 (March 1973). Marvel Comics.

Conway, Gerry (w), Mike Ploog (p), and Frank Chiramonte (i). 1973. "The Mystery of the Mad Monk." *Werewolf by Night* 3 (Jan 1973). Marvel Comics.

Coogan, Peter. 2006. *Superhero: The Secret Origin of a Genre*. Austin, TX: Monkeybrain Books.

Costello, Matthew. 2009. *Secret Identity Crisis: Comic Books and the Unmasking of Cold War America*. New York: Continuum.

Du Coudray, Chantal Bourgault. 2002. "Upright Citizens on all Fours: Nineteenth-Century Identity and the Image of the Werewolf." *Nineteenth Century Contexts* 24 (1): 1–16.

———. 2003. "The Cycle of the Werewolf: Romantic Ecologies of Selfhood in Popular Fantasy." *Australian Feminist Studies* 18 (40): 57–72.

Friedrich, Mike (w), Don Perlin (p), and Vince Colletta (i). 1974. "Vampires on the Moon." *Werewolf by Night* 19 (July 1974). Marvel Comics.

Haggerty, George. 1989. *Gothic Fiction/Gothic Form*. University Park, PA: Penn State University Press.

Hurley, Kelly. 1996. *The Gothic Body: Sexuality, Materialism, and Degeneration at the* Fin de Siècle. London: Cambridge University Press.

Killeen, Jarlath. 2009. *Gothic Literature: 1825–1914*. Cardiff: University of Wales Press.

Kristeva, Julia. 1982. *Powers of Horror*. Translated by Leon Roudiez. New York: Columbia University Press.

Lang, Jeffrey, and Patrick Trimble. 1988. "Whatever Happened to the Man of Tomorrow?" *Journal of Popular Culture* 22 (3): 157–73.

Moench, Doug (w), and Don Perlin (a). 1975. "The Darkness of Dr. Glitternight." *Werewolf by Night* 28 (April 1975). Marvel Comics.

Moench, Doug (w), Don Perlin (p), and Vince Colletta (i). 1974. "Eye of the Wolf." *Werewolf by Night* 20 (August 1974). Marvel Comics.

———. 1974. "One Wolf's Cure... Another's Poison!." *Werewolf by Night* 21 (Sept. 1974). Marvel Comics.

Priest, Hannah. 2017. "Like Father Like Son: Wolf-men, Paternity and the Male Gothic." In *Werewolves, Wolves and the Gothic*, edited by Robert McKay and John Miller, 19–36. Cardiff: University of Wales Press.

Pustz, Matthew. 2012. "'Paralysis, Stagnation and Drift': America's Malaise as Demonstrated in Comic books of the 1970s." In *Comic Books and Cultural History*, edited by Matthew Pustz, 136–51. New York: Continuum Books.

Round, Julia. 2014. *Gothic in Comics and Graphic Novels: A Critical Approach*. Jefferson, NC: McFarland Books.

Thomas, Roy. 1974. "Waiter! There's a Werewolf in My Soup!" *Giant-Size Creatures* 1 (July 1974). Marvel Comics.

Wolfman, Marv (w), Gil Kane (p), and Tom Sutton (i). 1973. "Comes the Hangman." *Werewolf by Night* 11 (November 1973). Marvel Comics.

Chapter 11

Misty, Mash-Ups, and the Marginalized in British Girls' Comics

Julia Round

Gothic has famously been described as "Frankenstein's monster, a collocation of materials drawn from other sources, bound together in a monstrous (dis)unity" (Otto 2013, n.p.). It is an encompassing mode of writing that absorbs and subsumes other genres and ideas: re-presenting them to us with a macabre edge. This often relies on some sort of adaptation, as existing texts and products are "gothicked up" (Byron 2012, 72). Famous recent examples might include *Pride and Prejudice and Zombies* (Seth Grahame-Smith, 2009), or the comic book series *Afterlife with Archie* (Robert Aguirre-Sacasa and Francesco Francavilla, 2013–present), which both disrupt their fictional worlds with a zombie apocalypse.

Comics are also known for their multiplicity, as many of their best-known stories and characters have spin-offs, adaptations, revivals, and reboots. The medium is multimodal: capable of sustaining many different communication channels, and digital comics may even bring in sound, virtual reality, or other enhancements. Stories may juxtapose or merge art styles, for example, combining photographs and caricature. Superhero stories often feature hybrid characters, team-ups, and multiverse franchises. Comics are also a collaborative medium, not just between creators of an individual title (writers, artists, letterers, editors, and more), but also in the sense that creators may work on a given title for a short time only: with the tale passing to someone else when they have finished their "arc." This means that the rights attached to comics characters and storyworlds have frequently been disputed, as publishers assert ownership of various properties. This approach to intellectual property encourages a sense of freedom and creativity but also practices of exploitation that align with the mash-up.

This chapter will analyze the British girls' supernatural mystery comic *Misty* (IPC, 1978–1980) to examine the ways that the British comics industry of the last century used mash-up titles, stories, themes, and characters. It first reviews recent academic work on Gothic and adaptation, noting how mash-ups and manipulation have been characterized. It then gives some background to British comics, explaining how both boys' and girls' titles followed the model of exploitation cinema by reworking versions of adult texts for younger audiences. It then moves to examine *Misty* more closely and discusses the mash-up methods it used, which ranged from superficial namechecks to the reworking and recombining of Gothic themes and stories. The analysis shows that while *Misty* sometimes used mash-ups and namechecks quite superficially to create an atmosphere of Gothic horror, in other respects it significantly reworked existing Gothic content into accessible and relatable storylines for young female readers. This dichotomy helped *Misty* to negotiate a line between conservatism and adventure (a requirement for all the girls' comics): disguising its shocking content under a veneer of acceptability and branding itself as a "mystery paper" rather than a "horror comic." It demonstrates the subversive potential of the comic book medium and the exploitative nature of the industry. These mash-ups therefore reveal tensions that underpin both Gothic and comic books.

CRITICAL FRAMEWORK

Gothic seems more popular than ever in recent years across multiple media. Mainstream television shows such as *Penny Dreadful* (Showtime/Sky, 2014–2016), *iZombie* (The CW, 2015–2019), and *Gotham* (Warner Bros, 2014–2019) center on horror characters and darker themes, often combining these with unexpected genres (the high school romance, the police procedural). Many established texts have also been given a monstrous facelift: the high school sitcom *Sabrina the Teenage Witch* (ABC, 1996–2003) re-emerged in 2018 as the dark and satanic *Chilling Adventures of Sabrina* (Netflix, 2018–2020) in which Sabrina Spellman's comedic mishaps are replaced by a pact with the Devil, cannibalism, sororicide, and insanity. While the adventures of a witch of course lend themselves to this sort of reimagining, other less likely Gothic adaptations have also appeared, like Tim Burton's *Alice in Wonderland* (2010).

Darker aesthetics and Gothic allegories are thus used to rebrand and remarket. Critics such as Fred Botting (2008) and Glennis Byron (2012, 2015) have argued that many contemporary texts are easily "gothicked" in this way (Byron 2015, 5), for example as "Clothes, puppets, masks, lifestyles, dolls, sweets, locate Gothic images in a thoroughly commodified context in which horror is rendered familiar" (Botting 2008, 9). Gothic becomes little more than a commodity or brand, and this claim often forms part of an elegiac argument that contrasts modern popular works unfavorably with older texts. Botting draws on the works of Baudrillard (1983), Lyotard (1984), and Derrida (1990, 80) to suggest that ghosts and other monstrous figures today are "recognisable, reiterated, familiar" and thus become "normal monstrosities" (Botting 2008, 10).

But for other scholars, such as Megan de Bruin-Molé, modern Gothic instead continues to expand and subsume, finding new ways to adapt and co-opt and even combine the traditions it exists within. One example of this is De Bruin-Molé's concept of "Frankenfiction," where works out of copyright are reworked into something new, such as *Pride and Prejudice and Zombies* (Grahame-Smith, 2009) or *Sense and Sensibility and Sea Monsters* (Ben H. Winters, 2009). These mash-ups are inherently subversive, capable of challenging the expectations and values attached to Gothic literature. Catherine Spooner's (2017) recent research also explores newer incarnations of Gothic, with adaptation and mash-up informing many of her ideas, such as the "whimsical macabre": a new mode of Gothic popular culture that merges carnivalized images of childhood with the "monstrous/cute." These often take the form of franchises modeled around particular characters, such as *Ruby Gloom*, *Emily Strange*, *Monster High*, and *Living Dead Dolls*. Traditional Gothic archetypes and tropes are blended with new settings or scenarios (e.g., *Monster High*'s fashion dolls include Frankie Stein and Draculaura). These newer Gothic forms seem to thrive on juxtaposition: Frankenfiction takes "classic" literature and inserts sensational violence or monstrosity; the whimsical macabre puts the cute and the creepy in dialogue with each other.

Value judgments also haunt the history of adaptation studies. Early debates privileged the pre-existing text and often used fidelity as a standard for judgment. However, later work from scholars such as Linda Hutcheon instead emphasizes the creativity that underpins adaptation, drawing on intertextual theory to argue that "adaptation is an act of appropriating or salvaging, and this is always a double process of interpreting and creating something new" (2006, 20).

Scholars may believe that modern Gothic forms are superficial and commodified, or alternatively might argue for their positive and creative attributes. But both critical angles suggest a disconnect between the "old" Gothic and the new (whether elegiac as in Botting and Byron's fears or celebrated as in De Bruin-Molé and Spooner's work). However, I wonder if this divide is more of a superficial scratch, rather than a deep cut. My own work has often drawn attention to Gothic's underpinning contradictions and tensions: since its early days the grisly genre has undermined simple divides and binaries. It blurs boundaries, is transgressive yet conservative, literary but sensationalist, attracts and repels, and finds monstrosity in both self and other. The mash-up's combination of old/new, its potential to offer the expected/unexpected, and, indeed, address the mainstream/marginalized accords with these dichotomies and will be investigated below.

BRITISH COMICS AND ADAPTATION

British comics were a vibrant and vast industry that dominated children's entertainment between 1950 and 1980: a survey by Fenwick (1953) reveals that 94% of 14- and 15-year-old girls read comics, and at its peak the industry was publishing hundreds of weekly titles, with individual circulations that could top one million copies (Digby 2017, Sabin 1996). There was a lot of pressure to produce content, and the relentless publishing schedule and small teams assigned to each title created a high-pressure set of circumstances that drove creativity through brutal competition. Two main publishing companies emerged: DC Thomson (a family-owned company based in Dundee, and publishers of titles such as *Beano*, *Jackie*, *Bunty*, and *Warlord*), and IPC, a holding company that swallowed up London-based publishers such as Fleetway and Amalgamated Press (responsible for titles such as *School Friend*, *Girl*, *Tammy*, and *2000AD*). There is a perception today that these comics were all very similar (ballet and boarding schools for the girls, war and sports for the boys) but nothing could be further from the truth. The breadth of titles was astonishing, with clear subgenres emerging at various points. For example, the first wave of British girls' comics (1950s) printed school stories alongside tales of adventure ("Kitty Hawke and her all-girl air crew," *Girl*) and expanded into multiple different formats, ranging from glossy color publications like *Diana* to cheap and cheerful looking comics like *Bunty*. A wave of romance comics arose from the mid-1950s and stretched into the 1960s (*Marilyn*, *Romeo*, *Valentine*, *Jackie*); followed by a more dramatic series of titles in the early 1970s with working-class protagonists and both urban and fantastic stories (*Tammy*, *Jinty*, *June*), including dedicated "supernatural mystery" titles such as *Spellbound* and *Misty*. The back-and-forth between the two publishers produced periods of intense industry growth as each tried to outdo the other by either releasing a similar title to compete in the same subgenre or developing in a new direction.

Adapting content from other media was common practice. For example, DC Thomson's *Diana* featured a full-color, licensed comic strip adaptation of *The Avengers* (1961–1969) in 1967 (#199–244, art by Emilio Frejo and Juan Gonzalez Alacrejo). These comic strip plotlines were original although had to be approved by the Avengers production office and sometimes ideas from the comic made their way into the television show (McGachey 2021). Other more subtle instances of reworking were also present. "The Girls from N.O.O.D.L.E.S." appeared in *Diana* c. #186–261 (September 10, 1966, to

February 17, 1968) (art by Phil Winslade and Geoffrey Whittam). It was about two young girls who are secret agents for the National Organisation for Order, Discipline and Law Enforcement in Schools: referencing the award-winning television show *The Man from U.N.C.L.E.* (1964–1968) through its dual protagonists, spy fantasies, and gadgetry (radios, homing devices). In both instances a high-profile contemporary television property was reworked with motifs suitable for younger female readers. For example, in *Diana* #212–215 (March 10–31, 1967) the Avengers pursue the jewel thief Black Heart and her Seven Dwarfs, who disguise themselves as children or teddy bears and use exploding toys as part of their robberies. Black Heart herself is a Maleficent-type figure with long cloak, high pointed collar, and heavily made-up eyes with arched eyebrows, even using "a special, closed-circuit television set in the shape of a crystal ball" (#214). "The Girls from N.O.O.D.L.E.S." replaces male leads with younger female protagonists "of outstanding character" (#187) and transposes the spy activity to more appropriate spaces for girls: for example they are dispatched to "The School for Adventure" (#187) and to investigate the mysterious leader of the Masked Ballet company (#260).

British boys' comics used similar tactics in some of their most popular series. Perhaps the most notorious example is the case of IPC's comic *Action* (1976–1977). This was devised by writer and editor Pat Mills to compete with DC Thomson's *Warlord* (1974–1986) following a previous attempt in the form of *Battle Picture Weekly* (IPC, 1975–1988). *Action* upped the ante by moving away from classic war settings into contemporary, urban stories with a heavy dose of gore and violence. Many stories adapted box office hits into comics format, such as "Hookjaw" (art by Ramon Sola, written by Ken Armstrong), which reimagined *Jaws* (1975) with the shark as an environmental anti-hero intent on eating corrupt criminals, and "Death Game 1999" (various artists including Costa, Ian Gibson, and Massimo Bellardinelli, written by Tom Tully), which stripped *Rollerball* (1975) down to its plot basics. These "dead cribs" (Barnard 2018) combined contemporary texts with a new slant and were extremely popular. In this they followed the model of exploitation cinema: an industry designed to create a fast profit and quick product by exploiting contemporary cultural fears (social problems, teenage rebellion, violence, and so forth). *Action* focused on many controversial subjects, from teenage gangs to football hooliganism, and this combined with the level of violence led to outcry in the press and on national television. The October 23, 1976, issue was withdrawn and pulped, and *Action* then continued in a much-sanitized form for the rest of its run (see Barker 1990 for further information).

Mills was also the co-creator of *Misty* (IPC 1978–1980), a supernatural mystery comic for girls that ran for 101 weekly issues alongside three holiday specials, and eight annual publications (1979–1986). It grew from his initial idea for a girls' horror comic that would be a vehicle for his serial story "Moonchild" (an adaptation of Stephen King's *Carrie*, discussed further below). The comic was passed to co-creator Wilf Prigmore to develop when Mills turned down an editorial role and it became a quite different comic than intended. This was doubtless in part to compete with DC Thomson's *Spellbound* (1976–1978): a creepy "mystery paper" that had taken over from *Diana* and contained a mix of supernatural stories (such as "The Haunting of Laura Lee" who becomes possessed by a ghostly musician), science fiction fantasies ("Supercats," about an all-female space crew; "Dangerous Days for the Tiny Taylors" who are shrunk by a strange potion), and investigative mysteries ("Whatever Became of Betsy?" in which a journalist tracks down an old schoolfriend she believes has been abducted).

Mash-ups were key to *Misty*'s conception. Mills's initial vision was "we should look at all the kinds of female adults' fiction that were around at the time, and do girls' comics versions of that" (Mills 2011) as this was a strategy that had worked well for him on previous titles. But in the hands of its editorial team (Malcolm Shaw, Bill Harrington, Jack Cunningham, and Ted Andrews), *Misty* became something quite different: a blend of supernatural mystery and horrifying cautionary tales, both present-day and historical, alongside regular slapstick comedy strips, and with a mysterious and alluring host who welcomed readers to each issue. The initial idea for a horror comic was toned down significantly, and it was branded as a "mystery story paper."

MASH-UPS IN *MISTY*

Misty was launched as "A great mystery paper for girls!" Other common cover straplines included ambivalent statements such as "Step into the unknown" and "Enter the midnight world," as well as the slightly more threatening "Stories not to be read at night!" But *Misty* relied entirely on horror and Gothic themes, as can be seen from examining its covers, story titles, and content. These often reveal a contradiction between its self-definition as a mystery comic and the stories and associated visuals which were quite often shocking and terrifying. For example, considering the entire collection of 101 weekly covers, 40% show a fearful reaction (wide eyes, screaming, running) and 36% show a hideous image (a skeleton, monster, or animal). Just 14% show an image of Misty herself, and 10% contain a benign or abstract image (horses, fairies). *Misty* was quite happy to overtly show fear on its front cover, with suggestive forms only narrowly outweighing explicit images.

However, the story titles pull back from these threatening references and mostly create mystery and suspense rather than outright fear. The majority tend toward the suggestive rather than the explicit, for example, by referencing a mysterious item without explanation, as in "The Window Box" (#93), "The Wicker Basket" (#63), "The Black Gauntlet" (#83), "The Green China Man" (Annual 1982), and so on. Similarly, many titles are puns or knowing references to the story's content, such as "Sweet Tooth" (#78), "Shadow of a Doubt . . ." (#58), "Run, Rabbit, Run!" (#64), and "It's a Dog's Life!" (#9). Gothic language (such as namechecking monsters, or using words such as fear, doom, darkness, death, evil, even magic) only appears in 28% of the story titles.

This meant that *Misty* was constantly looking for more subtle ways to conjure a Gothic atmosphere, and one way it did this was through its story titles, which often mashed up Gothic texts. For example, "The Four Faces of Eve" namechecks the 1957 movie *The Three Faces of Eve*, a dramatic treatment of dissociative identity disorder. The title of Pat Mills's serial "Hush, Hush, Sweet Rachel" echoes the movie *Hush . . . Hush, Sweet Charlotte* (1964), a psychological thriller about infidelity and a falsely accused murderess. It blends this with the TV movie *Sweet, Sweet Rachel* (1971), a pilot for a 1972 series about a murderer who uses extrasensory perception. "Whistle and I'll Come . . ," about runaway Toni and her ghost dog Albert, truncates *Whistle and I'll Come to You* (M. R. James, 1904; adapted for BBC in 1968). Although the titles might not be explicitly Gothic or horror-focused, they connote some quite strong stuff—death, murder, and psychic danger—by referencing big-name texts with Gothic, horror, and mystery overtones. This is backed up by other *Misty* content—there are features on writers like Edgar Allan Poe (Annual 1983), whose tales are recommended as "a 'must' for the *Misty* fan who has not encountered them." There are also feature articles on Dracula (*Annual* 1980), the Borgias (*Annual* 1980), and horror stars like Christopher Lee (*Annual* 1983).

Mills (2016) has spoken out repeatedly against the direction *Misty* took, particularly objecting to its use of one-shot historical tales, saying:

> the people who followed in my footsteps would look for the easy way rather than say "OK, well the reason Pat's done that Stephen King story is because there is a principle here that we can follow up on" so it would have been a natural thing for example to have other Stephen King stories and had a hotel, or a giant werewolf [but] they didn't want to [. . .] because it requires a commitment, you've got to sit down, you have to read a 400 page novel, in the case of *The Shining* or whatever it is, you've got to analyse it and then say "Can I make this acceptable for 11–12 year old girls?"

For Mills, adapting texts is not a cynical, easy, or convenient way to write—it is a process of hard work that demands creativity. This view of adaptation as an act of creation (rather than one of derivation where elements of the original are always lost) is borne out by scholarship and the success of texts that have taken their content in a new direction, such as those mentioned above, or other examples such as AMC's *The Walking Dead* (2010–2022, based on the comic by Robert Kirkman and Charlie Adlard) and HBO's *Watchmen* (2019, based on the comic by Alan Moore and Dave Gibbons).

Mills scripted five stories for *Misty* in total, of which two are reworkings of existing texts: "Moonchild" (based on Stephen King's *Carrie,* adapted into a film in 1976), and "Hush, Hush, Sweet Rachel" (based on Frank de Felitta's *Audrey Rose,* 1975, adapted into a film in 1977). In "Moonchild" Rosemary Black is a school outcast and abused child whose mother beats her. She discovers her telekinetic powers after a dangerous practical joke is played on her at school. Her only support throughout this is her friend Anne, and the discovery of telekinesis reveals a murky family history in which Rosemary's grandmother also had this power and accidentally killed her husband, meaning Mrs. Black was sent to an orphanage. It's soon revealed that her grandmother isn't actually dead, though, and while Rosemary tries to unravel this mystery, she is consistently bullied by school tearaway Norma and her gang. The story's climax is a birthday party that they throw for Rosemary, at which they give her mean gifts, a disgusting cake, spray her with paint, and blindfold her, causing her to fall off a balcony. Rosemary's reappearance rising into the air (figure 11.1) is pure Carrie—drawn from the bullies' perspective and with the menacing threat "You've had your turn. Now . . . it's mine" (#12, #13). As in *Carrie,* the building also catches fire (albeit due to Norma's smoking), but Rosemary's grandmother appears and saves the girls, although the strain is too much for her and she dies. Rosemary's mother leaves, her powers vanish, and she goes to live with her friend Anne: a new start, but "at a terrible price" (#13).

The rewriting directly reworks the key story elements into more juvenile forms, removing the sex, death, and gore. Rosemary's powers are unrelated to puberty; they are brought on by trauma when she is scared by an exploding chalk trick that is played on her. There is no competition over boys or hint of romance and no shower scene or bucket of blood—but resonances remain, such as when Norma's gang decide to throw a birthday party for Rosemary and begin chanting, "Shame! Shame!" (#9) rather than "Plug it up!" This preserves the animalistic bullying and mob mentality that are so disturbing in *Carrie*, and there are numerous other small nods to the pre-existing texts: Rosemary Black is an obvious antonym for Carrie White; gang-leader Norma takes her name from Chris's bully-in-chief in the De Palma movie; Rosemary has nightmares about being surrounded by flames with all her classmates laughing at her (#4); she knocks a boy off of his skateboard (#6; this is a bike in the novel), and Mrs. Black rants continually about the "wickedness" she is trying to save Rosemary from (#9).

Misty, *Mash-Ups, and the Marginalized in British Girls' Comics* 181

Figure 11.1 **"Moonchild" (*Misty* #1–13). Art by John Armstrong, written by Pat Mills.** Reproduced with permission of Misty™ Rebellion Publishing IP Ltd.; copyright © Rebellion Publishing IP Ltd., all rights reserved.

However, transposing this story into a girls' comic is not just a case of "tak[ing] out all the kind of sex and ultraviolence" (Mills 2016). Instead, Mills mashes up the common themes and motifs of girls' comics into the skeleton of *Carrie*'s plot. He has spoken about his other writing for girls' comics in terms of writing to a distinct set of formulae. These established story patterns included the slave story (about hardship and bullying, directed at a victimized individual/group that is systematically exploited and abused), the Cinderella story (an unlucky heroine in unfortunate circumstances), the Friend story (in which the heroine's desire for a friend is paramount), and the Mystery story (which could be as simple as "What's inside the box?") (Mills 2011, 2014, 2016). They are not unique to Mills's writing and often appear in girls' comics. Three of these formulae are recognizable in "Moonchild"—the bullying Rosemary receives creates the established structure of a slave story, where the heroine is subjected to increasing torment every week. Rosemary's desire for a friend and her relationships with loyal Anne and false friend

Dawn also underpin the story. Mystery is also continually present: first arising from Rosemary's powers, and once these have been identified as telekinesis, the mystery of her grandmother is introduced. Mills (2016) describes it as: "not just Stephen King but there was certain rules that could apply and this brings us back to the formula [. . .] all those kind of basic formula rules can just as easily apply to the mystery and the occult."

Mills (2016) also stresses the importance of bringing in his own experience, saying,

> you have got to find something of yourself in it. In other words you take a story like *Carrie* [and] say "OK, what can I bring to this? What works for me?" So I would have drawn on personal recollections of bullying or sort of mildly psychic events that I was familiar with personally [. . .] and I certainly did in the case of "Moonchild."

Here, personal energy and experiences are described as vital to engage readers and revitalize the adaptation.

A very similar process takes place in Mills's only other *Misty* series "Hush, Hush, Sweet Rachel" (art by Eduardo Feito). This retells Frank De Felitta's novel *Audrey Rose*, in which young Ivy Templeton comes to believe she is the reincarnated spirit of a dead child. The novel begins when Ivy's parents first become aware that a strange man is stalking her and believes she is the reincarnation of his daughter, developing into their acceptance of this supernatural event, a kidnapping court case, and ending in tragedy when regression hypnosis is attempted on Ivy. "Sweet Rachel" follows a similar pattern as Lisa meets the mysterious Mrs. Prendergast and then finds herself consistently lapsing into fugue states where she speaks and acts like a much younger child. After Mrs. Prendergast explains her reincarnation theory, the plot is based on Lisa's struggle to prevent herself lapsing into Rachel's personality, until ultimately Mrs. Prendergast dies, and the possession vanishes. As with "Moonchild," the sexual and unsavory overtones are removed (*Audrey Rose* is told from the point of view of Ivy's parents who have concerns about the motivations of Audrey's father); and Lisa is given a group of friends who try and support her through her ordeal (as well as a school enemy who consistently tries to bring these attacks on to humiliate Lisa). Whereas Ivy Templeton ends up dead in the book, Lisa escapes the supernatural and Rachel's control, and it is Rachel's heartbroken mother Mrs. Prendergast who dies instead (just as Rosemary's grandmother sacrifices herself in "Moonchild").

Mills was not the only *Misty* writer to use mash-up techniques in his stories. Malcolm Shaw was *Misty*'s editor for the bulk of its run and wrote many other girls' comics stories. His *Misty* stories include "The Sentinels" (art by Mario Capaldi, #1–12) in which Jan discovers a terrifying alternate dimension where Britain lost WWII and is Nazi-occupied, via a deserted towerblock building. This plot shares its alternate history setting of Nazi-occupied Britain with the film *It Happened Here* (1964) and perhaps also takes its title and scenario from *The Sentinel* (Konvitz, 1974; movie adaptation dir. Winner, 1977), in which protagonist Alison discovers that her Brooklyn apartment building contains the gate to hell.

"End of the Line" (Malcolm Shaw and John Richardson, #28–42) is about protagonist Ann, who is hunting for her father (whom she had believed dead) after seeing him through a tube train window as one of an enslaved force of Victorian workers underground. The setup is very like another existing text, the movie *Death Line* (or *Raw Meat*, 1972), in which missing people are being kidnapped by the cannibalistic descendants of a group of Victorian tube tunnel workers trapped underneath central London. As in the other examples discussed, there are some namechecks referencing the movie—the catchphrase "Mind the Doors" appears at the cliff-hanger end of #29, and the dramatic curving shapes of panels evoke endless tube tunnels (#31), just like in the film. However (and in counterpoint to the near-complete removal of violence in "Moonchild"), some fairly brutal images remain in the comic: we see starving and impoverished workers (#28, being whipped by foremen in #29) plus the threat of violence with workman's tools like a hammer (#31), which again both recall the movie. Ann's investigative role also parallels the movie, which has a female lead who becomes obsessed with the fate of a man found collapsed in the subway after his body disappears.

However, whereas "Moonchild" and "Sweet Rachel" both follow a very similar plot to their equivalents, "End of the Line" departs swiftly from the scenario of *Death Line*. After Ann becomes convinced her father is still alive, she learns about an older tunnel collapse in the same place. She shares her suspicions with reporters (who are abducted by the underground dwellers when they investigate) and then must constantly try and prove she isn't crazy while struggling to stop her mother marrying again. She escapes from therapists and sanatoriums, and follows the mystery to Vicary Hall, whose owner built the underground lines and was also a scientist who thought he had discovered the secret to eternal life. She enters the tube tunnels, infiltrates his underground village of laborers, is caught but allowed to stay on as a maid and makes friends with another child worker, Lucy. Ultimately, Ann convinces Lucy to help her rescue her Dad and although this plan fails, they are saved by the police with Lord Vicary killed in the process. The workers are sent to an island to be rehabilitated, Anne promises to keep it all a secret, and her father returns home.

In "End of the Line," then, a completely new plot is grafted onto the scenario of lost Victorian workers trapped underground. Like the Mills adaptations, we can see the girls' comics story formula being applied here: the mystery is introduced early and baffling developments drive each installment forward, and Ann's friendship with Lucy underpins the second half of the story. It therefore works similarly as a mash-up between an existing classic horror text and the themes/formulae of girls' comics—foregrounding two additional features. These are firstly the isolated heroine, as nobody believes Ann. She must investigate on her own and is repeatedly disbelieved and thwarted, for example the reporters who support her vanish (#31), and her mother and boyfriend have her sedated (#33) and take her to a psychiatric hospital (#32). As Ann says, "I can't go on having everyone think I'm either crazy or a clever liar!" (#31) and "You don't understand . . . none of you . . ." (#33).

This mash-up plot also emphasizes a second theme common to British girls' comics—that of parental mistrust. Ann's mother's boyfriend, Neville Chandler, is drawn as an unappealing bald fat man, and his thoughts reveal he is only interested in marrying into the family for their money. This accords with the common treatment of male characters in *Misty*, who appear most often as antagonists. There are no male protagonists and only a few stories have brothers, male friends, or other positive male figures. Fathers, stepfathers, and grandfathers are present, but their roles are quite variable, and they are often lying to the protagonist about something, or complicit in some sort of bigger deception ("Roots" [#1], "The Family" [#6]). They are also often representatives of institutional authority, like doctors or scientists ("The Secret World of Sally Maxwell" [#48–60], "The Silver Racer-Back" [#83–91]). Alternatively (and mainly in the historical tales) they may represent this sort of patriarchal power through social status, such as the cruel landowner in "Sure-Footed . . . to Eternity" (#3), the murderous Squire in "The Last Hunt" (#95), or Sir Mortimer in "Violets in the Moonlight" (#62), who unwittingly rejects his own daughter. Lord Vicary's enslavement of his workforce and his brutal treatment of them echoes this stereotyping.

This type of Gothic mash-up features often in the *Misty* serials but also appears occasionally in the one-off stories, where we might see fairy tales like "The Red Shoes" or "Red Riding Hood" being reworked. In "Danse Macabre" (#52, art by María Barrera Castell), Lois and Nadia are competing for the lead role in a ballet. Nadia cheats to get the role and steals their mistress's famous ballet shoes, but when she wears them, she is compelled to dance unendingly with a skeletal partner and chorus until she collapses. There are clear echoes of Hans Christian Andersen's "The Red Shoes" (1845) in which Karen buys a pair of red shoes against her guardian's wishes and is cursed to dance relentlessly until she dies. Like the other mash-ups, we have a recognizable Gothic motif (the cursed object), which is merged with the common themes and setups of girls' comics. The ballet setting provides the catalyst for the theft of the shoes, and like other stories the two characters are clearly marked as heroine and villain in both speech and action (figure 11.2). While Lois modestly muses "I'd so love to be the star of the show, but I'm not sure I'm a better dancer than Nadia," the other girl thinks "I've gotta make sure that little drip Lois doesn't get the part. I know I'm the best and I've gotta let the rest of the world know I am!" Nadia's thoughts are marked by lower-class slang and selfish arrogance. This is reinforced later in the story, both when she steals the shoes ("Stupid old trout. She didn't see me pinch her keys") and when she begins to dance ("I'm on stage. The centre of attention. All eyes watching me").

Mel Gibson's analysis of girls' comics and reader memory points out that "Parental disapproval and intervention in girlhood reading was largely based around issues of class and 'proper' femininity" (2013, 126) and that characters modeled important feminine qualities such as humility and "not showing off" (2010, 127). "Danse Macabre" reinforces this message as Nadia's

Figure 11.2 "Danse Macabre" (*Misty* #52). Art by María Barrera Castell, writer unknown. Reproduced with permission of Misty™ Rebellion Publishing IP Ltd.; copyright © Rebellion Publishing IP Ltd., all rights reserved.

behavior is motivated by arrogance and marked by lower-class speech patterns (even though the story's plot suggests she is richer than Lois who doesn't have a telephone and so must rely on Nadia to relay a message about the audition, which she lies about). The story's artwork also emphasizes this divide, and the characters are juxtaposed when they first appear (figure 11.2). Lois has short tousled blonde hair and freckles and outside of ballet is plainly dressed in a midi skirt (past the knee) and long-sleeved blouse—representing simple and unpolished femininity. Nadia has dramatic long black hair that is worn up with a few artful curls, made-up eyes, and wears patterned clothes and trousers—she has worked to enhance her appearance, and her clothes suggest a dynamic and rebellious attitude. So rather than sticking with the original tale's moral message of obedience and religious humility (as an angel curses Karen to dance ceaselessly), the story's plot instead rewards selflessness and personal modesty, and punishes selfish dishonesty: mashing up a dark fairy tale trope with a contemporary setting and established set of cultural messages.

The cursed shoes are also a good example of "commodity Gothic," which draws on the uncanny elements of commodity fetishization to depict objects that are able to wreak historical vengeance and reveal their own hidden grotesque origins (Lootens 2013, 132–3). These sorts of magical items litter the pages of *Misty*: 40% of its stories have some sort of external magic catalyst (an object, a magical charm or curse, or a haunted place) whose effect might be positive or negative (see Round 2019, 165). For example, a box of paints allows the finder to create haunting pictures that resolve a family mystery and right a wrongful death ("Paint it Black," #1–18); an evil car possesses its owner to relive its past as a gangster getaway car ("Journey into Fear," #14–27); and a stolen clock requires its new owner to wind it forever ("Slave of Time," #55). These examples all use mash-up tactics to blend the Gothic trope of the uncanny object with settings and temptations that are familiar and relatable to a younger audience.

CONCLUSION

The *Misty* mash-ups bring older texts into dialogue with younger concerns, creating tales that conjure a Gothic atmosphere but are also familiar and relatable to a younger audience. Existing stories are edited down and reshaped into allegories for the concerns of young female readers (friendship, bullying, isolation), with classic Gothic motifs or setups welded to the familiar plots, characters, and messages of British girls' comics. By reworking established Gothic forms into accessible and relatable tales for young female readers, the *Misty* stories negotiate a line between conservatism and adventure, disguising their horror content under a veneer of acceptability that looks back to prose story papers and the literary Gothic. They also foreground the concerns of girlhood, which are frequently marginalized and ignored, and whose literature and tastes are often denigrated. Ormrod (2011), Priest (2011), Spooner (2017), and Buckley (2018) all draw attention to the ways in which Gothic scholarship has historically devalued female creators, readers, and characters. My work on *Misty* continually seeks to illuminate and reclaim these stories, which were abundantly popular but today are critically underexplored and mostly forgotten—despite the ongoing and increasing presence of overtly Gothic material in literature for young female readers.

The mash-up subverts expectations of motifs, characters, and plots that we think we know. It revels in a juxtaposition of creativity and copying, exposing a tension between Romantic and collaborative views of authorship. This tension seems particularly applicable to comics, which has often been perceived as a subversive medium (caricature, political cartooning, working-class origins), but has frequently operated as an exploitative industry (creator rights, intellectual property, work for hire). By blurring these boundaries, the *Misty* mash-ups foreground tensions that underpin both Gothic and comics.

REFERENCES

Barker, Martin. 1990. *Action: The Story of a Violent Comic*. London: Titan Books.

Barnard, Steve. 2018. "Hook Jaw Omnibus by Pat Mills." Review of *Hook Jaw Omnibus*, by Pat Mills. *Finalguys.com*, June 7, 2018. https://finalguys.com/2018/06/07/hook-jaw-omnibus-by-pat-mills/. Accessed May 21, 2021.

Baudrillard, Jean. 1983. *Simulations*. New York: Semiotexte.

Botting, Fred. 2008. *Limits of Horror: Technology, Bodies, Gothic*. Manchester: Manchester University Press.

de Bruin-Molé, Megan. 2020. *Gothic Remixed: Monster Mashups and Frankenfictions in 21st-Century Culture*. London: Bloomsbury.

Buckley, Chloé. 2018. *Twenty-First Century Children's Gothic*. Edinburgh: Edinburgh University Press.

Byron, Glennis. 2012. "Gothic, Grabbit and Run: Carlos Ruiz Zafón and the Gothic Marketplace." In *The Gothic in Contemporary Literature and Culture: Pop Goth*, edited by Justin D. Edwards and Agnieszka Soltysik Monnet, 71–83. Oxford: Routledge.

———. 2015. "Introduction." In *Globalgothic*, edited by Glennis Byron, 1–10. Manchester: Manchester University Press.

Derrida, Jacques. 1990. "Some Statements and Truisms About Neologisms, Newisms, Postisms, Parasitisms, and Other Small Seismisms." In *The States of 'Theory': History, Art, and Critical Discourse*, edited by David Carroll, 63–94. New York: Columbia University Press.

Digby, Anne. 2017. Personal correspondence with Julia Round. Conducted by email, August 11, 2017.

Fenwick, L. 1953. "Periodicals and Adolescent Girls." *Studies in Education* 2 (1): 27–45.

Gibson, Mel. 2010. "What Bunty Did Next: Exploring Some of the Ways in Which the British Girls' Comic Protagonists Were Revisited and Revised in Late Twentieth-Century Comics and Graphic Novels." *Journal of Graphic Novels and Comics* 1 (2): 121–35.

———. 2015. *Remembered Reading*. Leuven, Belgium: Leuven University Press.

Hutcheon, Linda. 2006. *A Theory of Adaptation*. London: Routledge.

Lootens, Tricia. 2013. "Commodity Gothicism." In *The Encyclopedia of the Gothic*, edited by William Hughes, David Punter, and Andrew Smith, 132–35. Oxford: Wiley-Blackwell.

Lyotard, Jean-Francois. 1984. *The Postmodern Condition*. Translated by Geoff Bennington and Brian Massumi. Manchester: Manchester University Press.

McGachey, Daniel. 2021. Facebook comment. https://www.facebook.com/julia.round.98/posts/4075314185869515?comment_id=4075521929182074&reply_comment_id=4075534842514116&notif_id=1621513197974647&notif_t=comment_mention&ref=notif. Accessed 26 May 2021.

Mills, Pat. 2011. "Interview with Jenni Scott." FA – The Comiczine. http://comiczine-fa.com/interviews/pat-mills. Accessed October 26, 2020.

———. 2014. "THE FORMULA Part 1—Inspiration." Blog post. *Millsverse*, October 20, 2014. https://www.millsverse.com/formula1-inspiration. Accessed February 29, 2021.

———. 2016. Personal interview with Julia Round. Conducted by Skype, July 28, 2016. https://www.juliaround.com.

Otto, Peter. 2013. "Gothic Echoes/Gothic Labyrinths," sec. 9 of "Introduction." *Gothic Fiction: Rare Printed Works from the Sadleir-Black Collection of Gothic Fiction at the Alderman Library, University of Virginia*, 11–57. Marlborough: Adam Matthew Publications. https://minerva-access.unimelb.edu.au/bitstream/handle/11343/34575/67174_00003015_01_Otto002.pdf?sequence=1. Accessed April 18, 2021.

Ormrod, Joan. 2011. "Pa/trolling the Borders of the Federal Vampire and Zombie Agency Website." In *Fanpires: Audience Consumption of the Modern Vampire*, edited by Gareth Schott and Kirstine Moffat, 33–54. Washington, DC: New Academia Publishing.

Priest, Hannah. 2011. "What's Wrong with Sparkly Vampires?" *The Gothic Imagination*, July 20, 2011. http://www.gothic.stir.ac.uk/guestblog/whats-wrong-with-sparkly-vampires. Accessed February 27, 2021.

Sabin, Roger. 1996. *Comics, Comix and Graphic Novels*. London: Phaidon Press.

Spooner, Catherine. 2017. *Post-Millennial Gothic: Comedy, Romance and the Rise of Happy Gothic*. London: Bloomsbury.

Chapter 12

Mashing Up Magick
Bizarre Magick and the Fuzzy Gothic
Nik Taylor

> On the appointed night the audience find themselves seated around a table. The windows of the room are curtained, the door is locked and low, rather strange music can be heard in the room. Perfumed smoke rises from several sticks of smouldering incense and the room is illuminated by candlelight. There is an air of nervous expectancy, even those who really don't believe in the supernatural find themselves being strangely affected. (Cameron 1967)

So begins Charles Cameron's darkly Gothic performance magic routine *Voices from the Dead*, a routine that claims to draw upon "the strange and forbidden lore of the Black Arts" to contact the spirits of the deceased. Magicians such as Cameron believed that through mashing up the recognizable trappings of the popular Gothic, they could transform what would have been traditional performance magic effects into pieces of Gothic magic. We see in *Voices from the Dead*, the magician leading participants through a series of ritual offerings and incantations. Participants choose tarot cards, are asked to inscribe geometric shapes, record the name of a dead person, and write down questions to which they seek answers. All of these choices, hidden from the magician, are revealed during the climax of the ritual by a mysterious disembodied voice which speaks in "deep, ghostly tones" that resonate throughout the ritual space (Cameron 1967, 35). In terms of procedure, this experience could have easily been performed as a traditional multi-phase routine for a stage magician; however, it has been carefully reframed by Cameron into an intimate piece of Gothic performance magic, or as this genre would later be named, bizarre magick.

This routine or, more accurately in magician parlance, this "effect," was first published in the magician only periodical *The Cauldron* in 1967. Later, as bizarre magick became more popular as a form, Cameron revised the effect as *Voice from the Tomb* for his work *Devil's Diary* (1976). In this version, he chose to further emphasize the uncanny setting of the séance parlor by describing a heavily curtained room, illuminated only by three black candles, with the props used in the routine changed into a small ivory skull, an Eastern coin, and a tiny shrunken head (Cameron 1976, 33–7). In his earlier publication *Handbook of Horror* (1971) Cameron had described the philosophy of this type of "weird magic" explaining that it should only be performed "under the proper conditions" and only when "a suitable atmosphere has been created," the combination of which will allow "critical faculties [to] become suspended and age old beliefs take over" (Cameron 1971, 7). Cameron continued to develop this approach to performance magic, declaring in the first issue of *Invocation*, a quarterly magazine devoted to weird and bizarre magick which ran from 1974 to 1978, that the "average magician has long since given up dread [and] requires [. . .] *a sound Gothic revival!*" [my emphasis] (Cameron 1974, 1)

It is the Gothic revival of performance magic as bizarre magick that will be my focus. I will examine how bizarre magicians mashed up elements of the Gothic to shape a practice that was a dynamic, if rather dark, underground alternative to contemporary performance magic. For these magicians, this revival of magic drew from the Gothic's ability to facilitate the exploration of "borderline states of being [. . .] spirits, ghosts and demons and necromancy" (Bloom 2020, 13). Bizarre magicians used Gothic themes and texts to create new modes of presentation that were able to revitalize a performance magic that they saw as tired and disenchanted. As bizarre magician Tony Andruzzi observed, "in Magick, one will see no fountains of silk or flipover boxes painted garishly with ersatz hieroglyphs" (Andruzzi 1977). At its core, bizarre magick was a reaction against established popular tropes of performance magic; garish props, printed plaques, comedy, and presenting magic as tricks or puzzles had no place in the form. The aim was, as Eugene Burger suggests in his article "A Magazine in Search of a Mage," to elicit the "rediscovery of presentation" (1986a). In doing so, bizarre magicians would mash up and remix their effects to present a vibrant form of Gothic magic(k). The themes within these mash-ups are a kind of fuzzy Gothic in that they invite wide interpretation and allow for the provision of a "rich tapestry of material, which can be recognised as broadly Gothic in the popular sense" (Taylor 2015, 163). I am suggesting here that within bizarre magick there is a process of mashing up a broad range of material that has become associated with the Gothic for the purposes of the magician *playing* the Gothic. This might include, for example, borrowing from rich, popular notions of Dracula(s) that go beyond the original novel and include elements drawn from subsequent adaptations such as the Hammer Horror films (Taylor and Nolan 2015, 131–2).

MAGIC AS MASH-UP AND THE FUZZY GOTHIC

Before moving on to discuss examples of the mashed-up Gothic in bizarre magick, it is important to acknowledge that magicians, in the creation of their act, their persona, and the workings of their effects, have always been experts in mash-up. Thus, while Simon During states that the "magic assemblage" may have popularized "new technologies and new sorts of pleasures" (2002, 1), it is important to remember that this form of entertainment ultimately was, and still is, the most deceptive form of show business. Equally, there is a tacit acceptance of this deception in an audience; as James W. Cook quotes P. T. Barnum: "the public appears to be disposed to be amused even when they are conscious of being deceived" (Cook 2001, 16). Therefore, historically, many of the new technologies and new pleasures that were performed were carefully crafted falsehoods aimed at using mashed-up sources to create further falsehoods. So, while the father of modern conjuring Jean Robert-Houdin's "Ethereal Suspension" claimed to reveal the hitherto unknown properties of the newly discovered ether, it was in fact a magic trick using mashed-up tropes from popular science with appropriated themes drawn from the popular "illustrated lecture" model. Chung Ling Soo, the world-renowned Chinese magician remembered today for being fatally wounded when his bullet-catch effect failed, was in reality American magician William Robinson (1861–1918). Robinson mashed up notions of the Mystic East in order to pull off his "glorious deception" (Steinmeyer 2005) and present a performance persona of the kind identified previously by John Nevil Maskylne as "oriental jugglery" (Weatherly and Maskelyne 1891, 153). Equally, as Michael Mangan says of Houdini, perhaps one of the most famous characters in performance magic: "Houdini made up his own legends, weaving together fact and fantasy to create an illusory figure who became in many ways more real than the historical Ehrich Wiess who first invented him" (2007, 140). Without laboring the point too much here, magicians have throughout history relied on mashing up many sources to produce credible archetypes for both their persona and their act, whether this be the scientist, the "oriental," the handcuff king, or something else. These apparent truths, having been mashed up freely from a plethora of often disparate sources, ultimately form the core of a deceit which has allowed the magician to make their magic and pull off their deceptions.

As I have alluded to above, for the deception to be effective for the magician, the mashed-up material of which the deceit comprises needs to be necessarily vague, with only the most casual nod toward the veracity of the sign the magician is appropriating. We can often see evidence of this through the disclaimer of the magician. These short pieces of carefully scripted dialogue utilize the mash-up by being playful and ambiguous in their construction (Taylor 2018, 4) and by allowing the performer to distance themselves from any claim to them performing real magic. This simple form still allows for the possibility that the magician is the real thing, but simultaneously offers other avenues of possibility hidden in plain sight. A relatively recent example can be seen in the mashed-up themes within magician Derren Brown's initial disclaimer. He explains, "This program fuses magic, suggestion, psychology, misdirection and showmanship. I achieve all the results you'll see here through a varied mixture of those techniques" (Brown 2007). Disclaimers are therefore wide in scope offering many possibilities, but the content is vague enough to appear to provide apparent genuine context for the work. They act as fuzzy categories that illustrate broad principles of theming that are deliberately "muddy and unclear" in order to blur the boundaries between the "real" and the "pretend" (Goto-Jones 2016, 33), and after all isn't all magic pretend magic? Returning to bizarre magick, performer Tony Andruzzi's disclaimer for his persona Masklyn ye Mage runs for almost 300 words, beginning with an assertion that modern-day parapsychology is "clinical" and "mundane," and moving on to the claim that his work goes back to

> the genesis of Psi occurrences . . . back to the schools of Mysticism that existed eons before our sophisticated epistemologists closed their minds to magick, due to an ignorance spawned by fear, or a fear spawned by ignorance. Back to the goetic rituals and arcane rites, which are neither religious nor sacrilegious, but merely a reflection of the beliefs and philosophies of the sages of antiquity.
>
> There may be some of you who will say, Witchcraft!!" or Black Magick!"... No, my friends, it will simply be a psychodynamic experiment to determine the validity of those ancient writings in the old grimoire. Remember, what man knows, he calls science; what he is yet to learn, he calls magick! Both are real. (Masklyn ye Mage 1982, 95)

Privately to magicians, Andruzzi claims this dialogue will "blend enough fact with fantasy to draw the audience quickly within the framework of the presentation before they have the opportunity to discern the dichotomies" (Masklyn ye Mage 1982).

As this example also shows, the appropriation and mashing up of fuzzy sign systems is particularly prevalent in bizarre magick, where practitioners gather not only the signs and symbols of the Gothic, but also blur the difference between real and pretend magic much further than ever before. In fact, we often see that the areas chosen to be explored by the bizarre magician are taken from a wide assortment of popular Gothic tropes. Thus, when Charles Cameron argued that the magician required a "Gothic revival" he was referring not to an accurate reflection of Gothicism, but rather to a fuzzy distillation of the historical, the geographical, the environmental, the physiological, and the scenographic sign-system of the Gothic (Taylor 2015, 163).

Functioning much like the "Gothic motif" and achieving meaning "through evoking the Gothic" (Spooner 2006, 26–7), Cameron's own work in Castle Dracula plays freely with Gothic fictions, props, and locations. Castle Dracula, a performance space built above Edinburgh Wax Museum, "was a theatre of weird and bizarre magic, mystery and the supernatural" providing "magic, entertainment, laughter, suspense and icy moments of sheer terror." Cameron himself played Dracula and was assisted by Daemon, "a creature from the depths of Hell[,] and the 'Vampiress'" (Cameron 1997, 7). While the mashed-up tropes of the fuzzy Gothic in bizarre magick are predominantly drawn from popular Gothic fictions, attention is also paid to conjuring an atmosphere of the Gothic, whether this be serious or comedic. Castle Dracula effects such as *From Satan—with Love* where an audience member plays a game of fate framed as an experiment in ritual magic (Cameron 1997, 47–52), and *The Book of Demons* where the bizarre magician uses a book of horror tales and a hat pin to demonstrate the power of voodoo (Cameron 1997, 19–24) develop what Samuel Finegan identifies in his study of Gothic performance as a "heightened reality of fiction" (2015, 61), and this further accords with Robert Mighall's notion of a Gothic "mode" (2003, xix). Thus, its broad intention is to be an attitude or an *approach* to the past, rather than an accurate reflection of the Gothic itself. Bizarre magick is a genre that chimes with Clive Bloom's notion of Gothic forms "that can be recognised as of the 'Gothic genre'" and as having "similar attitudes to setting atmosphere and style" (Bloom 1998, 2). As such, the work often theatrically mirrors the popular Gothic seen in films such as those from the Hammer Studios which, according to Misha Kavka, have a clear "visual code" and are themselves "inheritors of a cultural legacy" (Kavka 2002, 210) of the Gothic (Taylor 2015, 168).

We should note, however, that it is not just the fuzzy Gothic that is mashed up to achieve the atmosphere of bizarre magick, as other fuzzy tropes are apparent across the form, and these are drawn from many genres of popular fiction. In Taylor (2016) I identified these elements as aligning closely to *fantastika*, a term appropriated by John Clute (2007) to embrace genres such as science fiction, horror, and fantasy. Even so, while the fantastika that is drawn upon in bizarre magick may often comprise many fuzzy genre signs which are then applied across a wide continuum of practice, the most prevalent signs are drawn from the fuzzy Gothic. The majority of bizarre magicians mash up the atmosphere and stylings of the Gothic to create a performance space that is Gothic-*like*, or simply a space where the Gothic-*like* happens. In terms of the physical space, we see frequently repeated settings, such as a magician's study in the effect *The Great God Pan* based on Arthur Machen's novella *The*

Great God Pan (1894) where sitters join a dark séance dedicated to Pan only to witness a wax effigy of a woman used in the ritual mysteriously broken into pieces when the god takes offense at being summoned (Shiels, Raven, and Fromer 1974, 23–5); or a ritual circle in *The Sacrifice* where a "fair novice" is seen to be ritually sacrificed in an hypnotic ritual that culminates in her disappearance in a shower of sparks leaving only her white robe on the floor (Masklyn ye Mage 1980). A popular setting is the heavily curtained parlor seen in effects such as in *Beyond the Grave* where a "Master of the Unknown" performs a séance incorporating a momentarily awakened Egyptian mummy that speaks, moves, and glows with a "strange greenish light," with eyes burning with a "queer reddish gleam" (Cameron 1971, 24–5).

BIZARRE MAGICK: ORIGINS AND CONTINUUM

In many ways, the mashing up of these numerous sources is baked into the form of bizarre magick itself. Stephen Minch argues that bizarre magick rose "wraith-like from the sod of two specialised schools of magick: pseudo-spiritism and mentalism" (2009, 732). In terms of performance magic practice, these schools represent a form of pretend magic that often makes more profound claims at being real (rather than a deception) than traditional conjuring might. "Pseudo-spiritism," being perhaps the more ambiguous and even less flavorsome area, was according to During a "problematic extension" of the magic assemblage (2002, 71). It does however conjure up images of the spiritualist séance, with its Gothic parlor setting and the ambiguous role of the medium/magician. The other school mentioned by Minch is "mentalism," which is itself a mash-up deriving from nineteenth-century discourses on personal development following the publication of Segno's *The Law of Mentalism* (1902) and later appropriated by magicians. Mentalism was being used as a wide-ranging label for mediumistic or mind-reading effects, and the term the "mentalist" was used as a title for the magician who performs mentalism (Wilson 1906; Sterling 1910; Wilson 1919). Bridging the gap between these sources and the subsequent development of the bizarre magick movement proper we can see the foundations being laid as magicians, particularly mentalists, would often experiment with Gothic modes in their work producing what we can call proto-bizarre material. Perhaps the best example of this work is Ormond McGill's "Psychic Series," a series of six volumes published by Supreme Magic between 1950 and 1951, in which the author promised to provide "magicians with some most unusual material with which they can entertain" (McGill 1950, 5). *Psychic Magic* covers effects based on mind reading, crystal seership, psychometry, x-ray vision, animal magnetism, manifesting spirits, an "East Indian" mystery act, pendulums, and occult "amazements." In the final volume, McGill suggests that a requirement of a miracle presentation is that "it must, by its very nature, imply the workings of some supernormal force or source for its accomplishment" (1951, 19).

However, the actual origins of bizarre magick are more complex than Minch suggests. If we were to set a date for the founding of bizarre magick as a genre in its own right it is likely to be around the time of the establishment of the bizarre magick focused periodical *Invocation* in 1974. Bizarre magician Brother Shadow later describes the beginning of the movement in an interview with *Oracle Magazine* in 2006. Here he recounts that "in Germany the great magician Punx was doing stage magic like no other," Charles Cameron was publishing several small books containing "weird and spooky routines," and magician Tony Shiels was publishing "weird and scary magic books." He concludes, "in 1974, Tony Raven published the first issue of *Invocation*, which brought us all together through the printed word." He adds that Tony Andruzzi joined them shortly afterward and "modern-day bizarre magic[k] was born" (Goodsell and White 2006). Indeed, a search of the Conjuring Arts Research Centre archives reveals that in 1974 the *Magic Circular*, the magazine of the Magic Circle (often seen as the legitimate face of the magic community in the United Kingdom), first mentions bizarre magick in volume 68, issue 156 (1974, 221), as does the U.S.-based *Linking Ring*, the magazine of The International Brotherhood of Magicians, in the same year in volume 52, issue 10 (1974, 88), both in reference to *Invocation* magazine. Bizarre magick had its heyday in the 1970s and 1980s and, at least initially, much of the work was based on Gothic horror and ritual; however, as magician Docc Hilford later reflected, "bizarre magick isn't just the ritual or arcane [. . .] bizarre is strange and unusual," and "the sky is the limit" (Hilford 1991, 742–3).

There is, therefore, a wide spectrum of what we can call a continuum of practice of bizarre magick that can employ Gothic mash-up. This can be described as spanning between the hard bizarre and the soft bizarre. Eugene Burger, in his book *Strange Ceremonies*, identifies fellow magician Harry Meier as first distinguishing these two styles of bizarre magick, with the soft being less about "blood and fear" (Burger 1991, 31). However, in reality this was a tricky binary for the bizarre magician to align to, and we see Jim Magus in his *Arcana of Bizarre Magick* referring to the practice as being played across a "spectrum" with the "theatrical" at one end and the "credible" at the other (2009, 20). Magus's work *The Arcana of Bizarre Magick* (2009) is framed as a journey, taking the bizarre magician through the wisdom of the major arcana of the tarot. Each card layers more potential themes for the bizarre magician to explore, resulting in a catalog of mashed-up techniques. These include creating the character, creating the atmosphere, and exploring the occult. Ultimately, however, it is the bizarre magician's response to the source material—that is, the mash-up—that determines where they might appear on this spectrum, and it is important to highlight that this framing is often unique and mutable for each performer. Thus, the bizarre magician's position across the continuum of bizarre magick is dependent on the fuzzy Gothic areas or themes that the magician chooses to draw from. To borrow from Doc Sheils, "bizarre Magick steals plots and settings from films and books [. . .] it plunders the works of Edgar Allan Poe, Arthur Machen, Bram Stoker, M. R. James, A. Merritt, Fritz Leiber, Stephen King and dozens of authors" (Shiels 1988, 41), and this is done freely across the genre.

This is perhaps most evident in the collection "And Then There were Three" (Shiels, Raven, and Fromer 1974) in which the majority of the effects are prefaced with a short introduction describing the Gothic source material that inspired the effect, with, for example, material borrowed from Machen's *The Great God Pan*, "The White People" (1904), and "The Novel of the Black Seal" (1895) in Roy Fromer's *The Black Seal*. *The Black Seal* is, in fact, a series of effects, tied together around a professor character recounting his investigations into a "prehistoric black seal from Babylon," which includes the mysterious appearance of a "glob of visceral abomination" (Shiels, Raven, and Fromer 1974, 29–32).

Work which mashes up Gothic signs predominately drawn from popular fictions can be loosely categorized as soft bizarre. The effects are generally lightweight, drawing from influences such as Hammer House of Horror or early Universal horror classics. An example here would be *Key to Dracula's Coffin* (Bridewell 1976) in which the magician recounts how, when disposing of the estate of his late uncle, he discovers a letter from Jonathan Harker accompanied by a padlocked box shaped coffin. The effect culminates with the spectator unwittingly releasing the spirit of Dracula into the world. Other examples include *Blood Harvest* (Devlyn 1983), in which the last bottle of "Chateau Dracul" wine is poured only to find that it slowly darkens and finally turns to ash, and *Shroud of the Vampire* (Cameron 1984) in which the ritual staking of a wax effigy results in a previously white "vampire shroud" magically turning blood red.

Midway within this continuum of practice we see work that takes itself a little more seriously although drawing again from popular fictions including those by H. P. Lovecraft and M. R. James. Here the fuzzy Gothic is presented for serious consideration in the sense that the bizarre magician provides, through magical method, apparent proof that the events recounted in their Gothic tales have real-world credence or have genuinely occurred. Thus, here the performance of bizarre magick is the vehicle to produce evidence with which to empirically demonstrate the apparent truth of the tale as recounted by the magician. This might be through the success (or failure) of a ritual, such as the effect *The Stigmata of Cthulhu* published in Minch's book of seven bizarre magick routines titled *Lovecraftian Ceremonies* (1979). The effects in this work are designed to draw spectators into the "drama of ritual and story" (Minch 1979, iii) and in this particular effect the participants are gathered to summon the "dread Cthulhu." The "Mark of Cthulhu" is drawn onto a piece of parchment while the magician chants a spell accompanied by the sound of bubbling water that gradually increases in volume. In the midst of all of this a spectator collapses suddenly, the parchment vanishes in a burst of flame, and the spectators find the Mark has appeared in various places on their bodies, demonstrating that "the mighty Cthulhu was with us" (Minch 1979, 2–4).

Finally, at the other end of the continuum we have a harder approach to bizarre magick, and this is often framed in terms of the pagan or the Gothic occult. The boundary between fantasy and reality is deliberately blurred in performance, and the work may border on the problematic with magicians passing themselves off as genuine occultists or scholars appearing to draw upon popular understandings and themes of the occult to speak to their own performance agendas. For example, Tony Andruzzi in the early 1970s fully embraced this when he became affiliated with a group called the *Pagan Way* in which he quickly learned that he could "out-bullshit the bullshitters," and he eventually set himself up as a "Priest of the Maganegro Coven" (Magus 2011, 170–1). However, to fellow magicians he was explicit about this sham: "I maintained the persona of being the great oracle, the wisdom of my traditional witchcraft upbringing which I invented the day before; and the beauty was that I could deceive these people without ever taking out the ball vase." (The Ball Vase is a classic magic trick often seen in children's magic sets. The vase allows a ball to vanish and reappear in a variety of different ways.)

More frequently, however, the subject matter drew on tales and themes of the Gothic occult, with occasional, rather specific, discussion of "real" ritual implements (Andruzzi 1977, 1–3; King 1977). The title and cover of *Invocation* itself suggest the trappings of high magick and the occult, and as Burger states in his *Foreword* to the collected volume, "*Invocation*, then, stands as a reminder to magicians that there is an older magic, a deeper and perhaps even darker tradition that has quietly spread underground for centuries" (Burger 1986a).

BIZARRE MAGICK AS MASHED-UP GOTHIC STORYTELLING

The persona of the magician continued to be of central importance in bizarre magick, and while the creation of the Gothic persona of the bizarre magician has been discussed previously in Taylor and Nolan (2015), it is worth revisiting briefly. The bizarre magician is a "Master of the Unknown" who demonstrates unusual powers (Cameron 1971, 24). This signals a multifaceted approach to developing a magic(k)al persona that came to be known as the "Van Helsing Approach" (Magus 2009, 17). Burger later argued that the persona of Van Helsing must stand as the "patron saint of bizarre magick" (1991, 34). The persona was a heady mash-up of an intellectual, occultist, storyteller, scientist, demonologist, and witness, who, again according to Burger, "may, or may not, know what he is doing!" and "leads us into areas that perhaps he can't handle" (1991, 35).

Many of these concerns were very much central to the performance of bizarre magick, with many practitioners experimenting with the framing of their work, in terms of both persona and effect, as genuine magic(k). There were, however, no hard and fast rules as to how to approach mashing up the Gothic in bizarre magick performance with magicians playing across the continuum by mashing up various fuzzy themes where necessary. The character of the bizarre magician largely determines, not only where they appeared on a spectrum of practice discussed above, but also the type of mash-up they will employ in the presentation of their effects.

This approach to presentation often saw physical manifestation in the books bizarre magicians wrote about their magic for other bizarre magicians. Often these would become objects that could be used in the performance of bizarre magick, each holding the affordance of the Gothic signs within them. More generally in performance magic, magic objects function, according to Burger and Neale, as "symbols and metaphors: pointing beyond themselves to a larger reality and a greater mystery" (1995, 9). The magical object is a thing that affords to be something else. Teemu Paavolainen, in his discussion of stage properties, calls this a powerful "static force of characterisation" (2010, 117). In bizarre magick, as compared to conventional magic, the difference is that the affordance of the objects is not mundane, and in most cases these affordances are not regular, but are performed as part of the effect. The object has been taken from the mundane. Props in bizarre magick function, as Andrew Sofer suggests in a different context, as "object(s) that go [...] on a journey," that "trace spatial trajectories and create temporal narratives as they track through a given performance" (2003, 2).

Andruzzi's *The Negromicon of Masklyn ye Mage* (1977) and *The Legendary Scroll of Masklyn ye Mage* (1983) function as not only as books of effects for magicians to work from, but also as magic objects to use in performance. Both were handmade and aged to look like ancient treatises on real magic. As a review from 1977 in *Invocation* magazine stated,

> What is it??? It's a unique book of tricks and routines . . . it's a prop to use in your shows . . . it's an unusual book to keep around the house to show your

guests. This is an ancient work of the black arts" . . . and then go into a ritual effect using the book. Produced in 8 x 11 page size hard-bound (by hand) in black imitation alligator with locking covers.

The standard practice with books for magicians is the writing up of a trick in two sections, the first being "the effect," in which the experience of the trick is recounted, usually from the audiences' point of view, and the second being "the method," in which the secret workings of the effect are explained. In bizarre magick publications, in keeping with the implicit occult themes, the method is often renamed the "Arcanum," and in turn the write-up of the effect is elevated to an extended, story-like, detailed description of the experience. This led Eugene Burger to observe that the creation of a bizarre magick effect had the danger of becoming a "literary exercise" rather than a wholehearted exploration of the form (1991, 28). This reimagining of the composition of the effect is essential to our understanding as to why so much of the fuzzy Gothic finds itself mashed into the bizarre and why bizarre magick can function as a Gothic storytelling experience. According to bizarre magician Tony "Doc" Shiels, the magician has "a powerful advantage over the story-teller in that he can, through trickery, make that 'something' apparently happen to his audience." Shiels quotes M. R. James as saying: "The reader of a ghost story must be put into the position of thinking to himself, 'If I'm not careful, something of this sort may happen to me'" (Shiels 1981, 58).

Many effects sections in bizarre magick books are heightened reflections of the genre from which they are drawn. The effect descriptions are often presented as heavy, occasionally overblown, mashed-up pieces of Gothic/ historical fiction, with the very act of writing underlining the highly theatrical nature of the work. The stories that frame the effects might draw material from Gothic fiction, mythology, the Cthulhu mythos, or from a more general pool of Gothic occult signifiers, such as tarot, crystal balls, and pentagrams. For instance, the aforementioned *The Legendary Scroll of Masklyn ye Mage* (1983) presents a collection of effects created by Andruzzi and fellow bizarrists such as Stephen Minch, Eugene Burger, and Anthony Raven. It is written in a heightened literary style; for example, the first effect, *The Blood of Dhste Kravahn* by Masklyn ye Mage, begins with the following sentence: "The elaborately ritualized Dessert for which the lugubrious dinner at the High Table of Miskatonic was quite famous rounded to a close and the Beak made his withdrawal." The effect continues in this mode describing how seven of the diners climbed the winding stairs to the "tower room" where they observe a container carrying an "obsequitious [sic] obscenity"; this being earth taken from the "Queen's Chamber in Cheops' pyramid." In the effect, the earth is shown to become burning hot, before leaving the "bloody red smear" of the blood of "Dhste Kravahn" (Andruzzi 1983, 2).

Stephen Minch much later, and somewhat dismissively, in his article "A Vivisection of the Bizarre," echoes Burger when he refers to bizarre magick as a "literary phenomenon" (Minch 2009, 61) rather than a coherent performance practice. Even so, Minch's most well-known work, *Lovecraftian Ceremonies* (1979) (noted above), follows the very literary design of which he is later so dismissive. This work, a collection of seven "ceremonies" is according to Minch, "a bastard blending of the subterfuges of the magician [. . .] with the horror fiction of the eminent genre-stylist, Howard Phillips Lovecraft" (1979, i). As interest in the bizarre expanded, some of the descriptions of effects that were produced for magicians relied heavily on storytelling and literary pastiche, often with little consideration of the effectiveness of the actual method for working the moment of magic. Minch in another article, "Evolution of the Bizarre" (1991), quotes performer Tony Raven as saying it is "the type of magic you'd expect to find in a Lovecraftian tale" (Minch 1991, 733). As suggested above, the Lovecraftian, or certainly some pastiche of the Cthulhu mythos, provided many reoccurring mashed-up themes within the genre. We see hints of this in the aforementioned *The Blood of Dhste Kravahn*, and much more explicitly in *Lord of Blood!—Lord of Lust!* (Charles and Janice 1977), which describes a complex routine involving a possession by Yog-Sothoth that playfully addresses the legacy of H. P. Lovecraft. In addition, some bizarre magicians were literally mashing up the physical to enhance the storytelling experience. We see, for example, in Kate Shiels's *Vermicularis* in Tony Shiels's *Bizarre* (1988), which is based on Brother Shadow's *Robin's Quest* (Shadow 1986), that the magician is required to construct a prop representing a hybrid creature from a squid and an octopus tentacle (Shiels 1988, 70), and Tony Andruzzi's *Temple of Cthulhu* (Maven 1986) utilizes a shelled oyster stained with blue-green food coloring.

Tony Shiels later argues that given the relative simplicity of the mechanics of many of the actual effects in bizarre magick, its framing must be serious, minute in detail, and not treated lightly (Shiels, Raven, and Fromer 1974, 17). Fellow bizarre magician Tony Andruzzi appears to agree when he refers to the secondary nature of the effect in *The Negromicon of Masklyn ye Mage* arguing that "the climax of a bizarre bit of weird Magick should seem incredible and a bit sinister . . . almost anti-climactic, at times," and the "resultant denouement should be a subtle and startling inexplicable 'happening'" (1977, 2). Throughout bizarre magick literature we find effects that are compact Gothic storytelling experiences that are designed to be played to small gatherings of participants. Reflecting on this, Stephen Minch suggests in *Lovecraftian Ceremonies* (1979) that the effects (Minch terms them "playlets") "are destined to be performed to an intimate grouping of three to eight persons" (1979, i), and Eugene Burger later quotes Andruzzi as saying, "the number of people in attendance is in direct ratio to the acceptability of the genuineness" (Burger 1986b, 90).

CONCLUSION

To conclude, in bizarre magick practice we see that the effects (tricks), the creation of atmosphere, the persona of the magician, the objects of magic, the storytelling experience, and the structure of narrative pull at the very essence of what performance magic practice can be. In particular, the practice allowed for a mashing up of a wider range of themes than traditional performance magic could, and these were predominantly drawn from the Gothic or the Gothic-like. Bizarre magician Tony Shiels believed that the performers should take time to "tread the path of the supernatural," ultimately developing their work to "convey the feeling of Gothic horror" (Shiels, Raven, and Fromer 1974, 3). The work should, according to Shiels in his collection of effects *13!!!* (1968), seem like "the real thing . . . not trickery, not deception, but genuine, spell-casting, spook-raising sorcery!" (1968, 2). The "real thing" described by Shiels is the heightened bringing to reality of the mashed-up fuzzy Gothic.

Bizarre magick with its intimate storytelling experiences represented an exciting experiment in performance magic. By treating Gothic themes as fuzzy, bizarre magicians could playfully mash up their presentations into new forms that experimented freely with the genre. As this was a countercultural movement there were no rules, and the "spectrum" of the work discussed above demonstrates this. Thus, the practice allowed for a wealth of creativity that questioned the very nature of performance magic. Bizarre magick was also, according to Max Maven in his foreword to the collected works of *Invocation*, "a fascinating failure" (Maven 1986). However, Maven is speaking in terms of magic innovation of method, rather than an expansion of theme and framing that moved the practice away from the mainstream. Certainly, while there was very little originality of method in Bizarre Magick, and Maven's dismissal echoes wider issues within the performance magic community concerned with the development of secrets, the mashing up of the fuzzy Gothic allowed the creation of new and vibrant material for presentation. While much of the practice waned in the early 1990s, there is evidence that interest in bizarre magick is growing, and while it still very much an underground movement, *Doomsday*, the annual UK meeting of bizarre magicians, is proving increasingly popular. Here card tricks are still "banned," or at the very least humorously frowned upon, in favor of work by magicians who might use bloodied Victorian autopsy photos or haunted first editions of M. R. James to frame their storytelling and effects in a darkly mashed-up Gothic mode. This new work echoes Catherine

Spooner's notion of the Gothic being a "series of revivals" (2006, 32), and thus bizarre magick appears to be rising again as magicians realize the storytelling potential of the Gothic mash-up.

REFERENCES

Andruzzi, Tony. 1977. *The Negromicon of Masklyn Ye Mage*. Chicago: self-published.

———. 1983. *The Legendary Scroll of Masklyn Ye Mage*. Chicago: Tom Palmer.

Bloom, Clive. 1998. *Gothic Horror: A Reader's Guide from Poe to King and Beyond*. Basingstoke: Macmillan.

———. ed. 2020. *The Palgrave Handbook of Contemporary Gothic*. Palgrave Macmillan. https://doi.org/10.1007/978-3-030-33136-8.

Braun, John. 1974. "Hocus in Focus." *Linking Ring*, 1974.

Bridewell, Jack. 1976. "Keys to Dracula's Coffin." *Invocation*, no. 8 (April): 120–3.

Brown, Derren. 2007. *Tricks of the Mind*. London: Channel 4.

Burger, Eugene. 1986a. "A Magazine in Search of a Mage." In *The Compleat Invocation*, edited by Bob Lynn and Tony Andruzzi. Washington: Kaufman and Co.

———. 1986b. *Spirit Theater: Reflections on the History and Performance of Seances*. 1st ed. Washington: Kaufman and Greenberg.

———. 1991. *Strange Ceremonies*. Washington: Kaufman and Co.

Burger, Eugene, and Robert E Neale. 1995. *Magic & Meaning*. 1st ed. Seattle: Hermetic Press.

Cameron, Charles. 1967. "Voices from the Dead." *Cauldron* 1 (4): 35.

———. 1971. *Handbook of Horror*. Devon: The Supreme Magic Co.

———. 1974. "Magic... or Magick!" *Invocation* 1 (1).

———. 1976. *Devil's Diary*. Devon: The Supreme Magic Co.

———. 1984. "Shroud of a Vampire." *The New Invocation*, no. 19 (February): 225.

———. 1997. *Castle Dracula Mentalism*. London: Breese Books.

Charles, Lambert, and Lambert Janice. 1977. "Lord of Blood!—Lord of Lust!" *Invocation*, no. 13 (July): 213–21.

Clute, John. 2007. "Fantastika in the World Storm." *Stuff* (blog). September 28, 2007. http://www.johnclute.co.uk/word/?p=15.

Cook, James W. 2001. *The Arts of Deception: Playing with Fraud in the Age of Barnum*. Harvard University Press.

Devlyn, Peter Adrian. 1983. "Blood Harvest." *The New Invocation*, no. 16 (June): 178–9.

During, Simon. 2002. *Modern Enchantments: The Cultural Power of Secular Magic*. Cambridge, MA: Harvard University Press.

Finegan, Samuel. 2015. "Closing the Circle: Presencing Gothic Space through Performance.'" *Aeternum: The Journal of Contemporary Gothic Studies* 2 (1): 60–71.

Goodsell, David, and Larry White. 2006. "Brother Shadow: A Conversation." *Oracle: Into the Unknown*, 2006.
Goto-Jones, Chris. 2016. *Conjuring Asia: Magic, Orientalism, and the Making of the Modern World.* Cambridge University Press.
Grossman, John Henry. 1974. "Americana." *The Magic Circular* 68 (156): 220–1.
Hilford, Docc. 1991. "Where Do We Go from Here?" *The New Invocation*, no. 61 (February): 742–3.
Kavka, Misha. 2002. "Gothic on Screen." In *The Cambridge Companion to Gothic Fiction*, edited by Jerrold E. Hogle, 209–28. Cambridge: Cambridge University Press.
King, Karnak. 1977. "Basic Ritual Implements." *Invocation*, no. 11 (January): 173–7.
Magus, Jim. 2009. *Arcana of Bizarre Magick*. Atlanta: James Salterella.
———. 2011. *UnSpeakable Acts: Three Lives and Countless Legends of Tom Palmer, Tony Andruzzi & Masklyn Ye Mage*. Atlanta: James Salterella.
Mangan, Michael. 2007. *Performing Dark Arts: A Cultural History of Conjuring.* Bristol: Intellect Books.
Masklyn ye Mage. 1980. "The Sacrifice." *The New Invocation*, no. 4 (April): 41–3.
———. 1982. "Leaves from the Black Book." *The New Invocation*, no. 8 (January): 95.
Maven, Max. 1986. "The House of Representatives." In *The Compleat Invocation*, edited by Bob Lynn and Tony Andruzzi, i–iv. Washington: Kaufman and Co.
McGill, Ormond. 1950. *Psychic Magic Volume One.* Devon: Supreme Magic Company.
———. 1951. *Psychic Magic Volume Six.* Devon: Supreme Magic Company.
Mighall, Robert. 2003. *A Geography of Victorian Gothic Fiction: Mapping History's Nightmares.* Oxford: Oxford University Press.
Minch, Stephen. 1979. *Lovecraftian Ceremonies.* New Jersey: Bob Lynn.
———. 1991. "Evolution of the Bizarre." *The New Invocation*, no. 61 (February): 732–3.
———. 2009. "A Vivisection of the Bizarre." *M-U-M*, October 2009.
Paavolainen, Teemu. 2010. "From Props to Affordances An Ecological Approach to Theatrical Objects." *Theatre Symposium* 18 (July): 116–34.
Segno, A. Victor. 1902. *The Law of Mentalism: A Practical, Scientific Explanation of Thought or Mind Force: The Law Which Governs All Mental and Physical Action and Phenomena: The Cause of Life and Death.* Los Angeles: American Institute of Mentalism. http://archive.org/details/lawofmentalismpr00segnuoft.
Shadow, Brother. 1986. "Robin's Quest." *The New Invocation*, no. 32 (April): 379–80.
Shiels, Tony. 1968. *13!!!* United Kingdom: Figurehead Press.
———. 1981. *Daemons, Darklings and Doppelgangers.* Devon: Supreme Magic.
———. 1988. *Bizarre.* London: Breese Books.
Shiels, Tony, Tony Raven, and Roy Fromer. 1974. *And Then There Were Three.* New Jersey: Bob Lynn.

Sofer, Andrew. 2003. *The Stage Life of Props*. Book, Whole. Ann Arbor: University of Michigan Press. https://doi.org/10.3998/mpub.11888.

Spooner, Catherine. 2006. *Contemporary Gothic*. Reaktion Books, Limited.

Steinmeyer, Jim. 2005. *The Glorious Deception*. New York: Carroll & Graf.

Sterling, Max, ed. 1910. "New York Magical Notes." *Magical World* 1 (16): 244.

Taylor, Nik. 2015. "Impersonating Spirits: The Paranormal Entertainer and the Dramaturgy of the Gothic Séance." In *New Directions in 21st-Century Gothic: The Gothic Compass*, edited by Lorna Piatti-Farnell and Donna Lee Brien, 163–74. Routledge.

———. 2016. "'Strange Ceremonies': Creating Imaginative Spaces in Bizarre Magick." *The Luminary*, no. 7 (September): 54–63.

———. 2018. "Magic and Broken Knowledge; Reflections on the Practice of Bizarre Magick." *The Journal of Performance Magic* 5 (April). http://eprints.hud.ac.uk/id/eprint/34494.

Taylor, Nik, and Stuart Nolan. 2015. "Performing Fabulous Monsters: Re-Inventing the Gothic Personae in Bizarre Magic." In *Monstrous Media/Spectral Subjects: Imaging Gothic from the Nineteenth Century to the Present*, edited by Catherine Spooner and Fred Botting, 128–42. Manchester: Manchester University Press.

Weatherly, Lionel, and John Nevil Maskelyne. 1891. *The Supernatural?* Bristol: J W Arrowsmith.

Wilson, A. M., ed. 1906. "Entertainers." *The Sphinx* 5 (1): 5.

———. ed. 1919. "Zenola - the Girl Who Knows (Advertising Copy)." *The Sphinx* 18 (1): 24.

Chapter 13

Gothic Gaming, Queer Mash-Ups, and *Gone Home*

Ewan Kirkland

At first glance, video games rarely follow the mash-up formula described in Megen de Bruin-Molé's 2020 publication on "Frankenfictions." There are undoubtedly examples inspired by Gothic literature and authors. Tanya Krzywinska (2009) writes of a video game translation of H. P. Lovecraft resulting in a particularly unforgiving interactive experience. Richard J. Hand notes the literary influences on the survival horror subgenre, including the work of Anne Rice, Bram Stoker, and Edgar Allan Poe (2004, 121–2). As has been argued (Kirkland 2012), the *Silent Hill* series, which ran from 1999 to 2015, producing eight main titles, several multiple-platform spin-offs, and two movies, contains many explicit references to Gothic literature and film, as well as being heavily indebted to a range of Gothic tropes. *Castlevania* (1986–) aside, what Kamilla Elliott labels the "foundational literary triptych" of Gothic film adaptation (2008, 24–5)—Dracula, Frankenstein and his monster, and Dr. Jekyll and Mr. Hyde—appears relatively rarely across the history of Western video games. Sherlock Holmes, or Herlock Sholmes in the latest legally savvy Phoenix Wright installment, has been a regular feature of the medium, appropriate given the way games often position the player as detective. Alice, of Lewis Carroll's children's books, has featured in several computer games, including one inspired by the adaptation directed by Tim Burton, a filmmaker persistently aligned with the Gothic. The original *American McGee's Alice* (2000) provides the iconic opening image for Krzywinska's influential discussion of horror games (2002, 206). But, as Michael Ryan Moore asserts, while the industry has close connections with film production, and variously draws upon comics and graphic novels, "classic prose" is less commonly a source of video game inspiration (2010, 186). There are no examples which immediately spring to mind of titles which self-consciously combine figures from different works of literature, or transport recognizable literary characters into the kind of zombie apocalypse scenario characterizing De Bruin-Molé's exemplary text *Pride and Prejudice and Zombies*. Given the significant presence of the undead across digital game culture (Kirkland 2016), this might seem peculiar. Nevertheless, despite the noticeable absence of explicit Gothic literary adaptations and video game Frankenfictions, video games have always been Gothic.

This chapter examines the celebrated exploration game *Gone Home*, a "walking simulator" released in 2013, developed and published by The Fullbright Company. In this game, players assume the role of a young woman, just returned from a year abroad, who finds her family home inexplicably deserted. By exploring this empty space, players uncover information pertaining to the protagonist's family. Situating this game in the context of Gothic literature, video game mash-ups, and queer culture, I begin by detailing the extent to which video games, like all modern media, have been influenced by the Gothic. While rarely drawing explicitly upon pre-existing Gothic novels, games have always featured spooky and unsettling environments, labyrinths and mazes, locked doors, secret rooms, and mysterious narratives from the past. The already playful nature of the Gothic, it is suggested, suits the ludic orientation of the digital game. Moreover, many writers identify something peculiarly Gothic about the video game as a medium: in the games' half-real worlds, uncanny avatars, and blurring of boundaries between reality and fiction. Although lacking specific qualities of the Gothic mash-up, video games have frequently drawn upon the Gothic, while incorporating an array of cultural forms into the experiences they generate. Video games combine different ludic experiences, but also appropriate, simulate, and remediate aspects of architecture, paintings, cinema, and print media. In this respect, digital games resemble the patchwork narratives of many works of traditional Gothic literature. Finally, it is argued that through their hybridity, nonlinearity, and heterogeneity, the digital game potentially embodies various queer qualities, also an ambiguous feature of Gothic fiction.

Gone Home is then discussed as a means of illustrating overlaps between the video game, the Gothic, the mash-up, and the queerness of ludic digital experiences. Like so many Gothic novels, films, and video games, this title takes place in a large, deserted, spooky house in the middle of the night. This typically Gothic tale of troubled domesticity is revealed through the player's sleuth-like investigation. This involves piecing together the family's narrative from the many discarded documents, objects, and artifacts scattered throughout the game space. Central to this family saga is the protagonist's sister, who recently began a lesbian love affair with a girl at her new school. As this prominent storytelling strand emerges from the sister's disembodied voice-over, it is argued, *Gone Home* presents itself as a ghost story. Like much literature before it, *Gone Home* uses this ambiguous format to tell hidden histories, raise silenced voice, and allow the marginalized, oppressed, and ostracized to tell their tales. While not a Gothic mash-up in the usual sense, *Gone Home* nevertheless illustrates the significance of Gothic storytelling traditions to contemporary video games, the mosaic of media formats through which games tell their stories, and queer overlaps among the Gothic, the video game, and the mash-up.

VIDEO GAMES AND THE GOTHIC

The claim that video games have been influenced by Gothic media is a far from radical proposition. When considering the pervasiveness of this style, and the longevity of the commercial video game as a 50-year-old form of popular culture, it would be strange if this digital medium had not been impacted by the Gothic. Clive Bloom argues the Gothic represents "one of the most influential artistic styles and artistic genres of the last four centuries." Its influences stretch to architecture, paintings, and photography, as well as computer games (Bloom 2010, 2). Scholars have traced Gothic influences across contemporary media, including film, television, music, and graphic novels. Given overlaps between the requirements of video game design and the affordances of horror culture, as explored by Richard Rouse III (2009), it is maybe not surprising that video games easily slip into Gothic registers. This has been a feature since the medium's inception. The descending cosmic horror of *Space Invaders* (1978), the medieval castle of *Adventure* (1980), *Pac-Man*'s (1980) pursuit by ghosts through a succession of mazes, and the architectural clichés of *Haunted House* (1982) reflect the inspiration early designers found in claustrophobic tension, ruined neo-medieval locations, labyrinths, spectral adversaries, and mysterious spaces. Romantic rescue structures continue to inform the long-running *Mario* series. Similar codes of chivalry pervade another Nintendo flagship title, *The Legend of Zelda*. Classic first-person shooters combined crossbows and chainsaws, zombies and cyborgs, satanic creatures, and science fiction scenarios in a ludic free-for-all of the medieval, the modern, and the futuristic. Video games are full of mazes and monsters, ghost and goblins, dungeons and dragons. Players are frequently tasked with finding keys to locked doors, hidden objects, and concealed manuscripts, representing the incorporation of Gothic tropes into video game mechanics.

If there is something Gothic about these ludic experiences, there is also something ludic about the Gothic. John C. Tibbetts, for example, writes of the old dark house genre being one which consistently "played a game with their readers"; writers are compared to stage magicians, revealing supposed supernatural elements to have been tricks, ventriloquism, a wax effigy, an escaped prisoner, rather than actual psychic phenomenon (2002, 100–1). Many scholars suggest that the playfulness of the Gothic explains its ubiquitous presence across video game media. Bernard Perron, in a substantial study of horror digital games, notes "the genre was from the outset playful and interactive in a manner which makes its transition to video game a logical progression" (2018, 81). Krzywinska draws attention to proximities between the Gothic detective and the game player, both of whom look for clues and solves puzzles to progress (2014, 506). Arthur L. Cooke details how the "explained supernatural" appealed to the rationality of eighteenth-century audiences. As readers were effectively tasked with second guessing the true explanation behind apparently supernatural occurrences, Gothic novels represent "a kind of elaborate brain teaser" (2004, 23). Again, there is something distinctly ludic to this formation. Rosemary Sweet (2014) points out that the literary and cultural Gothic emerged from the practice of antiquarianism. There are further comparisons with the video game player whose efforts often entail the unearthing and collation of various documents. Observing a similar phenomenon, De Bruin-Molé mentions the *Assassins Creed* series and the games' incorporation of letters and newspaper clippings (2020, 29). In a chapter defining the "ludic-gothic," Laurie N. Taylor parallels the protagonists of Gothic literature, who uncover lost histories hidden throughout spooky locations, with the survival horror player, who finds traces of the past in books, portraiture, sculpture, and pottery (2009, 53). Video games frequently involve following a paper trail of found manuscripts, which players piece together to form the game's back story. This represents a common method by which games tell fixed narratives, communicated through non-interactive media fragments such as diaries, memoranda, ancient tomes, and email conversations. These storytelling strategies connect ludic-Gothic games with traditional Gothic stories, which frequently resemble a collection of documents assuming different formats, employing different registers, written by different authors. This combination of the ancient and the modern, analog and digital, paintings, artifacts, notes, and electronic communication has also historically characterized the video game medium. It is this form of textual mash-up, connecting the Gothic and the Gothic game, which later sections of this chapter will explore.

Beyond the impact of the Gothic on games aesthetics, narratives, and structures, it can be argued there is something inherently Gothic about the video game medium itself. Such an argument echoes those of numerous theorists who identify peculiar Gothic dimensions in other forms. For example, as Heidi Kaye suggests, the Gothic has "natural affinity with cinema," both being "born in darkness" (2012, 239). Similarly, Julia Round argues there is something inherently Gothic in the nonlinearity and hallucinatory qualities of the graphic novel (2012, 347). Photography has frequently been associated with death, embalming, the *memento mori* (Sontag, 1979). Julian Wolfreys explores parallels between the specter and the literary text. In a Derrida-inspired commentary, Wolfreys observes that, like the specter, the book is not bound by borders; it appears simultaneously real and phantasmal, potentially surviving without the intervention of human readers, archivists, scholars, or authors. Numerous Gothic terms and metaphors are employed in Wolfreys's discussion of the necromantic nature of the text: "archival burial ground," "embalming process," "uncanny," and "spirit medium," the last being a common pun alluding to compelling connections between media and spiritual practices (2002, xi–xii). Similar ghostly, supernatural, uncanny qualities circulate digital games and the simulated worlds they create. A frequent point of reference for early video game authors such as Chris Crawford, Katie Salen, and Eric Zimmerman, was the "magic circle," a contested concept drawn from the work of Johan Huizinga suggesting ludic activity unfolds within a realm outside real life (Egenfeldt-Nielsen et al. 2008, 24–5). Jesper Juul (2005) in an early consolidation of video game scholarship, uses the term "half-real" to describe the either/or nature of the digital ludic experience. Games are real insofar as they are actual ludic experiences in which players invest; at the same time, the fantasy worlds they create are patently digital fabrications.

Popular discourses surrounding video games and their players frequently suggest a blurring of boundaries between gamer and game, reality and illusion, life and simulation. In such scenarios, the video game player resembles a Gothic protagonist who, unable to trust the veracity of their own senses, descends into a form of digital delirium. Video game academics have also noted something strangely hallucinogenic about the environments and relationships games generate. Sue Morris in a chapter exploring the apparatus of first-person shooter games, drawing upon a film studies application of psychoanalysis, notes the dream-like "otherworldliness" of game spaces (2002, 88). Diane Carr (2006) describes the player/avatar relationship as one of uncanny doubling, a theme Angela Tinwell (2015) develops in relation to digital games and animation, applying the established concept of the "uncanny valley." There is something intangible about the video game experience, which makes it a notoriously slippery object of textual analysis. Video games are a combination of digital assets, full motion videos, and sound files, often worked upon by hundreds of individuals across years of development. Contemporary games can be in a constant state of beta, being updated, often without warning, as bugs are fixed and patches downloaded. There is something incorporeal, intransient, and insubstantial about the video game. As Jay David Bolter and Richard Grusin argue, "there is nothing behind or beyond the interface, as there appears to be with a perspective painting or photograph" (2000, 91). Add to this the obvious point that every play of a video game is different, that many games have multiple endings, and that it is often possible to play through an entire game while missing branching story paths, hidden rooms, and areas which are inaccessible on first play through. As a text, if the term is even appropriate for an interactive medium, the video game appears increasingly spectral.

From their early years, video games have appropriated the Gothic iconography of ghosts, labyrinths, old-god alien invaders, and giant apes. As the medium has matured it continues to draw upon Gothic tropes in presenting players with perilous situations, filled with elaborate puzzles and traps, populated by monstrous adversaries intent on their destruction, all organized around the goal of escape. The neo-medievalism of Gothic romance, the psychological horror of weird fiction, the techno-Gothic of cyborg sci-fi have all provided fertile generic material for video game aesthetics, worlds, narratives, and gameplay mechanics. The close relationship between the Gothic and the video game depends upon the former's ludic qualities and the latter's spectral dimensions. Games' ability to generate ambiguous alternative realities, playful liminal experiences, the digital uncanny, and the sublime, all contribute to the medium's phantasmagorical dimensions. In short, video games have always been Gothic.

VIDEO GAMES AS QUEER MASH-UPS

In addition to being Gothic, video games have always been mash-ups. Discussing the tension between play and narrative elements, Geoff King and Tanya Krzywinska consider video games a hybrid medium, combining storytelling and ergodic interaction (2002, 25). Most video games are an uneven, arguably antagonistic, combination of game and narrative. The former encompasses a range of playful activities, including sports, puzzles, board and card games, pinball, shooting ranges, and gambling, as well as dress-up, hide-and-seek, and treasure hunts. Video games' storytelling and aesthetic elements fuse many genres, styles, and narrative traditions. While, as noted, classic literature appears infrequently in their repertoire of inspiration, there are close connections between the games and film industries (Moore 2010, 186). Jonathan Bignell considers the multiple influences upon some classic video games, which include Disney films, popular American and Japanese fantasy cinema, comic books, and *Star Wars* (2000, 212–13). Robin J. S. Sloan concludes a paper exploring nostalgia in contemporary video games by noting the medium is "capable of referencing virtually all of the media forms of the 20th century" (2015, 547). The history of digital play is one of hybridity, synergy, adaptation, and appropriation. Mia Consalvo explores how three major Japanese games companies represent exemplary instances of Henry Jenkins's convergence culture, their background in toys and amusements resulting in diffused media environments where no single product occupies primacy (2009, 135–7). Also drawing on Jenkins, Juul notes that games exist within an ecology of transmedia storytelling, but also within a general *game ecology* based on relationships with other ludic titles, genres, and franchises (2005, 17). Both convergence culture and transmedia storytelling can easily incorporate Gothic tropes, aesthetics, and digital experiences. One of the most successful international franchises, *Pokémon*, began life as a video game, although these origins may be obscured in the range of media throughout which this intellectual property has appeared. As any fan of the series will tell you, the franchise has its own Gothic branch in the form of ghost Pokémon. A recent mobile version of the series had players searching for apparitional Pokémon projected onto everyday environments using the augmented reality facilities of smartphone technology.

Like most popular entertainment, video games draw on many multimedia points of reference. They are also themselves multimedia experiences. Bolter and Grusin, whose term "remediation" has become an established way of exploring relationships between traditional and digital technologies, have much to say on the experiences and interfaces of the computer game. Gaming technologies effectively repurposed home computers, the television, the remote control, and the pocket calculator. Domestic games effectively adapted arcade experiences, integrating film, television, desktop icons, and, in the case of one celebrated early computer game, the book (2000, 89–94). Video game environments conspicuously integrate architecture, interior decoration, furniture, posters, paintings, photography, and music, both diegetic and non-diegetic. Cut sequences remediate the editing techniques of popular cinema and television, while orchestrated scenes unfolding within the game world often resemble theatrical performances. Games include elements of digital operating systems, such as icons, maps, menus, and GPS systems, which themselves have origins in a pre-digital era. Cartography remains one of the most significant components of the medium. A player's inventory might contain analog objects such as polaroid photographs, handwritten letters, newspaper clippings, stone tiles, jewelry, textiles, post-it notes, or sweet wrappers. As Taylor suggests, the ludic-Gothic combination of different forms of communication scattered throughout a horror game's world do not just serve a narrative function. They simultaneously express a traditional Gothic theme, illustrating "cycles of miscommunication," while "repeatedly emphasizing the importance of written texts, textual materiality, and its processing" (Taylor 2009, 52–3). Video games promise players the opportunity to live different lives, inhabit different subjectivities, and design their own Frankenstein bodies from selections of body parts and sliding scales of size and tone. In this and other respects, the video game shares postmodern qualities of the Gothic and the Gothic mash-up. Video games are postmodern in their indeterminacy, their decontextualization of aesthetic styles, their de-corporealization and re-corporealization of the playing subject, and their simulation of bodies, spaces, and activities. As a medium of bricolage, drawing from different media, genres, and aesthetics, of which the Gothic is but one, contemporary video games are characterized by the same hybridity, pastiche, and imitation of dead styles which Fredric Jameson argues is all that remains for late capitalist culture (1998, 132–3).

Video games are digital mash-ups combining styles and media forms. They are also *queer* mash-ups. The queerness of video games is a further point of intersection between games and the Gothic, which is particularly pertinent to this chapter's case study. Queerness is a highly contested feature of any popular medium, yet many authors have identified something queer in Gothic fiction's concern with the perverse, the abject, the marginal, and the maligned. The "unspeakable" tales and frantic narrators of Gothic fiction (Sedgwick 1986, 14) often imply deviant sexual desires, acts, and identities. Gothic, Eve Kosofsky Sedgwick argues, was the first literary genre to depict male homosexuality, providing a unique opportunity for authors to explore homosocial desire (1985, 91). Ellis Hanson notes that many significant Gothic scholars are also prominent queer theorists, including Sedgwick, George Haggerty, and James Kincaid. Despite the fit between queer and Gothic, Hanson acknowledges such criticism is "fraught with ambivalence and contradiction." Gothic fiction often reproduces homophobic paranoia and moral anxieties, while also serving as a site where excessive and transgressive depictions of unconventional sexualities resist containment (Hanson 2007, 176).

Throughout its history Gothic fiction has developed an increasingly complex and sympathetic disposition toward unspeakable sexualities, as has Gothic literary criticism. As E. L. McCallum states: "The relation between the Gothic and the queer [. . .] is by now a well-established aspect of this very mixed literary genre." Indeed, the author argues, with some relation to the Gothic mash-up, that the genre's queerness arises from the mode's hybridity, its combination of genres, of high and low culture, and of artificiality and realism (McCallum 2014, 71). Turning to one classic publication, Avril Horner and Sue Zlosnik describe Rebecca in Daphne du Maurier's 1938 novel as a queer vampiric character. Rebecca's body is unstable and associated with transgressive sexuality, as a desiring promiscuous heterosexual and as an implied lesbian. This invisible antagonist disrupts boundaries between gender, life and death, and sexual identity, emerging as an abject, ambiguous, in-between figure (Horner and Zlosnik 2014, 65). In their analysis, Horner and Zlosnik make clear the associations between queer identity, the vampire, the ghost, and the invisible female protagonist. In recent writings Gina Wisker identifies a "recuperation of the Other," which serves to "reconfigure difference as something to celebrate rather than fear and destroy." Such shifts in interpretation and representation are seen in both queer academic theory and in works by authors of lesbian and queer Gothic (Wisker 2009, 126–7). The Gothic has also been incorporated and recontextualized within popular culture, with some revealing instances of subcultural appropriation. Referencing the poster advertising a "polysexual" London club night, Hanson points to the perverse pleasures to be found in bounded, simulated, consensual traumatic experiences, indicating the desires accommodated by BDSM events coincide with those of Gothic literature (2007, 180).

McCallum's suggestion that "the gothic has always been queer" (2014, 85) resonates with the title of Bo Ruberg's 2019 publication presenting an identical statement about the nature and history of video games. This is an undeniably provocative assertion. No shortage of evidence indicates the extent mainstream games focus on the activities of white, male, cisgendered heterosexual protagonists, while facilitating activities defined by competition, domination, and the violent eradication of difference. The recent Gamergate controversy saw the magic circle of straight male gaming, perceived as under attack from non-traditional players, designers, and commentators, defended in the form of online rape and death threats. Nevertheless, as this controversy also evidences, video game cultures are far from uniform, and may exemplify a heterogeneity rarely seen in other popular media. As such, further implying a Gothic liminality, "'video game' is, by nature, neither a single nor a stable ontological category" (Ruberg 2019, 8–9). Video games incorporate many different platforms, genres, production models, and modes of gameplay. The medium includes arcade, console, computer, portable, and social media-based activities. While the first-person shooter, most aligned with hegemonic gamers, may have a primacy not afforded other genres, both mainstream and independent markets accommodate a profusion of game types. Play itself offers a range of possibilities. Ruberg persuasively argues that video game queerness resides in various qualities of exploration. discovery, closeness, physicality, intimacy, affect, embodiment, silliness, the possibility of resisting authority, breaking the rules, and "playing against the grain," even in games which contain no queer characters. In common with many contemporary writers, Ruberg argues that debates around identity and games need to move "beyond representation" (2019, 14) to include appreciation of aspects including game mechanics, controllers, and fandoms (2019, 12).

In common with other queer academics, Ruberg illustrates how straight texts can be effectively unstraightened through radical interpretive methods. The act of play, like the act of resistant reading, has the potential for "disrupting and dismantling heteronormativity itself" (Ruberg 2019, 15). Modding, an established practice throughout gaming history which entails literally rewriting game data, effectively reifies this counterhegemonic strategy in practices which "enact queerness by reshaping the game's very code through non-normative player agencies" (Ruberg 2019, 12). This represents a form of remix culture which approaches the Gothic mash-up De Bruin-Molé (2020) describes. In a subsequent publication, Ruberg (2020a) turns attention to the "queer games avant-garde," a subculture of independent production dating back nearly ten years. Games of this stable are often made by LGBTQ designers, inspired by their own queer experiences, adopting a scrappy, zine-like aesthetic. Employing distribution methods and funding strategies which bypass established business models, these are low budget titles, produced by small teams for queer players, inspired, among other impulses, by a desire to "explore alternative ways of being" (Ruberg 2020a, 1–3). Many games Ruberg considers express various Gothic qualities. Their narratives involve bondage and cross-dressing twins, teenagers fighting the devil at summer camp, and abusive relationships, accompanied by monstrous images of tentacled creatures, a decapitated wolf, and a witch on the moon. The sample Ruberg explores suggests compelling overlaps among the queer, the Gothic, and the video game.

GONE HOME AS GHOST STORY

From its first moments, *Gone Home* situates itself as a Gothic game. Players arrive on the doorstep of a large empty house in the middle of a thunderstorm. Assuming the role of Katie Greenbriar, who returns from a year traveling to find her family home strangely deserted, play involves investigating the mansion, searching for evidence explaining the mysterious whereabouts of her parents and sister. The labyrinthine house is a maze of rooms, corridors, and secret passageways. Suggestions the building is haunted by its former owner contribute to a spooky atmosphere of menace and foreboding. Like many Gothic family narratives, the story that players uncover is one of dysfunctionality, sexual repression, and generational conflict. It tells of a depressive father, a dissatisfied mother, and Katie's younger sister, Sam, who during her sibling's absence has developed a romantic relationship with a girl at school. *Gone Home* evidences the Gothic in games, but also Gothic mash-up culture. Taking place in 1990s America, it is among two titles considered by Sloan in an exploration of nostalgia in contemporary video games. The maturation of the market, Sloan notes, has led to "an increasing number of video games that seek to integrate cross-media references into their design to satisfy the wider nostalgic urges of consumers." In an assessment uncannily familiar to scholars of the Gothic, the postmodern, and the mash-up, Sloan observes "the embedding of nostalgic references within nostalgic references, to the point where historicity is replaced by an ambiguous image of the past" (2015, 526–7). The Greenbriar home is filled with digital versions of food, textiles and furnishings, cereal boxes, board games, and dot matrix documents which simulate 1990s design styles. Accompanied by references to Gothic media and television shows, including *The X-Files*, *Picket Fences*, and *American Gothic*, *Gone Home* engages in a familiar mediation of the past through a combination of digital facsimiles, clichés, and representations. Its very process of narration is rooted in nostalgia, a quality itself heavily associated with Gothic fiction and protagonists. A substantial part of the story is delivered by Sam's voice-overs, activated by interactions with particularly pertinent objects. As Sloan points out, this narrative self-consciously follows the confessional format of 1990s teen dramas (2015, 544). Replacing the imagined Dark Ages of traditional Gothic with late twentieth-century culture, *Gone Home* is engaged in a complex remediation of history similar to De Bruin-Molé's Frankentexts (2020, 16–17).

Crucial to the Gothic ludic experience it delivers, *Gone Home* takes place within a family home. Barry Curtis (2008) details the importance of haunted houses to cinema, while Perron acknowledges the presence of houses across classic scary video games, including *Resident Evil*, *Eternal Darkness*, and *Amnesia* (2018, 321). The horrors of the family home, supernatural or otherwise, have concerned Gothic fiction since its inception, often suggesting an uncanny synergy between the family and the walls within which it is contained. A portrait showing Terry, Janice, Katie, and Sam hangs in the mansion hallway and is one of the first pieces of media that players encounter. Suggesting overlaps between the Gothic and video game narrative techniques, Dimitrios Pavlounis observes how *Gone Home* has been celebrated as an example of "environmental storytelling," a process which involves "uncovering and reanimating the past" (2016, 579–80). Jenkins influentially argues for a critical approach to video game storytelling which privileges "spatial exploration" over the "causal event chains" of classical linear narrative (2004, 121–2). King and Krzywinska write of a Gothic animation and anthropomorphizing of digital environments, arguing: "More than simply a background setting, the world of the game is often as much a protagonist, or even antagonist, as its inhabitants" (2006, 76). The home of *Gone Home* functions as a substitute for the absent Greenbriar family. The study evidences Terry's despondency. A failed writer, stacks of unsold copies of his novel lie in boxes in the cupboard. The bar in his den suggests the man is turning to alcohol for consolation. The couple's bedroom indicates the dissatisfaction Janice feels in her marriage. By her bedside lies a copy of Walt Whitman poetry, on loan from a work colleague with whom Janice is clearly enamored. Sam has turned the mansion's basement into a workshop where she produces her own photocopied riot grrrl fanzine.

As discussed, video game players frequently assume the role of detective, and *Gone Home* positions the player as amateur sleuth (Veale 2017, 660) investigating the reason behind the parents' absence and the conclusion to Sam's story. *Gone Home*'s narrative emerges through a patchwork of media fragments, including letters, photographs, scribbled notes, portraits, newspaper clippings, and postcards, concealed within the game's virtual drawers, cupboards, and closets. In a discussion of architecture, narrative, and the environment's personification of the absent family, Kevin Veale observes that the house is littered with objects which reveal the last year of the family's history, but also extend back decades (2017, 659). The house is burdened with documentary and material reminders of the past, functioning to flesh out the Greenbriar's family saga. There is something of the Frankenfiction in this multimedia mash-up, recalling Fred Botting's description of *Frankenstein* itself as "a novel composed of frames," which, in its fragmented nature, reflects the creature at its center (2007, 102). This game is far from "neat, comprehensive, or well-formed in the traditional sense." Instead it is "a messy conglomeration of texts from various media, registers, and narrative traditions" (de Bruin-Molé 2020, 9). There is often something ghostly about these documents. Communications from Terry to his daughter, notes from Sam to Lonnie, and letters between Janice and her old college roommate resonate with the haunting quality which Wolfreys (2002) argues surround all texts, stories, and narratives. These characters are never met, and therefore only exist in these media remains. Together with other Gothic qualities this suggests that *Gone Home* is a ghost story. One commentator whom Rowan Tulloch et al. cite writes of "waiting for the inevitable ghost," producing for one player a terrifying gaming experience (2019, 339). Play is directed toward the locked attic, a space that traditionally resonates with foreboding. Sam's disembodied messages and spectral narration contribute to the impression her voice emerges post-mortem. Modern media is replete with narratives of dead queer characters. Even stories depicting homosexuality in a sympathetic manner frequently end in tragedy. Sam's story progresses from courtship to passion to anguish, as her girlfriend Lonnie announces she is leaving to join the armed forces. The young woman's suicide would seem in keeping, not only with the Gothic horror story, but also a homophobic culture which cannot imagine a happy ending for two young gay lovers.

The fact Sam is very much alive does not preclude *Gone Home* from being considered a ghost story. As Simon Hay writes, this is a loose generic category, in which many hauntings reveal themselves to be "hoaxes or misunderstandings" (2011, 22) similar to the ones this game engineers. Characterized by its short form, its marginal status, and engagement in politics of domestic oppression, the ghost story has attracted particular critical attention of late. One quality *Gone Home* shares with the genre is brevity, a feature noted by many investigating the format. Using typical architectural terms to emphasize its economy, Julia Briggs compares the "bare scaffolding" of the ghost story to "the rambling mansion of the Gothic novel" (1977, 13). More recently Victoria Margree argues the short story format is hospitable to ghosts, whose credibility becomes much harder to sustain across the duration of a standard novel (2019, 9–10). *Gone Home* is a comparatively modest title. As Sloan notes, this was a game made by an independent studio with just four members of staff (2015, 528), while Dean Bowman notes the exploration game's short play time (2019, 156).

Like many ghost stories (Curtis 2008, 15), both the ghost and the medium through which they communicate are female. Consistent with Gothic themes of doubling, the game elicits various uncanny parallels between the two sisters. Investigating the unfamiliar family home, Katie follows in her sister's footsteps, finding the hidden passageways Sam has mapped out on documents concealed throughout the house. If, as the player may suspect, Sam is a departed spirit, Katie is unconsciously reproducing her sibling's pursuit of the supernatural. An Ouija board shows Sam and Lonnie spent much time hunting Oscar, a deceased relative believed to haunt the building. Katie herself is somewhat spectral, a consequence of the non-corporal nature of the game's first-person perspective. The point is frequently made by feminist literary critics that patriarchy renders women "ghost-like" (Wallace 2004, 57), affecting an association with the *ghostly* (Margree 2019, 6), suppressing and consequently ghosting women's experiences (Smith 2010, 6). Ghost stories, like *Gone Home*, unearth hidden histories, characterized by domestic oppression, injustice, and abuse. Margree notes how women writers working in the early twentieth century continued a tradition developed in oral storytelling whereby the ghost returns to deliver justice "from beyond the grave" (2019, 3). Consequently "women's ghost stories repeatedly stage scenarios of women's silencing and exclusion" (Margree 2019, 15). Similar points might be made about the lesbian community's historical erasure. Within such a framework, it is significant that *Gone Home* voices the experiences of a queer teenage girl who suffers homophobic bullying from her peers, indifference from school authorities, hostility, and denial from her parents.

The queerness of *Gone Home* resides not only in its principal character, but also its ludic structure. The game is commonly considered a "walking simulator," a slow-paced first-person genre privileging exploration and narrative over action and competition. Actual tasks required to complete the game are comparatively few: finding a combination lock, uncovering a series of secret panels, and locating the key to the attic where Sam's journal lies waiting. The title's engagement with Juul's (2005) "game ecology" involves appropriating gameplay mechanics of the first-person shooter, a genre which Morris notes typically entails hostile environments, weapon accumulation, and monstrous enemies (2002, 82–3). It is politically significant, Bowman argues, that *Gone Home* reorients such a hypermasculine genre, associated with what Kline et al. term "militarised masculinity" (qtd. in Bowman 2019, 156) into a domestic story about a queer teenage woman. Referencing recent work on identity politics and contemporary games, Bowman argues that such titles are central to struggles concerning "changing definitions and material realities of videogame consumption and production, linked to the emergence of disruptive female and queer player and creator identities" (2019, 150). Insofar as *Gone Home* and other walking simulators emphasize exploration over combat-based point scoring, their gameplay deviates significantly from the normativity of dominant gaming experiences. It is no coincidence that examples of this cycle contain unusually high proportions of female and queer protagonists (Ruberg 2020b, 637).

Mindful of the multiple ways games engage with identity politics, Ruberg argues *Gone Home* constitutes "a game that expresses queerness through its gameplay as well as through its LGBTQ representation" (2020b, 634). In characterizing the title's mode of engagement, Ruberg draws on Melissa Kagen, Dietrich Squinkifer, and Gaspard Pelurson's discussion of the walking simulator as positioning the player as "queer *flâneur*" (2020b, 637). Pelurson mobilizes Walter Benjamin's theorizing of this figure, as developed by postmodern queer scholarship (2018, 922). A historically ambivalent individual, the *flâneur* is characteristically idle, curious, detached, and directionless, wandering the arcades of the metropolitan city, with no particular place to go. Considering a comparable queer video game, Pelurson notes the experience's leisurely pace, how play does not operate within standard time constraints, and does not adopt traditional systems of reward and achievement (2018, 928). *Gone Home* and other walking simulators offer similar non-normative game pleasures. In such titles "gameplay seems to be structured around queer wandering, moving not straight (as along a straight line) but instead meanderingly through the game's temporal and spatial dimensions" (Ruberg 2020b, 633). As observed, Sedgwick's discussion of Gothic's fascination with "unspeakable" horrors is awkwardly reflected in the genre's willingness to depict groups characterized by queer sexualities as shrouded in secrecy and shame. So "unspeakable" are such matters that the early Gothic text itself collapses rather than reveal its true subject (Sedgwick 1985, 94). In contrast, while *Gone Home* does end when Katie discovers the manuscript of her sister's diary, denying players the opportunity to read it with her, the document's work has already been done. Sam's experiences have been clearly communicated throughout the game's play through. We have learned of her bonding with Lonnie over playing *Street Fighter*, of their trip to see *Pulp Fiction*, of their shared love of riot grrrl music, an inclusion on the game's diegetic soundtrack which, far from the shallow nostalgia Sloan

(2005) suggests, or the playful postmodernity of De Bruin-Molé's (2020) Frankenfiction, Tulloch et al. argue is central to the game's politics of female agency and voice (2019, 338).

Despite all cues to the contrary, this is not a ghost story, a horror game, or a tragic dead lesbian narrative. The voice-over we hear belongs to a woman very much alive. The object hidden in the attic is not Sam's body, but her body of work. *Gone Home* does not close with the marriage of the heroine, the traditional conclusion of the Gothic romance. Neither does it end in the death or insanity of the lesbian heroine, the fate of so many queer characters in popular culture. The game concludes with the revelation that Sam has left the oppressive family home and run off with her girlfriend. The theme of containment and escape, Susanne Becker argues, is central to Gothic fiction. Escape implies both "the *thematic* enclosure of the female subject within the house" and "the *formal* enclosure of the text" (1999, 19). Sam manages to escape on a number of levels. She escapes the patriarchal family home, the homophobic school in which she has been persecuted, and the military institution which would take away the love of her life. She also escapes the literary restraints of her character type, avoiding her predetermined fate as mad woman in the attic or dead queer. Sam also escapes the text itself, and remains represented only by her own words and the documents she had left behind.

CONCLUSION

The video game can be understood as a mash-up format. Games appropriate a combination of aesthetics, media, and modes in the generation of a wide range of digital experiences. Spaces in games primarily draw upon architecture, but also interior decoration, theater, paintings, and photography. Virtual environments are often populated as much by media artifacts as they are by people. The incorporation of the Gothic does not rely so much on specific characters as it does settings, aesthetics, and mechanisms which have been employed in the service of the game's specific needs: providing uncanny adversaries, baroque puzzles, and hazardous interiors which must be overcome, solved, and navigated. Video games have always been Gothic, and they have always been queer; and it is tempting to see connections between these two ubiquitous qualities. *Gone Home* certainly functions in dialogue with both to generate ludic mystery, heavily suggesting its central character is speaking from beyond the grave, or rather, from beyond the attic. A video game ecology heavily reliant on Gothic tropes sets the scene for a supernatural, tragic, or grizzly end to Sam's tale. Similarly, a legacy of dead gays within popular culture, itself not inseparable from Gothic queerness, primes players for a conclusion involving suicide. That *Gone Home* ends on a high point, with Sam and Lonnie escaping into the night, subverts such expectations. While a site of celebration in the context of a heteronormative video game climate, there are limitations to the game's queerness. *Gone Home* may be progressive in its representation of sexuality, but its content is less diverse regarding class and ethnicity. Briggs points to two strategies that ghost story writers employ to evoke a recognizable world: they either locate the story in an ordinary middle-class setting or in an outlandish environment which is nevertheless described in a naturalistic manner (1977, 18). The "ordinariness" of the Greenbriar household, as Tulloch et al. observe, is a white and upper-middle-class normativity reflecting the orientation of both riot grrrl music and games journalism (2019, 346). Part of its evocation of 1990s media, the game's confessional tone reproduces the voice-overs of television shows which "typically focused on the angst and troubles of teenage, White, middle-class Americans" (Sloan 2015, 544). Ruberg also argues that despite offering queer free-form exploration, *Gone Home* conforms to a more rigid, linear structure than many commentators acknowledge (2020b, 633.) Various "gating" techniques can be identified which determine players' movement through the mansion. Exploration is thereby organized to follow a particular, often chronological, pathway (Ruberg 2020b, 640–2). The point where players discover Sam's journal might constitute a moment of heterosexual straightening whereby the queer strands are brought together in a hermeneutic whole. Nevertheless, despite such criticisms, *Gone Home* constitutes a progressive video game title, evidencing the ways critical approaches to Gothic literature and queer scholarship can be productively employed to understand this developing digital medium.

REFERENCES

Becker, Susanne. 1999. *Gothic Forms of Feminine Fictions*. Manchester: Manchester University Press.
Bignell, Jonathan. 2007. *Postmodern Media Culture*. Edinburgh: Edinburgh University Press.
Bloom, Clive. 2010. *Gothic Histories: The Taste for Terror, 1764 to the Present*. London: Continuum.
Bolter, Jay David, and Richard Grusin. 2000. *Remediation: Understanding New Media*. London: MIT Press.
Botting, Fred. 2007. *Gothic*. London: Routledge.
Bowman, Dean. 2019. "Domesticating the First-Person Shooter: The Emergent Challenge of *Gone Home*'s Homely Chronotope." *Press Start* 5 (2): 150–75.
Briggs, Julia. 1977. *Night Visitors: The Rise and Fall of the English Ghost Story*. London: Faber.

de Bruin-Molé, Megen. 2020. *Gothic Remixed: Monster Mashups and Frankenfictions in 21st-Century Culture*. London: Bloomsbury Academic.

Carr, Diane. 2006. "Space, Navigation and Affect." In *Computer Games: Text, Narrative and Play*, edited by Diane Carr, David Buckingham, Andrew Burn, and Gareth Schott, 59–71. Cambridge: Polity.

Consalvo, Mia. 2009. "Convergence and Globalization in the Japanese Videogame Industry." *Cinema Journal* 48 (3): 135–41.

Cooke, Arthur L. 2004. "Some Side Lights on the Theory of the Gothic Romance." In *Gothic: Critical Concepts in Literary and Cultural Studies*, edited by Fred Botting and Dale Townshend, 19–26. London: Routledge.

Curtis, Barry. 2008. *Dark Places: The Haunted House in Film*. London: Reaktion Books.

Egenfeldt-Nielsen, Simon, Jonas Heide Smith, and Susana Pajares Tosca. 2008. *Understanding Video Games: The Essential Introduction*. London: Routledge.

Elliott, Kamilla. 2008. "Gothic-Film-Parody." *Adaptation* 1 (1): 24–43.

Hand, Richard J. 2004. "Proliferating Horrors: Survival Horror and the *Resident Evil* Franchise." In *Horror Film: Creating and Marketing Fear*, edited by Steffen Hantke, 117–34. Jackson: University of Mississippi Press.

Hanson, Ellis. 2007. "Queer Gothic." In *The Routledge Companion to Gothic*, edited by Catherine Spooner and Emma McEvoy, 174–82. London: Routledge.

Hay, Simon. 2011. *A History of the Modern British Ghost Story*. Basingstoke: Palgrave Macmillan.

Horner, Avril, and Sue Zlosnik. 2014. "Gothic Configurations of Gender." In *The Cambridge Companion to the Modern Gothic*, edited by Jerrold E. Hogle, 55–70. Cambridge: Cambridge University Press.

Jameson, Fredric. 1998. "Postmodernism and Consumer Society." In *The Anti-Aesthetic: Essays on Postmodern Culture*, edited by Hal Foster, 127–44. New York: The New Press.

Jenkins, Henry. 2004. "Game Design as Narrative Architecture." In *FirstPerson: New Media as Story, Performance, and Game*, edited by Noah Wardrip-Fruin and Pat Harrigan, 118–30. London: MIT Press.

Juul, Jesper. 2005. *Half-Real: Video Games Between Real Rules and Fictional Worlds*. London: MIT Press.

Kaye, Heidi. 2012. "Gothic Film." In *A New Companion to the Gothic*, edited by David Punter, 239–51. Blackwell.

King, Geoff, and Tanya Krzywinska. 2002. "Cinema/videogames/interfaces." In *ScreenPlay: Cinema/videogames/interfaces*, edited by Geoff King and Tanya Krzywinska, 1–32. London: Wallflower Press.

———. 2006. *Tomb Raiders and Space Invaders: Videogame Forms and Contexts*. London: I. B. Tauris.

Kirkland, Ewan. 2012. "Gothic Videogames, Survival Horror and the *Silent Hill* Series." *Gothic Studies* 14 (2): 106–22.

———. 2016. "Undead Avatars: The Zombie in Horror Video Games." In *Vampires and Zombies: Transcultural Migrations and Transnational Interpretations*, edited by Dorothea Fischer-Hornung and Monika Mueller, 229–45. Jackson: University Press of Mississippi.

Krzywinska, Tanya. 2002. "Hands-on Horror." In *ScreenPlay: Cinema/videogames/interfaces*, edited by Geoff King and Tanya Krzywinska, 206–23. London: Wallflower Press.

———. 2009. "Reanimating Lovecraft: The Ludic Paradox of *Call of Cthulhu: Dark Corners of the Earth*." In *Horror Video Games: Essays on the Fusion of Fear and Play*, edited by Bernard Perron, 267–87. London: McFarland and Company.

———. 2014. "Digital Games and the American Gothic: Investigating Gothic Game Grammar." In *A Companion to American Gothic*, edited by Charles L. Crow, 503–15. John Wiley and Sons.

Margree, Victoria. 2019. *British Women's Short Supernatural Fiction, 1860–1930: Our Own Ghostliness*. Basingstoke: Palgrave Macmillan.

McCallum, E. L. 2014. "The 'Queer Limits' in the Modern Gothic." In *The Cambridge Companion to the Modern Gothic*, edited by Jerrold E. Hogle, 71–86. Cambridge: Cambridge University Press.

Moore, Michael Ryan. 2010. "Adaptation and New Media." *Adaptation* 3 (2): 179–92.

Morris, Sue. 2002. "First-Person Shooters: A Game Apparatus." In *ScreenPlay: Cinema/videogames/interfaces*, edited by Geoff King and Tanya Krzywinska, 81–97. London: Wallflower Press.

Pavlounis, Dimitrios. 2016. "Straightening Up the Archive: Queer Historiography, Queer Play, and the Archival Politics of *Gone Home*." *Television & New Media* 17 (7): 579–94.

Pelurson, Gaspard. 2018. "Flânerie in the Dark Woods: Shattering Innocence and Queering Time in *The Path*." *Convergence: The International Journal of Research into New Media Technologies*. 25 (5–6): 918–36.

Perron, Bernard. 2018. *The World of Scary Video Games: A Study in Videoludic Horror*. London: Bloomsbury.

Round, Julia. 2012. "Gothic and the Graphic Novel." In *A New Companion to the Gothic*, edited by David Punter, 335–49. Oxford: Blackwell.

Rouse III, Richard. 2009. "Match Made in Hell: The Inevitable Success of the Horror Genre in Video Games." In *Horror Video Games: Essays on the Fusion of Fear and Play*, edited by Bernard Perron, 15–25. London: McFarland and Company.

Ruberg, Bo. 2019. *Video Games Have Always Been Queer*. New York: New York University Press.

———. 2020a. *The Queer Games Avant-Garde: How LGBTQ Game Makers are Reimagining the Medium of Video Games*. Durham: Duke University Press.

———. 2020b. "Straight Paths through Queer Walking Simulators: Wandering on Rails and Speedrunning in *Gone Home*." *Games and Culture* 15 (6): 632–52.

Sedgwick, Eve Kosofsky. 1985. *Between Men: English Literature and Male Homosocial Desire*. New York: Columbia University Press.

———. 1986. *The Coherence of Gothic Conventions*. London: Methuen.

Sloan, Robin J. S. 2015. "Videogames as Remediated Memories: Commodified Nostalgia and Hyperreality in *Far Cry* 3: *Blood Dragon* and *Gone Home*." *Games and Culture* 10 (6): 525–50.

Smith, Andrew. 2010. *The Ghost Story, 1840–1920: A Cultural History*. Manchester: Manchester University Press.

Sontag, Susan. 1979. *On Photography*. London: Penguin.

Sweet, Rosemary. 2014. "Gothic Antiquarianism in the Eighteenth Century." In *The Gothic World*, edited by Glennis Byron and Dale Townshend, 15–26. London: Routledge.

Taylor, Laurie N. 2009. "Gothic Bloodlines in Survival Horror Gaming." In *Horror Video Games: Essays on the Fusion of Fear and Play*, edited by Bernard Perron, 46–61. London: McFarland and Company.

Tibbetts, John C. 2002. "The Old Dark House: The Architecture of Ambiguity in *The Turn of the Screw* and *The Innocents*." In *British Horror Cinema* edited by Steve Chibnall and Julian Petley, 97–115. London: Routledge.

Tinwell, Angela. 2015. *The Uncanny Valley in Games and Animation*. London: Taylor and Francis.

Tulloch, Rowan, Catherine Hoad, and Helen Young. 2019. "Riot Grrrl Gaming: Gender, Sexuality, Race, and the Politics of Choice in *Gone Home*." *Journal of Media and Culture Studies* 33 (3): 337–50.

Veale, Kevin. 2017. "*Gone Home*, and the Power of Affective Nostalgia." *International Journal of Heritage Studies* 23 (7): 654–66.

Wallace, Diana. 2004. "Uncanny Stories: The Ghost Story as Female Gothic." *Gothic Studies* 6 (1): 57–68.

Wisker, Gina. 2009. "Devouring Desires: Lesbian Gothic Horror." In *Queering the Gothic*, edited by William Hughes and Andrew Smith, 123–41. Manchester: Manchester University Press.

Wolfreys, Julian. 2002. *Victorian Hauntings: Spectrality, Gothic, the Uncanny and Literature*. Basingstoke, Palgrave.

Chapter 14

Hypertext of Horrors

A Post-Mortem of Evermore: A Choose Your Own Edgar Allan Poe Adventure

Adam Whybray

POE AND HYPERTEXT: CREATING UNITY FROM FRAGMENTS

The stories of Edgar Allan Poe epitomize the tendency of Gothic fiction toward the mash-up. On the surface, this might seem to contradict the author's own statements of aesthetic philosophy. Poe, in his 1846 essay "The Philosophy of Composition," expressed the importance of "unity of effect" whereby all elements in a work should contribute to the achievement of a "novel" and "vivid effect" (2017, 2). James Wilson, summarizing the essay, explains that Poe "holds the totality of effect to be the end towards which every art device must be trained" (1926/1927, 679). Yet, in apparent contradiction to its focus upon compositional unity, Marshall Brown uses "The Philosophy of Composition" to illustrate that the author's principal method of creation was one of blending heterogeneous elements (2005, 20). Indeed, Brown suggests that Poe was not unique in this collagist tendency, which he sees as typical of the Gothic genre. In particular, Brown also locates the approach in works by Henry James and Mary Shelley.

Shelley's 1818 novel *Frankenstein; or, The Modern Prometheus* was the first classic Gothic text to be adapted into digital hypertext. It was mashed up with L. Frank Baum's *The Patchwork Girl of Oz* (1913) by Shelley Jackson using Eastgate System's hypertext-creation software Storyspace and released as *Patchwork Girl* in 1995. Jackson's repurposing of Shelley's text deliberately reflects the fact that *Frankenstein* was itself already a Gothic mash-up of early nineteenth-century science and the myth of Prometheus. Jackson not only combines fragments of the disparate works together with her own writing, but she foregrounds the theme of fragmentation and re-composition by rendering the concept of text *corpus* ickily literal by requiring the reader/player to navigate the work by clicking on disassembled body parts and the labeled sections of a phrenology diagram. Hypertext is navigated by the reader via hyperlinks between nodes. In *Patchwork Girl*, for instance, these different body parts, which link to different fragments of text, are nodes. This navigation ensures that hypertext possesses a degree of interaction and tends toward a nonlinear and associative (rather than purely sequential) structure. The World Wide Web is one example of an especially large and sprawling hypertext. My 2016 game *Evermore: A Choose Your Own Edgar Allan Poe Adventure* is a much smaller, more contained hypertext. As with Jackson's selection of Shelley's novel, I chose to adapt stories, poems, and essays by Edgar Allan Poe due to their formal qualities. Poe's self-reflexivity, use of pastiche, and penchant for ambiguous endings make his stories uniquely suited to the hypertext form. In fact, after further elucidating these characteristics, I will build upon the work of prior critics to argue that Poe's stories could even be considered proto-hypertexts. I will then proceed to discuss how *Evermore* exemplifies, illustrates, and builds upon the mash-up tendencies in Poe's own work.

HYPERTEXTUAL CHARACTERISTICS IN POE

Today we tend to think of Poe primarily as a writer of Gothic horror, but it is more accurate to see him as a nineteenth-century man of letters—the equivalent of, say, H. G. Wells, Jules Verne, or even Mark Twain—who made his living from writing and publishing in a variety of different forms and commenting upon the writing of others. Poe was, among other things, an author of grotesque satires who would use elements from Gothic horror to play upon popular scientific or philosophic topics of the day. Subjects covered by Poe include ballooning, communication with the undead, and treatises on philosophy and the universe. Similarly, Poe's tales cannot be easily categorized as belonging to one single genre, for they generally contain elements associated with multiple genres, including detective fiction, adventure narratives, and the Gothic. His writing also slips perversely between the nonfictional and the fictional, moving between falsified events, pure fabulation, and quasi-scientific reportage with little differentiation. Sometimes this tendency was reinforced by Poe publishing his work anonymously or under a nom de plume. This allowed him to perpetuate several journalistic hoaxes—most successfully in 1844 with his publication of fictitious diary extracts by the balloonist Monck Mason in the New York paper *The Sun*. Indeed, many of Poe's anthologized short stories were originally published in newspapers and periodicals, though he also released four poetry collections, a textbook on seashells, many essays and reviews, a pamphlet on mesmerism, and the novel *The Narrative of Arthur Gordon Pym of Nantucket* (1837/1838) within his lifetime.

It is Poe's considerable plurality of thought and ability to jump between different genres and cultural discourses that make his writing ideally suited to hypertext. In contrast to more linear forms of storytelling, Astrid Ensslin characterizes hypertext as having a rhizomatic structure (2007, 21 and 63). This means that hypertexts tend not to have a single beginning which leads inexorably to a singular end, but exist in perpetual *medias res*, pointing readers in multiple directions, instead of only one. While Poe ostensibly worked in the linear medium of print, the rhizomatic structure of hypertext is mirrored in the lack of closure that a lot of his stories end upon. Sometimes—as in "The Business Man" (1840) or "The Man of the Crowd" (1840)—we do not know what happens to the characters after the stories end, or else—as in "Some Words with a Mummy" (1845) or "The Facts in the Case of M. Valdemar" (1845)—they deal with people who are both alive *and* dead at the same time. These characters seem trapped in hideously liminal in-between states, as though their stories are not allowed to fully end or begin. The narrators of "The Black Cat" (1843), "The Imp of the Perverse" (1845), and "The Tell-Tale Heart" (1843) finish their stories having confessed to murderous crimes, but we never hear of their subsequent executions, as though they are left confessing in a perpetual purgatory. For instance, the narrator of "The Imp of the Perverse" finishes his account with a questioning lament, left forever suspended and unanswered: "To-day I wear these chains, and am here! To-morrow I shall be fetterless—*but where?*" (Poe [1845] 2009, 265).

Poe's narrators are often nameless, as is also the case in the second-person address of much hypertext and interactive fiction (e.g., "You are standing in a forest"; "You travel North"; etc.). This allows for Poe's first-person narratives to be converted without much difficulty or resistance into second person. The namelessness of many of Poe's narrators and their related lack of biographical details create an absence at the heart of the fictional subjectivity in stories like "The Tell-Tale Heart" and "The Black Cat." In a traditional linear reading of those stories, this absence is filled imaginatively by readers, who put themselves in the shoes of the narrator—providing Poe's Gothic narratives with much of their disturbing power. In a hypertext game, this identification is carried further through interactivity, with the reader/player making decisions on behalf of the narrator.

Chris Benfey argues that Poe's stories are ultimately about how we are always enigmas to one another (1993, 27–44). The subjectivity of another's mind is only ever experienced at a remove, glimpsed piecemeal. We are reminded of this disquieting fact both when writing a work of hypertext *and* when reading one. This is because the coding language in which hypertext is (at least partially) written is unseen by—and likely unknowable to—the reader/player, who only sees the surface-level output of this coding. It is as though the text read by the reader/player veils a secondary more obscure or gnomic text, like in a reversal of the cryptogram in Poe's "The Gold-Bug" (1843). Kenneth Silverman writes that there is often an inscrutable, menacing paranormal world "lurking behind the workaday world" (1993, 7) in Poe's stories. We might, if reading hypertext based upon Poe's stories, think of this secondary hidden world as being the world of the writer-programmer. Astrid Ensslin (2007, 12), after Marie Laure-Ryan (2001), notes that the freedom of the hypertext reader is always relative because it is always wholly contingent upon choices already made by the writer/programmer, whose presence haunts the text. You are never quite alone when reading hypertext, and you are never quite as free as you would like to feel you are. This idea of freedom being illusionary because the choices available to the individual have already been circumscribed is highly apposite to Poe's protagonists who often read as though their thoughts and actions have been engineered by the Imp of the Perverse (or, indeed, Poe).

George Landow's influential theory of the "wreader" (1992, 1997) holds that the players or readers of hypertext should be understood as *simultaneously writing* hypertext as they read it. Through making choices and interacting with the hypertext, Landow argues, the reader helps determine the form it takes. Since one reader will encounter the text in a different order to another reader (or, indeed, may only encounter some parts of it at the expense of others) their specific iterations of the hypertext are uniquely created in the process of its reading. While this is a romantic notion, I ultimately agree with Ensslin that Landow's theory of the "wreader" is flawed because, while the reader of hypertext may be making choices, these choices have already been anticipated by the writer/programmer (Ensslin 2007, 31). The reader of hypertext is not a full participant in what they read but neither are they a completely passive reader. Landow's formation is more accurate if it is reversed, with the reader configured instead as a "rewriter," with a hand in shaping a narrative which they explore often intuitively and haphazardly. Like the doomed Fortunato of Poe's "The Cask of Amontillado" (1846), the reader/writer stumbles through the dark, led by the hand of the writer/programmer, who is always one step ahead—the only true freedom afforded them, the freedom of leaving or quitting the game. "Player," therefore, ascribes too much free agency to the reader of hypertext, who often does not navigate the hypertext tactically with a specific goal in mind or a settled notion of how to win.

Instead of the term "player," it is more accurate to use a term attributed to Roberto Simanowski (2004, 81) by Ensslin (2007, 32), who describes the reader of hypertext as an "unsettled traveler." This perfectly fits Poe's propensity toward the figure of the *flâneur*, the idle urban wanderer. This figure, according to Benjamin Fisher, enabled Poe

> to make deft transitions from panoramic to individual scenes, which in turn reflect the psychological makeup of the narrator [. . . .] [T]he curiosity in such an onlooker enhances the visual element in a tale as he (or she, in "A Predicament") mulls possibilities for meaning in what is beheld, be his/her thoughts the musings of an idler or shock reactions to startling or appalling visual scenes. (2008, 62)

The *flâneur* gathers to him/herself sensory fragments of experience which are arranged and assimilated into a holistic impression of the environment. These impressionistic fragments exist both in terms of their interrelations and in-and-of-themselves individually. Poe's ultimate aim is, Silverman writes, "[t]o achieve a tale in which every word, sentence, rhythm, and structural device expresses a single end, in which everything depends upon everything else" (1993, 10). This project, however, "lies beyond human ability, requiring a structural mega-memory and a transcendent ingenuity" (Silverman 1993, 10). To modern eyes, this can only read like the description of hypertext, the Internet, or a neural network. For me, it recalls Ted Nelson's utopian proto-World Wide Web hypertext project Xanadu (1960–), which was meant to be an encyclopedia of all world literature linked together associatively with no start and no end.

So, to recap, Poe's works fit the hypertext form because they: hop between genres and different styles, often through the use of pastiche; eschew closure in favor of heterogeneity, multiplicity and openness; often have nameless narrators, suiting the switch from first to second person; have an allegorical tendency toward a second world of meaning hidden beneath the surface-level world; and tend to be composed of images, effects, and motifs that arrest the reader's attention individually while also forming part of a greater aesthetic whole. They also often include the figure of the *flâneur*, who is perfectly matched to the "unsettled traveler" (Simanowski 2004, 81) of hypertext.

Further, to quote Silverman, almost every tale by Poe "dramatizes some means by which one can die and still live" (1993, 22). What is a video game or hypertext but a story in which, as a reader/player, you can die and then live again repeatedly? Indeed, we might even see Twine, the program in which a lot of modern hypertext is written, as a series of coffin-like enclosures, from which the reader/player can yet reawaken or, reversing time, go back from to make another decision. Ensslin (2007, 15) implies there is an inherent morbidity to the hypertext form via a quotation from Terry Harpold (1991): "Hypertexts are dismembered sorts of texts, marked by wounds at each irreducible turn of the narrative, and [. . .] reading these texts is a kind of ritual binding of the wounds, and an elevation of the fragmented corpus to a totemic object." Indeed, there are so many violent deaths in old "Choose Your Own Adventure" (CYOA) books that they rival Poe for the amount of space they give over to details of demise and dissolution.

It has been established that Poe's stories bear many of the characteristics of hypertext, but it is worth considering whether we can go further and see some of his works as proto-hypertext, which anticipate and even surpass the form in some regards.

POE'S WORK AS PROTO-HYPERTEXT

"Poe in Cyberspace" columns have run in *The Edgar Allan Poe Review* since 1998, largely written by Heyward Ehrlich, with early articles simply recommending various Edgar Allan Poe related websites, databases, CD-ROMs, projects, and societies. By 2002, articles were being written upon the broader implications of scholarly activity on the Internet, but these articles were often only tangentially related to Poe. By 2007, more sophisticated scholarship had begun to emerge, with Ehrlich's article "Populating Cyberspace" situating Poe as sympathetically aligned with New Media. While Ehrlich in the same year still published more straightforwardly descriptive articles like "Machines, Humans, and Web 2.0," which surveyed the transformation of online resources on Poe caused by the ascendancy of Web 2.0 formats like blogs and videos, much of his scholarship would shift to considering Poe's work as a precursor to the World Wide Web. In "Tipping Points: Tales of Obsession, Revenge, and the Internet," he refers to Poe's characters Dupin and Montressor as "technological forerunners of computer programmers" (2010, 156). Similarly, in a 2014 article, Ehrlich argues that Poe used his "Brevities" or "Pinakidia" (short reflections often paraphrased from Isaac Disraeli's "Curiosities of Literature" that Poe published in the *Southern Literary Messenger*) to appeal to his audience in a way akin to writers on social media.

Ehrlich (2011) has charted Poe's fascination with the mechanical means of reproduction in the forms of the telegraph and anastatic printing, both of which are mentioned in "The Thousand-and-Second Tale of Scheherazade" in 1845. While stopping short of stating that Poe anticipated the Internet, Ehrlich implies that Poe was keen to adopt technologies which allowed him to take greater control of the publication of his own works by circulating them in networked relationship to one another (rather than as merely self-contained pieces). He concludes his clear-sighted article on this topic with the reflection that "[a]fter a century and a half, Poe's dream of a personal revolution in publishing is finally materializing, although in ways he never expected" (Ehrlich 2011, 111).

Poe's work now being in the public domain, accessible freely on sites like Project Gutenberg, allows for webmasters to curate it in such a way that the interrelations among the different pieces of his oeuvre are emphasized so that readers can understand these works as parts of a greater aesthetic and philosophical project (rather than, say, as lone iconic stories). For instance, the University of Virginia's online copy of Poe's paired texts "How to Write a Blackwood Article" (1838) and "A Predicament" (1838) are hosted under the "Hypertexts" section of their American Studies page so that you can click upon hyperlinked footnotes which explain the references Poe is making to other contemporaneous authors and journals.

However, this hyperlinked quality is already present in the texts themselves. "How to Write a Blackwood Article" is a parodic piece of "how to" advice lambasting the sensationalism of articles published in *Blackwood's Magazine*. The fact that many of Poe's stories were exactly the kind of grotesqueries that he sends up in the text gives the piece a strong element of self-parody. Nonetheless, "How to Write a Blackwood Article" is—according to its fictitious authorship—not penned by Poe at all, but by the transcendentalist writer, the Signora Psyche Zenobia, who is commissioned by Mr. Blackwood to write an article detailing some autobiographical misadventure in which she narrowly escapes death. "A Predicament" is, then, seemingly the piece which Zenobia writes, even though it is written in the past tense after the author has been accidentally decapitated.

Both texts thus exist in symbiotic relationship with one another. For instance, in "How to Write a Blackwood Article," Mr. Blackwood instructs Zenobia to adorn and elevate the sentence, "The river Alpheus passed beneath the sea, and emerged without injury to the purity of its waters" (Poe [1835] 2009, 313). In "A Predicament," written by Zenobia, we find the line, "Thus it is said the immense river Alfred passed, unscathed, and unwetted, beneath the sea" (Poe [1838] 2009, 317). The humor in Zenobia's use of the word "unscathed" is only apparent when we recognize, through reference to "How to Write," that far from properly dressing up the sentence provided to her, she has merely turned to a thesaurus and used a synonym. Moreover, "unwetted" is amusingly nonsensical on its own merits, but funnier if we recognize it as a second-hand bastardization of Virgil, illuminating how preposterous (and randomly chosen) the original reference is—a parody of Poe's own habitual references to Ancient Greek texts in his stories. We are unlikely to remember such a small detail from "How to Write," where it sits alongside numerous other deliberate mistranslations, fudged references, and pretentious bunkum, unless we flit as readers between the two, keeping—for instance—two tabs open in our browser.

Furthermore, the highly adjective-laden, vivid, and overemphasized description that Zenobia provides of her own decapitation, cannot but recall grandiloquent—even *fruity*—passages from Poe's tales published under his own name or anonymously. Some of these tales, like "King Pest" (1835), were published prior to "A Predicament" and "How to Write"—while others, like the vicious and grotesque "Hop-Frog" (1849), were penned many years later. That is to say, the reader of Poe (as with the reader of later maximalist authors like William Faulkner, Thomas Pynchon, or Joyce Carol Oates) charts associations, patterns, and repetitions both forward and backward across an author's oeuvre. While it would be excessive to make claims of a hyperdiegetic "Poe-verse," reoccurring motifs such as premature burial and the death of a beautiful woman, as well as the character of C. Auguste Dupin featuring in three separate stories, provide an impression of interconnectedness across Poe's output. While associatively mapped—rather than foregrounded at the level of the stories' diegesis—there are enough similarities among the subject matter, style, and tone of Poe's disparate works that it was comparatively straightforward to adapt and combine them into one colossal overarching hypertext form.

EVERMORE AS EXEMPLAR OF POE AS HYPERTEXT

Evermore: A Choose Your Own Edgar Allan Poe Adventure was submitted to the 22nd Annual Interactive Fiction Competition in October 2016, where it was placed 34th with the second highest standard deviation in scoring. This hypertext game, produced with the software Twine, attempted to adapt, truncate, and mash together over 60 of Poe's short stories, poems, and essays into a single branching hypertext form. As such, while large portions of the game consist of sections of pastiche written by the present author, *Evermore* must be considered partially authored by Poe himself, from whose writings the majority of the game was directly adapted.

The work is split roughly 50-5 between Poe's own words—often transposed into second person—and sections imitating Poe's style. Sometimes these take the form of connective paragraphs; sometimes they are wilder deviations from Poe's original stories. Often these passages were written as a means of "filling in the blanks" as needed to flesh out a sense of place or increase immersion for the reader/player. The overall aim was to achieve a unity of effect, uniting disparate fragments into a holistic whole that would retain the dominant impression—the "Poe-ness"—of Poe's writings.

The title *Evermore: A Choose Your Own Edgar Allan Poe Adventure* is something of a joke in and of itself, playing on the fact that, as Kenneth Silverman notes in his introduction to *New Essays on Poe's Major Tales*, many readers of Poe tend to conflate the tales with the man, "fusing," to quote Silverman, "the two in a single impression of eerie melancholy" (1993, 1).

Thus, the "Edgar Allan Poe" part of the title gestures toward this commodification of Poe's character and the concomitant lack of differentiation between the man and his stories.

The "Choose Your Own Adventure" (CYOA) part of the title, meanwhile, refers to an imprint of books created by Edward Packard and published by Bantam Books from 1979 to 1998, beginning with Packard's original *The Cave of Time*. These books were advertised as immersive, interactive experiences in which "you" the reader were "the star of the story," choosing between multiple possible endings. As such, an impression of breadth and heterogeny is important to the CYOA format, even while these elements are necessarily constrained by a print medium unable to accommodate the sophisticated variables and algorithms of a digital medium. *Evermore*, by contrast, was developed in Twine, a digital tool that allows for the use of HTML and CSS to create webpage-based interactive fiction. While the piece tracks a small number of variables, it is more static than dynamic, its interactivity stemming from the choices the player makes that determine the order in which they experience the fiction's branching paths. These choices are supplemented by typographic and formatting effects programmed in the coding languages previously mentioned.

Being closer, therefore, to pure hypertext than to a game, *Evermore* accomplishes its impression of being an open rather than closed text through the sheer breadth of the sources that it draws from. Silverman notes that Poe published some 70-odd stories in his lifetime (1993, 7). *Evermore* transfigures, references, or otherwise adapts approximately 85% of these, as well as over a dozen more poems, dialogues, and essays. As such, *Evermore* maintains a certain consistency of theme, characters, and motifs, while also allowing for the opportunity of multiple branching paths and possible endings without deviating significantly from the events of the original stories.

Essentially *Evermore* splits early on into two separate narrative branches. One of these branches is composed of those stories set within or on the grounds of ancestral mansions, while the other branch veers more into Poe's tales of travel, exploration, and adventure. This speaks to one of the realizations I had when surveying Poe's work for inclusion in *Evermore*—the sheer breadth of the popular nineteenth-century genres that he tackled.

We have already established the appropriateness of Poe's stories to the hypertext form, but which of his tales to include and which to not? As said, I included the vast majority, but with the notable exception of those three tales involving the detective Dupin (1841, 1842, and 1844) and other mysteries like "The Gold Bug" (1843). This was essentially due to a difference in the mode of engagement expected by the reader of these stories, which are puzzles in which the reader is invited to decode a message or find a solution before the detective. Benjamin Fisher in *The Cambridge Introduction to Poe* points out that many critics have established that these tales are somewhat different in form and style to Poe's other stories, though Fisher disagrees with this himself (2008, 58). He argues that these stories still have a root in the supernatural and the Gothic, even while they may seem to disavow that root. For me, however, omitting these stories was essentially a matter of practicality since I found they required a fuller kind of puzzle solving than was permitted by the hypertext navigational system. This deeper level of interaction would require a text-only adventure game rather than hypertext format. I did consider creating a small spinoff game involving just those five detective stories, which would allow the players to type responses, but this was hard to integrate with the hypertext I developed in Twine.

When considering Poe, we find some stories are widely considered canonical, while others are much less so. So, for instance, we have well-known stories like "The Fall of the House of Usher" (1839) or "The Tell-Tale Heart"; but then we also have stories like "The Man That Was Used Up" (1839) or "Hop-Frog," which are far less anthologized and unknown by many readers. Now, if some of Poe's stories are considered worthier or more canonical than others, then we are confronted with a problem when it comes to hypertext, since textual fragments in hypertext are afforded the same weight by virtue of the commonality of the hyperlink. Jay David Bolter reflects:

> Although in a printed book it would be intolerably pedantic to write footnotes to footnotes, in the computer we have already come to regard this layered writing and reading as natural. Furthermore, the second page is not necessarily subordinate to the first. One linked phrase may lead the reader to a longer, more elaborate page. All the individual pages may be of equal importance in the whole text, which becomes a network of interconnected writings. (2001, 27)

As such, the notion of canonizing hypertext as proposed by Astrid Ensslin is inherently problematic. Admittedly, Ensslin is not naive to this. She herself problematizes the very title of her book *Canonizing Hypertext* repeatedly across the work. In fact, the chapter "Hypertext and the Question of Canonicity" (2007, 44–65) necessarily contains far more caveats in addressing the question of establishing a hypertext canon than it does a system of rules with which we might establish this. Indeed, the rules that she proposes are broad and speculative—for instance, works of the hypertext canon should involve "topicality," "thematic message," "self-reflexivity," "metatheoretical concept," and "intertextuality" (Ensslin 2007, 65). I would suggest that most works of hypertext are going to fulfill one of these criteria at least. The largest section is one on "reception," which would be evaluated by a work's number of awards, critical acclaim, readers, and so on. This verges upon being a self-fulfilling prophecy. If those works that received the most awards become part of the hypertext canon, they then, in turn, will receive the most readers, subsequently receiving the most retrospective awards.

The process of writing *Evermore* cemented in my mind the impossibility of respecting canonicity within hypertext. This was due not only to my personal desire to include as many of Poe's works as possible within *Evermore*, but also because the prominence I gave to certain works was primarily dictated by formal necessity rather than aesthetic criteria. So, for instance, those stories grouped together in a mansion were useful to put geographically close to one another so the player could navigate these without jumping divergently through space and time; whereas any stories set in a more exotic location needed to be reached via a boat journey, which necessitated them being buried a bit deeper within the hypertext, less likely to be seen. Finally, the notion of canonicity becomes more precarious still if we accept George Landow's aforementioned concept of the "wreader" (1992, 1997), which holds that a hypertext is only ever authored in the process of its reading. Like Ensslin, I feel this concept risks overemphasizing the amount of freedom that the reader/player has when engaging with hypertext (2007, 31), but I would also go further by noting that it decentralizes the experience of the writer/programmer *as a reader in the process of making hypertext*. Recent tools for authoring hypertext, such as Twine, emphasize the visual structure of hypertext. As such, the experience of making such interactive fiction becomes increasingly hard to distinguish from the experience of consuming it.

During the process of writing *Evermore*, the sheer scale of the project, and the sheer number of stories that I was dealing with, sometimes engendered in me an almost vertiginous effect in which I would forget which passages had been written by Poe and which passages were my own pastiche. Moreover, the geography of the game was so vast, I would sometimes forget what was at one end or the other of my Twine mind-map, neglecting narrative dead ends I had left, until weeks or months later when returning to work on the project. I was an unsettled traveler among my own writing, perhaps only worsened by the fact that I was often writing and programming late into the night. Working from the assumption that a hypertext's writer/s and reader/s can blur, it follows that close analysis of reader response can illuminate the original work responded to.

From this critical position, a post-mortem of a work of Edgar Allan Poe fandom like *Evermore* can help reveal the hypertextual potentialities within Poe's own work, which exhibits aspects of the mash-up even before being further mashed-up by myself in the creation of *Evermore*. While this runs the risk of forging a critical *mise en abyme*, such regressive metafictionality has already been shown to be typical of Poe's own writing.

FALLING FRAGMENTS OF A HYPERTEXTUAL HOUSE OF USHER

Benjamin Fisher argues that an equivalency is drawn between a character's internal landscape, the external setting, and the text itself in many of Poe's stories (2008, 30). Similarly, and more specifically, Louise Kaplan equates the structure of the house in "The Fall of the House of Usher" with both the text of the story and the mind of the titular Roderick Usher (1993, 5). This, to me, presages the formal techniques of early 1990s Macintosh hypertexts like John McDaid's *Uncle Buddy's Phantom Funhouse* (1993) or even the first graphical adventure game, Sierra's *Mystery House* from 1980. It speaks to the blurring of interior and exterior realities in Poe's works—that sense that we move in the stories from an outer to an inner space (or vice versa). Perhaps that is something of what I was experiencing when I was working on *Evermore*. It is that vertiginous quality of losing a sense of self as a player/reader/writer while experiencing the work that I really hoped to create—the idea of being (to refer to John Barthes's 1968 proto-hypertext novel) *Lost in the Fun House*.

Kaplan writes that the House of Usher "decays, crumbles, and falls into oblivion but it does so in a manner eminently lawful and orderly" (1993, 49). You can see that ambivalence captured in *Evermore*'s hypertext rendering of the story. The reader/player finds Roderick Usher in the front-most bedroom of the mansion where just over a third of the hypertext unfolds. Within this chamber, the events of "The Fall of the House of Usher" play out as though within a house within a house, the short story contained within the larger structure of the hypertext. Usher explains, "I have sequestered myself in the front-most bedroom because there really is no end to this house's windings—to its *incomprehensible* subdivisions" (Whybray 2016). This informs the reader/player that they have passed a threshold within the hypertext, entering a section of narrative sequestered away from the other stories, characters, and events found within the larger house. It also reassures the reader/player that though they may feel as though they are stumbling from place to place, this has been anticipated on the part of the writer/programmer. Finally, the line works as a reference to the pioneering text game *Colossal Cave Adventure* (Crowther and Woods 1975/1977) in which part of a cave system is infamously referred to as "a maze of twisty little passages, all alike."

As the story progresses, moments of aporia or visual disturbance reflect simultaneously the troubled, fragmentary, and compromised state of Usher's mind and the similarly problematic nature of hypertext. For instance, when Usher tells the reader/player about his sister, hovering the cursor over the text changes the sister's name from Madeline to Berenice. This not only draws a comparison between the character of Madeline and the similarly prematurely buried character of Berenice from the 1835 story of the same name, but functions as a slippage between two of Poe's different texts, as though distinctions between them are collapsing. In terms of Usher's emotional and cognitive disintegration, the "hover text" effect reveals strong emotions hidden behind more restrained expressions of decorum. For instance, the sister's gradual "wasting away" is replaced with "putrescent degeneration"; Usher's "sobbing" when hovered over is replaced by "stifled screams."

As the story continues, sound effects start to intrude upon the otherwise silent experience. In "Usher," an Arthurian romance narrated by Usher seems to be rendered into sound through pathetic fallacy—however it soon becomes apparent that Madeline has escaped from her grave and the noises belong to her. The intrusion of sound effects into what had hitherto been a silent reading experience is intended to not only shock the reader/player, but also momentarily collapse their sense of reality, for they do not know at what level of the diegesis the noises are occurring.

As the action of the romance escalates in intensity, so too do the sound effects. The very orientation of the text then begins to change, with one paragraph slanting at such an angle that it overlaps the hypertext's menu bar in most browser windows. This intentional glitchiness continues with the revelation of Madeline Usher's walking corpse. The paragraph which describes this is given a recurring red shadow effect. However, the words "trembling and reeling" literally vibrate upon the screen as though trembling and reeling. This also causes the red shadow to vibrate, causing a break in the visual illusion. As Usher's mind and the house both begin to fall apart, so too does the hypertext.

After this climactic encounter, the reader/player can choose to venture deeper into the mansion or to flee down the stairs and through the front door. If they do this, the whole screen shakes. Some sentences describe your theft of a horse and escape from the house. However, a visual effect makes the letters of the words disappear when hovered over by the cursor. The story, the House of Usher, and the hypertext itself disintegrate before the reader/player's eyes.

Ultimately, for choosing to escape the manor instead of plunging deeper into the hypertext, the reader/player is struck by a brick of falling masonry (a reference to Infocom's 1984 text-adventure *The Hitchhiker's Guide to the Galaxy*) and so is returned to the tomb where they started the story, having to begin over again. While there are more traditional endings to *Evermore* (two canonical endings and one secret bonus ending) this is easily the most appropriate. Hypertext never really finishes or reaches a definite conclusion because there always remains the potential for more links and connections. The same should be said of the writings of Edgar Allan Poe and the analysis of this writing—it is inexhaustible and infinitely recursive.

POE-ST SCRIPT

Reviews for *Evermore* were generally positive. However, some reviewers of the game, such as Jenni Polodna (2016) and Kyeli Smith (2016), argued that *Evermore*'s pastiche was not significantly differentiated from the patriarchal and colonialist ideologies underpinning Poe's work, leading the piece to replicate the oppressive dynamics of the material that I was seeking to deconstruct and parody.

In 2018, two years after writing *Evermore*, I worked with Polodna, and many other interactive fiction (IF) writers, upon a collaborative tribute game to Michael Gentry's text-only adventure game *Anchorhead* (1998), itself a pastiche of the writings of H. P. Lovecraft. *Cragne Manor* (2018) is an enormous nonlinear IF game, in which you play a woman who has come to the mysterious New England town of Backwater to inherit a manor. Each author was assigned a room, which we wrote independently using the coding language Inform—a natural language that consists of logical propositions based around objects. Each room having been written, Ryan Veeder and Polodna did the remarkable job of assembling the game into a semi-coherent Gothic patchwork.

Having reflected upon the reviews of *Evermore*, it was important to me that I avoided replicating the vicious racism in Lovecraft's work and deconstructed this ideology more adequately than I had achieved with *Evermore*. My strategy in writing my room for *Cragne Manor* was to place Lovecraft's colonial sentiments not into the voice of the player character (whom the player would have to occupy), but instead displace them onto a text within the text. As contributors, we were encouraged to put books within our rooms. My location was a riverbank, and so I put a book on the riverbank, a guide to lobster fishing. That year, right-wing psychology professor Jordan Peterson had notoriously begun his self-help book *12 Rules for Life: An Antidote to Chaos* with an extended comparison between humans and lobsters (2008, 4–9). Drawing connections between the right-wing ideology of Peterson and Lovecraft would make my own ideological position clearer and draw contemporary parallels to illustrate that Lovecraft's racist and colonialist thinking is not far behind us, but still with us in the alt-right online spaces that champion Peterson's ideas. Lovecraft's own focus upon creatures of the sea as a sublimated site for his racist anxieties in the form of Deep Ones and Cthulu allowed me to reimagine Peterson as Jeremiah Padoson, author of a book on the crawfish of Maine.

Most integral to a more successfully progressive vision for *Cragne Manor*, however, was the collaborative nature of the project, ensuring that a multiplicity of voices was contained within the hypertext. Ultimately the transformative power of the mash-up comes, I believe, from its radical reconfiguration of the ideas of authorship and canonicity—a necessary challenge to individualism in an increasingly interconnected world.

REFERENCES

Benfrey, Christopher. 1993. "Poe and the Unreadable: 'The Black Cat' and 'The Tell-Tale Heart.'" In *New Essays on Poe's Major Tales*, edited by Kenneth Silverman, 27–44. Cambridge: Cambridge University Press.

Bolter, Jay David. 2001. *Writing Space: Computers, Hypertext, and the Remediation of Print*. New York and London: Routledge.

Brown, Marshall. 2009. *The Gothic Text*. Palo Alto: Stanford University Press.

Ehrlich, Heyward. 2007. "Poe in Cyberspace." *The Edgar Allan Poe Review* 8 (2): 99–106. https://www.jstor.org/stable/i40073912.

———. 2007. "Poe in Cyberspace: Populating Cyberspace." *The Edgar Allan Poe Review* 8 (1): 91–6. https://www.jstor.org/stable/i40073899.

———. 2008. "Ten Years of 'Poe in Cyberspace' (1998–2008)." *The Edgar Allan Poe Review* 9 (1): 40–8. https://www.jstor.org/stable/41506281.

———. 2010. "Poe in Cyberspace: Tipping Points: Tales of Obsession, Revenge, and the Internet." *The Edgar Allan Poe Review* 11 (2): 156–60. https://www.jstor.org/stable/i40073919.

———. 2011. "Poe in Cyberspace: How Poe's Anastatic Printing Became Self-Publishing, POD, and Social Networking." *The Edgar Allan Poe Review* 12 (2): 107–12. https://www.jstor.org/stable/41506461.

———. 2017. "Poe in Cyberspace: His Contribution to Internet Pre-History." *The Edgar Allan Poe Review* 18 (2): 267–74. https://www.jstor.org/stable/10.5325/edgallpoerev.18.2.0267.

Ensslin, Astrid. 2007. *Canonizing Hypertext: Explorations and Constructions*. London: Continuum.

Fisher, Benjamin F. 2008. *The Cambridge Introduction to Edgar Allan Poe*. Cambridge: Cambridge University Press.

———. 2009. "Edgar Allan Poe." In *The Handbook of the Gothic*, 2nd ed., edited by Marie Mulvey-Roberts, 67–74. London: Palgrave Macmillan.

Kaplan, Louise J. 1993. "The Perverse Strategy in 'The Fall of the House of Usher.'" In *New Essays on Poe's Major Tales*, edited by Kenneth Silverman, 45–64. Cambridge: Cambridge University Press.

Landow, George. 1997. *Hypertext 2.0*. Baltimore: Johns Hopkins University Press.

Poe, Edgar Allan. [1835] 2004. "How to Write a Blackwood Article." American Studies at the University of Virginia. Last modified August 15, 2004. Accessed October 23, 2021. http://xroads.virginia.edu/~Hyper/POE/blackwod.html.

———. [1835] 2009. "How to Write a Blackwood Article." In *The Collected Works of Edgar Allan Poe*, edited by Helen Trayler, 310–16. Ware: Wordsworth Editions.

———. [1838] 2004. "A Predicament." American Studies at the University of Virginia. Last modified August 15, 2004. Accessed October 23, 2021. http://xroads.virginia.edu/~Hyper/POE/predicam.html.

———. [1838] 2009. "A Predicament." In *The Collected Works of Edgar Allan Poe*, edited by Helen Trayler, 317–28. Ware: Wordsworth Editions.

———. [1845] 2009. "The Imp of the Perverse." In *The Collected Works of Edgar Allan Poe*, edited by Helen Trayler, 261–5. Ware: Wordsworth Editions.

———. [1845] 2017. "The Philosophy of Composition." In *The Raven and The Philosophy of Composition*, edited by Taylor Anderson, 1–13. Scotts Valley: CreateSpace Independent Publishing Platform.

Polodna, Jenni. 2016. "IF Comp '16 – Adam Whybray & Edgar Allan Poe's Evermore!". *Pissy Little Sausages*. Last modified October 2, 2016. Accessed October 29, 2021. https://pissylittlesausages.wordpress.com/2016/10/02/if-comp-16-adam-whybray-edgar-allan-poes-evermore.

Polodna, Jenni, Ryan Veeder, et al. 2018. *Cragne Manor*. Quixe/Ryan Veeder. PC/Mac/Phone. https://rcveeder.net/cragne/play.html.

Silverman, Kenneth, ed. 1993. *New Essays on Poe's Major Tales*. Cambridge: Cambridge University Press.

Whybray, Adam, and Edgar Allan Poe. 2016. *Evermore: A Choose Your Own Edgar Allan Poe Adventure*. Itch. PC/Mac/Phone. https://adamwhybray.itch.io/evermore-a-choose-your-own-edgar-allan-poe-adventure.

Wilson, James Southall. 1926/1927. "Poe's Philosophy of Composition." *The North American Review* 223 (833) (December 1926–February 1927): 675–84. https://www.jstor.org/stable/25110283.

Index

12 Rules for Life (Peterson), 238
13!!! (Shiels), 201

Abbott and Costello Meet Frankenstein (film), 9, *11*
abhuman characters, 162–63
"Abjection and Body Horror" (Aldana Reyes), 162, 163
Abraham Lincoln, Vampire Hunter (Grahame-Smith), xi, 35, 92–93
absorption, of Universal by larger corporations, 15
Action (comic series), 177
adaptability, of Dorian Gray, 57
adaptation, 5; mash-ups contrasted with, xiii; from other media into comic books, 176–77, 179–80, 186–87; Romantic, 30–31
"Adaptation and New Media" (Moore, M.), 205–6
Addams Family (TV series), 14
Adler, Nathan Niigan Noodin, 140
Adrian (historical Roman character), 134
"The Adventure of the Empty House" (Doyle), 115
advertising, by Universal, 7
After Dracula (Peirse), 12–13
Afterlife with Archie (Aguirre-Sacasa and Francavilla), 173

Against Nature (À Rebours) (Huysmans), 126–29
Aguirre-Sacasa, Robert, 173
Ainsworth, William Harrison, 94, 95
Aisha (fictional character, *Henry VIII: Wolfman*), 102
Aldana Reyes, Xavier, xi, xv, 3–4, 17–18, 162, 163
Alice in Wonderland (film), 174
Alien Imposters (TV episode), 77–78
"Allison Williams Reveals What White People Ask Her About *Get Out*" (TV episode), 85–86
Altered States (film), 29
American McGee's Alice (video game), 205
Amunet (goddess), 64
Anchorhead (game), 238
Anderson, Hans Christian, 184
Andre (fictional character, *Get Out*), 79–80
Andrea (fictional character, *Werewolf by Night*), 159, 164
Andrews, Jennifer, 139, 142–45, 149
Andruzzi, Tony, 190, 192, 197–201
"And Then There were Three" (Shiels, Raven, and Fromer), 196
"Angel in the House, Devil in the City" (Rocha), 67

241

Angelique (fictional character, *Penny Dreadful*), 59–61
Ann (fictional character, "End of the Line"), 183–84
Anne (fictional character, "Moonchild"), 180, 181
Antinous (historical Roman character), 134
anxieties, of Shelley, M., 33–34
"apeturismo" (legal loosing of ideological mores), 38
appearance, of Dorian Gray in *Penny Dreadful*, 58–59
Appleford, Rob, 146, 149–50
"Approaching Abjection" (Kristeva), 66
The Arcana of Bizarre Magick (Magus), 195–96
Armitage family (fictional characters, *Get Out*), 80–81, 83–85
Armstrong, Ken, 177
The Arts of Deception (Cook), 191
Asian character, in *Get Out*, 78–79
assimilation, of *Penny Dreadful* characters to mundane world, 56
"At the Rialto" (Weiler), 12
attitude toward homosexuality, in *Teleny*, 135–36
Atwood, Margaret, 140
Aubrey (fictional character, "The Vampyre"), 33
auction scene, in *Get Out*, 84
Audrey Rose (de Felitta), 182
auteurism, in filmmaking, 46–47
"Authorship and Authenticity in Sherlock Holmes Pastiches" (Nyqvist), 109
The Awful Dr. Orlof (*Gritos en la noche*) (film), 39–40

Baron Gregory Russof (fictional character, *Werewolf by Night*), 164
Bartels, Kathleen S., xiii
Barzun, Jacques, 25
Basil (fictional character, *The Picture of Dorian Gray*), 134

Bava, Mario, 43
BDSM, Gothic literature and, 213
Beautiful Untrue Things (Mackie), 123
Becker, Susanne, 219
Beerbohm, Max, 123
Ben (fictional character, *Night of the Living Dead*), 83, 85
Benfrey, Christopher, 227
Between Men (Sedgwick), 218
Beyond the Grave (Cameron), 194
B'gwus (folklore character), 139, 142, 145–49, 151
Bignell, Jonathan, 210
Bizarre (Shiels), 196
bizarre magick, xvi, 189–90, 194–201
Black horror mash-ups, 76
black humor, 73–74
Black Sabbath (*I tre volti paura*) (film), 42
The Black Seal, 196
Black Sunday (*La maschera del demonio*) (film), 37, 39, 41
Blood and Black Lace (*Sei donne per l'assassino*) (film), 43
Blood of Dhste Kravahn (Masklyn ye Mage), 199, 200
Blood of the Rose (Pearce), 100
Blood Quantum (film), 140
Bloody Pit of Horror (*Il boia scarlatto*) (film), 42, *43*
Bloom, Clive, 190, 193, 207
blurring, of line between fantasy and reality, 197
Boleyn, Anne, xv, 91–92, 94–95; as evil, 99–100; ghost of, 96; Gothic revenge narratives of, 96–97; as undead avenger, 96–99; as vampire, 97–98; as vampire slayer, 103–4; as werewolf, 102–3
Boleyn, George, 97
The Boleyn Necklace (Bramley), 96
Boleyn: Tudor Vampire (Cinsearae), 97–98
Bolter, Jay David, 234
books, for magicians, 199

Bordo, Susan, 104
Borham-Puyal, Miriam, 93
Botting, Fred, ix, 174–75, 216
Bowman, Dean, 218
Braidotti, Rosie, 55
Bramley, Zoe, 96
Bride of Frankenstein (film), 7
The Brides of Dracula (film), 40
Briggs, Julia, 217
British: comics for boys, 177–78; comics for girls, 176–77, 184; comics industry, 173–74, 176
British Trash Cinema (Hunter), 23
British Women's Short Supernatural Fiction, 1860–1930 (Margree), 217
Brooks, Kinitra, 73
Brother Shadow (magician), 195
Brother Voodoo (fictional character, *Werewolf by Night*), 170
Brown, Derren, 192
Brown, Marshall, 225
Buck Cowan (fictional character, *Werewolf by Night*), 164
Buffy the Vampire Slayer (TV series), 100, 103
Burger, Eugene, 197–201
Burke, Chesya, xv
Burton, Tim, 174
Byron, George Gordon (Lord), 29–30; portrayal of in *Gothic*, 31–32; as vampire, 32–33
Byron, Glennis, 174

The Cabinet of Dr. Caligari (Das Cabinet des Dr. Caligari) (film), 40
The Cabin in the Woods (film), 75, 76
Caleb, Amanda, 129
The Cambridge Introduction to Edgar Allan Poe (Fisher), 229, 233–34, 238
The Cambridge Introduction to Satire (Greenberg), 73–74
Cameron, Charles, 189–90, 192–93, 195
Camille Des Grieux (fictional character, *Teleny*), 130–35
Campbell, Maria, 141

Canada, "haunted wilderness" of, 140, 141, 143, 151
"Canadian Monsters" (Atwood), 140
canonicity, 235
Canonizing Hypertext (Ensslin), 227–29, 234–35
Capital (Marx), 25
capitalist drive, 41
Captain America (comic book character), 156
Carpenter, Cari, 141
Carr, Diane, 209
Carrie (King, S.), 178, 180–81
"The Cask of Amontillado" (Poe), 228
Castle Dracula (performance space), 193
Castle Dracula Mentalism (Cameron), 193
The Castle of Otranto (Walpole), xi–xii, 94
Castriciano, Jodey, 144
Catherine Hunter (fictional character, *The Tangled Skein*), 119–20
The Cauldron (magazine), 189
The Cave of Time (Packard), 233
characters, abhuman, 162–63
The Chilling Adventures of Sabrina (TV series), 100, 174
"Choose Your Own Adventure" (book series), 230, 233
Chris (fictional character, *Get Out*), 74, 81–84
Christianity, in *Boleyn: Tudor Vampire*, 98
cinema, exploitation, 38, 41, 46, 49n4, 174
"Cinema/videogame/interface" (King, G., and Krzywinska), 210, 215
Cinsearae, S., 97–98
Clairmont, Claire, 29–30; as portrayed in *Gothic*, 32
Classic Monsters, 4–6, 15–18
"Classic Monsters" (video set), 15–17
"Close, Very Close, a b'gwus Howls" (Appleford), 146, 149–50

Clouds of Glory (TV show), 22–23
Cold Steel (Shiel), 95–96
Cold War, 156
Coleman, Robin R. Means, 75–76
Coleridge, Samuel Taylor, xii
colonialism, as monster, 145–51
Colossal Cave Adventure (game), 236
comic books: Gothic characters in, 155–56, 173; Gothic novels compared with, 157–59
Comics Code, 155–56
The Committee (fictional characters, *Werewolf by Night*), 169
"commodity Gothic", 186
"Complicating the Image of Model Minority Success" (Ngo and Lee, S.), 79
concept, of "wreader" in hypertexts (Landow), 228, 235
concerns, of girlhood, 187
conglomerate era, early, 13–14
The Conjured Vengeance of Anne Boleyn (East), 98–99
Consalvo, Mia, 210–11
"The Contemporary Gothic" (Aldana Reyes), xi
Contemporary Gothic (Spooner), 202
"A Contemporary Gothic Indian Vampire Story" (Taylor, H.), 140
continental horror, 38
conventions, of Gothic novel, 139
"Convergence and Globalization in the Japanese Videogame Industry" (Consalvo), 210–11
Convergence Culture (Jenkins), 6
Conway, Jerry, 155
Cook, James W., 191
Cooke, Arthur L., 208
Coons, Robbin, 9, 12
Cosima (fictional character, *Lisztomania*), 24, 28
Costello, Matthew, xvi, 156
Du Coudray, Chantal Bourgault, 163, 165
Count Dracula (fictional character, *Dracula*), xv, 107, 111, 121; in *Sherlock Holmes VS Dracula*, 112; in *The Tangled Skein*, 119–20
"counterfictions", 109
Cowdin, J. Cheever, 8
Cragne Manor (game), 238–39
Crane, Jonathan, 77
The Creation of Anne Boleyn (Bordo), 104
creativity: of British comics, 176; with established myths, 48
Creature from the Black Lagoon (film), 13
"The Critic as Artist" (Wilde), 130
Cromwell, Oliver, 67
Cromwell, Thomas, 97
crossover fan fiction, 109
Cthulu (mythological character), 197, 200, 238
Curti, Roberto, 38–39, 42, 44
Cut-Wife of Ballentree Moor. *See* Joan Clayton (fictional character, *Penny Dreadful*)

Daemons, Darklings and Doppelgangers (Shiels), 199
The Daily Chronicle (newspaper), 127
Dance of the Seven Veils (film), 25
"The Danger Game" (*Werewolf by Night* issue), 167
Danny (fictional character, *The Shining*), 80
"Danse Macabre" (*Misty* issue), 184–86, *185*
The Dark Eyes of London (film), 40
dark humor, 86n1; in Black community, 73, 85, 86
Dark Universe, 3, 15–17
Davies, David Stuart, 112–13
Davis, Angelique M, 82
DC Thompson comics, 176
"Death Game 1999" (Tully), 177
Death Line (film), 183
de Bruin-Molé, Megen, x, xi, xiv, 41, 93; on Frankenfiction, 103, 109–10, 142, 149, 151, 175, 205, 216

deception, of magicians, 191–92
Decherney, Peter, 6, 13
Deliberate Regression (Harbison), 25–26
de Ossorio, Amando, 49n3
Des Esseintes (fictional character, *Against Nature*), 126–29, 135, 136
detective, video game player as, 216
Deuze, Mark, 84
devaluation, of female creators in Gothic scholarship, 187
The Devils (film), 22
Devil's Diary (Cameron), 190
"Devouring Desires" (Wisker), 212–13
Diana (comic series), 176–78
Di Chiara, Francesco, 41
Dick Hallorann (fictional character, *The Shining*), 80
Diehl, Nicholas, 73
Dimaline, Cherie, 140
"Director's Foreword" to *MashUp* (Bartels), xiii
disclaimers, of magicians, 192
diversity, lack of, in *Gone Home*, 220
"Domesticating the First-Person Shooter" (Bowman), 218
"Domestic Films Made for Export" (Di Chiara), 41
Doomsday (convention), 201–2
Dorian Gray (fictional character, *Penny Dreadful*), 57, 61–62, 69; appearance of, 58; as queer character, 59–60
Dorian Gray (fictional character, *The Picture of Dorian Gray*), 57, 124–26, 128–29
Dormer, Natalie, 104
Doyle, Arthur Conan, 107
Dracula (film), 3, 5, 6, 8, 17
Dracula (Stoker), 5, 27, 103, 109, 113–14
Dracula's Daughter (film), 7–8
Dracula series, 41
Dr. Christopher Banning (fictional character, *Penny Dreadful*), 64–65, 68, 69

Dr. Florence Seward (fictional character, *Penny Dreadful*), 68–69
Dr. Glitternight (fictional character *Werewolf by Night*), 170
Druids (fictional characters, *Blood of the Rose*), 100–101
Dr. Watson (fictional character, *The Adventures of Sherlock Holmes*), 110–13; in *Sherlock Holmes and Count Dracula*, 115–16; in *Sherlock Holmes and the Plague of Dracula*, 118–19
Duke Metger (fictional character, "KKK Comeuppance"), 76–77
Dumas, Chris, 34
Dundes, Alan, 97–98
During, Simon, 191, 194

early conglomerate era, 13–15
East, Jonathon, 98–99
Edgar Allan Poe Review (online journal), 230
Edwards, Justin, 141
Edwards, Kyle, 11
Ehrlich, Heyward, 230
elements of Gothic horror, in *Teleny*, 133
Elizabeth I (queen), 103–4
Elmo (fictional character, *Werewolf by Night*), 168
Emily (fictional character, *Alien Imposters*), 78
"End of the Line" (Shaw and Richardson), 183–84
Ensslin, Astrid, 227–29, 234–35
Ernst, Rose, 82
eroticism, of Gothic horror films, 45–47
escapism, 12
established myths, creativity with, 48
Estleman, Loren, 111
Ethan (fictional character, *Penny Dreadful*), 63
European horror, golden age of, 37, 49n1
Evermore (game), xvi, 226, 232–38

"Evolution of the Bizarre" (Minch), 200
The Exorcist (film), 43
experiences, ludic, 209
explanations, of lesser known stories of Poe in *Evermore*, 234
exploitation cinema ("Filone"), 38, 41, 46, 49n4, 174
Eyes without a Face (Les Yeux sans visage) (film), 40

The Face of Terror (*La cara del terror*), 40
"The Fall of the House of Usher" (Poe), 236–37
family home, in Gothic fiction, 215
fan community, of Sherlock Holmes, 108
Fantasmagoriana (ghost stories collection), 29–30
"Fantasmas de amor" (Curti), 38–39, 42, 44
fantastical elements, of *Lisztomania*, 27
the Fantastic Four (comic book characters), 156
fantastika genre, 193
Farizova, Nina, 59
The Fast and the Furious (film franchise), 3
fatal woman trope, 39
father, of Robinson, 146–48
Father Joquez (fictional character, *Werewolf by Night*), 164
"Fear" (YouTube Channel), 17
de Felitta, Frank, 182
female protagonists, of Gothic horror, 45–46
Ferdinand Lyle (fictional character, *Penny Dreadful*), 63
filmmaking, auteurism in, 46–47
film mash-ups, television and, xiv, 1–86
films: "sex-vampire", 46; slasher, 43, 46
"The Final Problem" (Doyle), 115
The Final Programme (film), 27
first-person shooter games, 209, 217–18
"First-Person Shooters" (Morris), 209

Fisher, Benjamin F., 229, 233–34, 236
Flanagan, Kevin M., xiv
"Flânerie in the Dark Woods", 218
flâneur (idle urban wanderer), 218, 229
"Foreword" to *Universal Studios Monsters* (Sommers), 14
formulae, for comics for girls, 181–84
"The Four Faces of Eve" (*Misty* issue), 179
"Fragment of a Novel" (Byron, George), 32
Francavilla, Francesco, 173
Franco, Francisco, 38, 48
Frankenfiction, x, xiii, 21, 55, 93; Sherlock Holmes and, 109–10
Frankenstein (film), 3, 5, 6, 8
Frankenstein (Shelley), xii–xiii, 5, 21, 22, 225–26; *Gothic* and, 28–35; *Lisztomania* and, 27–28
Frankenstein's Bloody Terror (*La marca de hombre lobo*) (film), 39, 40
Frankenstein's Monster (fictional character, *Van Helsing*), 16
Frankenstein's monster-Hitler hybrid, 28
Franz Liszt (fictional character, *Lisztomania*), 26–28
Freeman, Matthew, 6, 7, 17
French Decadent genre, 124–25
frequent death: of Black characters in horror films, 75–76; of gay characters in popular media, 216, 219–20
From Dawn to Decadence, 1500 to the Present (Barzun), 25
Fromer, Roy, 196
Fuseli, Henry, 30–31
fuzzy Gothic, 193, 201

Gabriel Van Helsing (fictional character, *Van Helsing*), 16; bizarre magick and, 198; in *Sherlock Holmes VS Dracula*, 112; in *The Tangled Skein*, 113
Gaertner, David, 140

Galvan, Jill, 63–64
game ecology, 211, 217–18
Gamergate controversy, 213
games, first-person shooter, 209, 217–18
"Games Design as Narrative Architecture" (Jenkins), 211
Gaslight (film), 82
gaslighting, 81
Genette, Gérard, 22
genre, *giallo*, 43–44
Gentry, Michael, 238
Get Out (film), xv, 73, 86; Asian character in, 78–79; auction scene in, 84; ending of, 82–83; *The Shining* and, 81; *The Stepford Wives* and, 81–82; subtle racism as portrayed in, 80–81; as zombie film, 83–85
ghost, of Boleyn, A., 96
The Ghost of Frankenstein (film), 10, *10*
"The Ghost of the Counterfeit in the Genesis of the Gothic" (Hogle), xi
ghost story, *Gone Home* as, 216–17
Ghostwatch (film), 21
giallo genre, 43–44
Il Giallo Mondalori (novel series), 43
Gibson, Mel, 185
"The Girls from N.O.O.D.L.E.S" (*Diana* issue), 176–77
The Girl Who Knew Too Much (*La ragazza che sapeva troppo*) (film), 43
Gisele Du Grand (fictional character, *The Vampires*), 45
Gogol, Nikolai, 41
"The Gold-Bug" (Poe), 228, 233–34
golden age, of European horror, 37, 47n1
Gomez, Joseph A., 22
Gone Home (video game), xvi, 206–7, 214–15, 218–20; as ghost story, 216–17
Good Night, Mr. Monster (*Buenas noches, señor monstruo*) (film), 37
Gothic: approach to magic shows, 193–96, 198, 201; family home and, 215; revenge narratives on Boleyn, A., 96–97;; texts as mash-ups, xi; transgressive sexuality and, 56-57, 212, 218; video games, 205–10
Gothic (Botting), ix, 216
Gothic (film), 21–24, 28–35
"Gothic, Grabbit and Run" (Byron, Glennis), 174
Gothic Afterlives (Piatti-Farnell), x
Gothic and the Comic Turn (Horner and Zlosnik), xii, 75
"Gothic Bloodlines in Survival Horror Gaming" (Taylor, L.), 208, 211–12
The Gothic Body (Hurley), 161
Gothic Canada (Edwards, J.), 141
Gothic characters, in comic books, 155–56
Gothic Cinema (Aldana Reyes), 3–4, 17–18
"Gothic Echoes/Gothic Labyrinths," (Otto), 173
Gothic elements: in video games, 206–10, 219; in *Werewolf by Night*, 164–65
"Gothic Fiction" (Lynch), xii, xiii
Gothic Fiction/Gothic Form (Haggerty), 158
Gothic Forms of Feminine Fictions (Becker), 219
Gothic Histories (Bloom), 207
Gothic Horror (Bloom), 190, 193
"Gothic Horror" (Marlow-Man), 39
Gothic horror films: eroticism of, 45; female protagonists in, 45–46; tyrannical figures in, 48
Gothic iconography, of video games, 210
Gothic Literature (Killeen), 163
Gothic novels, comic books compared with, 157–59
Gothic Remixed (de Bruin-Molé), x, xi, xiv, 41, 93; on Frankenfiction, 103, 109–10, 142, 149, 151, 175, 205, 216
The Gothic Text (Brown, M.), 225
Grahame-Smith, Seth, x, xi, 35, 92–93

Grant (fictional character, *Werewolf by Night*), 168
Gray, Jonathan, 7
Gray, Robert, 131
Greenberg, Jonathan, 73–74, 82
Green Lantern (comic book character), 156
Grenville, Bruce, xiii
Grey, Jane, 95
de Groot, Jerome, 92

Haefele-Thomas, Ardele, 56
Haggerty, George, 158
Haisla people, 139, 141–42, 144, 148
Halfbreed (Campbell), 141
Half-Real (Juul), 209, 211
"half-real" nature, of video games, 209
Hall, Billy, 146–47
hallucinogenic quality, of video games, 209
Halperin, David, 56
Halsall, Alison, xiv
Handbook of Horror (Cameron), 190
"Hands-on Horror" (Krzywinska), 205, 208
Hangman (fictional character, *Werewolf by Night*), 166, *167*
Hanson, Ellis, 212, 213
Harbison, Robert, 25–26
hard bizarre, 197
Harpold, Terry, 229–30
Harrison, Nate, 6, 14–15
Harrison's Reports (trade journal), 12
Hart-Davis, Rupert, 124
Hassler-Forest, Dan, 10
haunted houses, in horror video games, 215
Haunted Summer (film), 29
The Haunted Wilderness (Northey), 140–41
"haunted wilderness," of Canada, 140, 141, 143, 151
Hawkins, Joan, 34
Hay, Simon, 216
Hays Code, 8

Heine, Heinrich, 25
Henry VIII (king), 91, 94, 95
Henry VIII: Wolfman (Moorat), 101–2
Herne the Hunter (fictional character, *Windsor Castle*), 95
Hilford, Docc, 195
Hirsch, Charles, 129–31
historical fiction, about Boleyn, A., 92, 94–95
The Historical Novel (de Groot), 92
Historicising Transmedia Storytelling (Freeman), 6, 7
History and Cultural Memory in Neo-Victorian Fiction (Mitchell), 121
"History Bites" (Salvati), 93
A History of the Modern British Ghost Story (Hay), 216
Hogle, Jerrold E., xi
"Holding onto Hulk Hogan" (LaRue), 86
Hollywood's Copyright Wars (Decherney), 6, 13
"Hollywood Sights and Sounds" (Coons), 9, 12
The Holmes-Dracula File (Saberhagen), 111, 112, 120
homosexual elements, in *The Picture of Dorian Gray*, 124–25, 133–35
"Hookjaw" (Armstrong), 177
Horner, Avril, xii, 75
horror: frequent death of Black characters in, 75–76; industrial, 15; Italian Gothic, 38–39; mixture with humor, 74–76; racist history of, 77; Tudor, 95. *See also* Gothic horror
horror-comedies, 14
Horror Noire (Coleman), 75–76
"Hot Profits Out of Cold Shivers" (Edwards, K.), 11
Houdini, 191
House of Frankenstein (film), 12
"'House of Frankenstein' with Boris Karloff and Lon Chaney" (*Harrison's Reports*), 12
"House of Horrors" (Edwards, K.), 11–12

Index

"The House of Representatives" (Maven), 201
hover text function, in *Evermore*, 236–37
"How to Write a Blackwood Article" (Poe), 231
Hughes, William, 62
humanized superheroes, of 1960s, 156
humor, horror mixed with, 74–76
Hunter, I. Q., 23
Hurley, Kelly, 161
"Hush, Hush, Sweet Rachel" (Mills), 179, 180, 182
Hutcheon, Linda, 108, 175
Huysmans, Joris-Karl, 126, 128–29
hybrid medium, video games as, 210
Hypertext 2.0 (Landow), 228, 235
hypertexts, 225–35; problematic nature of, 236–37

"I, Werewolf" (Thomas, R.), 160–61, *160*
Icon & Idea (Read), 23
Immoral Tales (Tohill and Tombs), 45
"The Imp of the Perverse" (Poe), 227
inclusion criteria, for use in *Evermore*, 233–34
incorporation, of Gothic elements into story of Boleyn, A., 96
Indigenous Gothic Canadian works, 140–42, 151
industrial horror, 15
industrialization, 6
"Inside Stuff—Pictures" (*Variety*), 8
interconnected characters, in stories of Poe, 232
interpretation, of "mash-up", xiii–xiv
intertextuality, 22
intertextual references, in *Get Out*, 74, 79
"Interview with Jenni Scott" (Mills), 179
"Introduction" to *Alternative Europe* (Mathijs and Mendik), 48–49
"Introduction" to *Mashup* (Grenville), xiii

"Introduction" to *Queering the Gothic* (Huges and Smith), 62
"Introduction" to *Teleny or The Reverse of the Medal* (Caleb), 129
invisibility, of hypertext code, 227–28
The Invisible Man (fictional character, *Abbot and Costello Meet Frankenstein*), *11*
Invisible Man (film), 17
Invocation (magazine), 190, 195, 198–99
IPC comics, 176
Irene Adler (fictional character, "A Scandal in Bohemia"), 116–17
Iron Man (comic book character), 156, 170
Italian Gothic horror films, 38–39
Ivy Templeton (fictional character, *Audrey Rose*), 182

Jack (fictional character, *The Shining*), 80
Jack Russell (fictional character, *Werewolf by Night*, "I, Werewolf"), 157–71, *160*
Jackson, Shelley, 225–26
Jack Stapleton (fictional character, *The Tangled Skein*), 112–13
James Moriarty (fictional character, *The Tangled Skein*), 114; in *Sherlock Holmes and Count Dracula*, 115
Jameson, Fredric, 108
Janice Greenbriar (fictional character, *Gone Home*), 215
Jenkins, Henry, 5–6, 211
Jeremiah Padoson (fictional character, *Cragne Manor*), 238
Jimmy (fictional character, *Monkey Beach*), 143, 144, 147–48
Joan Clayton (fictional character, *Penny Dreadful*), 66–68
Joanna (fictional character, *The Stepford Wives*), 81–82
jock (fictional character, *The Cabin in the Woods*), 76

Jonathan Harker (fictional character, *Dracula*), 113–14
Josh (fictional character, *Monkey Beach, Traplines*), 144, 150
Joshua Kane (fictional character, *Werewolf by Night*), 167, 168
Justine (fictional character, *Penny Dreadful*), 60–61
Juul, Jesper, 209, 211

Kane, Gil, 166
Kaplan, Louise, 236
Karaoke (fictional character, *Monkey Beach, Traplines*), 144
Karloff, Boris, 6–7, 9
Katie Greenbriar (fictional character, *Gone Home*), 214–15, 217–19
Keep, Christopher, 131
Ken Russell (Gomez), 22
Key, Keegan-Michael, 77–78
Key & Peele (TV series), 77
Killeen, Jarlath, 163
King, Geoff, 210, 215
King, Stephen, 180
Kirkland, Ewan, xvi
Kitamaat, British Columbia (village), 143, 144
"KKK Comeuppance" (story in *Tales from the Hood*), 76
Klapcsik, Sándor, 109
Klaver, Christian, 115
Knights Templar, 48, 49n3
Kohlke, Marie-Luise, 56, 60, 61
Kraig (fictional character, *Werewolf by Night*), 159
Kristeva, Julia, 66, 161
Krzywinska, Tanya, 205, 208, 210, 215

Laemmle, Carl, Jr., 5, 8
Landow, George, 228, 235
language of Poe, treatment by Whybray, in *Evermore*, 233
Lanza, Joseph, 24
LaRue, Robert, 86
Late Night with Seth Meyers (TV show), 85–86

Lathom, Francis, 94
Laura Ford (fictional character, *Cold Steel*), 95
The League of Extraordinary Gentlemen (film), 16
The League of Extraordinary Gentlemen (Moore, A.), xiv
"Learning to Talk with Ghosts" (Castriciano), 144
Lee, Christopher, 26
Lee, Stacey J., 79
legal loosening, of ideological mores (*apeturismo*), 38
The Legend of Zelda (video game), 207
The Legendary Scroll of Masklyn ye Mage (Andruzzi), 198, 199
Leolin (fictional character, *Mystic Events*), 94–95
Leonard, Sandra M., xv
The Letters of Oscar Wilde (Hart-Davis), 124
Letters to Reggie Turner (Beerbohm), 123
Lily (fictional character, *Penny Dreadful*), 60–62
Limits of Horror (Botting), 174–75
Linking Ring (magazine), 195
Lips of Blood (*Lèvres de sang*) (film), 47
Lisa (fictional character, "Hush Hush, Sweet Rachel"), 182
Lisamarie Hill (fictional character, *Monkey Beach*), 139, 142, 143, 147–50
Lissa (fictional character, *Werewolf by Night*), 165, 169–70
Liszt, Franz, 21, 24, 25
"Lisztomania" (Heine), 25
literary mash-ups, xv, 91–151
"Living as a Zombie in Media is the Only Way to Survive" (Deuze), 84
Liztomania (film), 21–26, 34–35; *Frankenstein* and, 27–28
locations, of Gothic horror media, 44, 215; in Canada, 141, 143, 151
Logan, John, 55, 69

Lois (fictional character, "Danse Macabre"), 185–86
Lonnie (fictional character, *Gone Home*), 216–20
Lord Henry (fictional character, *The Picture of Dorian Gray*), 58, 127, 128, 131, 132
Lord of Blood!—Lord of Lust! (Charles and Janice), 200
Lord Ruthhaven (fictional character, "The Vampyre"), 33
Louisa Altmamount (fictional character, *Séance for a Vampire*), 120
Lovecraft, Howard Phillips, 200, 238
Lovecraftian Ceremonies (Minch), 194, 196–97, 200
loyalty, of mash-ups to source texts, 109–10
Lubin, Frank, 7
Lucy (fictional character, "End of the Line"), 183–84
Lucy Westenra (fictional character, *Dracula*), 103, 111, 117
ludic experiences, 209
Lugosi, Bela, 6–9
LuPone, Patti, 68
"The Lures of Neo-Victorianism Presentism" (Kohlke), 56, 60, 61
Lynch, Deidre Shauna, xii, xiii

Mackie, Gregory, 123–24
Madeline (fictional character, "The Fall of the House of Usher"), 237
Mad Monk (fictional character, *Werewolf by Night*), 164–65
madness, in horror films, 44
"A Magazine in Search of a Mage" (Burger), 197–98
magic, performance, 189–90
magical items, in *Misty*, 186
"magic circle," of video game worlds, 209, 213
The Magic Circular (magazine), 195
magicians: books for, 199; deception of, 191–92; skill in mash-ups of, 191
"Magic... or Magick!" (Cameron), 190

magic shows, Gothic approach to, 193–96, 198, 201
Magus, Jim, 195–96
Mahler (film), 25, 27
Mahler, Gustav, 25, 27
Maier, Sarah E., xv
"Making a 'Monster'" (Mellor), 33
male figures, in *Misty*, 184
Malía (comic series), 42
Mallory, Michael, 8, 13
Ma-ma-oo (fictional character, *Monkey Beach*), 148
Mangan, Michael, 191
Margree, Victoria, 217
Mario (video game), 207
Marlow-Mann, Alex, 39
The Marrow Thieves (Dimaline), 140
martyr/whore dichotomy, 96, 103–4
Marvel Comics, 155
Marvel Spotlight (comic book series), 155
Marx, Karl, 26
Mary Watson (fictional character, *Sherlock Holmes and Count Dracula*), 115, 118–19
the Mashed Potato (dance), 14–15
"Mashing up Jane Austen" (Mulvey-Roberts), xiv, 144–45
"mash," origin of term, 14–15
Mashup (Augaitis, Grenville, and Rebick), xiii
"Mashup" (Harrison and Navas), 6, 14–15
mash-ups: Black horror, 76; film and television, 1–86; Gothic texts as, xi; interpretation of, xiii–xiv; literary, 91-151; loyalty to source texts, 109–10; skill of magicians in, 191; video games as, 206, 210–12, 219
Masklyn ye Mage (magician), 192
Mathijs, Ernest, 48–49
Maturin, Charles Robert, 125
du Maurier, Daphne, 212
Maven, Max, 201
MCA. See The Music Corporation of America

McCallum, E. L., 212, 213
McGill, Ormond, 194–95
Mellor, Anne K., 33
Melmoth (fictional character, *Melmoth the Wanderer*), 125–26, 136
Melmoth the Wanderer (Maturin), 125
Mel's Matinee Movie (TV series), 13–14
Mendik, Xavier, 48–49
mentalism, 194
merchandising surge, 15
Meyer, Nicholas, 110
Meyers, Seth, 85–86
Mills, Pat, 177–82
Mina (fictional character, *Dracula*), 65
Mina (fictional character, *Penny Dreadful*), 63–65
Minch, Stephen, 194, 196–97, 200
mirroring motif, in *The Picture of Dorian Gray*, 133
Misty (comic series), xvi, 173–74, 177–83, 185, *185*; concerns of girlhood in, 187; Gothic atmosphere of, 179; magical items in, 186; male figures in, 184
Mitchell, Kate, 121
modding, 213–14
Modern Enchantments (During), 191, 194
A Modest Proposal for Preventing the Children of Poor People From being a Burthen to Their Parents or Country, and For making them Beneficial to the Publick (Swift), 74
Monkey Beach (Robinson, E.), 139–42, 144–51
monster, colonialism as, 145–51
monster films, popularity of, 8–9
"The Monster Mash" (song), 14
"monster mashes", ix
monster rallies, 10–12
monstrous Anne narrative, 99–100
Monterrubio-Ibáñez, Lourdes, 57, 61–62
Moodie, Susanna, 141
"'Moody Three'" (Hawkins), 34

"Moonchild" (Mills), 178, 180–81, *181*
Moon Knight (fictional character, *Werewolf by Night*), 169–70
Moorat, A. E, 92–93, 101–3
Moore, Alan, xiv
Moore, Michael Ryan, 205–6
Mordred (mythological character), 103
More, Thomas, 102
Morgaine (mythological character), 103
Morris, Sue, 209
The Most Dangerous Game (film), 167
Mr. Blackwood (fictional character, "How to Write a Blackwood Article"), 231
Mrs. Prendergast (fictional character, "Hush, Hush, Sweet Rachel"), 182
Mulvey-Roberts, Marie, xiv, 144–45
The Mummy (1959) (film), 13
The Mummy (1999) (film), 15
The Mummy (2017) (film), 3, 16–17
The Munsters (TV series), 14
music, in *The Picture of Dorian Gray* and *Teleny*, 132–33
The Music Corporation of America (MCA), 14
Mystic Events (Lathom), 94

Nadia (fictional character, "Danse Macabre"), 185–86
narrators, of Poe, 227
Naschy, Paul, 39
Native American presence, in *The Shining*, 80
"Native Canadian Gothic Refigured" (Andrews), 139, 142–45, 149
Navas, Eduardo, 6, 14–15
Nazi-era superheroes, 156
Nazism, 25–26, 156
The Negromicon of Masklyn Ye Mage (Andruzzi), 190, 198–200
Nelson, Ted, 229
neo-Victorian texts, 55, 107, 121
"New Adventures in Old Texts" (Borham-Puyal), 93

New Essays on Poe's Major Tales (Silverman), 229, 232
new technologies, fascination of Poe with, 230
Ngo, Bic, 79
The Night Evelyn Came Out of the Grave (La notte che Evelyn uscì dalla tomba) (film), 44
The Nightmare (painting), 30–31
Night of the Living Dead (film), 83, 85
Night Visitors (Briggs), 217
Noakes, Richard, 65–66
Northey, Margot, 140–41
nusa, 146
Nyqvist, Sanna, 109

"Oral Sex" (Sceats), 114
origin: of *Teleny*, 130–31; of term "mash", 14–15
Orpheus (Liszt), 24
Oscar (fictional character, *Gone Home*), 217
Oscar Wilde's Plagiarism (Tufesco), 123
Otto, Peter, 173
Overlook Hotel, 80

Packard, Edward, 233
Palimpsests (Genette), 22
"A Parade of Curiosities" (Halsall), xiv
paratexts, 7
parental mistrust, in British comics, 184
parody, pastiche contrasted with, 108
pastiche, parody contrasted with, 108
pastiches, 108
Patchwork Girl (Jackson), 225
"Pauline Johnson's 'As It Was in the Beginning' and Drew: Hayden Taylor's *The Night Wanderer*" (Carpenter), 141
Pearce, Kate, 100
Peele, Jordan, 74, 77–79, 82, 86
Peirse, Alison, 12–13
Pelurson, Gaspard, 218

"Penny Dreadful" (Monterrubio-Ibáñez), 57, 61–62
Penny Dreadful (TV series), xi, xv, 35, 55–69
performance magic, 189–90
Performing Dark Arts (Mangan), 191
Perron, Bernard, 208
"The Perverse Strategy in 'The Fall of the House of Usher'" (Kaplan), 236
Peterson, Jordan, 238
Phallic Frenzy (Lanza), 24
Phillip Russell (fictional character, *Werewolf by Night*), 164
"The Philosophy of Composition" (Poe), 225
Piatti-Farnell, Lorna, x
Pickett, Bobby "Boris", 14
The Picture of Dorian Gray (Wilde), xii–xiii, xv, 57, 126; homosexual elements in, 124–25, 133–35; mirroring motif in, 133; music in, 132–33; *Against Nature* compared with, 128; "poison book" in, 127; *Teleny* contrasted with, 130–36; theme of influence of, 127–28
Pierce, Jack, 7
plagiarism, of Wilde, 123
playfulness, of Gothic media, 207–8
pleasure, sensual, 126
Ploog, Mike, 155
Poe, Edgar Allan, 225, 228–29, 232–37; fascination with new technologies, 230; narrators of, 227; as proto-hypertext, 230–31; wide range of, 226–27
"Poe and the Unreadable" (Benfrey), 227
"Poe in Cyberspace" (Ehrlich), 230
"Poe's Philosophy of Composition" (Wilson), 225
"poison book," in *The Picture of Dorian Gray*, 127
Pokémon (video and mobile game), 211
Polidori, John William, 22, 29, 31
Polodna, Jenni, 238

popularity, of monster films, 8–9
portrayal: of Canadian settlers, 141; of women in Sherlockian pastiches, 120, 121
Post-Millennial Gothic (Spooner), ix–x
postmodern, video games as, 212
Postmodernism (Jameson), 108
Postmodern Media Culture (Bignell), 210
Powers of Horror (Kritsteva), 161
"A Predicament" (Poe), 231
Pride and Prejudice and Zombies (Grahame-Smith), x, xiv, 92–93, 173, 206
Prigmore, Wilf, 178
Princess Carolyn (fictional character, *Lisztomania*), 24, 27
problematic nature, of hypertext, 236–37
process, of Romanticist genius, 34
pseudo-spiritism, 194
Psychic Magic (McGill), 194–95
Psycho (film), 44
Punch (magazine), 127

Queen Victoria: Demon Hunter (Moorat), 92–93
queer: character, Dorian Gray as, in *Penny Dreadful*, 59; elements of Gothic stories, 212, 218; medium video games as, 212–13
The Queer Games Avant-Garde (Ruberg), 214, 220
"Queer Gothic" (Hanson), 212, 213
queer issues, in *Penny Dreadful*, 56–64
"The 'Queer Limits' in the Modern Gothic" (McCallum), 212, 213
Queer Others in Victorian Gothic (Haefele-Thomas), 56

Rachel (fictional character, "Hush, Hush, Sweet Rachel"), 182
"Racial Gaslighting" (Davis and Ernst), 82
racial hierarchy, 79

racism, scientific, 84
racist history, of American horror, 77
Radcliffe, Ann, xii, 142
rallies, monster, 10–12
Rape of the Vampire (Le Viol du vampire) (film), 46
rational thoughts, of werewolf in *Werewolf by Night*, 162
Raven, Anthony, 196
Raw, Laurence, 34
Read, Herbert, 23
Rebecca (du Maurier), 212
Rebecca (fictional character, *Rebecca*), 212
recursion, in *The Picture of Dorian Gray* and *Against Nature*, 128, 133
"The Red Shoes" (Anderson), 184
Regina-Wiltshire Theatre, 8, 12
remediation, of video games with traditional technologies, 211
René Teleny (fictional character, *Teleny*), 130–32, 135
residential schools, 144, 150
rewriter, hypertext reader as, 228
Richardson, John, 183
Richard Wagner (fictional character, *Lisztomania*), 24, 28; depiction of as vampire, 26
rights, theater, 5
Rihya (fictional character, *Werewolf by Night*), 168
Rise and Growth of the Anglican Schism (Sander), 99
Robinson, Eden, 139, 142, 145–46, 151
Robinson, William, 191
Rocha, Lauren, 67
Rod (fictional character, *Get Out*), 85
Roderick Usher (fictional character, "The Fall of the House of Usher"), 236–37
Rogers, Charles, 8
Rollin, Jean, 46–47
Romantic adaptation, 30–31
Romanticism, 22–23, 25–26
Romanticist genius, process of, 34

"Romantic Poetry and the TV Series Form" (Farizova), 59
Romero, George A., 83
Rosales, L. N., xv
Rosalind Llewellyn (fictional character, *Blood of the Rose*), 100
Rose (fictional character, *Get Out*), 74, 84
Rosemary Black (fictional character, "Moonchild"), 180
Roughing it in the Bush (Moodie), 141
Round, Julia, xvi, 157–58, 208
Rowing with the Wind (film), 29
Ruberg, Bo, 213–14, 218, 220
Russell, Ken, xiv, 21–22, 33–35
Russo, Stephanie, xv
Ryan, Marie-Laure, 228

Saberhagen, Fred, 111, 112, 120
Sabrina the Teenage Witch (TV series), 174
"The Sacrifice" (Masklyn ye Mage), 192
Saint Foucault (Halperin), 56
Sally (fictional character, *The Holmes-Dracula File*), 120
Salvati, Andrew J., 93
Sam Greenbriar (fictional character, *Gone Home*), 214–20
Sander, Nicholas, 99
Sasquatch (folklore character), 139, 145, 146
The Sasquatch at Home (Robinson, E.), 145–48
satire, 73; use of to address injustice, 74, 77–78
"Satire, Analogy, and Moral Philosophy" (Diehl, Nicholas), 73
Satyricon (book in *Against Nature*), 129
"A Scandal in Bohemia" (Doyle), 116–17
Sceats, Sarah, 114
Science Fiction, Fantasy, and Politics (Hassler-Forest), 10
scientific racism, 84

Screen Gems, 13
Séance for a Vampire (Saberhagen), 112, 120
The Secret History of Elizabeth Tudor, Vampire Slayer (Weston), 103–4
Secret Identity Crisis (Costello), 156
Sedgwick, Eve Kosofsky, 218
Seitz, Stephen, 113
Sense and Sensibility and Sea Monsters (Winters), 175
sensual pleasure, 126
"The Sentinels" (Shaw), 182–83
settings, for Gothic magic shows, 193–94
settlers, indigenous Canadians contrasted with, 145–51
The Seven-Per-cent Solution (Meyers, N.), 110
sexual depravity, 44–45, 114
sexual desires, of Vanessa, 64
sexuality: Gothic stories and, 212; vampires and, 114
"sex-vampire" films, 46
Seymour, Jane, 96; as portrayed in *Henry VIII: Wolfman*, 102–3
"Shadows of the Fantastic Over Baker Street" (Klapcsik), 109
Sharp, Dee Dee, 14–15
Shaw, Malcolm, 182–83
Sheils, Doc, 196
Shelley, Mary, xii–xiii, 5, 22, 23; anxieties of, 33–34; as portrayed in *Gothic*, 29–31
Shelley, Percy Bysshe, 29–31
Sherlock Holmes (fictional character, *The Adventures of Sherlock Holmes*), xv, 107; Dracula and, 111–15; fan community of, 108; in video games, 205; women and, 116–17
Sherlock Holmes and Count Dracula (Klaver), 115, 118
Sherlock Holmes and the Plague of Dracula (Seitz), 113, 117, 118
Sherlock Holmes VS Dracula (Estleman), 111–12, 117

Sherlockian pastiches, 110–19, 121; portrayal of women in, 120
Shiel, M. P., 95–96
Shiels, Tony, 196, 199, 200
The Shining (film), 80; references to in *Get Out*, 81
Show Sold Separately (Gray), 7
Siegfried (fictional character, *Lisztomania*), 24, 27–28
Signora Psyche Zenobia (fictional character, "How to Write a Blackwood Article," "A Predicament"), 231–32
Silent Hill (video game series), 205
Silverman, Kenneth, 229, 232
Sir Malcolm (fictional character, *Penny Dreadful*), 63, 70
skill in mash-ups, of magicians, 191
slasher films, 43, 46
Sloan, Robin J. S., 210, 214–15, 220
Smeaton, Mark, 97
Smith, Andrew, 62
soft bizarre, 196
"Some Side Lights on the Theory of the Gothic Romance" (Cooke), 208
"'Something in Between'" (Gaertner), 140
Sommers, Stephen, 14, 16
Son of Frankenstein (film), 9
source texts, loyalty of mash-ups to, 109–10
"Space, Navigation and Affect" (Carr), 209
Spain, 39, 48
Spellbound (comic series), 178
Spirit Theater (Burger), 200–201
"Spiritualism, Science and the Supernatural in Mid-Victorian Britain" (Noakes), 65–66
Spooner, Catherine, ix–x, 175, 202
Steele, Barbara, 39
The Stepford Wives (film), 81–82
Stoker, Bram, 5, 27
story titles, in *Misty*, 179
storyworlds, 10

Strand (magazine), 108
Strange Ceremonies (Burger), 199
subtle racism, as portrayed in *Get Out*, 80–81
superheroes: of 1960s, 1970s and, 156–57; transhuman, 162
supportive community, in *Teleny*, 135–36
surge, of merchandising, 15
Swan, R. B., 96
Swift, Jonathan, 74, 85, 86
Sybil (fictional character, *The Picture of Dorian Gray*), 60, 127
symmetrical, portrait and Dorian as in *The Picture of Dorian Gray*, 133
The Sympathetic Medium (Galvan), 64

Tales from the Hood (film), 76
The Tangled Skein (Davies), 112–15, 119
Taylor, Hayden, 140
Taylor, Laurie, 208, 211–12
Taylor, Nik, xvi
Tegan, Mary Beth, xvi
Teleny (Wilde), xv, 123–24, 129–31, 134; attitude toward homosexuality in, 135–36; music in, 132–33; supportive community in, 135–36
Terror and Everyday Life (Crane), 77
Terry Greenbriar (fictional character, *Gone Home*), 215
textual effects, in "The Fall of the House of Usher" section of *Evermore*, 237
theater rights, 5
theme: of influence in *The Picture of Dorian Gray*, 127, 131–32; of parental mistrust in British comics, 184
A Theory of Adaptation (Hutcheon), 175
A Theory of Parody (Hutcheon), 108
Thomas, Joan, 139
Thomas, Roy, 160–61
"The Thousand-and-Second Tale of Scheherazade" (Poe), 230
"Tipping Points" (Ehrlich), 230

Tit-Bits (magazine), 108
Tohill, Cathal, 45
Tombs, Pete, 45
Tombs of the Blind Dead (*La noche de terror ciego*) (film), 48
Tommy (film), 24, 28
Topaz (fictional character, *Werewolf by Night*), 165
The Tower (Ainsworth), 95
The Tower of London (Swan), 96
"To William Wordsworth" (Coleridge), xii
traditional technologies, remediation, of video games with, 211
transgeneric fiction, about Boleyn, A., 92
transhuman superheroes, 162
transmedia franchise, 3–5, 15
transmedia worldbuilding, 10–11
Traplines (Robinson, E.), 144
Travis Anderson (fictional character, *Bloody Pit of Horror*), 42
Tricks of the Mind (Brown, D.), 192
T'sonoqua (folklore character), 149–50
Tudor horror, 95
The Tudors (TV series), 91, 104
Tufescu, Florina, 123
Tully, Tom, 177
Twine (software), 232–34
tyrannical figures, in Gothic films, 48

Umann, Emil, 8
Un-American Psycho (Dumas), 24
"An Uninterrupted Current" (Gray and Keep), 131
Universal Studios, 3–6; advertising by, 7
Universal Studios Monsters (Mallory), 8, 13
"unsettled traveler," hypertext reader as, 228–29
"Upright Citizens on all Fours" (Du Coudray), 163, 165
ur-texts, 57–58
Us (film), 77

vampire: Byron, George, as, 32–33; sexuality and, 114; Wagner as, 26
"The Vampire as Bloodthirsty Revenant" (Dundes), 97
The Vampires (*I Vampiri*) (film), 37, 45
"The Vampyre" (Polidori), 22, 32
Vanessa Ives (fictional character, *Penny Dreadful*), 56, 62–63, 66–69; experience of in asylum, 65, 69; as queer character, 67; sexual desires of, 64
Van Helsing (film), 3, 16
Vanity Fair (magazine), 82
Variety (magazine), 8
variety, of characters in *Penny Dreadful*, 55–56
Veeder, Ryan, 238
Victor (fictional character, *Penny Dreadful*), 57, 62
Victorian Hauntings (Wolfreys), 209
Victorian London, 63
video game player, as detective, 216
video games: Gothic elements in, 206–10, 219; "half-real" nature of, 209; hallucinogenic quality of, 209; haunted houses in, 215; as mash-ups, 206, 210–12, 219; as postmodern, 212; as queer medium, 212–13
"Videogames as Remediated Memories" (Sloan), 210, 214–15, 220
Video Games Have Always Been Queer (Ruberg), 213–14, 218
Villa Diodati, 21, 29
"A Vivisection of the Bizarre" (Minch), 200
"The Viy" (Gogol), 41
Voices from the Dead (Cameron), 189
Volk, Stephen, 21

Wagner, Richard, 25
The Walking Dead (TV series), 180
Walpole, Horace, xi–xii
Weiler, A. H., 12
werewolf (mythological character), xvi, 155, 157, 162–63, 170

Werewolf by Night (comic book character), 155, 157, 163
Werewolf by Night (Conway and Ploog), xvi, 155, 157–58, *158*, 159–61; Gothic elements in, 164–65; Jack as were werewolf in, 166–71; rational thoughts of werewolf in, 162, 163
The Werewolf Versus the Vampire Woman (*La noche de Walpurgis*) (film), 37, 39
Weston, Lucy, 103–4
Whale, James, 5
"What Bunty Did Next" (Gibson), 185
"Where Do We Go from Here?" (Hilford), 195
whimsical macabre, 175
white supremacy, 76–77, 84–86
Whybray, Adam, xvi, 226, 232–36
wide range, of Poe, 226–27
Wilde, Oscar, xii–xiii, xv, 124–31, 135–36; plagiarism of, 123
Williams, Allison, 85–86

Williams, Jesse, 76
Wilson, James Southall, 225
Windsor Castle (Ainsworth), 94, 95
Winters, Ben H., 175
Wisker, Gina, 212–13
The Wolf Man (film), 9, 165–66
Wolfreys, Julian, 209
women: in *Dracula*, 117, 120–21; in Gothic horror, 45-46; in Sherlock Holmes universe, 116–17
The World of Scary Video Games (Perron), 208
"wreader," hypertext reader as (Landow), 228, 235
Wrist (Adler), 140
Writing Space (Bolter), 234
Wyatt, Thomas, 101

Xanadu (encyclopedia), 229

Zlosnik, Sue, xii, 75
zombie film, *Get Out* as, 83–85

About the Contributors

Natalie Neill is an assistant professor of English at York University who specializes in the Gothic, women's authorship in the Romantic period, parody and satire, and adaptation studies. She has published articles and book chapters on Gothic parodies, Gothic novels as historical fiction, the commodification of *Frankenstein*, and adaptations of *A Christmas Carol* (among other topics). She has edited two early nineteenth-century comic Gothic novels—*The Hero* and *Love and Horror*. She is currently working on an edition of Mary Charlton's *Rosella; or Modern Occurrences*.

Xavier Aldana Reyes is a reader in English literature and film at Manchester Metropolitan University and a founding member of the Manchester Centre for Gothic Studies. He is the author of *Gothic Cinema* (2020), *Spanish Gothic* (2017), *Horror Film and Affect* (2016), and *Body Gothic* (2014), and editor of *Twenty-First-Century Gothic: An Edinburgh Companion* (with Maisha Wester, 2019) and *Horror: A Literary History* (2016).

Kelly Baron (née Whitehead) is a SSHRC-funded PhD candidate at the University of Toronto, where she studies sensory depictions of intergenerational memory and trauma in contemporary Canadian novels. Her work has either been published or is forthcoming in *Philip Roth Studies*, the *Journal of Latin American Cultural Studies*, and *Modern Language Studies*, and in the edited collections *Exploring Narratives of Trauma and Memory in the Graphic Novel* and *Digital Memory Agents in Canada: Performance, Representation, and Culture*. She is the publisher of *The Puritan Literary Magazine* and serves on their editorial team as a co-editor of the book reviews.

Megen de Bruin-Molé (@MegenJM, she/her) is a lecturer in digital media practice with the University of Southampton. Her book *Gothic Remixed* (2020) examines contemporary remix culture through the lens of monster studies, and her co-edited collection *Embodying Contagion* (2021) explores how fantastical metaphors of contagion have infiltrated the way news media, policymakers, and the general public view the real world and the people within it. Megen is also an editor of the *Genealogy of the Posthuman*, an Open Access initiative curated by the Critical Posthumanism Network. Read more about Megen's work on her blog: frankenfiction.com.

Chesya Burke is an assistant professor of English and U.S. literatures at Stetson University. Having written and published nearly a 100 fiction pieces and articles within the genres of science fiction, fantasy, comics, and horror, her academic research focuses primarily on the intersections of race, gender, and genre. Her primary areas of study are in African American literature, race and gender studies, comics, and speculative fiction. Burke is the co-chair of the Anti-Abuse Team of Wiscon, a national feminist science fiction conference, and the president of her university chapter of American Association of University Women. *Let's Play White*, her story collection, is being taught in universities around the country.

Matthew Costello, professor of political science at Saint Xavier University in Chicago, explores the role of popular culture—particularly comics—in the construction of national identity. His recent works appear in *Drawing the Past* (2022), *The Cambridge Guide to American Science Fiction* (2015), and *PS: Political Science and Politics* (2014). His book *Secret Identity Crisis: Comic Books and the Unmasking of Cold War America* was published in 2009.

Kevin M. Flanagan, term assistant professor of English at George Mason University, is the author of *War Representation in British Cinema and Television: From Suez to Thatcher, and Beyond* (2019). He is editor of *Ken Russell: Re-Viewing England's Last Mannerist* (2009) and has edited special issues of *Screen* and *Widescreen Journal*. His essays have been published in *Framework*, *Critical Quarterly*, the *Journal of British Cinema and Television*, *South Atlantic Review*, and in numerous anthologies. He teaches courses in film, composition/rhetoric, and literature.

Rachel M. Friars is a doctoral candidate at Queen's University in Kingston, Ontario. Her work centers on neo-Victorian lesbian narratives and nineteenth-century lesbian history, with secondary research interests in true crime, life writing, and the Gothic. Her writing has appeared in *The Journal* of *Neo-Victorian Studies* (2020) and *Neo-Victorian Madness: Rediagnosing Nineteenth-Century Mental Illness in Literature and Other Media* (2020).

Ewan Kirkland has published extensively on video games, particularly focusing on survival horror and the *Silent Hill* series. Exploring such issues as storytelling, self-reflexivity, gender, genre, and psychoanalysis, Ewan's chapters and articles have appeared in journals such as *Games and Culture*, *Convergence*, *Gothic Studies*, and *Camera Obscura*. Routledge's Advances in Game Studies book series recently published Ewan's most recent study exploring the influence of Gothic literature on contemporary video games, which contains chapters on *BioShock*, *What Remains of Edith Finch*, and *Night in the Woods*. Ewan is the course leader for the Animation and Games Art & Design degree programs at the University of Brighton.

Sandra M. Leonard is an assistant professor of English at Kutztown University, where she teaches composition, literature, and linguistics. She has a research interest in nineteenth-century transgressive authorship and the aesthetic potential of plagiarism. Her articles on Oscar Wilde's aesthetic plagiarism have appeared in *The Journal of Narrative Theory* and *English Literature in Transition 1880–1920*.

Sarah E. Maier is a professor of English and comparative literature at the University of New Brunswick. She has published extensively on the Brontës; edited special issues on Sir Arthur Conan Doyle, neo-Victorian considerations, and Charlotte Brontë at the bicentennial; as well as published articles on biofiction, neo-Victorian vampires, transmedia adaptations, and Anne Lister. Maier has co-edited (with Brenda Ayres) and contributed chapters to the following: *Neo-Victorian Madness: Rediagnosing Nineteenth-Century Mental Illness in Literature and Other Media* (2020); *Neo-Gothic Narratives: Illusory Allusions from the Past* (2020); *Animals and Their Children in Victorian Culture* (2020); and *Reinventing Marie Corelli for the Twenty-First Century* (2019). Maier co-wrote *A Vindication of the Redhead: The Typology of Red Hair Throughout the Literary and Visual Arts* (2021) and the forthcoming *Neo-Victorian Things: Re-Imagining Nineteenth-Century Material Cultures* (co-edited with Ayres and Danielle Dove).

L. N. Rosales is an adjunct instructor of English at Southeast Community College in Lincoln, Nebraska. She has previously published on such subjects as the domestic Gothic elements of Shirley Jackson's short fiction and the relationship between queerbaiting and the Gothic in BBC's *Sherlock*. Her research interests include Victorian and neo-Victorian literature and culture, detective fiction, Gothic narratives, and popular culture studies.

Julia Round is an award-winning writer and scholar whose research examines the intersections of Gothic, comics, and children's literature. Her books include *Gothic for Girls:* Misty *and British Comics* (2019), *Gothic in Comics and Graphic Novels: A Critical Approach* (2014), and the co-edited collection *Real Lives Celebrity Stories* (2014). Forthcoming publications include a co-authored *Guide to Essential Criticism of Comics and Graphic Novels* (2022) and a co-edited *Companion to Literary Media* (2023). Julia is an associate professor at Bournemouth University, an editor of *Studies in Comics* journal, and the book series *Encapsulations*, and an organizer of the annual International Graphic Novel and Comics Conference (www.IGNCC.com). She shares her work and her own short comics at www.juliaround.com.

Stephanie Russo is an associate professor in the Department of English at Macquarie University, Sydney, Australia. She specializes in women's writing of the early modern period, as well as historical fiction. She is the author of *The Afterlife of Anne Boleyn: Representations of Anne Boleyn in Fiction and on the Screen* (2020) and *Women in Revolutionary Debate: Female Novelists from Burney to Austen* (2012), and has published widely on representations of revolution, celebrity, monarchy, fashion, work, and marriage. Her recent research has centered on representations of early modern women in contemporary historical fiction. Currently she is working on a project on the use of deliberate anachronism in historical fiction, film, and television.

Nik Taylor is subject lead for drama, theatre and performance at the University of Huddersfield. He is co-editor of *The Journal of Performance Magic*. He has worked as a performer, writer, and director. His numerous projects in the United Kingdom, Germany, and France include Discurs'96 and the Festival of Contemporary European Plays. He has designed for Performance City, FestCEP, and Sapajou, produced a low budget feature, and performed as a dancing penguin. As a research magician, he is coordinator of the Magic Research Group and has recently completed a research project on Performing Real Magic(K): The Conjurer and Audience in Bizarre Magick. He is currently writing a monograph examining the cultural history of performance magic. As a performer, Nik specializes in Bizarre Magic, Sideshow, Séance, and Divination. Nik co-curates Mr Punch's Cabinet of Curiosities, a dark museum of weird and haunted artifacts, and is currently working on a short film capturing the Victorian Parlour Séance. He recently advised on the Thackray Medical Museum's "The Magic of Medicine" exhibition and Proper Job Theatre's *Nosferatu* and performed in Hester Reeve's YMEDACA at the Yorkshire Sculpture Park. He is a member of the International Brotherhood of Magicians and The British Society of Mystery Entertainers.

Mary Beth Tegan, professor of English at Saint Xavier University in Chicago, writes on female novelists' formal management of affect. Her most recent contributions are to *The Eighteenth Century: Theory and Interpretation* and *Material Transgressions: Beyond Romantic Bodies, Genders, Things*. Her monograph project *Vanity's Heirs: Popular Romance and the Reproduction of Women Writers* pursues questions raised by the persistent links among vanity, imitation, and popular romance reading found in the literary reviews and conduct literature of the long eighteenth century.

Adam Whybray currently lectures in film studies and works in the library at the University of Suffolk. His book *The Art of Czech Animation: A History of Political Dissent and Allegory* was published in 2020. He has previously published a chapter on post-irony in *Nathan Barley* (2005) in the 2013 essay collection *No Known Cure: The Comedy of Chris Morris*. He also co-hosts the podcasts *Still Scared: Talking Children's Horror* and *The Legendary Pink Dots Project Podcast*.

www.ingramcontent.com/pod-product-compliance
Lightning Source LLC
Chambersburg PA
CBHW061708300426
44115CB00014B/2602